READY,
STEADY,
GO!

D1021347

ALSO BY SHAWN LEVY

Rat Pack Confidential

King of Comedy:
   The Life and Art of Jerry Lewis

SHAWN LEVY

THE
SMASHING
RISE AND GIDDY FALL
OF
SWINGING LONDON

READY, STEADY, GO!

BROADWAY BOOKS NEW YORK

Book design by Terry Karydes.

The Library of Congress has cataloged the
Doubleday hardcover edition as follows:
Levy, Shawn.
Ready, steady, go! : the smashing rise and giddy
fall of Swinging London / Shawn Levy.
p.   cm.
Includes index.
1. London (England)—History—1951–
2. London (England)—Social life and customs—
20th century.   3. Popular culture—England—
London—History—20th century.   4. Arts,
English—England—London.   I. Title.
DA684.2.L48 2002
942.1085—dc21   2002019203

ISBN 978-0-7679-0588-6

FOR MARY,
FINALLY. . . .

CONTENTS

PART ONE

It happened to happen. All at the same time. Every day was a party. It was like a child who has been under the parents' control, and all of a sudden on the eighteenth birthday, they say, "Here is the key to your Ferrari, here is the key to your house, here is your bank account, and now you can do whatever you like." It was enough to go mad! The new century started in 1960. After that, it's only been perfecting what we started.

—Alvaro Maccioni,
restaurateur

Awesome intro.

Gray.

The air, the buildings, the clothing, the faces, the mood.

Britain in the mid-1950s was everything it had been for decades, even centuries: world power; sire of glorious intellectual, aesthetic and political traditions; gritty vanquisher of the Nazis; civilizing docent to whippersnapper America; bastion of decency, decorum and the done thing.

But somehow, in sum, it was less.

Its colonies were demanding freedom and getting it; its unilateral forays into geopolitics were fiascoes; its cuisine, fashion, cinema, popular entertainment and architecture succeeded—barely—only when mimicking Continental or American models; it stood stubbornly outside a centralizing Europe while shrinking alongside the U.S. as standard bearer of Western values in a crystallizing cold war; it was a noncompetitor in the arms race, the space race and, more and more, the prestige race. With Winston Churchill still in Parliament and the spoor of antique manners still thick in the air, it seemed a nation not so much in decline as one left behind. _Change is occuring everywhere, but not in England._

The States, France, Italy all felt modern. Rock music and the rise of the teenager as tastemaker made the American scene come on, naturally, loudest, while decadent, savvy, grown-up style made existential Paris and La Dolce Vita Rome meccas for both the international jet set and an emerging global bohemian underground. England, by contrast, was dowdy, rigid and, above all, unrelentingly _gray,_ gray to its core.

In 1953—fully eight years after the war ended—Britons were still eating rationed food, answering nature's call in backyard privies and making their daily way through cities that bore the deep scars of Luftwaffe bombing. Germany, Italy and Japan—the _losers,_ mind you—were seeing their economies revitalize; France, which had been ravaged, was in recovery. But in Britain, the hard days—harkening back twenty-odd years by then—seemed still alive; to many Britons, the mid-fifties were materially and psychologically a lot like the mid-thirties. It was, in the words of critic Kenneth Tynan, a "perpetual Dunkirk of the spirit," made more bitter, perhaps, with the false glimpse of spring that was a young queen's coronation.

Within a few years, however, that was to change. By 1956, the British economy had finally relaunched itself: Key industries were denationalized by a Conservative government; American multinationals were choosing Britain as the home base for their expansion into Europe; unemployment dipped, spiking the housing, automobile and durable goods markets; credit restrictions were eased, encouraging a boom in consumerism; the value of property—particularly bombed-out inner-city sites—soared. In just three years, the English stock market more than doubled in value, and the pound rose sharply in currency markets.

Inevitably, as in America, prosperity led to complacency and nostalgia for a prewar era that only in retrospect seemed golden. There was no widely held notion of "cool" or "hip." The mood, taken at large, was smug—or would have been, if smugness were considered good form. The prime minister, Harold Macmillan, patting himself on the back in 1957, declared, "You've never had it so good." And in many respects he was right—if you were of certain tastes and strains of breeding.

The common conception of big city excitement—women in long skirts, men in dinner jackets, dance band music, French cuisine, a Noël Coward play and a chauffeured Rolls—was just as it might have been in the twenties. "London was kind of a grown-up town," remembered journalist Peter Evans. "It was an old-man's town. Nightclubs were where you went if you wanted to hear people playing the violin. There was nowhere to go. Even Soho closed early. There were drinking clubs, but they were private." "There was nothing for young people," remembered fashion designer Mary Quant, "and no place to go and no sort of excitement."

But as, again, in America, there were intimations of a burgeoning dissatisfaction with the status quo that had become the landscape. And, perhaps because it had been beaten down for so long, or perhaps because its increasing marginalization on the world stage liberated it from grave responsibilities, Britain seemed particularly fertile ground for this sort of seed.

At a pace that seemed wholly un-British, various strains of unofficial culture—defiant, antiauthoritarian and hostile to such commonplaces of tradition as modesty, reserve, civility and politesse—were coalescing not so much in unison as in parallel. Bohemians in Chelsea and Soho; radical leftists from the universities and in the media; teens with spending money, freedom and tastes of their own: These three groups would evolve and meld over the next several years to bring forth a dynamic that would center in London and become a global standard. You could point to a few shops, pubs, coffee bars, theaters and dance halls where it all started; you could walk to all of them in a single fair day; and you would, in so doing, encompass an entire new world.

Ten years, maybe fifteen, maybe six.

London rose from a prim and fusty capital to the fashionable center of the modern world and then retreated.

The fifties were Paris and Rome.

The seventies, California, Miami and New York.

But the sixties, that was Swinging London—the place where our modern world began.

Hardly any of the elements were unique: There had been bohemian revolutions and economic renaissances and new waves in the arts and popular culture and lifestyle before. There had even been other moments when youth dominated the scene: the Jazz Age of the twenties, the brief rock 'n' roll heyday of the fifties.

But in London for those few evanescent years it all came together: youth, pop music, fashion, celebrity, satire, crime, fine art, sexuality, scandal, theater, cinema, drugs, media: the whole mad modern stew.

Decades later all of that came to seem organic: Whole empires would rise and fall on the mix, the bread and circuses and lifeblood of the contemporary mind; no one could imagine life without it or remember when things were different. But prior to the day when London hit full swing—some time, more or less, in August '63—it hadn't existed before. Within three miles of Buckingham Palace in a few incredible years, we were all of us born.

It wasn't youth culture that England invented: From James Dean to Levi's to Elvis, that was America through and through. But where American official culture at the end of the fifties had effectively tamped down the expressive impulses of young people, England embraced them as a way of emerging from decades—maybe centuries—of slumber. It let them grow, coalesce, strut. London was where youth culture finally cemented its hold on all forms of expression, and made itself loudly and exuberantly known. Youth, once something to endure, transformed in the span of a few years of British sensations into a valuable form of currency, the font of taste and fashion, the only age, seemingly, that mattered.

The Brits who created Swinging London were unique in their resilience, their ability to absorb and transform elements of American and Continental culture and the cocksureness with which they flaunted their invention of themselves. "Quite a tough bunch of kids made it through the war," reflected tailor Doug Hayward. And their toughness was one of their chief assets in their attack on tradition, as boutique owner Barbara Hulanicki, who outfitted so many of the hip young girls, concurred: "The postwar babies had been deprived of nourishing protein in childhood and grew up into beautiful skinny people. A designer's dream. It didn't take much for them to look outstanding."

It was as much a revolution in English society as any the island nation had ever experienced. "My generation," recalled the actor Sir Ian McKellen, "was brought up to think that you would peak in middle age. There was such a thing as the prime of life. And when you were secure financially and secure in what you believed in the world and what you could contribute to it, then your big years would come, and it would be in your forties or your fifties. And suddenly it was all knocked on the head. Suddenly forty was old."

David Puttnam, then working in advertising, felt it firsthand: "I had a little office that I had taken pains to make attractive, putting up the ads that I was responsible for. But I used to wear a white suit, and my hair was longish. And when they were showing a new client 'round the agency, invariably, they would kind of walk rather quickly past my room. Within a year, my room became a stopping-off point: 'Look at this crazy young guy'—I looked about twelve—'and here's his room with all his ads.' It moved literally within a year from being a liability to being an asset."

Like all capital cities, London was used to hosting sensations, but this one wowed 'em not only in the provinces, but everywhere on Earth. By the early sixties, the city positively overflowed with out-of-nowhere high energy. At night in London, anything could happen: You might attend a concert by a band of geniuses who would create music worth remembering for decades or see a fortune come and go gambling at an elegant casino in Mayfair or learn the Twist at a trendy discotheque near Piccadilly or smoke pot at an after-hours Caribbean joint in Notting Hill or laugh out loud at the old fart prime minister being lampooned on a West End stage or at a nightclub in Soho.

And those were just the outward signs: If you looked harder you could find a bold, spirited and, crucially, *employed* generation of young people with education, access to birth control, freedom from mandatory military service, a new culture of morals and sensations being reinvented daily and no particular sense that the old ways were set in stone. These were English people who'd absorbed the sensibilities and attitudes of the French and the Italians and grafted them onto the materialism and energy of the Americans. They'd invented themselves as living works of art in a way no Britons had since Oscar Wilde.

More, too, than any freethinkers in the history of England, they felt themselves unimpinged by any of the caste conditioning that had divided them for centuries; their world would never truly be classless, as some of them liked to swear it was, but the illusion that it was was valuable, and there were specks of truth in it. If the American sixties were about breaking away from the establishment, England in the sixties was, at first at least, about joining in—*finally*. By mid-decade, a new aristocracy was in place—a popocracy, a hipoisie, a stratified pantheon of pop bands and actors and models and new-style entrepreneurs and a few titled and moneyed and privileged sorts who were hip enough to fit into the mix. It wasn't a wide open world, but it was perforated in ways it never was before.

And streaming through the holes were foreigners eager to have a close-up look at things. London had suddenly become the hottest place in the world: New York and Paris and Los Angeles and Rome combined. Nowhere previously had such an agglomeration of globally noted talents combined at one time and with one such sense of common tenor—not to mention the inestimable advantage of tender age. For a few years, the most amazing thing in the world to be was British, creative and young.

"The fashion and the art and everything was just exploding," said American hepcat Dennis Hopper, who made the trip over more than once to take part in the party. "Music. It was just amazing. The dance clubs and the jazz and these packed places, it was just incredible. There was excitement *here*, but it was basically coming out of England. I've never been anywhere that had that kind of impact on me, culturally. You can think of Haight-Ashbury and the hippie thing later, but this was more of a style and cultural explosion. It wasn't the anti-, drop out, tune in whatever thing that we did. It was really about culture, painting, music, sculpture, fashion, clothes. I'd say for about five years, no one could touch them. They were dictating culture to the rest of the world."

It changed, in a while, as it would, as it was discovered and imitated and grew pleased with itself. By the middle of the decade, it wasn't just a matter any longer of being talented and eager and lucky enough to be invited to sit at the adult table. The adult table itself was being shunned, along with everything that was eaten off it and what the diners wore and how they spoke to one another and what they smoked by the fire afterward. The sharp, clean-shaven cool of the first phase of Swinging London was replaced by a defiant new mien: hairy and druggy and enamored of strange fabrics and eccentricities acquired on foreign travels or in granny's attic. By 1966, it was as if the young were so confident that they'd won that they didn't need approval any longer. The most switched-on cat of 1963 could pass for straight; three years later, hip and square were different continents.

Things became political—always a divisive step. And it was importing the cool new way of being, too. The preferred new lifestyle of the young wasn't quite built for London. Hippie may have looked swell in Hyde Park in July and August, but try it in January or November, making your way to some club through a downpour barefoot or in a peasant skirt. The aesthetic was far better suited to California or Majorca or the countryside. And, in fact, it was being practiced and defined in such places, making the whole world seem hip when just a few years earlier only a handful of postal districts north of the Thames qualified. In 1963, a cool-looking person could only be from London; by 1969 standards, a person who looked with-it could be from anywhere.

Same with a pop record or a movie or a wild new outfit or haircut or art gallery or *anything*, really: London wasn't alone any longer and it surely was no longer the center or even the top. It was alongside New York and Los Angeles, Paris and Rome and Berlin and even Tokyo and Amsterdam and even, for a few minutes, Prague. The world had soaked up everything London could think up and was still thirsty, so it started brewing its own. In a real sense, London was losing because London had won. Its passing may have been inevitable—it had, ironically, helped cement the very notion of ephemerality in popular culture—but it was nevertheless a shame.

And for all the sweep of history and all the pop artifacts and all the indescribable meteorology of human taste, attitude and passion, Swinging London was built of individuals. People became icons because they did something first and uniquely. Everybody overlapped and partied together and slept and turned on and played at being geniuses together, but a few stood out and even symbolized the times: eminent Swinging Londoners, wearing their era like skin.

It would be possible, in fact, to explain the age by telling their stories.

The Snapper, David Bailey, was one of the first on the scene, an East End stirrer and mixer and the most famous of the new breed of fashion photographers who helped revolutionize the glossy magazines and popularize the new hairstyles, clothing and demeanor.

The Crimper, Vidal Sassoon, also from an East End background, but Jewish and, amazingly, a real warrior, who freed women from sitting under hairdryers and ascended into an unimaginable ether: flying to Hollywood to cut starlets' hair and branding himself into an international trademark.

The Draper, Mary Quant, took a Peter Pan–ish impulse to not grow up and sicced her craft, inspiration and diligence on it, creating a new kind of women's fashion that spoke to the rapidly expanding notions of what it meant to be cool, free and young.

The Dreamer, Terence Stamp, another one from the stereotypical Cockney poverty, who wound up winning acting prizes, with his face on magazines, the most beautiful women in the world on his arm and a home among peers and prime ministers in London's most prestigious address—and then wandered out the back door of the decade into spiritual quest.

The Loner, Brian Epstein, who failed miserably at everything until he helped create the greatest entertainment sensation of the century while warring internally against the self-doubts he'd borne his whole life.

The Chameleon, Mick Jagger, a suburban boy with a bourgeois up-

Fashionest = people who erupted from London.

bringing, who could mimic whatever he wished: black American music, the stage manner of raunchy female performers, the go-go mentality of rising pop bands, the chic manners of slumming aristocrats and the arcane sexual and narcotic practices of bohemians both native and exotic—a quiver of cannily selected arrows that let him survive the decade unscathed while the road behind him was littered with the corpses of friends.

The Blue Blood, Robert Fraser, with every tool that traditional English life could offer a man—birth, schooling, military appointment, connections, polish, bearing—but a restless imagination and a decadent streak that led him into art dealing and sensational living that brought him down.

Lay these lives alongside one another, bang them together, hold them up to the light and you could open an entire time.

You could see how people lived and rose and changed and stumbled and faded or kept on rising until they disappeared into the sun.

You could see how people made a glory of their day or their days into a glorious apotheosis of themselves.

You could hear the music, feel the energy, see the paisley and the op art and the melting, swirling colors.

You could go back to Swinging London.

PART
TWO

A CLOUD OF PINK CHIFFON

The story of David Bailey's early life and career would come to sound a cliché: Scruffy East End (or maybe northern) boy aspires to a field normally reserved for the posh and sets the world on its ear without bending his personality to fit the long-established model. But like the jokes in Shakespeare or the Marx Brothers, it was only familiar because it was repeated so often from the original. All the pop stars, actors, dressmakers, haircutters, club owners, scenesters, satirists and boy tycoons who exploded on the London scene in the early sixties did so after Bailey, often in his mold and almost always in front of his camera.

Before mod and the Beat Boom, before Carnaby Street and the swinging hot spots of Soho and Chelsea, before, indeed, sex and drugs and most of rock 'n' roll there were the laddish young photographers from the East: Bailey, Brian Duffy and Terence Donovan, "the Terrible Three" in the affectionate phrase of Cecil Beaton, an iconoclastic snapper of another age whose approval of the new lot made it that much easier for them to barge in on what had been a very exclusive and sedate party.

The trio—and a few others who came along in the rush—dressed and spoke and carried on as no important photographers ever had, not even in the putatively wide-open worlds of fashion magazines and photojournalism. They spoke like smart alecks and ruffians, they flaunted their high salaries and the Rolls-Royces they flashed around in, they slept with the beautiful women who modeled for them, they employed new cameras and technologies to break fertile ground in portraiture and fashion shoots. They were superstars from a world that had previously been invisible, perhaps with reason. "Before 1960," Duffy famously said, "a fashion photographer was somebody tall, thin and camp. But we three are different: short, fat and heterosexual."

Duffy could enjoy such self-deprecating boasts because, recalled Dick Fontaine, who tried to make a documentary about the trio, "He was really the kind of architect of the guerilla warfare on those who control the fashion industry and the press."

But it was Bailey who would bring the group their fame and glory. Bailey was the first bright shiny star of the sixties, a subject of jealous gossip, an inspiration in fashion, speech and behavior, an exemplar of getting ahead in a glamorous world, and, incidentally, the great, lasting chronicler of his day.

Bailey was born January 2, 1938, in Leytonstone, east of the East End, a block over, he always liked to brag, from the street where Alfred Hitchcock was born. When Bailey was three, the family home took a hit from a Nazi bomb and they relocated to Heigham Road, East Ham, which was where Bailey and his younger sister, Thelma, were raised.

Their father, Herbert, was a tailor's cutter and a flash character who dressed nattily, ran around on his wife and like to have a roll of fivers at hand; his wife, Gladys, kept house but also worked as a machinist, especially after Bert finally split on her. The family wasn't rich, but they were comfortable—they were among the first people in the block to have a telephone and TV set, and Bailey was made to dress smartly, to his chagrin ("What chance have you got in a punch-up in East Ham wearing sandals?" he later sighed). But they weren't entirely free of money worries, and one of their ways of dealing with them was, to Bailey, a blessing: "In the winter," he recalled, the family "would take bread-and-jam sandwiches and go to the cinema every night because in those days it was cheaper to go to the cinema than to put on the gas fire. I'll bet I saw seven or eight movies a week."

Bailey fell, predictably enough, under the spell of rugged (and mainly American) actors at around the same time that his parents' marriage was foundering. But Bert Bailey was nonetheless a little worried about his son's fancy for birdwatching and natural history, which loves led the boy into vegetarianism. "My father thought I was fucking queer," Bailey said, "but queer didn't mean homosexual. In those days it just meant a bit of an oddball."

Part of Bailey's queerness was taking and developing photos of birds—he preferred the latter process, as it involved playing with chemicals. But he didn't think of taking pictures as a career ambition—"photography was something you did once a year on Margate beach"—and he had enough on his hands at school, where his learning disabilities (undiagnosed at the time) made for a hellish routine. "I can't read and write," Bailey said. "Dysgraphia, dyslexia—I've got them all. I went to the silly class—the school for idiots—and they used to cane me when I couldn't spell. It was quite tough knowing that you're smart and thinking you're an idiot."

At fifteen, he dropped out of school altogether and started a series of unpromising jobs: copy boy at the Fleet Street offices of the *Yorkshire Post,* carpet salesman, shoe salesman, window dresser, time-and-motion man at the tailoring firm where his dad worked and debt collector. He developed a taste for jazz and spent nights checking out the music and women at the handful of venues the East End offered someone his age. His musical interests were underscored in his oft-quoted quip about his roots: "You had two ways of getting out in the fifties—you were either a boxer or a jazz musician." So perhaps it was inevitable that he followed an artistic muse, especially as he quickly learned how ill-suited he was to make a living with his fists: "The Krays, the Barking Boys and the Canning Town Boys were the three gangs at the time," Bailey remembered. "They weren't gangsters, they were just hooligans. They just went around beating people up if you looked at them wrong in a dance hall. I got beat up by the Barking Boys because I danced with one of their girlfriends. They left me in the doorway of Times Furnishing."

Bailey's dreamy aimlessness was finally punctured by the call-up: In the spring of 1956, he was ordered to report for a physical for the National Service. He tried to duck it—he stayed up two nights straight and consumed a huge quantity of nutmeg ("Someone said it made your heart go faster"), but it didn't work. He might have requested assignment to a ographic unit, but that meant a longer hitch than he was ready to sign for. In August, he reported for basic training in the Royal Air Force, and by December he was stationed in Singapore as a first-level aircraftman with duties such as helping to keep planes flight ready and standing guard on funeral drill.

On the whole, Private Bailey found the situation pleasant enough. "I had a good time in the National Service," he confessed years later. "I hate to sound like a right-wing middle-aged man, but I think it was very good for me." There were, he admitted, drawbacks: "The snobbery! They had a toilet for privates, a toilet for sergeants and a toilet for commissioned officers, as if all our arses were different. It made me angry, the way we were treated, almost like a slave. You were dirt compared with an officer."

Indeed, it was a run-in with an officer that would prove pivotal in shaping Bailey's future. He was still on his jazz kick—his "Chet Baker phase," as he later deemed it—and trying to teach himself to play the trumpet. But when an officer borrowed his horn and failed to return it, he was forced to seek another creative outlet. Cameras could be gotten cheap in Singapore, so Bailey—who'd been as enamored of the photos of Baker on the trumpeter's album jackets as by the playing inside—bought a knockoff Rolleiflex. He was sufficiently hard up for money that he had to pawn the camera every time he wanted to pay for developing his film, but he caught the bug.

The camera suited Bailey's growing bohemianism. He had begun to read, and where his barracks mates had pinup girls hung over their beds, he had a reproduction of a Picasso portrait of Dora Maar. His pretensions didn't go unnoticed: "I did used to get into fights," he said. "But because I was from the East End I could look after myself. I also had the best-looking WAAF as my girlfriend, so they knew I wasn't gay."

When he demobbed in August 1958, Bailey acquired a Canon Rangefinder camera and the ambition to make a living with it. He applied to the London College of Printing but was rejected because he'd dropped out of school. Instead, he wound up working as a second assistant to photographer David Olins at his studio in Charlotte Mews in the West End. He was a glorified gofer—not even glorified, actually, at three pounds, ten shillings a week—and was therefore delighted a few months later to be called to an interview at the studio of John French, a some-

His career begins to kick off with French.

what better-known name and a man who had a reputation for nurturing his assistants' careers.

French, then in his early fifties, was the epitome of the fashion photographer and portraitist of the era: exquisitely attired, fastidious, posh and gay (although, as it happened, married). "John French looked," Bailey remembered, "like Fred Astaire. 'David,' he said, 'do you know about incandescent light and strobe? Do you know how to load a ten-by-eight film pack?' I said yes to everything he asked and he gave me the job, but, at that time, I didn't even know what a strobe was. We became friends and after six o'clock Mr. French became John. One night I asked him why he gave me the job. 'Well, you know, David,' he said, 'I liked the way you dressed.' Six months later everyone thought we were having an affair, but in fact, although we were fond of each other, we never got it on."

In fact, French—"a screaming queen who fancied East End boys," according to documentarian Dick Fontaine—was the first person to really recognize something special in Bailey. Partly it was his bohemian style—Cuban-heeled boots, jeans, leather jacket and hair over the ears, all before the Beatles had been heard of; partly it was his aptitude for the craft. French liked to compare his young protégé to the unnamed hero of Colin MacInnes's cult novel about bohemian London, *Absolute Beginners*—a savvy insight—and he was perfectly willing, as he had with many previous disciples, to see Bailey get ahead in his own work.

"He was an incredibly decent type of man," Bailey would say of his mentor after French died in 1966. "I don't think he was very good as a photographer, but he had a good attitude. His photography sort of slowed me down a bit, because I had to break away from his way of doing things, but I benefited from his attitude."

Even more, he would say years later, "I owe my success to two gay men, really, who told me I was wonderful and pushed me. Being a Cockney and working class, I was an outsider, and in those days gays were outcasts, too. So we felt an affinity. Anyway, John French introduced me to the picture editor of the *Daily Express*, and John Parsons, the art director of British *Vogue*—the second gay man—saw my pictures in the newspaper and offered me a job at the magazine."

It was in the *Daily Express*, in fact, that Bailey published his first really important photo—an image of the model Paulene Stone wearing a dark

① John French
② John Parsons

knee-length skirt and a bright turtleneck mohair sweater and crouching on the leaf-strewn ground to commune with a squirrel, who was nibbling on an ort. Terence Donovan, who didn't yet know Bailey, was among the people who reacted strongly to the image, pronouncing himself "disturbed by its freshness and its oblique quality." On the strength of that shot and a few other striking pictures, Bailey found himself hired in May 1960, as a full-fledged photographer at John Cole's Studio Five, earning thirty to forty pounds a week.

The money came in handy, as Bailey had in February of that year married Rosemary Bramble, a typist whom he'd met at Soho's Flamingo Club a few months previous. The couple lived in a small apartment near The Oval cricket ground in South London. Bailey's salary wasn't grand, but it was good, and when John Parsons of *Vogue* called on Bailey later that year to ask him about joining the staff of the magazine, Bailey refused because he was doing so well with Cole.

"They were offering me less per week than *Woman's Own* was paying me per picture," Bailey remembered. "I didn't realize that *Vogue* was different from any other fashion magazine. . . . I thought it was just another magazine that used pictures. I wasn't that interested in fashion and preferred reportage and portraits, but fashion gradually took over because of *Vogue*." The next time Parsons asked, though, Bailey agreed. His first small piece appeared in the magazine in September 1960, followed by full-page work the next month and, in February 1961, his first cover. The Bailey legend was about to be made.

Bailey's arrival at deluxe fashion magazines couldn't have come at a more perfect time to suit his ambitions. The media business, so long a stolid presence in English life, had grown increasingly itchy in the preceding years. English magazine culture was in the throes of an invigorating shake-up that had begun in the least likely of places. *Queen*, a hundred-year-old society magazine, had undergone a radical change at the hands of its new owner/editor, Jocelyn Stevens, who transformed it from a dry lifestyle report for the upper classes and those with a passion for following their lives (Stevens sniffed that the old *Queen* was all about how to "knit your own royal family") into the most vital publication in the country, with fresh concepts in photography and layout and a wry new attitude toward its putative subject: British tradition.

*1959 → Fashion hits a Boooom! Magazines
are filled with fashion.*

Queen began branching out into areas that had never before been within the purview of a society magazine: articles about the Cuban revolution, a four-issue photo essay about Red China by Henri Cartier-Bresson (who was then hired by Stevens to cover the annual Queen Charlotte's debutante ball "like a war") and a series of articles and features that tried to capture the changing mood of Britain. In one, a parody of the Eton College *Chronicle* (Stevens had attended the school), the establishment of the day, insofar as *Queen* saw it, was sent up as a bunch of schoolboys. In 1959, an entire issue was dedicated to the "Boom . . . Boom . . . BOOM"—the new decorators, dress designers, cars, art treasures and overall lavish living ("When did you last hear the word *austerity*," the lead article asked, and then went on to chronicle England's rise as a producer of advertising, a consumer of champagne and a piler-up of consumer debt); surveys were published on the New Thinkers (including fashion designer Mary Quant, satirist Jonathan Miller and interior designer Terence Conran), the Challengers (including actor Terence Stamp) and New Faces; charts of Who Revolves Around Who were run. Within three years, the magazine nearly tripled in size to accommodate all the advertising its heat had drawn.

Queen encouraged an upsurge of native British talent, including, of course, photographers, none of whom would become more spectacularly famous than Anthony Armstrong-Jones, who had parlayed an admirable career as a photojournalist and society portraitist into the most amazing coup of all: marriage to the Queen's sister, Princess Margaret, in one of the most celebrated matches of the time.

The wedding between the commoner (who took the name Lord Snowdon) and the Princess was held up as a principal exhibit for the claim that England in the early sixties was becoming a "classless" society in which wealth and breeding didn't matter as they had only a few years before. Promulgators of the theory pointed to the appearance of members of the upper class in such formerly outré professions as show business, fashion boutiques and nightclub ownership, as well as the vogue for lower-class accents among the upper classes and the initiation of new styles in clothes and dances not by the aristocracy but by working-class youth. "There was a jolly collision," remembered Mary Quant. "People came together, and they tended to be rather one extreme or the other. Both were smart; the boring thing was to be anything in the middle."

The effect, especially on the upsurgent lower classes, was miraculous, utterly transformatory. "In France," reflected Terence Stamp, "they have that saying, *nostalgie de le boue*, which refers to aristocratic men who like to shag washerwomen. In the sixties, amongst ourselves, our age group, there was an absolute coming together. And what made the coming together was basically music and dancing. In a way it was a new aristocracy. But the main thing was that there was suddenly access between the classes. Had the sixties not happened, I would never have been able to spend the night with a young countess because I would never have met her. And as the great Mike Caine once said to me, 'You can't shag anyone you don't meet.' Rather Aristotelian logic!"

For the upper classes, the idea that a centuries-old stasis was coming unsettled could be either exhilarating or alarming. Young people from moneyed, privileged families felt impelled to change with the times—and as many seemed to greet the situation with a sense of liberation as with desperate entrenchment in old ways. "People with country houses either assimilated or vanished," remembered David Puttnam. "You could count on the fingers of one hand the number who got in. They were quite few, and you knew who they were, and they assimilated, quite successfully in some cases."

In fact, of course, the idea that England's centuries-old traditions of class prejudice had suddenly vanished was a canard that effectively couched the stifling realities in a country where birth still trumped ability in virtually every case. As the sixties emerged, proponents of the theory of classlessness could point to the likes of Quant and Stamp and the Beatles and a dozen other exceptions—people who'd broken into a new class where talent and the wealth that followed success mattered more than who your parents were. But it was inarguably the case that this meritocracy—with its members-only restaurants and nightclubs—was just as exclusive as the old upper class of money and birthright; you may no longer have needed to be born to position but earning it was, arguably, a harder and rarer feat. And, too, entrance to the new world only lasted as long as the traditional elite chose to allow it. "The rich people let us play in their back garden for a few years," said tailor Doug Hayward, "and then they said, 'Right, lads, very nice, you've all had a good time, now let's get back to it.' "

Still, there was a loosening, and it was accompanied by another shift that made the rise of the Baileys and Quants and Stamps possible. English society, the British were more and more frequently being told at the dawn of the sixties, was becoming more permissive—and if the reality was only that England was loosening up as much as the Continent and the States already had, it was nevertheless more true than thinking that the royal family were happy to fit in with the mob. There was the evidence of teenage promiscuity: more talked about if not more practiced than in previous generations. There was the soon-to-be-available birth control pill, a boon to sexual adventurers the world over finally available to Britons at the start of 1961. And there was the embarrassing blow to censors in the 1960 prosecution of Penguin Books on obscenity charges for the publication of a paperback edition of *Lady Chatterley's Lover*, a novel written by D. H. Lawrence in 1928 but banned in Britain ever since. It was a ludicrous, last-century business, with the prosecutor, Mervyn Griffith-Jones, asking jurors in his opening statement, "Is it a book that you would even wish your wife or your servants to read?" and debating the novelist's use of such words as "womb" and "bowels" with literary critics who had been called as witnesses for the defense. After a five-day trial and several days of adjournment during which jurors read the novel, a three-hour deliberation led to Penguin's acquittal; a week later, a new edition of the novel, dedicated to the jury, sold more than 200,000 copies in twenty-four hours—and five times that during the coming year.

And while Griffith-Jones was making an ass of himself in an Old Bailey courtroom, Englishmen of his stripe were being openly mocked on West End stages: Satire, a brand of hipster comedy initially practiced by Americans like Lenny Bruce and Mort Sahl but alchemized into a vital, all-encompassing movement by young Brits, was the rage. Four well-bred young men—comedian Peter Cook, polymath physician Jonathan Miller, history teacher Alan Bennett and the Oxford-educated pianist Dudley Moore—were goring every sacred cow of British life in their smash hit stage show *Beyond the Fringe*. A revue that spared neither the crown nor the prime minister nor Shakespeare nor memories of the war nor sexual mores nor Britain's geopolitical role, it liberated and legitimized years of antiestablishment grumbling and inspired a pan-cultural explosion of new venues for acid commentary. Coming down the pike were Cook's Establishment Club in Soho, where an even more scabrous review was held; the wicked magazine *Private Eye* and a hit TV series,

That Was the Week That Was (starring David Frost, that old person's idea of a young person), which capped (and, indeed, pricked) the satire boom by making subversive humor a weekly staple of domestic life.

"This was very new indeed," remembered Alexander Walker, then reviewing films in the *Evening Standard*. "Very quickly, an atmosphere of mockery and cynicism regarding public life and 'our betters,' to use the Somerset Maugham phrase, was created." But in spreading, satire, of course, lost its bite. Cook, the boy wonder who was the sharpest and, at first, most successful satirist, watched with chagrin as something that had begun as an undergraduate impulse to mock and deflate became an institution: "The heyday of satire was Weimar Germany," he reminded people, "and see how it prevented the rise of Adolf Hitler!" But if his invention didn't crush the status quo, it certainly knocked it back on its pins for long enough so that several similarly subversive new strains of culture could emerge.

In the context of these social and moral upheavals, Bailey's photographs seemed particularly vital and one of the things that Parsons had surely noticed was that Bailey's work had more of a sense of movement and energy than that of most of the British fashion photographers who'd preceded him. In part it was the young man's inherently brash attitude, which bled into his pictures to create out of his models seemingly normal human beings, not inaccessible mannequins removed from the world of the viewer. "Bailey was user-friendly," remembered photography buff and sometime snapper Dennis Hopper. "The models seemed to love him. A lot of fashion photography is how well you get along with people. And Bailey had a good bedside manner. He seemed to be able to be on the level with a lot of different types of people."

But in part, too, it was Bailey's affection for the work of American masters like Richard Avedon and Irving Penn, whose photos he studied for technical details, small effects and emotional impact. By the spring of 1961, Bailey had taken the lessons he learned from his masters and put them to work in a new idiom. He had acquired a 35-mm Pentax camera, which liberated him from the tripod and allowed him to shoot his models in a kind of erotic dance (imitated in the film *Blow-Up* and later in the Austin Powers films). "He was sort of like [bullfighter] El Cor-

Positive feed back on Bailey

dobés when he worked," remembered Terry O'Neill, who took iconic photos of the expressive, energetic Bailey conducting a fashion shoot.

Away from the studio, in environments such as the grandstands of a racetrack or the busy streets of a city, Bailey's new cameras allowed him to shoot wherever the fancy struck; *Vogue* fashion editor Marit Allen recalled jumping into "Bailey's brand-new Jaguar E-Type and taking off on the M-1 to go to Liverpool to photograph girls in clothes at the Cavern because it would be fun, it would be a riot, we should do that maybe. And just picking up girls when we got there because we liked them." The result was extraordinarily fresh imagery—a whole new feel for *Vogue*, for the men's magazine *Man About Town* and for advertising clients such as El-Al, BOAC, Fortnum & Mason and the synthetic fabrics manufacturers Acrilan and Terylene.

As for Bailey, it all amounted to a ticket to a new life. He always joked about his motives into signing on to *Vogue*—"It did allow me to pursue my three main interests: photography, women and money"—and probably he told a lot of truth in the jest. But he also relished the opportunity to work at a machine-gun pace—he developed a reputation during these years as a workaholic, and never lost it—and to try new techniques once he'd earned the confidence of his editors. "Fashion is a good way to explore photography," he explained. He wasn't pretentious about it, exactly: "I didn't really think about it as art. It just seemed a nice thing to do. I've never really been clear what art is. I couldn't believe it when *Vogue* gave me a contract to photograph women and get paid for it.

"They—from Mars or wherever they are—said I wouldn't be a fashion photographer because I didn't have my head in a cloud of pink chiffon," he bragged. "They forgot about one thing. I love to look at all women."

As his stock rose at *Vogue* and elsewhere, he became a kind of craze—the cute Cockney who took such wonderful shots. "Up at the *Vogue* studio," he remembered, "one of the editors actually patted me on the head and said, 'Doesn't he speak cute?' " (And he added with a characteristic giggle, "Three years later, the managing director was asking me if I could move my Rolls so that he could get his Rover out.")

It was, in many ways, a calculated posture: Dick Fontaine, who grew friendly with Bailey over the years, noted, "He's a deeply serious person, and I would say that to him, and he'd say, 'Fuck off. I just wanna make money, have a good time, have dinner, drink a lot, fuck a lot.' All true, of course."

Bailey used his reputation for lower-class cheek to his advantage. "All the posturing with the editors—'I'm not going on that gig!'—was always to do with something else," remembered Fontaine. "Bailey just would be the court jester, playing the trickster."

And he cavorted as much with his subjects as with anyone else. Within a year of Bailey's arrival at *Vogue*, jazz singer and pop critic George Melly sat for him, and he recalled the excited atmosphere the photographer brought to the session: "Here was this unposh, blatantly heterosexual young man dressed all in black. . . . David made no attempt to disguise his Cockney accent—I suspect he may even have put it on a bit—and jumped around like a grasshopper taking what he called 'snaps' of us from every angle, rather than setting the whole thing up in a stiff, formal way like most fashion photographers did in those days. I remember he used lots of funny expressions when taking pictures like, 'Lose that arm, Chief.' "

Melly was in the studio to be photographed with one of the magazine's newest models as part of a feature Bailey was shooting for the "Young Idea" section. The idea for the feature was to photograph the new girl in a variety of outfits alongside a number of men who were just making a splash on the London scene: Kenneth Tynan, Peter Cook, Dudley Moore, David Frost, Vidal Sassoon, Terence Donovan and Stirling Moss included. There was a problem, though: Claire Rendlesham—*Lady* Rendlesham, the magazine's imperious editress—didn't want to use the girl he had in mind. Bailey fought her and finally won out on the condition that he would reshoot the feature no questions asked if, as Rendlesham feared, it didn't turn out well enough.

The girl was Jean Shrimpton, and, soon after Bailey photographed her with all those up-and-coming men, she would transform in his hands into virtually the first model in England to become famous solely on the strength of posing for pictures.

Unlike the noted models of previous eras, Shrimpton wasn't a movie star or a debutante or aristocrat. "Prior to then," journalist Peter Evans remembered, "a model was an anonymous creature. One or two might have had a name but mostly because they were society girls. The top models were either married to or were themselves aristocrats; they could afford to do it because it wasn't a highly paid job."

Shrimpton wasn't well-educated or rich or from an old family. She had attended Lucie Clayton's modeling school, which she entered after indifferent tuition at the Langham Secretarial College. Barely eighteen years old when she first set eyes on Bailey, she was, in her own phrase, "waifish, coltish and cack-handed," but she was a stunning natural beauty—if uncultivated—who had been turning heads in her native Berkshire since childhood. She was only slowly making her way into the modeling world, but it would be hard to imagine that someone as per-spicacious as Claire Rendlesham didn't see her obvious potential.

Bailey noticed it right away in late 1960, when he walked into a Stu-dio Five shoot that Brian Duffy was doing with Shrimpton for Kellogg's cornflakes. "I looked in his studio and saw this vision," Bailey remem-bered. "He was taking the picture against a blue background. It was like her blue eyes were just holes drilled through her head to the paper be-hind." Afterward, he had a chance to ask Duffy who this fabulous girl was and the older man warned him off: "Duffy said, 'Oh, she's too posh for you.' I said, 'Well, we'll see about that, mate.' "

A few weeks later, Bailey requested her for one of his first *Vogue* jobs.

"I'm Bailey," he told her by way of introduction.

"Just Bailey?"

"Just Bailey."

And that would be all she'd ever call him.

Shrimpton was taller than Bailey, even with his Cuban heels; she knew he was married and she was still living in the country with her par-ents. Still, she confessed, "We were instantly attracted to each other. Whenever we worked together this attraction created a strong sexual at-mosphere."

Over the coming few months, they would inch closer and closer to acting on that attraction. In that time, Bailey taught her how to dress and how to model, but he never tried to make her into something she was not. Rather, relying on the aesthetic he was developing in his life and in his photography, he encouraged her naturalness. "She took modeling with a bit of dignity," Bailey said. "Honestly, I don't think she really cared if she did it or not."

But the results, he said, were almost always the sort he was after:

"With Jean you never had to reshoot anything. Ever. She was always in perfect synch with the camera. It's funny, though; in terms of personal style, Jean didn't have any. She just dressed in any old rags. Most of the time she looked like a bag lady."

She concurred with his assessment of her attitude toward the business of fashion: "Modeling meant little to me till I met him," she said when she became famous. "I was just lucky getting work. Bailey has been the greatest influence in my life so far. He says when I met him I was a county chick. All MGs and Daddy and chinless wonders." And she defined the look that he and she had cultivated as "not beatnik and not classical exactly—but more beatnik than classical."

Their technique when they worked together was remarkably simple: "We would just drive out to the country with some clothes," he said, "and Jean did her own hair and makeup." *Vogue* editors were initially ambivalent toward the off-the-cuff feel of the stuff he was giving them, referring to the results as "Old Bailey and his scruffy look." But Bailey was perfecting his theory about how to shoot fashion: "If you look at my fashion pictures, there's a personality to the girls. The girl is always the most important, then the dress. If she's not looking stunning, then I figure the dress doesn't either. The girl is the catalyst that brings it all together." And when they saw what he managed with his new model, the editors couldn't deny that Bailey had discovered a star; their work together became a sensation. Shrimpton—at first anonymous but soon heralded as the Shrimp—was becoming a pinup darling throughout the country.

Shrimpton was a sensation not only because of her fabulous looks or the extraordinary photos Bailey took of her. The two would eventually become famous—infamous even—for their lives together. Despite the obvious obstacles to a romance, Bailey courted Shrimpton as diligently as had the lovesick public school suitors she was accustomed to, with his own personal twist. He would take her out to dinner, not to chic West End restaurants but rather to a favorite chop suey joint on East Ham High Street. With their late working hours and their increasingly common socializing, Shrimpton wasn't always able to go all the way home at night, and she stayed once or twice at Bailey's parents' home, where she was given an understandably cold shoulder. Rather than repeat the unpleasantness, Bailey took to renting them a chaste pair of rooms at the Strand Palace Hotel. Finally, it happened: On a hillside near her home, they made love for the first time.

With their passion consummated, they had to confront Bailey's marriage and the hostility of Shrimpton's parents who, astounded that their daughter—still not nineteen—was carrying on with a married man, threw her out of the house and shunned her for some time; she and her dad didn't speak for a year. By the summer of 1961, Bailey and Shrimpton were living in a flat in Primrose Hill with a dog and Bailey's birds (he would remain an amateur ornithologist his whole life) in a rough bohemian setting that was at stark odds with their increasingly glamorous lifestyle and public profile.

In the next year, Bailey would become a source of excitable scandal in London: "David Bailey/Makes love daily" went the salacious refrain. And he would become the poster boy for the rise of what one writer would call the "photogenes," the wild young men, primarily, associated with the world of fashion magazines, models and piles of money in the hands of unlikely lads. "I think the photographer is one of the first completely modern people," Bailey was famously quoted as saying. "He makes a fortune, he's always surrounded by beautiful girls, he travels a lot and he's always living off his nerves in a big-time world."

Much was made of how cocky East End types like Bailey had broken so completely into what had been a rarefied line of work, and, later on, Bailey acknowledged how timing and history had abetted his rise: "Until the sixties, the class structure here was almost like the caste system in India. If things had gone on as they were, I would have ended up an untouchable. But that all broke down."

He didn't, of course, break it down alone. His key collaborator, who kicked at the status quo with real relish and wicked wit, was Terence Donovan, Bailey's chum, coeval and fellow Cockney crasher of the gilded gates of fashion photography. Big, stout, booming, soft-hearted Donovan was even more of a character than Bailey, a serious practitioner of the martial arts, a man so adverse to cutting a fashionable image that he bought dozens of identical outfits so he'd never have to think about dressing and a prodigious font of comic verbal fancies—rather than admitting to wasting his money on "wine, women and song," say, he claimed he'd blown a fortune on "rum, bum and gramophone." Donovan was more restless than the other photographers: He was the first to publish a book (*women throooo the eyes of smudger TD*—the title was his, as was the free-association text inside), and he owned a number of businesses completely unrelated to his nominal work: a hardware store in the King's Road, a building contractor company, a chain of dress shops, a restaurant. Eventually, he tried to segue out of still photography altogether, shooting commercials for the majority of his commissions.

But fashion photography, of all fey pursuits, was what he became famous for, and he was soon shooting for *Vogue* and *Queen* right alongside Bailey and Brian Duffy. They were always thought of in a group, cowing editors and clients with Cockney sass. "Duffy laid it out," said Dick Fontaine. "They got access to the fashion business by producing this kind of hysteria among the upper-class women who controlled the fashion magazines. They would go in there and be totally East End, acting out in fashion offices. Lady this-and-that was being beset by these East End boys who were being facetious and not respectful." Once they had their feet in the door, the three stereotypically dashed from one exciting assignment to another, partied in chic restaurants and clubs and ran with beautiful women (Donovan left his first wife for, among others, model Celia Hammond, a classmate of Jean Shrimpton's at Lucie Clayton's—such a school!).

Being a photographer, in fact, became a curse for them, just as being pop stars did for the Beatles and the Rolling Stones. Bailey became bristly when asked about the clichéd image of his life: "The whole thing about the East End fashion photographer is that it is perfect for cheap journalism. They always have me talking like a Cockney but I don't think I speak particularly Cockney. And in fact I've never been out with girls who wear white boots. And I've never called a woman a bird."

He did a lot of documentary work along with his fashion stuff, some of it quite fine, as his 1962 studies of the East End, which had an otherworldly quality reminiscent of Eugene Atget nearly a century earlier. But it was for "shifting frocks," as he derisively referred to the art of fashion photography, that he was famous. And rightly: His April 1962 *Vogue* feature, "Young Idea Goes West," in which Shrimpton was shot on the streets of New York in documentary style, was a landmark that looked breathtaking decades later. There Shrimpton stood—fully clothed and yet somehow at once naked and fragile, aloof and reserved, a talismanic teddy bear in hand—in Harlem and Chinatown and Greenwich Village, with men ogling her or just as often walking by without a glance. Some of the scenes were dynamically filled with detail, others so spare as to seem posed: brilliant, organic, breakthrough stuff.

New York had been an education for both photographer and model. The British *Vogue* office had been somewhat nauseated by the prospect of unleashing their bright new Cockney on outsiders: "To give you an idea of what it was like then," Bailey remembered, "Ailsa Garland, the editor of *Vogue*, phoned me before we left and said, 'Don't wear your leather jacket at the St. Regis. Remember, you represent British *Vogue*.' " But Bailey dressed as he pleased: The *Vogue* chauffeur sent to take him to the airport was horrified to find him waiting to go in a sweater and jeans. In New York, Miki Denhof, the editor of *Glamour*, which gave Bailey his first stateside work, remembered her shock on first seeing him: "*Nobody* came to the office in *jeans*." But Diana Vreeland, who'd only recently taken over at American *Vogue*, knew the real thing the moment she saw it, interrupting the subordinate who was introducing Bailey and Shrimpton with "Stop! They are adorable! The English have arrived!"

The majority of American editors weren't, however, any more prepared to give free rein in their pages to Bailey and his handheld, freewheeling imagination and imagery than their English counterparts had been. "You're all over the map," he was told. In *Women's Wear Daily*, the great Richard Avedon dismissed Bailey as "a Penn without ink." And Bailey was even more disappointed at the treatment afforded Shrimpton: "It was very square, very 'professional.' And what they did to Jean was amazing: They tried to turn her into a kind of doll—stiff hair, too much makeup, overproduction. By the time they were finished, it wasn't really Jean anymore. And it had nothing to do with what we were doing in London at the time, which was much more natural."

So they became a revolution of two. For the next couple years—be it in London, New York, Paris or the countryside—Bailey and Shrimpton worked almost exclusively together and, until the rise of the Beatles, were the most glittering jewels in the diadem of the New Aristocracy, the set of young pretties and go-getters whose rise and adventures filled the newspapers and the dreams of young strivers in the East End, South London and the hinterlands.

How big were Bailey and company, and how early? Consider how they overwhelmed the competition: When Bailey suggested to *Vogue*'s

Ailsa Garland in mid-1963 that he shoot Shrimpton with the Beatles, the editor fixed him with a puzzled look: "Who are the Beatles?"

And *Vogue* wasn't alone: Marit Allen, then at *Queen*, remembered her first encounter with the knockabout musicians from up north: "Caterine Milinaire and I were coming back from Liverpool on the train, and we bumped into them and we all sat together and hung out. And we thought they were very funny, and we got to Euston station and I said, 'What do you think about doing a photographic session?' And they said, 'We'd love it: models and clothes and that kind of thing!' And I went rushing into the office on Monday morning and I said to (editor) Jocelyn Stevens, 'I met these mad guys, absolutely wonderful, they're flaky, they're incredible, they're such fun, and they've got this new record out called "Please Please Me" and I think we ought to include them in our fashion spread, and it would be a gas.' And Jocelyn said, 'But this is for the January issue: They'll be over for years by then.' "

THE WORLD WAS FULL OF CHANCERS

For as long as there's been a Bond Street in Mayfair, it's been a fashionable place to shop, be pampered, live and stroll. Shirtmakers and silversmiths, stamp dealers and hosiers, auction houses, art galleries, antique dealers and tobacconists—always the finest and most expensive, always catering to upper-class money. It's a place where the fictional Clarissa Dalloway saw Queen Victoria buying flowers, where both the real Admiral Nelson and his fictitious inheritor Horatio Hornblower lived, where shops have been in business—and serving royalty—for centuries.

Hardly the setting for a revolution, in short, and yet, in 1963, in a beauty salon at number 171, that was exactly what was going on. Sitting having her hair done was Mary Quant, the Chelsea fashion wizard and madcap. Behind, beside, above and around her buzzed Vidal Sassoon, owner and eponym of the establishment, working away with short scissors—five-inchers, which let him get closer to the hair, he felt—and applying a theory he'd been developing about haircutting to her already famous Buster Brown bangs.

A few days earlier, Quant had asked Sassoon to come up with something new for the hair of the models who would present her new fashion line in an upcoming show. Sassoon had joked, "You could cut the whole damn lot off."

Quant laughed, but he was serious. "I'm going to cut the hair like you cut material," he explained. "No fuss. No ornamentation. Just a neat, clean, swinging line."

The idea had come to Sassoon through his study of architecture, particularly the works of the Bauhaus, pioneers of the International style of rigorously straight, clean lines that gave even massive skyscrapers an affecting lightness. "I dreamt hair in geometry," he remembered, "squares, triangles, oblongs and trapezoids." More specifically, he had intuited that it was possible to cut a woman's hair so that it would hold a shape without recourse to gels, chemicals or applied heat, so that its shape would persist because of its structure, as it were, rather than the way in which it had been sculpted. "It is not the hemline but the outline that matters," he reckoned. He had been working gradually toward the ideal form of his vision; his 1960 design known as the Shape came close. But he hadn't ever really applied his theory to its fullest extent: What he wanted to do was crop the models' hair into a squared-off shape of straight lines, short back and long sides—a modern approximation of a flapper's bob but without any fixatives or styling: a bob *cut*.

Quant was excited by the prospect and said he should go ahead and use it for her upcoming show. But Sassoon pointed out that it was only an idea—he'd need to try it out first on an experimental subject.

"It'll work," she declared, "and I'll be your guinea pig, so what the hell."

And so she sat, and when it was over, she was delighted, insisting that the girls in the premiere have their hair done just the same way. On the morning of the show, Sassoon cut all the models' hair just as he had Quant's—and then covered them up in scarves so as to deploy the new look as a surprise on the runway.

At the show, the haircut was even more of a sensation than the clothes. A *Vogue* editor rhapsodized, "At last hair is going to look like hair again," and went in for the cut herself. An editor at the *Sunday Times* lashed out against the look in print. David Bailey, of all people, sided with the antis, arguing with Sassoon heatedly until they came to this tart pass:

"Well, at least, Bailey, I've made some sort of a mark!"

"Is that what you call it? It looks more like a bloody scar to me!"

But the thing had grown beyond the bounds of critique. A few weeks after its debut, the new haircut, which Sassoon still called the Bob but which was becoming known in the business as the Quant, received an enormous boost when the actress Nancy Kwan, preparing to shoot *The Wild Affair* (in clothes designed by Quant), was brought to Sassoon's salon for the new look. Kwan was famous for her long, thick, straight curtain of jet-black hair, but Sassoon went to work on it all the same while the actress played chess with her manager. When it was over, she offered no commentary save a smile. A few days later, Terence Donovan was hired by *Vogue* to help show off the new look in both the British and American editions of the magazine; when Sassoon arrived at the photo studio to help get Kwan ready, he found her beaming: "I like it. Everybody likes it." Donovan took the photo—one of the most famous of his career—and began a long association with Sassoon, whose work, he felt, made a splendid subject: "Because the cuts were so strong they were very easy to photograph," he explained.

Donovan's shot of the Bob—now also known as the Kwan—went everywhere in the world: a real style sensation. One of those inspired by it was the French designer Emmanuelle Khanh, who flew to London for it (yes, it now became known in some places as the Khanh) and then ordered it for all the girls in her coming show. The gimmick in this one was that the models would all come onto the runway wearing gigantic hats, then simultaneously remove them and shake their heads—astonishing the crowd of fashionistas as their new haircuts fell naturally into shape.

The ensuing publicity pushed Sassoon's thriving business and growing reputation to unprecedented heights. There had always been celebrity crimpers around London's posher neighborhoods—Sassoon had worked for some, such as "Teasy Weasy" Raymond, and others, such as Leonard of Mayfair, had worked for him in the near decade he'd been running his own salon. But none of them—not even the ones who won prizes in hairdressing competitions—had anything like the fame that was now enveloping Sassoon. He was in magazines and newspapers, both as an interview subject and as a matter of debate. Business on Bond

Street increased dramatically—so impressively, in fact, that the managers of the Grosvenor House Hotel invited Sassoon to open a second salon on their premises; they'd been surreptitiously eyeing the traffic at various chic salons and observed that Sassoon's Mondays and Thursdays were as busy as other people's Saturdays.

And beyond even all the fame and success, Sassoon had discovered that the Bob/Quant/Kwan/Khanh had made concrete all his abstract thoughts about hair, haircutting, hair care and the new lifestyles that were sweeping London. In another few months, he would create another cut, the Five-Point Cut, "the finest cut I have ever created, the geometric design in its purest, most classical form."

More impressive even than this triumph—the obsessive's realization of his dream vision—was the totality of the achievement: Sassoon's new vision of hairstyling changed the lives of looks-conscious women everywhere. Before Mary Quant submitted to his ministrations, women— even the most modern and chic—went to salons to have their hair dressed: permed, gelled, fried, baked and bent into shapes that enslaved them both to their coiffeur and to the people who had built it; semi-weekly visits to salons were common. Sassoon's new cuts liberated women from the tyranny of the hairdresser; he had become a hair*cutter*, providing women with a look that they could maintain on their own without costly, even dangerous treatments and finicky protective measures—space helmet hair dryers, curlers, hair spray, sleeping with their heads wrapped in tissue paper, that sort of thing. A chic hairstyle—a flip or a beehive or some other bit of sculpture—had once been the province of ladies of leisure and means; now anyone could have it.

Like most overnight successes, it was painful years in the making. Sassoon declared: "It took me from '54 to '63 to do my work, which was to untangle what was there—the teasing, the backcombing, the hairdressing—and turn it into a haircutting art form. I'm not disparaging in any way the hairdressing art form, because it was very clever, and it made people look extremely pretty. But it wasn't for me. My work had to look much more architectural."

And when his theory had been realized, an entire world embraced it. In less than a year, Sassoon had perfected his ideas and become known for them all around the world—you could realistically compare him to the Beatles, who were doing the same to pop music at exactly the same time. And his innovations, like those of the Beatles, completely remade the field he'd mastered. The only thing more impressive, perhaps, was the path he took to his singular station.

Like so many of the people who made London swing, Vidal Sassoon was an East Ender, born in Shepherd's Bush in the west of the city but moving to Aldgate in the east in 1932 at the age of four. His father, a Sephardic Jew who sold carpets and had the gift of guile, had just left his mother, Betty, who, to support Vidal and his younger brother, Ivor, moved the family to Wentworth Street near the mythic Petticoat Lane so that she could work—under Dickensian conditions and for Dickensian wages—in the area's garment district sweatshops. After a year of struggle, she felt she had no choice but to hand the boys over to the Orphanage for Sephardic Jews in Maida Vale, where for the next six years they saw her only during Sabbath services and a regular monthly visit.

When Betty remarried, she brought her boys home, but the Nazi blitz found them relocated to Wiltshire and then, when London was safe again, to a condemned house in Lawrence Road, West Ham. Sassoon, now an adolescent, skirted school for a job as a messenger boy and a life of hijinks with friends. And his folks didn't like the trend. One night they sat him down to tell him outright that he would have to learn a trade and that they'd chosen one for him: He was to report to Professor Adolf Cohen in Whitechapel Road where he would be apprenticed as . . . a hairdresser.

Sassoon, who liked the rough-and-tumble of football and larking through bomb sites, couldn't believe his ears: "They were trying to make a ladies' hairdresser out of me!" But he was a dutiful son and reported in his one good suit at the appointed hour. Cohen, who wasn't really a professor but certainly had a donnish air, asked a few questions, ascertained Sassoon's aptitude (if acknowledging his disinterest) and announced that he would take the boy on—for the standard apprenticeship fee of one hundred guineas. He might as well have asked the Sassoons to square the circle. They apologized and started to leave.

And then Sassoon did something: By one of his accounts, he tipped his cap and then held the door open for his mother; by another, he thanked Cohen for his time as he made to leave. Whichever, Sassoon's deferential mien caught Cohen's eye, and the old master bade them stay: "It's not every day I see a polite boy around here," he told Betty. "Let's forget about the fee."

And so Sassoon began his career, partly as a janitor, partly as a shampooer, for a grand total of five shillings a week. For two-and-a-half years, Sassoon studied under Cohen—really studied, practicing every technique over and over again until he got it right, attending whatever night school classes Cohen recommended, honing his skills on models and down-and-out men at an East End homeless shelter.

When the time came for him to leave, his ambitions pointed west to the posh salons of Mayfair. He was an apt boy and presentable, but, despite his earnest efforts to imitate the actors he'd watched in West End plays, he spoke with a raw Cockney accent. The most polite salon proprietors suggested he was too young to work for them; others responded as if to a trained monkey looking for a position. He found a job in a Shaftsbury Avenue salon that catered to the streetwalker trade—classy streetwalkers, mind you—and then moved on to salons in Putney, Bayswater, Stamford Bridge, Camberwell, Knightsbridge and Maida Vale: just another youngster learning a trade, building a clientele, making a living.

Well, almost just another. Unlike most of the legions of aspiring young hairdressers, Sassoon was a Jew—not Orthodox, but certainly observant—and was well cognizant of the fact. He had been raised, after all, in a Jewish neighborhood that, especially before the war, had been besieged by Fascists marching against the Jews whom they accused of poisoning the global economy. "The East End of London was a very political place," he remembered, "an area of disquiet with loads of anti-Semitism. You had to be careful where you walked. I never went into Bethnal Green because it was a very Fascist area." Just before the war, the English Fascist Party had been outlawed and some of its leaders jailed. But they were given their liberty after the war and, amazingly, used it to once again march against England's Jews. Said Sassoon, "They started holding their meetings and wearing Fascist uniforms—if you can believe Fascist uniforms in London—sometimes helped by the police, depending on which neighborhood they were in. And you thought, Didn't we defeat all this?"

Others had the same reaction—and not just young men, but war veterans from the Jewish East End who'd come home from battlegrounds in Germany and Poland with reports of the Holocaust. These men were decorated combat heroes—tough guys, to their bones—and they weren't going to sit still for any hint of anti-Semitism in their midst. When the reemergent Fascists began making their presence felt in Jewish neighborhoods in the East End and North London, these veterans, loosely confederated in a gang known as the 43 Group, decided to fight them in the streets.

Sassoon wasn't a born fighter, but he knew some of the neighborhood tough guys, such as the human colossus known as Big Jacky Myerovitch, who worked as a bouncer for a Soho gangster and came calling on the Sassoon brothers one night in the winter of '47–8, asking them to attend a meeting of London Jews who were massing against the Fascists. The rendezvous point was a room near Leicester Square that drew young Jewish men from all over the city—"any of us," Sassoon remembered, "that were fit enough and could run fast enough and could actually conquer the fear, the extraordinary fear, of being a foreigner in your own country. When I was a kid we were made to feel as if we were foreigners in the country that we were born in. You had to conquer the fear before you could conquer the Fascists."

A few nights later, several 43 Group members attacked a Fascist meeting in Hackney; after the Jewish combatants were arrested, they appeared in court to face charges wearing the decorations they had won from the Crown for fighting the Nazis. Sassoon and other East End boys who decided to join the 43s were taught how to fight—and not à la Marquis of Queensberry, but scrappy stuff: real guerilla combat. They engaged in attacks on Fascists in Whitechapel Road, Kilburn High Road and the West End. These were carefully mounted battles, with carloads of backup fighters called in at crucial moments and other tactics of military warfare. Sassoon got beaten—he'd show up at work occasionally in bandages, bruised—and he was arrested once. But he was thrilled by his actions, by the defeats the Fascists suffered—"they were beaten in the streets, it was as simple as that"—and by the sense of belonging to something bigger than himself and his world.

When another meeting was called, this time to recruit young London Jews to help fight for Israeli independence, he heard the call. He hadn't served England, but he would join the Israeli army. This was, technically, illegal: England had only recently sanctioned the partitioning of Palestine, and British subjects were banned from joining the infant nation's armed forces. Sassoon and his fellow recruits were forced to travel to France in small, secretive groups, pretending to be tourists. Then they assembled in a tent city near Marseille, where they were evaluated and trained. After several weeks, they were flown, via Rome and Athens, to an airfield near Haifa and assigned to training camps. Eventually, Sassoon was outfitted and armed and sent into the Negev desert to fight the Egyptian army.

Even compared to melees in the London streets this was terrifying stuff—the front lines of a real war. Sassoon fought in a seventeen-day campaign intended to capture and secure a nameless desert hill in the Gaza Strip, surviving both aerial bombardment and frontal attack by Egyptian soldiers, witnessing the deaths and maimings of friends and acts of mortal bravery on both sides. When it was over, victorious, he was taken to a kibbutz to recuperate and regain his strength. While he was resting up for another rotation to the front, a cease-fire was declared; the Israelis had won. He joined in the wild celebration, but then he was left with the reality: He was English, not Israeli, and the battle was only his—no matter how he'd paid with fear and sweat and effort—in an idealistic sense. He would return to London, to hairdressing. It was, for better or worse, who he was.

"During that year in the Negev," Sassoon reflected, "I developed a sense of self that I'd never had before." But back home, he found himself drifting from job to job, not entirely sure he was at all following the right path. He was hired on at a salon on the Edgware Road, where he became interested in the world of competitive hairstyling—designing new looks which were executed and judged tournament-style. He moved on to a posh shop on Albermarle Street—Mayfair proper—and then thought about going to Paris to study and work. Finally he surfaced, through connections, at Raymond's in Grafton Street, the most prestigious salon in Britain.

Raymond, also known as "Teasy Weasy," was a grand master of theatricality and quasicelebrity, a man who breezed campily into a room and air-kissed and tutt-tutted and charmed, if you were charmed by that sort of thing—a professional character (and, by the way, a fine judge of horseflesh who owned a successful stable for decades). But he was also a master hairdresser, innovative, energetic and encouraging to his young staff, including Sassoon, to whom, after a few successful months, he offered the opportunity to run a salon that would soon open in Cardiff. Sassoon had confided to his boss that he wanted to open his own shop, and he liked the look of the new setup in Cardiff, but he wanted some input and, more, recognition: "How about calling it Vidal Sassoon at Raymond's," he asked. No dice. "How about publicity, then? I'd like my name mentioned on all photographs taken." Uh-uh. Ah, well: They parted on friendly terms.

Which was fine with Sassoon, whose ambition had come to the attention of a client who offered to help him fund a new venture. When the meeting came, Sassoon had his pitch ready:

> In most salons, the client tells the hairdresser what she wants and he gives it to her, no matter how hideous, how ludicrous the result. In my salon they will get what I think is right for them. If they don't want it, they can take their business elsewhere. In some salons the smarm is all-important—the "yes madam"-ing and "no madam"-ing, the bowing and scraping. In mine, clients will get simple, downtown politeness. We're not going to waste our breath on compliments that cost nothing and mostly mean nothing. We're going to put all our energies into producing great work. There's going to be no stuffiness, no cathedral atmosphere, no plush-lined hush. We're going to have cool, cool jazz and fabulous classical music, Mahler and Sibelius, playing in the background. Those who don't like it can find a morgue of their choice.

Most importantly, he had a financial plan: He would keep costs down—he himself would work on salary—and his brother, Ivor, now a licensed accountant, would see to the money. The financiers agreed, and in mid-1954, Sassoon opened his first salon in a third-floor premises above a shoe store and a photo studio at 108 Bond Street.

It was cramped—with room for only twenty bodies at a time and an elevator that held only three at most (and they'd better be on friendly terms, at that)—and funky for the neighborhood. Sassoon ran it true to his word, refusing to follow the "madam-knows-best" dictates of wealthy women who'd occasionally wander in, ask for some antiquated look or treatment and then leave in a huff, their hair untouched.

Slowly, the salon's reputation for quality work and a relaxed new feel spread. Business—and staff—grew. Sassoon hired Peter Laurence Taylor, a master tinter and lifestyle experimentalist, a protohippie whose wardrobe was a source of daily amused scandal among both employees and customers. He hired Leonard Lewis, another Shepherd's Bush Jewish boy with a yen for the grand life; later on, after disagreeing with Sassoon over techniques, he would leave and become Leonard of Mayfair, almost as famous as his old boss. And he hired Nigel Davies, another clothes horse, this time from North London, who called himself Mr. Christian. Davies wasn't at all serious about hair—or, in fact, much else besides looking sharp, getting paid and getting laid. He insulted customers and disappeared for knee tremblers in the elevator and generally drove Sassoon mad. Sassoon finally sacked him in a fury: "Out—and stay out! Never let me see you in this salon again!" Davies grinned: "Blimey, would you listen to old God, going on!" But leave he did, only returning after several years had passed and he had renamed himself Justin de Villeneuve and discovered Twiggy.

These colorful characters—plus an assortment of clients from the theater and jazz circles in which Sassoon had begun to run—gave the salon a hot name. But it wasn't making enough money to satisfy investors, who had hoped to compete with the stuffy sort of Mayfair salons that Sassoon was revolting against. So he bought out his backers and sought new capital. "There were many times," he remembered, "when you walked into the bank and said, 'I need. Please.' It was not easy. Once London became *it*, then, of course, it became much easier. Then the City wanted to invest in you and all kinds of people were after you." But when the lease became available on a large, old-school salon on New Bond Street—number 171—another backer emerged, a brassy Australian named Charles Prevost. Maybe because he was a visionary, maybe because he wanted to meet girls, Prevost gave Sassoon forty thousand pounds to redecorate and open the place. Sassoon hired the celebrated society interior decorator David Hicks to apply his hand to all four floors, which he did up in stark and airy black and white. In April 1959, it opened.

The change in location—just a few blocks—wasn't nearly as important as the timing. Where just a few years earlier Sassoon had to dig up old friends who'd tasted fame to give his shop a bit of chic cachet, now his salon was a destination for celebrities, well-to-do ladies and others feeling the flush of "never had it so good" prosperity. Women who were wearing clothes made by Mary Quant started to come in for the loose new style Sassoon had designed, the Shape. Some of the adventuresome London men who'd been leaning toward new styles came in, including young acting stars: Peter Sellers, Peter O'Toole, Christopher Plummer, Terence Stamp. (In recruiting such manly customers, Sassoon was no doubt aided by the fact that he was an East End boy with a known reputation as both a scrapper and a skirt-chaser; by the time he opened his second salon, in fact, he had one marriage behind him and another on the horizon.)

Energized by what was going on around him, Sassoon began sparking ideas: Handheld blow-dryers were used to create body in hair and eliminate the use of big space helmet dryers; conditioners and other treatments were created to nurture the hair of clients who'd been subjected to years of harsh chemicals, gels and sprays; electrically heated rollers helped speed up the setting time. He had become such a sensation that Clairol, the American hair product company, sent him around the U.S. in 1960 on a barnstorming demonstration tour; he followed up with a similar trip through the U.K.

And for all this success, he was still haunted by his ideas of hair sculpted geometrically and freed from all the encumbrances that many of even his newest styles still required. He pursued studies of shapes and forms—even sitting down with architect Philip Johnson to show him some sketches. He knew there was another way; he could feel it simmering under his feet.

And then in 1963 Mary Quant showed up and told him she wanted something new for her girls.

Kaboom.

Quant had that kind of power—indeed, she had virtually invented it. She had single-handedly reinvigorated the idea of modern English fashion with designs that bubbled up out of her head and into the window of a boutique on the King's Road in Chelsea, a thoroughfare which, though a ten-minute taxi ride from Piccadilly, was considered by most Londoners to be the heart of some quaint remote river village.

The impetus to Quant's starting a revolution in quiet, arty Chelsea was her marriage to Alexander Plunket Greene, one of the very first old-line Britons in whom something like the spirit of the sixties blossomed. Born to a family of English eccentrics who included among their lovers, friends and acquaintances such diverse lights as Paul Robeson, Bertrand Russell and Evelyn Waugh, he was a teenage scene unto himself in the early fifties, wandering through Chelsea in his mother's disused pajamas and slacks, hanging around Soho jazz bars, where he aspired to play the trumpet, and showing up only when he felt like it to classes at Goldsmiths College, an art and technical school in New Cross, near Deptford, where he tried to further distance himself from his fellow students—as if it were possible or necessary—by walking about with a film script under his arm. He was, in short, the sort of nutter one expected to find in Chelsea, London's nearest answer to Montmartre: moneyed, bred to leisure, artistically inclined—a definitive bohemian, if he said so himself.

Among the mere mortals who found themselves dazzled by Plunket Greene's antics at Goldsmiths was Quant, a pixie-size but blunt and strong-willed student who'd been raised variously, as her parents followed schoolteaching careers, in Kent, Wales and, after the war, in Blackheath, south of Greenwich, which would always be, in her mind, home. Quant, who was born in 1934, was attending Goldsmiths out of a compromise arrangement with her exasperated folks, who thought they could channel her penchant for designing and sewing her own clothes into a useful career: teaching art or some such. But she found herself swept into an exciting new way of life by Plunket Greene, with whom she became romantically involved, and she forsook the chance to get a teaching certificate for a life of gadding about with her beau and the ragtag bunch who came to be known as the Chelsea Set.

As much as the Jazz Age and the Beat Generation (and, later, Swinging London), the Chelsea Set was a creation of myth and media that nevertheless had a basis in the real lives of its so-called members. "The Chelsea Set was invented by gossip columnists—or promoted and publicized and brought to the public's attention that way," reflected Christopher Gibbs, the antique dealer and scenemaker who seemed always at the heart of the groovy, starting with his inclusion in the Chelsea Set. But just because the media propped it up didn't mean it didn't happen.

In the mid-fifties, at a few pubs, clubs and coffee bars mainly along the King's Road, various restless and creative young people—many from old families, some with money—began to hang out, live fast and look for kinkier diversions than the norms of the day allowed. The first real instance of jeunesse dorée in England since the Bright Young Things of the 1920s, they dressed outrageously, partied hedonistically, consorted with rough types—including gangsters—and courted headlines beyond the usual society page notices reserved for the activities of young people of their background and breeding. Chelsea Set folks did sensational things like holding a maverick drinking party on the Circle Line of the London Underground that climaxed in a chaotic free-for-all or throwing a pajama party at a Soho nightclub which, again, ended in near riot. They became famous—the men, especially—for what they were seen wearing: ethnic outfits from colonial outposts; exaggerated versions of gentlemen's clothes from previous generations of English fashion; colorful, form-fitting pants and flowing shirts; even blue jeans, then generally worn only by laborers.

They had good educations and trust funds and other advantages and perhaps that's why they were among the first Britons to act out on their frustrations with the long post-war malaise that gripped the country. Some of them had jobs—they kept small shops or photo studios or worked in advertising or public relations or the media—but mostly they gave themselves over to scene-making and the husbandry of outrage in others. "We were all very spoiled and very tiresome," recalled Simon Hodgson, who ran with the Chelsea Set. "Most of us were subsidized by our families and our lives were built around going to parties and getting drunk and meeting gangsters. Nobody had ever spoken to gangsters before—they seemed rather chic. But we were really frightfully snobbish. Everyone had to be rich, funny or famous, or at least notorious."

"Chelsea was very much removed from the rest of London," remembered Gibbs. "There were people who hung out in Chelsea who might not go east of Sloane Square for months. West of Sloane Square was a kind of dark land. You went perhaps to an amusing Italian restaurant or a snappy coffee bar. It was [a] very bohemian world. It had long-established, well-off people who were living on Cheyne Walk and such. It was a daytime culture, really; there weren't any nightclubs in Chelsea."

For those sorts of entertainments, Chelsea Setters gravitated toward the bohemian enclave of Soho, where you could feel some of the upsurging change—or, rather, feel an energy that was distinct from the prosperous after-dinner hum that Harold Macmillan bragged about. Soho was, with Chelsea, the one place in London you could count on running into artists, writers, drunks, loons and the daft on a regular basis—with the difference being that in Soho you also rubbed shoulders with gangsters, pimps, hookers, strippers, pornographers and slumming actors from nearby West End theaters rather than the aged soldiers and genteel shopkeepers of the King's Road. Soho was hardcore bohemia, a place where foreigners ran the restaurants and pubs, where homosexuals felt relatively safe, where vice businesses were permitted if not free rein, then certainly lots of elbow room.

"Soho was more louche and more cross-fertilized," remembered Gibbs. "There were East End kids coming up for a good time in the West End. There were jazz clubs and night spots and coffee bars and a sprinkling of gay bars and such. It drew a lot of people from the provinces and east London."

The best jazz music could be heard in Soho, often in tiny little basement dumps that had been converted, with self-avowed grandness, into clubs. There were a number of after-hours (and, given the erratic licensing hours of the era, afternoon) drinking clubs in the area. And it was the best neighborhood to haunt in search of ethnic food other than haute cuisine: French, Italian, Jewish and Chinese families in particular did substantial business there as restaurateurs.

But if you had the right spirit, daytime in Chelsea offered sufficient opportunities. "The world was full of chancers from all over the place," Gibbs recalled, "a lot of wild colonial boys from Australia, Canada, New Zealand, South Africa, the Caribbean. You could live on ten pounds a week. You could take a taxi ride to Hampstead for seven shillings. Just as in the nineteenth century you could live the life of a gentleman on seven hundred pounds a year, you could skate by on not very much."

Quant, who hadn't been raised with money or privilege and was, perhaps, less jaded, had a slightly different take on the scene: "I think it grew out of something in the air which developed into a serious effort to break away from the establishment. It was the first real indication of a complete change of outlook." For her, the Chelsea Set—or the loose group of people who went by that name in the papers—was like a genial extension of art school: "We felt very much a sort of isolated group because there was so little else in Chelsea. So as a group, the Chelsea lot would sort of hang together." She saw the humor and the essential frivolity of the scene, as evidenced in her pleasure in recounting the story of the elderly publican at the Markham Arms who thought that the newspapers had been referring to the "Chelsea *Six*," and had reckoned that Quant, Plunket Greene and a couple of their drinking buddies constituted the entire gang.

But then, Quant probably felt kinder toward the idea of the Chelsea Set because she stood so distinctly apart from it, distinguished by her raw talent and by ideas that no one else had ever had. Ever since girlhood, Quant had designed her own clothes in pursuit of a Peter Pan–ish idea about what constituted—or ought to constitute—women's fashion: "I grew up not wanting to grow up," she explained. "Growing up seemed terrible. It meant having candy-floss hair, stiletto heels, girdles and great boobs. To me it was awful; children were free and sane and grown-ups were hideous." Even as she hit her twenties, she still refused to kowtow to the fashion dictate that she morph into some sort of stoic, matronly mannequin. When, in mid-1955, she and Plunket Greene had the idea to go into business together, they agreed to open a boutique for young Chelsea women that offered the sorts of gear that Quant couldn't find anywhere else for herself: jewelry, clothes, accessories and the hats that Quant had been designing and selling to a handful of shops and friends. They discussed the idea with Archie McNair, one of the lot they ran with and a fellow who had a track record of succeeding with unlikely inspirations.

McNair was the owner of The Fantasy, a rising King's Road hot spot, the first coffee bar in the district and one of the first anywhere in London outside of Soho. In the early 1950s, Soho became the center of a trend that would serve as an important catalyst to the lifestyle changes of the following decade: the vogue for Italian-style coffee bars. In 1953, Frith Street was home to the first Gaggia espresso machine imported into England, and the hot little cups of steamed coffee became, along with a taste for Italian food and fashion, a staple of au courant city life. The new Italian lifestyle—the famous Dolce Vita that hadn't even been named yet in Federico Fellini's movie—was imported to England by a small army of young Italian men who had come to the U.K. to avoid serving in the real Italian army back home. When the Italian government renewed national service after the war, it allowed men to defer their conscription up to the age of thirty-six, provided they were working abroad and left before they had their induction physicals. There wasn't need for much incentive to leave in the first place—unemployment was at nearly 30 percent. And as the United States had clamped down on immigration, England found itself filling up with a steady stream of Italian workers who, naturally, brought their tastes and manners and clothes and foodstuffs with them.

The appetite for espresso and Italian fashions for men opened English eyes to a great many things, remembered restaurateur Alvaro Maccioni, one of the throng who came: "They realized that on the other side of the channel there was life after the war." More and more Italian restaurants could be found. "They didn't want to eat roast lamb anymore," he said of the English customers who flocked to the new trattorias. "Before, food was like gas or electricity: Then it became another form of entertainment."

But even more than the taste for pasta, the craze for Italian coffee swept England along with the growing prosperity: In every town, it seemed, the young people who had jobs but weren't old or jaded enough to frequent pubs turned a coffee bar into the local hip spot. Archie McNair had been one of the first to hit on this trend, and his good fortune had left him with a little capital and the desire to compound it. He joined forces with Quant and Plunket Greene, and with eight thousand pounds of seed money, they got a lease for a King's Road building that had an ideal shop space on the street level and, below, just the place for Plunket Greene to open the jazz club of his dreams. In November of 1955, the boutique, named Bazaar, opened its doors.

Among the items for sale that day were a pair of pajamas that Quant designed—the only thing she'd made for the opening, in fact, other than some hats. The gaily colored bedclothes were photographed by *Harper's Bazaar* and bought by an American clothier who said he planned to copy them for sale back home. Quant resented being ripped off but was also inspired to make more of her own pieces for the shop. Buying ready-made sewing patterns, which she revamped according to her tastes, going to Harrods for yards of cloth of the sort not normally used for women's clothes, she began working feverishly in her Chelsea bedsit, whipping up enough stock each day to replace whatever had been sold the day before. "I just went at it like any other design thing," she said, "which was clothes for the way I lived or the way one lived in Chelsea."

Both the very concept of the shop and Quant's novel designs for it were hits. "It was almost a violent success," she recalled. "People were sort of three-deep outside the window. The Royal Court Theatre people were mad about what we were doing. And it was very much the men who were bringing their girlfriends around and saying, 'This is terrific. You must have some of this!'" Because of its erratic hours—drinking with their customer-friends, Plunket Greene and Quant sometimes forgot to close until midnight—and because each day promised an entirely new look as dictated by Quant's mood or the materials she found, Bazaar became an essential destination, with young Chelsea girls popping in several times daily to see what had just been set out for sale.

What they got were simple, bold designs: bright colors, stripes or polka dots, dresses and suits that broke away from the closed-necked, pinch-waisted style of French-dominated haute couture and short—and, in time, even shorter—skirts. You didn't see stuff like it in Paris, you didn't see stuff like it in New York and you certainly didn't see anything like it anywhere else in London. The Chelsea girls ate it up. Literally, too, as Plunket Greene used the downstairs premises not to open a jazz club but rather a French-style bistro called Alexander's, one of the first new wave restaurants in all London and a decidedly trendy and popular dining spot for the crowds that hovered around Bazaar.

Outside of the predictably enthusiastic locals, however, there was at first little ballyhoo. "The trade ignored us," Quant recalled. "They called us degenerate. They raised their eyebrows in mystified amazement. Later, when they realized how successful Bazaar was proving, they called our success a 'flash in the pan.'"

But Quant had hit a nerve with her work. She was making clothes that distinguished those who wore them from their mothers—or, more exactly, the girls from the women—and which proclaimed to the world that virginity and propriety, so long the basis of English women's fashion, weren't absolute values. Her clothes were sexy—hell, *sexual*—and the sense of color, freedom and youthfulness that they imparted gradually became more and more fashionable until they finally became the norm. "The street," recalled an admiring Vidal Sassoon, "was her atelier."

Said a fashion writer then with the *Daily Express*, "Suddenly someone had invented a style of dressing which we realized we had been wanting for ages. Comfortable, simple, no waists, good colors and simple fabrics. It gave anyone wearing them a sense of identity with youth and adventure and brightness."

Quant, who, as another of their mad whims, would have her pubic hair shaved into a heart shape by Plunket Greene, saw the impact more explicitly. The look of her clothes, she explained, said, "'I'm very sexy.

I enjoy sex, I feel provocative, but you're going to have a job to get me. You've got to excite me and you've got to be jolly marvelous to attract me. I can't be bought, but if I want you, I'll have you.' "

Yes, she really said that, and more. As the most visible exponent of a new slant on life, Quant became a fount of pithy, outrageous comments.

On her ideal of a stylish woman: "She is sexy, witty and dry-cleaned."

On jewelry: "Too much jewelry makes you look old, as if you were rejected by lots of rich, old men who paid you off."

On the new vogue for youthful fashions: "Suddenly, every girl with a hope of getting away with it is aiming to look not only under voting age but under the age of consent."

On her own success: "Egg and chips, egg and chips, egg and chips—and finally we got a bit of steak!"

Not, in short, the traditional standard of English girlhood.

But that standard was starting to be swept away.

TUGBOAT TERRY

The great cities all bide by the water—rivers and oceans mainly, or a confluence of the two. It was water that brought the people there to start with; water that made their profit taking and empire building possible; water that gave their poets a living metaphor for eternity, nature, change. However the centuries have altered the buildings, the goings-on, the people, the surging, sweeping, neverending, everchanging water is the same—the oldest, most unknowable part of a city.

The Thames, for one, is a world unto itself. Murky, swift and perilously tidal, it connects the city to the world and has done since the Roman army first built a bridge across it in the age of the caesars. Psychologically it divides the metropolis in two—the capital and capitol and culture of the north, the vast, scruffy residential boroughs of the south. But it constitutes a third city, an evermoving medium of trade, tourism, crime, sensation and, being water, romance. The Thames has its own police force—the world's oldest—and ancient tunnels and bridges and docklands. Now and again it reminds those who live beside it that it is as much estuary as stream, flooding its banks with devastating frankness. Whole generations of families have lived by the Thames, worked it, eaten from it, died on it. Within London, they're a breed among themselves, urbanite yet marine, as authentically of the place as the first people who ever knew it as home.

Tom Stamp was a Thamesman, born in Poplar, the canal-laced area of northeast London between the isthmus of the Isle of Dogs and the Cockney stronghold of Bow. His father was a Thamesman, too, and Tom followed him to sea as a teen. But marriage and fatherhood brought him back onto land. On Boxing Day, 1936, Tom married Ethel Perrott, a Bow lass whom he'd met during the harvest in a Kentish hop field—a common seasonal employment for young Cockneys. For a while, to stay near Ethel, Tom worked in town as a delivery boy. But when it became clear in 1939 that war was imminent, and as he feared being called up to the army, back to the water he went—stoking coal in the guts of great ships, a "donkey man . . . one step up from a galley slave," as his eldest son would describe it.

The boy was only an infant when Tom went off, and the man who came home wasn't the same who'd left: Hellish labors had left Tom back-bent and prematurely gray. Now there would be no thought of employment on land: Water work was all he could conceive. Tom returned to the stoking, in tugs on the Thames, and after fifteen years of effort was rewarded with promotion out of the bowels of the boat. By the spring of 1961, he was a tug driver.

He was working the river that May, the twenty-third, and perhaps he steered as far west as Waterloo Bridge. If he had, he probably didn't notice the little knot of newspaper reporters and photographers on the embankment surrounding a young man who was eating an ice-cream cone and trying to wrap his mind and words around a new world. It was Tom's eldest boy, Terence, and as he sat there he was becoming famous. He was talking about a part he was going to play in a new movie; the part of a seaman.

Terence Stamp: Thames boat man [handwritten annotation]

Terence Stamp wasn't the first East End boy to become a Face in the six-ties—the photographers Bailey, Donovan and Duffy preceded him, as had Vidal Sassoon. But none of them had anything like his sudden, widespread fame, an absolute rocket to the moon that stunned the people around him and even the most jaundiced observers of the British celebrity scene. Within a year of that May afternoon, he was an Oscar nominee who commanded thousands of pounds a week in salary, escorted the most desirable women in London and was considered one of the most beautiful men in the world.

The metamorphosis turned even Stamp's own head: "For the first three or four years of my success," he would remember, "I thought the sixties were happening only to me."

Perhaps that was because Stamp was raised to feel one of a kind. He didn't acquire the sense from the family's circumstances: For most of his young life, they inhabited a typical two-up, two-down attached home with loo out back on Chadwin Road, Plaistow, a working-class enclave east of Bow with a slightly genteel air. (Terence Donovan would rib him about his relatively cushy upbringing: "Don't believe all that guff about Stamp being a Cockney. He was brought up in Plaistow, and that's like chalk and cheese.")

Rather, he was imbued with a curious notion of his special qualities by his mum, who encouraged him with nice clothes, pennies for candy, trips to the movies and indulgence of his childish tastes, affectations and, when she could afford it, desires: "Having encouraged me to think of myself as special," he remembered, "she wanted to see what I would make of myself." He had fantasies of being rescued from his dogsbody life by a mysterious woman in a black gown, who would pull up in a limousine, inform him that he was no Stamp but rather heir to some unclaimed fortune and whisk him off to a new life of comforts and wonders. He was a dreamer and an introvert and, no wonder, a mama's boy, a status driven home with the arrival on the scene of his brother Chris, in 1942.

Conceived while Tom was on leave, Chris became his dad's favorite. Terry was never, as Chris was, invited to join Tom for a day out on the tug, and where Chris was taught to scrap and fight by his father. Tom never bothered to teach his older boy how to use his fists; eventually, Stamp recalled, he stopped fighting with Chris because "it was too dangerous." Indeed, though three years younger, Chris grew burlier than Terry, who was only to discover years later that his lifelong finickiness at table was a symptom of food allergies and not a tendency toward femininity.

To be fair to Tom, Ethel, too, had her doubts about her eldest boy: "Mum's big fear," he would recall, "was that I would turn out to be a pansy. It was for this reason that I was never allowed to wear jeans. Apparently, during her evenings as a barmaid at the Abbey Arms she had served a male couple; the extremely feminine one had been encased in a pair of denims and this, combined with a fully made-up face, had given her a shock."

Yet fears of this sort didn't stop Ethel from encouraging Terry to take dancing classes or to primp in nice clothes or even, after the onset of puberty, to continue to indulge in his taste for the Rupert Bear story books of Alfred Bestall—a fancy so abhorrent to Tom that he was once actually caught in the act of throwing one of Terry's beloved volumes into the trash. (Years later, still atavistically enthralled by thoughts of his beloved Rupert, Stamp tried to buy a bear cub from Harrods as a pet at a time when he was sharing a flat with another young actor, a fellow by the name of Caine. His mate put his foot down: "It's a bear, and they bloody well grow up!")

At school Stamp evinced no special aptitude or ambition: "I don't know about you, Stamp. You're a monkey puzzle," a teacher told him. He drifted into acting in a local amateur theatrical, managing the rare trick of being singled out for opprobrium in a small East London newspaper for his brief performance. Sent to the local gymnasium to build up his body, he found a group of friends and a sport—*table tennis*, as it turned out, another point of worry for his distrustful dad, who had taken to calling his oldest son "Lord Flaunt" after Little Lord Fauntleroy, for his vanity.

He tried his hand at being a golf pro—another means, perhaps, of fulfilling his mother's intuition that he would stand out. But he flopped and soon was taken by his mum to the Youth Employment Bureau, where he was pointed toward a job as a boy Friday-slash-messenger at an advertising firm in Cheapside, just east of St. Paul's and the farthest west in the city he'd ever ventured regularly in his life. He was sixteen years old, and he had no clue where he was going.

One night a year or so later, as he sat nicely dressed in his family's tiny front room watching the new television Tom and Ethel had managed to acquire, he came to the conviction that the English actors he was watching weren't particularly skilled at their profession. He'd had this impression previously, but this time he voiced it: "I could do better than that myself!"

Tom, still unsure about the boy, turned firmly toward him: "People like us don't do things like that," he declared. And then, before Stamp could offer a rebuttal, he nailed the door shut: "Just don't talk about it anymore. I don't want you to even think about it."

"He didn't say it unkindly," Stamp recalled. "In retrospect, I'm sure he felt he was saving me a lot of heartache. I never spoke about it again."

So he kept at the ad game, rising—through some lies about his experience and a combined talent for handwriting and mimicry—to the rank of typographer at a tonier firm in Soho. He had taken to lazing about the West End after work, becoming a semiregular at movie houses and chatting up the sorts of girls he would never meet back at home. The taste for this new life in his mouth, he did something few in his situation dared: He found a flat—cheap and a bit mean but at a posh address on Harley Street, where Mayfair's priciest doctors lived—and he moved away.

It was a stunning decision—another thing "people like us" never did—and Stamp's own closest friend, with whom he planned the getaway, couldn't find the nerve to make the leap with him at the crucial moment, choosing to continue living with his parents. Later, reflecting on the limited sense of horizons bred into his fellow East Enders, Stamp could get huffy: "They're scared of nothing except being told they're putting on airs and acting posh. And that stops them from trying to do *anything*. They're smart and good-looking and sharp and tough as nails. But the nits waste their lives because they don't know that there's so much lying around, waiting to be picked up by the boy with a bit of talent."

But that was the movie star talking, the toast of the trattorias and the discotheques, and he hadn't been born yet. In his place was a vague young wanderer, killing a year before his compulsory military service with life as a would-be among the rich and swell.

It turned out that the army didn't want him: flat feet, or the analog thereof. The guaranteed two years of regimentation and routine vanished: poof! It was like a free play on life's pinball machine, and he was determined to use it audaciously. He'd been musing along with a buddy from work about taking acting classes. Now he would reward himself with two years' pursuit of the chimera of a thespian career. He'd be no worse off, he reckoned, than if he'd spent two years on a rifle range or digging latrines.

It being the fifties and he a James Dean fan, he decided he'd study the Method, signing up with guru Jos Tregoningo's Dean Street studio in Soho. It was quite the hip scene, with pretty girls and even, one night, a BBC TV crew taking in the exotic goings-on. Stamp and his classmates were filmed performing various exercises, one of his mates standing out in particular with his impression ("rather wonderful," Stamp remembered) of a tree; asked by the interviewer what the experience was like, he held his pose and declared, "I can feel the sap rising within me."

The Method failed, though, to answer some of Stamp's basic questions about the acting game, and he itched for something more formal in the way of training. He and his acting mates had conned to the fact that there were scholarships available at some of the really good acting schools: the Royal Academy of Dramatic Art, the London Academy of Music and Dramatic Art, the Webber Douglas Academy of Dramatic Art. It was at the latter that Stamp was awarded a scholarship: two years' free tuition plus eight pounds per month stipend—not enough to live on, but sharing a flat and doing odd jobs, he could maintain himself reasonably as an acting student, if not yet an actor.

And so he learned proper acting—and to earn extra money he took to stage-crewing in the big houses of theaterland: He saw the original London production of *West Side Story* scores of times. Then a break: He played Iago in his school's year-end showcase and piqued the interest of an agent, Jimmy Fraser, an old Piccadilly hand widely admired as an essentially decent fellow in a racket full of heels: "My God, that's the sexiest Iago I've ever seen," Fraser spouted. "Thank goodness he's not loose on the streets!"

Fraser signed Stamp up and he got him work straight off: twelve pounds a week to play a Geordie soldier in a suburban production of *The Long and the Short and the Tall,* the World War II play that had launched Peter O'Toole to stardom. When that brief run closed down, the producers decided to mount a touring version of the show, and Stamp was asked to carry on in his role. At the first cast meeting, held at the Duke of Argyll pub in Soho, he got a glimpse of the actor who would play the lead—O'Toole's understudy, in fact, from the original West End production: a blond guy, insolent, sardonic and possessed of the most striking, hooded blue eyes. He was several crucial years and many, many life lessons more experienced than Stamp, and he would almost right away come to dominate the younger man's next few formative years: Maurice Micklewhite by birth, he was known as Michael Caine to the trade.

If Stamp had a cameo in Caine's life story, Caine had a feature role in Stamp's. He was six years older, he had served in the Korean War (indeed, one grim night he stood sentry at the very front of the demilitarized zone, the tip of the spear of Democracy pointed across the black abyss at the Red hordes), he was divorced—with a child—and he had dozens of film, stage and TV jobs under his belt. Stamp, always looking for gurus, now had a South London know-it-all as his personal guide to the stage life. Caine was a little suspicious of Stamp's wide-eyed admiration at first go: "So you're one of the lads, then?" he said to him once they'd become better acquainted. "Blimey! I thought you were a poof!" But he felt kinship with any fellow working-class boy with the gumption to give the acting game a go: "You've got more front than bloody Woolworth's!" he pronounced, approvingly.

As soon as the touring company took to the road, Caine began showing Stamp the ropes—how to get a good hotel room, the idiosyncrasies of various theaters and, most vitally, where to find the likeliest girls in a given town: "Mike ran amok with sexual theory even when sitting down," Stamp said. When the tour neared an end, Caine mentioned he was between addresses back in London, and Stamp offered him a share of the Harley Street flat. Presently they acquired lodgings of their own in Ennismore Gardens Mews, south of Hyde Park and east of the Royal Albert Hall in a Kensington that they had only inhabited in dreams.

Here the modernization of Terence Stamp began: Caine introduced him to the latest novels, movies, coffee bars. They would plan whole days around doing nothing: where to nurse a cup of tea for hours, which library to haunt to read the newspapers, whether to spring for two lamb sandwiches for lunch or just the one, what pub or party or night spot was aptest to yield up a pair of game young ladies (Stamp was in awe of Caine's skill as a puller of birds). There were auditions and calls to their agents and now and again the flickering prospect of good work; Caine gave Stamp hints and wise advice that constituted something of a makeshift master class in acting; they even—decades before their time—wrote a screenplay together, *You Must Be Joking*, about two South London lads who try to break out of their native world. Mostly, as Stamp recalls, there were the luxuries of time and time spent together. "The young Mike Caine was heaven to be with," Stamp remembered. And in some ways, he was as happy during these lean days as he ever would be.

They were working together in a Wimbledon theater in the spring of 1961, playing in the premiere of one of the very rare misses in the ascendant career of songwriter Lionel Bart, *Why the Chicken*, when Stamp got an excited call from Jimmy Fraser. He was to report to an office in Golden Square, Soho, that afternoon; Peter Ustinov wanted him to audition for the new film he was directing, *Billy Budd*.

"What's the part?" Stamp asked.

"The lead: Billy Budd."

He couldn't believe his ears: "They must really be scraping the barrel if they want to see me!"

Fraser leveled with him: "They are. They've already seen every young actor in town."

P.S.: He got the part. Ustinov met him and had him read and asked him to come back for a screen test the next day. He took a quick lesson from Caine in how to respond to the intimidating presence of a camera (he'd never even acted for TV before), he wore one of his dad's old sweaters from the navy for good luck and he was off. With the camera rolling, Ustinov asked him to listen to a heap of abuse and false charges and *not* respond—just as Herman Melville's seaman Budd is unable to respond to a slander and is thereby impelled into striking an officer. Relying on a bit of Method trickery, Stamp recalled how he felt when he was unfairly caned at school and had to, mutely, take it. When the test was over, Ustinov came and patted his cheek: "That was . . . tumultuous."

A little time passed; Stamp despaired, thinking he'd made a botch of so good a chance; and then he heard: He was in. And Ustinov chose to kick off the production with a splashy press conference to introduce his handsome young Cockney leading player to the world. The setting was a lunchtime cocktail party at the Savoy. Wearing his second-ever suit, a shirt borrowed from Lionel Bart and hair that had just recently been dyed blond for the movie, Stamp stepped into the limelight on May 23, 1961, telling his brief life story while enjoying an ice cream along the river on which his father was busy at work.

The next day newspapers carried accounts of "Tugboat Terry," a name, Stamp recalled, "that would cling like a hair in my mouth."

Months later, when he came home to London after filming *Billy Budd* in Spain, Stamp quickly recognized that the world immediately around him was changing. It wasn't only the instant fame that the papers heaped at his feet. The city itself and all the young, creative people in it were moving in heady new ways.

His flatmate, Caine, always with an ear to the ground, had heard of a hot new club, the Saddle Room, where the patroness, a former flame of Prince Phillip's named Helen Cordet, egged her customers into trying the new dance craze, the Twist. "Can't get in there," Caine explained. "It's a real toffee place, full of high-class crumpet." But Stamp was no longer some East End bum with neither prospects nor sway. He told Caine to get dressed and not worry; when they arrived at the club, he told the doorman "I'm Stamp, and he's with me," and bang: In they were.

It was like that everywhere. La Discotheque (where a couple of notorious bad girls, Christine Keeler and Mandy Rice-Davies, caught his eye), the best restaurants, posh shops: Stamp's face was his passport to everything. It almost didn't matter that, as he showed in *Budd*, he could act and act well. He was a one-man vanguard, embodying whatever sense there was in the culture at large that young Britons had arrived. Flush with instant success, drunk on fame, Stamp entered the commotion in early midstream but at full pace. He could rightly consider himself the center—the first of the new generation to make it smashingly big.

And you couldn't blame him. His role in *Billy Budd*, effectively his debut, would garner him an Oscar nomination for Best Supporting Actor and worldwide recognition. He was in the middle of something that he had no way to grasp—nor, indeed, did anyone else. Taken up by the press as a symbol of a new wave in British life, he was presented as a standard of his generation, and he was perfectly willing to tell the press as much: "People like me, we're the moderns," he pronounced. "We wear elastic-sided boots and we smoke Gauloises, we work hard and we play hard. We have no class and no prejudice. We're the new swinging Englishmen. And it's people like me who are spreading the word."

It wasn't just in England that people were noticing, either, in his view. Though he'd barely seen a little bit of the world, he spoke as if he understood perfectly his place in it: "There's a new kind of Englishman that I think the general public will be interested in," he declared. "He's very masculine, very swinging, very aware, well-dressed and all that but with great physical and mental strength. He's the working-class boy with a few bob as opposed to the chinless wonder. French girls and American girls used to look on Englishmen as idiots because they only saw the ones that could afford to travel. Now they're seeing the new type and they think they're great."

And no one, in his view, was more a paragon of this new English animal than he: "I would like to start a Terence Stamp trend, but of course to do this I would have to be in a more important position than I am now."

That was a foolish young man talking, of course, unused to having microphones in his face and great swaths of history to describe for the world's consumption. In later years, Stamp could explain better what that adrenaline-drunk whelp was thinking: "The whole point of the sixties was that it was like coming out of prison," he said. "I was twenty-two when the sixties started. I just couldn't have been better placed. The working class were just dogsbodies up until then. Suddenly we were Jack the lads. Everybody wanted to be like us. I can't begin to express what it was like after the Pill and before AIDS. It was a golden section."

Ah, the Pill.

When he was cast in *Billy Budd*, Stamp was emerging as a sexual being, engaging in one-off trysts with fellow acting students and an ongoing fling with a wealthy Chelsea lass who lived near the flat he shared with Caine, but certainly no one's idea of Casanova. By the following summer, with his face on movie screens and all over newspapers, his sexual horizons had become seemingly limitless.

The eagle-eye Caine beheld with wonder his flatmate's astounding success with women. With the boost their household finances had received from Stamp's film work—*Budd* was immediately followed by a turn as a juvenile delinquent in *Term of Trial*, on which set Stamp was snubbed by Laurence Olivier—their menage had shifted to a flat on Ebury Street, an address close enough to Chelsea to put them right in the heart of the burgeoning new scene. As opposed to their tiny one-bedroom flat in Ennismore Garden Mews, where they'd perfected a trick of pulling the other fellow's mattress, bed linens and all, into the sitting room in one fell (and, to some dollies' eyes, alarmingly proficient) swoop, here they each had a room, Stamp, the rent payer, claiming the larger. But the extra room couldn't quite make up for the added female traffic occasioned by Stamp's new fame and money.

"For the first time," Caine recalled, "I saw what an irresistible aphrodisiac these two can be when combined. . . . The succession of individual dolly birds turned into a flock and I was the flight controller. Getting them in and out of the very busy airfield that our flat had become, without collision, meant keeping them on a very narrow and definite flight path. . . . The job, though stressful, was not without its compensations as the odd damsel in distress was guided, as an emergency, onto my own private runway, bedroom two."

As Stamp's reputation and confidence grew, he became almost frighteningly successful as a seducer, even in the eyes of so jaundiced an observer as Caine. There was the time, for instance, when Caine came home perturbed because, as he explained to Stamp, he'd heard a rumor that the two of them were homosexual lovers. Stamp asked who'd been spreading the rumor, and Caine gave him the names, then became alarmed that his friend was going to try to sort the gossips out with his fists. Stamp had no such plan. A few weeks later, he came into the apartment in a merry mood: "Remember all those blokes who said we were queers?" he asked Caine. "Well, I've screwed all their girlfriends!"

For all his newfound bacchanalian proficiency, Stamp still retained his youthful dreaminess and persisted in falling in love with great beauties he'd seen on TV or in magazines. At times, he was brilliantly successful in seeing these schoolboy crushes through to grown-up affairs. There was Julie Christie, whom he'd swooned over in a TV commercial before she was a name and met through Caine, who knew her through a few connections he had in the business; after a whirlwind romance, Stamp found himself dumped when Christie went off to Bradford to make *Billy Liar* and become a star. Presently, he hooked up with Caterine Milinaire, an assistant editor at *Queen* and stepdaughter of the Duke of Bedford. The romance was, in Stamp's mind, indicative of the great changes going on in English society: "Some yobbo like me could get into the Saddle Room and dance with the Duchess of Bedford's daughter, and get hold of her, and get taken down to Woburn Abbey to hang out for a long weekend and have dinner in the Canaletto room with the Duke's sons!"

And all this while, there was another girl he had in mind: Doe-eyed, long-legged, with a pert expression and a modern mien and yet somehow comfortably suited to all the lovely clichés about what an English girl ought to be. He'd seen her in fashion layouts and advertisements in magazines and was smitten. And he knew he wasn't alone: "Her cover shots were pinned to the underside of prefects' desks and bedsit walls across the country," he recalled. Caine warned him away, telling him that the girl, Jean Shrimpton, was living with the photographer who took most of those shots, David Bailey; Bailey had even left his wife and set up house with Stamp's dream girl. "Sounds like they're almost cut-and-carried (Cockney slang: cut-and-carried = married)," Caine told him. "Besides, I hear he hails from down your manor. Probably a nice bloke."

Ah well, another dream. . . .

Aside from becoming terribly famous and getting laid in grand houses, of course, Stamp was about the work of finding a follow-up to *Billy Budd*, no small matter in itself. Following the advice of Peter Ustinov, Stamp had grown picky—indeed, difficult—in selecting new parts, demanding four thousand pounds for a mere ten days of work on *Term of Trial*.

The producer of that film was Jimmy Woolf, a garrulous, outsized figure who was the son of a producer and the brother and business partner of another. For Stamp, who'd never had much support of his acting ambitions at home, the oversized Woolf was to become a Falstaffian mentor, popping pills, smoking cigars and dispensing insights into the film industry that, in Stamp's mind, trumped even Michael Caine's canny advice. "He became the superbright adult I'd always wanted in my life," Stamp admitted. "I was dazzled by the man's brilliance. Other friendships appeared childlike by comparison."

Woolf, in fact, tried explicitly to prize Stamp away from Caine's ministrations, particularly from Caine's advice that Stamp take any job that came along. "Michael Caine is not you," Woolf told him when Stamp reported over one of their frequent lunches together that his flatmate was suggesting he take a part he'd been offered. "Michael Caine would do anything. Stars are choosy, they only come out at night. There are lots of fine British actors, but not so many stars. Don't be in such a rush."

And so he turned up his nose at such pictures as *Youngblood Hawke*, a Hollywood adaptation of Herman Wouk's novel about a hot young writer and the mean old publishing world. After the producers offered him thirty thousand pounds to sign and two hundred fifty pounds a week while working, he said, "They sent me the script. It was bad enough reading the lines in this room. To get up in a studio and say them would have been impossible. Far too embarrassing. I turned it down. Being Americans they thought it wasn't enough money. So they offered double. I still couldn't do it." (Imagine Caine's horror upon reading *that* in the paper!)

Hounded by a press that wanted to know when he'd follow up *Budd*, Stamp complained that the industry wasn't making it possible for him: "You know, the only two English actors they think they can build up internationally are O'Toole and me. I reckon I'm now worth around thirty thousand pounds a picture and the reason I've done nothing this last year is that I've been offered nothing but rubbish."

But the truth wasn't so much that he'd priced himself out of work as that he'd grown too much to believe Woolf's protestations that he was utterly unique. By 1964, when, two years after *Billy Budd*, he was still sifting through offers diffidently, everywhere around him young English actors were taking off. And he—the most handsome and among the most talented—was putting himself in danger of being left out.

In the wake of *Look Back in Anger* and the 1959 film of it, a string of movies about the hard times and rough passions of young men and women of the provinces revived the British film much in the way the *nouvelle vague* was reviving the French. "Kitchen sink" cinema, as it came to be called, featured a crop of young performers who, though in many cases classically trained, lacked the homogenizing polish associated previously with fine British acting: Albert Finney, Tom Courtenay, Rita Tushingham, Oliver Reed, Alan Bates. Regional actors with regional voices, they crashed into the public eye playing drunks and lashers-out and fornicators, characters who railed, like *Look Back in Anger*'s Jimmy Porter, against the age-old system yet succumbed to it, sometimes out of choice, just as often out of erosive inevitability. In the ironic way of the times, they were becoming glitzy media stars, celebrated by the very social and economic machinery their films decried.

Lynn Redgrave, who was a Londoner by birth and was well trained and *could* speak properly, was one beneficiary of these changes, playing the sort of role that might have gone to traditional beauties just a few years before. "I became an actor, I suppose, at a lucky time," she admitted. "The young actors suddenly weren't aspiring to skip through the French doors looking beautiful. There was this new style of acting. It wasn't really new, because great acting was always great acting. But suddenly people did behavior. They didn't just stand in the perfect position looking beautiful."

The movies these actors starred in were, picture for picture, as strong as any national cinema had to offer: *Room at the Top, The Loneliness of the Long-Distance Runner, This Sporting Life, A Kind of Loving, A Taste of Honey, Billy Liar, Saturday Night and Sunday Morning, Tom Jones, The Damned, The Leather Boys.* If, as a group, they seemed to condemn English life and traditions, they also made a great case for London as the capital of world cinema, with new directors availing themselves of some of the techniques that were developed in the French *nouvelle vague* or Italian *neorealismo* and an impressive corps of actors who could play classical or modern with equal flair. At the same time, as the result of arcane legal and financial obligations, American film companies found themselves making more and more films in Europe, England in particular.

With all this activity, and with the public's new appreciation of lower-class and provincial actors, directors and stories, the early sixties was the first time in the history of British film when a native performer could become a real international star without having at least one foot in classical drama or serious stage work. And Stamp, who was, for a while anyhow, among the most promising of faces in this great new bloom of English cinema, patiently followed Jimmy Woolf's advice that he only accept the plummiest of parts—much to the suspicion of Stamp's friends, who thought that Woolf would rather have had the actor as a regular lunch date than see him work steadily. Stamp suspected the same: "Although I knew he was somehow preventing me from working," he admitted later on, "I didn't care: I thought I could handle it. Jimmy Woolf must have laughed. He read me like a book. Spun me like a top."

And yet, finally, an offer came that even Woolf agreed that Stamp could not ignore. In the midst of a stupendous age for English cinema, with the whole world looking to Britain for new directions in film technique, in acting and in style, Stamp agreed to go off to Los Angeles and act for William Wyler, who'd been directing Hollywood movies since 1925.

The film was *The Collector*, and it was actually a hell of a good project. Wyler, of course, was a giant, with a résumé that included such works as *Dead End, Wuthering Heights, The Best Years of Our Lives, The Little Foxes, Mrs. Miniver, Roman Holiday* and *Ben-Hur*. His new picture was based on John Fowles's internationally bestselling, prize-winning novel. Stamp was cast in the role of Freddie Clegg, a wormy little clerk who wins a fortune in the football pools and then spends the money in pursuit of a scheme to kidnap a woman and convince her to love him, a terrific chance for Stamp to expand his screen persona beyond the strong, decent, stuttering angel that was Billy Budd. Playing opposite his old drama school chum (and *Budd* premiere date) Samantha Eggar, Stamp would reinvent himself as a twisted, obsessive sociopath, as far a cry as could be imagined from his last role—and, presumably, from himself.

He had dreamt up an entirely new life.

AN ORDINARY PERSON COULDN'T DO IT

In 1962, businessmen commuting between Liverpool and London didn't fly or drive but plumped themselves into British Rail carriages at Lime Street or Euston station and spent several hours incommunicado, gazing at the countryside, catching up on paperwork, browsing newspapers, sampling the dodgy railway cuisine. The two-hundred-mile journey was literally a trip between worlds: the prestige, power, wealth and sophistication of the capital at the southern end; a provincial port city with a queer local dialect and as many cultural and sentimental ties to Ireland as England at the northern. To the extent that there was any notion of a flow of traffic between the two cities, it was a given that one left Liverpool in search of *more*: more work, more money, more opportunity. Londoners didn't even go to Liverpool to holiday; if they went there at all, it was to conduct business or see family.

On the evening of February 7, 1962, Brian Epstein, the twenty-seven-year-old manager of central Liverpool's best record store, boarded the northbound train at Euston in a state of gloom and disappointment. He had recently become a semiregular among the hopeful southbound travelers from his hometown, but now he was heading home, tail between his legs, his dreams of *more* dissolving in front of him.

The day before, he had taken lunch with executives of Decca, one of England's largest and most prestigious record labels, to discuss a new business venture on which he had embarked and staked his name and reputation, such as they were. Epstein prided himself on his ability to predict the public appetite for pop music: Record company sales reps dined out on stories of his gargantuan orders for little-heralded discs—some of which they themselves had tried to talk him out of—which then became massive hits. Now he thought he could apply the same instincts to managing a pop group; he had just the month before contracted to represent an unknown musical quartet from his hometown. Leveraging his standing as a big account, he had stuck a foot in the door at Decca and insisted that their top artist and repertoire men get a load of his new discoveries.

Decca's chief of A&R at the time was Dick Rowe, a somewhat sourpussed music industry veteran who had risen during the era of smooth fifties pop and gotten a foot into the youth market with such acts as Tommy Steele and Billy Fury. He liked to boast that he knew nothing about music except that he knew what he liked. And one thing he didn't, he admitted some years later, was Brian Epstein: "It's very difficult for me to say a nice word about Epstein. I just didn't like him. He was too conscious of the fact that he'd been well educated and fancied himself as a gent." At the time he made those remarks, Rowe had become world famous for the cost of his aversion to Epstein: "It's unfortunate," he admitted, "that I didn't get on with the person I should have got on with the most." But in the winter of 1962, nobody knew that Epstein's act would go on to do just what the presumptuous Liverpool record merchant said they would—"be bigger than Elvis."

For all his personal distaste for the man, Rowe didn't give Epstein the bum's rush; he knew how much his custom meant to Decca. He had the Liverpool band record an hour's worth of material for him and then spent a month sitting on it, ignoring Epstein's pleas for a reaction. Then, he and an assistant had Epstein over to the executive restaurant in the company's Albert Embankment office tower to discuss the band during lunch. They made small talk about business and then, over coffee, the kiss-off: "Not to mince words," Rowe said, "we don't like your boys. Groups are out; four-piece groups with guitars particularly are finished." Epstein protested; Rowe cut him dead: "The boys won't go. . . . We know these things. You have a good record business in Liverpool. Stick to that." (Asked later about the Decca dismissal, Paul McCartney said of Rowe, "He must be kicking himself now," to which John Lennon responded flatly, "I hope he kicks himself to death!")

The next evening, after a final rebuff, Epstein phoned Liverpool to ask the members of the band to meet his train. He had been their manager for a matter of weeks, and nothing he'd tried had worked: They'd been rejected by EMI, Pye, Phillips, Columbia, HMV, Oriole and now Decca, which had showed the most interest in them (or, rather, the least willingness to say no to Epstein) to date. It would be hard news for the band to hear. And it would be even harder, perhaps, for Epstein to deliver it: In so doing, after all, he would be admitting that, as in school, in the military, in an acting career and even in romance, he was once again a failure.

The pity of it was, Brian Epstein wasn't some scruff whose life of failures represented an inability to reach goals that lay beyond his grasp. He was the sort, rather, who, by the long-standing rules of English society, ought to have done well enough at *something*.

He had been born into middle-class comfort and privilege, the eldest son of a respected Jewish merchant family in Childwall, a well-appointed, leafy suburb of Liverpool. His father, Harry, worked in *his* own father's successful furniture store; his mother, Queenie, came from a family that produced a popular line of furniture that the Epsteins sold. By the time Brian arrived on September 19, 1934 (Yom Kippur, auspiciously) the little family—which would grow only by one more son—was installed in a five-bedroom, two-bathroom house. Save for a wartime evacuation to a northern seaside community during the Nazi air assault on Liverpool's ports, it was the only family home Brian would ever know.

As the firstborn son of a well-off Jewish family, Brian was naturally presumed to be destined for great things: scholastic excellence, perfect manners, social standing. He would have a career, make a name, sire a family. In all of this, for years, he would disappoint Harry and Queenie. "I was not," he would one day admit, "the best of sons."

Once Brian began attending school, his presumed future began to dissolve. He had no particular scholastic aptitude. He disliked sports (though he did, schoolmates recall, like wearing dashing sporting uniforms). He was, by his own confession, something less than a people person: "With little to offer in the way of brilliance and nothing in the way of acceptable personality," he remembered later on, "I was not a very popular individual . . . I was not very good at forming friendships."

Partly due to the family's need to evacuate Liverpool, partly due to his own slovenly school habits and petulant manner, partly due to the fact that he failed to forge one single, enduring bond to any classmate or institution, he attended five grammar schools and two colleges before removing himself altogether from academe and the hopes of a profession in letters, law, medicine or science. Just before his sixteenth birthday, he came to work for Harry; it would have to be business for him—and the family business at that.

At the time, I. Epstein and Sons, the store run by Harry with his Polish immigrant father Isaac, was sufficiently respected and popular to prosper even in the lingering shadow of rationing and economic stagnation that smothered English confidence in the early 1950s. Everyone shopped there for furniture, musical instruments and the like, even families who had to count their pennies like the James McCartneys of Speke; wee little Paul first played "Chopsticks" on a piano sold to his dad by Harry Epstein. Brian, maturing into something of a proper young man, with a new, becoming fussiness about his dress and manner, took to the responsibility of being a third-generation furniture peddler. At last something seemed to engage his attention and maybe even his ambition.

He began, too, to socialize, dating some of the daughters of Liverpool's most prominent Jewish families and slipping—with caution but undeniable engagement—into the city's world of closeted homosexuals. There would long be a side of Brian that was drawn sexually to women—at least one local lass whom he chatted up at a boozy soiree in the early sixties remembered him as "a better necker than anyone else at that party." But increasingly he found himself attracted to men in a fashion more profound and lasting than the groping, bonding, transitional one stereotypical of English public school life; he had matured and grown sufficiently sure to confess his bent to his parents and brother who, disappointed, nevertheless stood with him.

With his bit of money and his blossoming poshness and the taste of success at *something, finally* on his tongue, he was building a complete life for himself. And then came the letter: December 9, 1952: An able-bodied, eighteen-year-old man, Brian Epstein was conscripted into His Majesty's armed forces. It's a measure of how much Epstein had absorbed Harry and Queenie's notion of what sort of man he should be that he immediately thought he belonged in the RAF, the most elite corps he could think of (and, he somehow surmised, the easiest). Instead, he was assigned to the army and sent to train in Aldershot, the Fort Dix of England, a nondescript spot forty or so miles southwest of London in Hampshire.

Brian hated Aldershot: "If there is a more depressing place than this in all Europe," he remembered, "then I would not be interested to know of it." And he hated the army as much as he had hated any of the colleges he struggled through: "If I had been a poor schoolboy, I was surely the lousiest soldier in the world." Agreeing with Brian's self-assessment, his commanders turned him into a clerk and assigned him to the staff of the Royal Army Service Corps and stationed him in Regents Park.

If conscription seemed a prison sentence, then this specific station was the most hoped-for of reprieves. Brian had relatives in West London and now he had the whole capital as his furlough ground. He dove into the city's pleasures—the restaurants, the coffee bars, the theaters and nightclubs, the gay demimonde—with ready ease.

A little too ready, actually. He rolled back to his barracks one night in a large hired car and dressed like a City gent: bowler, pinstripe suit, brolly—the works. The guards and several others took him for an officer, and he accepted their salutes; the next morning, a testy superior charged him with impersonating an officer. He lost his liberty privileges and, with them, his equilibrium. Before long, he was seeing a psychiatrist and, less than a year after showing up for induction, he was given a medical discharge. "I ran like a hare for the Euston train," was how he remembered his release.

Back to the furniture racket, then, and the Liverpool social whirl. Brian and his chums—similarly elegant young homosexual sons of comfortable families—became gourmets and night owls, now driving out to sample the fare at well-appointed country inns, now frequenting one of the city's secreted gay bars, now taking in a performance of the Liverpool Playhouse repertory company and, after, lounging with the players in a pub or coffee bar. It was in this latter setting that the next unlikely fancy popped into Brian's head: Surely nature had bred him so grandly for the stage. With the help of a few friends attached to the theater, he would enroll in the Royal Academy of Dramatic Art; he would be an actor.

Like school and soldiering, it made a poor fit: "Brian was not a natural mover," recalled the actress Helen Lindsay, who helped him prepare for his RADA audition. "He had no flow in his movements. His movement was completely unrelated to his speech." But he applied himself and, on his twenty-second birthday, he passed the audition and was accepted into the most prestigious acting school in the world.

Once again, he had London available to him, and he took to it with Epicurean zeal. There were concerts and parties and restaurants and liaisons with both men and women. His teachers weren't overwhelmed with him, but they recognized that he projected a palpable presence and might yet learn to be an artist. But he was miserable, drinking too much, lonely for all his apparent company and antipathetic to the actorly personality he was meant to be cultivating in himself: "The narcissism appalled me," he would recall. Before the first academic year had ended, he resolved to leave.

And this wouldn't be the worst news he would bring home. On the Wednesday night after Easter 1957, Brian stepped off a subway train at the Swiss Cottage tube station, en route to his Hampstead bedsit. He used the station men's room and, when he emerged, noticed a young man eyeballing him. The look they exchanged hit a nerve in Brian immediately: This was a gay man, he realized, and, although he had recently turned his mind to quelling his homosexual inclinations, he was undeniably excited. He walked around the tube station a few times, continuing to return the other man's gaze, and then, agitated and self-conflicted and a little scared, stepped out into the street. When he saw that he was being followed, he exchanged a few words with the fellow, a conversation that was entirely innocent in the strictest sense but utterly explicit in another. Brian broke away, and a minute or three later saw the man again, this time in the company of another man; both were watching him. He walked away; he loitered; he agonized: What did they want?

They wanted to arrest him: "Persistently importuning for immoral purposes" they called it, claiming that it wasn't just a single undercover officer but four (and then, the next day in Marylebone Magistrate's Court, *seven*) men with whom Brian had conducted this tremulous, abortive courtship dance. Lies, of course, but he pled guilty to them—heeding the suggestion of the investigating detective—so as not to endure the ignominy of an open hearing in which his life and habits would be bared. The court, piteously, merely fined him. Once again, it was back to Harry and Queenie, another failure stuck to the sole of his shoes, and a horrifying shame on top of it.

In his diary, recounting these days, he wrote of his deep self-loathing: "Through the wreckage of my life by society, my being will stain and bring the deepest distress to all my devoted family and few friends." And yet he was drawn, again and again, to the same sort of furtive, dangerous sexual encounter the very prospect of which got him framed and convicted in London. Cottaging at a public lavatory in Derby, a good drive out of Liverpool, he was attacked and beaten by a man dressed as a construction worker (Brian always, according to everyone who ever cruised with him, preferred the rough types); bloodied and robbed of his wallet, he made his way to a friend's house in Liverpool to recuperate; a few days later, his assailant showed up at his home, threatening public exposure unless Brian paid him off. At the advice of his parents, Brian brought in the police; using Brian as bait, they caught the man and put him away for three years.

This was, seemingly, bottom: Ashamed and humiliated, a bust at everything his parents might reasonably have hoped for him, Brian submitted without struggle to the business of selling furniture to Liverpool's families. But now, for once, luck was with him. At the end of the 1950s, the British economy had finally reawakened from its tedious postwar lethargy. The Epstein business was expanding into central Liverpool, first with an outlet on Charlotte Street and then into the heart of the shopping district, Whitechapel Street. For this move downtown, a new name was adopted: North End Music Stores, or NEMS.

It wasn't so much the fact that there were more shops to man that formed the basis of Brian's good fortune but that the nature of the business was changing. Whereas the original I. Epstein and Sons forsook decoration for function and location, the central Liverpool NEMS stores would require a bit more dash to stand out. Brian, the creative, theatrical son with the nice way about him, made a neat fit with the new image. He was given a responsible position first at Charlotte Street, where he indulged in revolutionary—and very successful—experiments in window design (he displayed chairs with their backs facing out, for instance, in an effort to approximate how they'd look in an actual parlor), and then at Whitechapel Street, where NEMS had planned to augment its booming business in phonographic equipment with a record department. It was like the invention of a new medium. And in it Brian would express something like genius.

NEMS Whitechapel was, by all accounts, a *great* record store. It stocked *everything:* imports, jazz, classical, pop, you name it—and if you did and it wasn't in stock they would knock themselves out to get it. Typically for the time, it was stocked with listening booths in which shoppers could sample various discs; the pre-Epstein Beatles wiled away many idle afternoons there listening to American records they had no intention of actually buying. Like Rick's Cafe in *Casablanca, everybody* went to NEMS and *everybody* knew the enigmatic, elegant proprietor, the posh, cool number known to his staff as Mr. Brian.

Mr. Brian had his moods and his sometimes snobbish attitudes, but he was seen as a fair boss and nobody on his staff questioned his knowledge of how to run the business, his uncanny ability to forecast smash hits where everyone else saw nice little tunes or his encyclopedic knowledge of the records he sold. "We use to have a game with Brian," Ringo Starr remembered, "where we'd say to him, 'Okay, "C'mon Everybody"—what was the B side?' and he'd tell us. So we'd say, 'What number did it reach?' and he'd know. It was thrilling."

So it must have been with at least a slight sense of perturbation that Brian began to sense that something important musically was going on right under his nose—right there in central Liverpool—without his knowledge. A local act, the Beatles, had gone to Hamburg, Germany, and cut a record with a third-rank Cliff Richard named Tony Sheridan, and a handful of excitable kids—girls mainly—were asking for it at NEMS. For reasons that have never been made clear, Brian hadn't ordered the record, and his assistant, Alistair Taylor, contrived to invent a fictional customer—one Raymond Jones—and put his name in the order book as requesting the disc. The record arrived from Germany and sold out lickety-split, and Brian, antennae twitching, sensed that something was up. He found out that the Beatles played in a basement club, the Cavern, a few blocks from his shop, and he had a secretary call over to let management know he'd be dropping in for one of the band's lunchtime sessions.

On November 9, 1961, Brian Epstein, wearing his usual natty businessman's attire, descended into the sticky, humid air of the Cavern and stood among the Coke-and-sandwich–snarfing teenage clerks and school skippers who watched in a rapt frenzy as the Beatles, four handsome young toughs in black leather, pounded through their repertoire. So parochial was the little world of Liverpool—and the even littler world of fans and players of what would come to be called Merseybeat music—that Brian was actually announced by house manager/DJ Bob Wooler as a celebrity guest to the audience.

Brian was electrified—in fact, he was overcome with another of his whims. He turned to Alistair Taylor, secret instigator of this bizarre mission, who had come along to satisfy his own curiosity: "They *are* awful," he admitted, "but I think they're fabulous. What do you think about me managing them?"

In a short life dotted with suspicious enthusiasms and pipe dreams, this may have been the most absurd yet. Brian knew absolutely nothing about showbiz management. Not only were the intricacies of running a pop musician's career beyond his experience and, perhaps, abilities, but the racket was strictly a London affair: Even more than being gay or Jewish, being a Liverpudlian, however well-bred, would be a massive obstacle.

But Brian's question was rhetorical anyway. He was once again in the throes of fancy. He introduced himself to the band after their set, then returned several times over the coming weeks to see if his initial excitement had abated. He asked around town about the band: What sort of boys were they? Were they reliable? Were they, *you know?* Everyone told him not to waste his time. Nevertheless, on November 30, after another lunchtime session, he asked the band if they would come by NEMS Whitechapel to talk something over with him the following Sunday. They shrugged their consent.

When he sat them in his office at the otherwise empty store, Brian put his proposition to them bluntly: "Quite simply, you need a manager. Would you like me to do it?"

There was some talking about it among them, and they, as Brian had, asked around town (Paul McCartney's dad, who remembered Harry Epstein, thought a Jewish manager would be a real boost: "He thought Jewish people were very good with money," his son remembered).

But, essentially, the thing was agreed to there, terms pending: Brian Epstein had acquired the Beatles as artistes, and the Beatles had, on that Advent Sunday, acquired their John the Baptist.

If it seemed an unusual blend—the twenty-seven-year-old classical music and show tune fan with the refined air and the secretive private life and the quartet of still-teen (mostly), roughneck, pill-popping rockers with laddish tastes and rooms in their parents' houses—it was also an instance of absolute kismet.

In the Beatles, Brian found a medium for him to express his sense of daring and flamboyance while still maintaining his discretion and reserve. "Brian wanted to be a star himself," said Beatle producer George Martin, "and he couldn't do it as an actor, so he did it as a man who was a manipulator, a puppeteer." The Beatles were smartass and sexy and rough-and-tumble and extroverted—everything, in short, that Brian wished for himself (and, it can't be avoided saying, that he sought in sexual partners). Too, his proximity to them gave him, in time, something that life had all but denied him thus far: friends.

For their part, the Beatles found in Brian someone with class—his own car, nice clothes and manners, a prestigious job—who made a dignified impression, took them seriously, recognized them as a cut above the motley Merseybeat fray and was willing to pitch them to the London pop music elite. Brian taught them—about food, clothes, social niceties, the larger world—and instilled in them a sense of their right due. And he had wild-eyed, messianic faith in them, swearing to one and all that they would be the biggest act that England—nay, the *world*—had ever seen.

It was an ideal partnership: an extraordinarily talented group with no career path to follow and a man of eclectic, impetuous tastes and dubiously founded but substantial self-belief. Brian would lead the way, would help create the Beatles, would prepare the world to receive them. As at least one cool-eyed observer of the Liverpool scene noted, he was arguably the most uniquely qualified prophet they might have found.

"An ordinary person couldn't do it," declared Yankel Feather, owner of one of the city's very few gay nightclubs. "If he had been a young married man with two children, would his wife let him out to spend time with four unruly boys? No, it couldn't have happened. For the Beatles to make it, they had to have somebody as strange as him."

Strange, no doubt, but managing the Beatles—a contender for first place in the litany of foolish chimeras that had constituted his life to now—would be the purest form of self-expression Brian would ever find. His need for amiable companionship, his eye for rough young men, his sense of the done thing and the clothes and style in which to do it, his egoistic ambition, his unfounded yet enormous self-confidence, his ability to spot what people liked just before they realized they liked it: It all came to bear in a single job—impresario. In concert with the accident that a band of musical geniuses happened to be playing around the corner from his office, it all seems like a divine plan. There couldn't have been three people on Earth who could bring just the right mix of attitude, dedication, taste and assuredness to proctoring the Beatles. The odds that one of them happened to be in Liverpool and looking for a way to make his mark on the world—well, they wouldn't even be worth computing.

It could also be argued that landing Brian as a manager was the Beatles' first important break: For all the rough moments waiting for them in the coming months, his interest was the first real sign they had from outside their cultish little world that they meant something. And, as it involved a posh fellow like Brian, it boosted their morale. Subconsciously, at least, in the eyes of one observer, the band knew they had it made as soon as they'd landed him: "Four tough, working-class lads had come to accept the benefits of acting coquettishly for a wealthy middle-class homosexual," observed Simon Napier-Bell, one of the posh young hotshots who followed Brian into the pop management game. "People said their image was that of a boy next door, but it wasn't. To anyone who'd seen it before, their image was instantly identifiable. It was the cool, cocky brashness of a kid who's found a sugar daddy and got himself set up in Mayfair."

Beguiling proof of this can be found in the mythic tale of Brian's spring 1963 trip to Barcelona with John Lennon. Brian was nutty for Iberia: He holidayed there whenever he could and became such an aficionado of the corrida that he would eventually spend some time managing the English toreador Henry Higgins (known in Spain as Enrique Canadas) and have his private bathroom decorated with a gigantic photographic image of El Cordobés, the flamboyant bullfighter known as "the Spanish Beatle." (He had the opportunity once to dine with the great Mexican bullfighter Dominguín and considered it one of the great moments of his life; the *torero*, on the other hand, seemed not quite sure whom he had met.) At a time when the English culinary palate was expanding to accommodate new tastes, he regularly had his Spanish housekeepers prepare him gazpacho. And he would, inevitably perhaps, go to Spain in search of sexual gratification; like Morocco, it was a famous destination for English gays seeking the ready company of young men.

With that in mind, perhaps, Brian asked John to travel there with him in April 1963, a mysterious trip during which, depending on which version you believe: John took advantage of a free vacation to make it clear to Brian that the Beatles were his band (the McCartney surmise); John quizzed Brian about what it was like to be a gay man (the account John repeated throughout his life); John granted Brian, who was head over heels for him, a sexual encounter (the much-surmised theory around Liverpool, reported several times by Lennon's boyhood chum Pete Shotton and, at Paul's twenty-first birthday party in his Auntie Jin's garden, to Lennon's face by Cavern Club DJ Bob Wooler, who got walloped by John—using fists and a shovel—in return). Bolstering the nastiest whispers was the fact that John had always liked to cover his middle-class upbringing with an insolence and toughness he'd adapted from the examples of more hard luck Liverpudlians. His leather gear, his cocky, chin-out posture, his never-ending stream of verbal abuse—he was the picture of Scouse rough trade—just the sort, by all accounts, for which Brian was weakest.

But if sexuality factored into Brian's private relations with the band (and it would always be a big if), it was explicitly absent from Brian's two-pronged strategy for turning the Beatles into stars: He would smarten them up, give them a more professional aspect, and he would assail the London record and concert industry with news of his brilliant act. Gone were the Beatles' leather jackets and blue jeans; gone were such stage antics as swearing and chatting up the girls and drinking, smoking and eating between numbers; gone were their cheap cigarettes (filter tips only) and the curly ends of guitar strings sticking out on their pegboards. Henceforth, the Beatles would perform in smart suits and boots, would stick to the most professional sort of stage manner, including a full bow from the waist—straight out of Brian's RADA days—after each number. They wore suits from Dougie Millings, the Soho tailor who outfitted Cliff Richard and other eager-to-please boy pop stars; they wore zip-up, wedge-heeled Cuban boots, which would quickly come to be known as Beatle boots (though, in fact, David Bailey had beat them to the look).

Some in Liverpool saw these new bits of polish as a dilution of the band's essence, a sellout, in short, that had nothing to do with music and everything to do with image. But that wasn't how the Beatles themselves felt. As John Lennon said, "It was a choice of making it or still eating chicken onstage." And the suits? "Yeah man, all right, I'll wear a suit— I'll wear a *balloon* if somebody's gonna pay me. I'm not in love with leather *that* much!

"He wasn't trying to clean our image," Lennon went on. "He said our look wasn't right, we'd never get past the door at a good place." Paul concurred: "We knew Brian had good flair, and, when you're onstage, you can't see yourself, so it's often very important to have someone sitting in the stalls to tell you how you looked. Brian's memos used to reflect that: 'You're playing Neston tonight. I'm looking for a rebooking here, please wear the shirts and ties.' " And, said Ringo, "He really was instrumental in bending our attitude *this* much so that the public would bend theirs *that* much to accept us."

All that remained, then, was to convince the world. Thus began Brian's fruitless trips to London: no, no, no, no and no. Always a little knot of Beatles would wait for him at the Punch and Judy coffee shop in Lime Street station; always he would descend dejected from the train with the sorry news. "By then," remembered John, "we were close to him, and he'd really be hurt. He'd be terrified to tell us that we hadn't made it again."

But he had this faith, this zealous, intangible belief in them and his vision of their potential. To some, like aspiring young music scenester Andrew Loog Oldham, Epstein's certainty was contagious: "You knew you were dealing with a man who had a vision for the Beatles and nobody was going to get in the way of that vision. He was convinced that eventually everybody was going to agree with him. That gave him the power to make people listen."

But by May 1962, just five months into his tenure as manager, Brian had run out of people to buttonhole and cajole. He had gone door to door, virtually, with the tapes of the Decca sessions and, tired of schlepping the reels with him, decided to cut an acetate demo record of them during yet another bleak trip to London. The engineer at the HMV record store on Oxford Street listened to the band and liked them, suggesting that Brian talk with his boss. That meeting led to a call to EMI, where there was one last A&R man, a chap who'd been on vacation when Brian first came around a few months earlier.

His name was George Martin and he was, in all practicality, the last hope: He would simply have to say yes.

From Brian's mouth to God's ear: He did.

The Beatles were signed to EMI on the mere strength of Martin's having listened to the audition tapes that Decca had recorded; in September they flew—flew!—to London and cut their first record, "Love Me Do."

The rest everyone knows: Within eighteen months of that first recording session, they had released five singles—a number seventeen ("Love Me Do"), a number two ("Please Please Me") and three number ones ("From Me to You," "She Loves You," "I Wanna Hold Your Hand"), for a total of 109 weeks in the charts—and two albums (*Please Please Me* and *With the Beatles*), both of which reached number one, the first one holding the spot for thirty weeks only to be supplanted by the next, which held it for twenty-one weeks, making for a solid year at the top.

And for a while, in a sense, they weren't even Brian's biggest act. In the wake of his success at getting the Beatles a record deal, he signed other Cavern acts. The first of his bands to score a number-one record was Gerry & the Pacemakers, an agreeable Merseybeat combo who gladly sopped up a record—"How Do You Do It?"—that the Beatles, with their deep love of authentic American rock 'n' roll and their in-house songwriting duo of Lennon and McCartney, wouldn't touch. Gerry and the lads followed that one up with "I Like It," another number one, and that one with "You'll Never Walk Alone," which hit the top as well. That was their whole wad, but it was a hell of a run. Toss in—and why not?—another of Brian's finds, Billy J. Kramer and the Dakotas, who hit number one with "Bad to Me," and you get a total of thirty-two weeks in 1963 in which Brian Epstein acts were at the absolute top of the British charts.

But there was nothing, truly, ever, like the Beatles.

The personalities, the songwriting, the freshness of their look and sound, the palpable exuberance they radiated onstage, on record or simply talking off the cuff. Pop music had never known the like—if *ever*, which could seriously be debated—since the brief initial explosion of Elvis Presley. And no British act had ever come remotely close to generating the same degree of heat, hysteria and pan-cultural recognition.

They started out the year semiobscure, with just one number seventeen record to their names, and then worked their asses off: 229 live appearances in three countries, fifty-three radio gigs, thirty-seven performances for TV, plus recording two whole albums (the first of which was cut in one knockout day) and three singles' worth of entirely new material—a year-long testimonial to the efficacy of diet pills chased with scotch and Cokes.

When the calendar turned, they'd been the subject of documentaries and stars of their own BBC radio show, *Pop Go the Beatles*. In *The Times*, a writer went on, completely sober, about the group's use of "pandiatonic clusters" and "Aeolian cadences." They'd virtually invented a market out of the teenage girls and boys whom the U.K. record industry had previously courted with only mixed results and were rewarded with the sorts of accolades and performance opportunities normally reserved for older-style performers: a Variety Club award, two appearances on *Sunday Night at the London Palladium*, a chance to perform before the Queen Mother and Princess Margaret (on a bill which included, among others, Marlene Dietrich and Buddy Greco), even their own Christmas pantomime—thirty shows of music, comedy and traditional holiday sketches at the Astoria Cinema in Finsbury Park, London, in front of more than 100,000 seats total, all filled.

The papers could barely move quickly enough on their feet to keep up with the public demand for news about the band and the phenomenon dubbed Beatlemania: fans—mostly young girls—surrounding hotels and theaters, choking airports and lining motorcades to see their heroes come and go. There were accounts of the band's concerted efforts to survive this frightening level of adoration; "Operation Beat-the-Beatlemania," as the *Daily Mirror* called it: disguises and body doubles and false exits through vehicles that went nowhere while the boys sped off in second vehicles and so forth.

The timing of the Beatles' rise was impeccable. England had been rocked with tabloid travesties throughout 1963—the Argyll divorce, in which upper-class depravity and female sexual appetite emerged from the closet of gossip into the glare of a sensational, endless trial; and the Profumo scandal, a thrilling paella involving a Tory cabinet minister with a movie star wife, a Russian spy, a couple of floozies (one from a family with a hyphenated name!), Caribbean dope peddlers, common whores, a Polish gangster slumlord, the scion of one of England's greatest families, gunshots, flights from justice, a two-way mirror and, in the middle, an osteopath and society portraitist with predilections for all sorts of deviant sexual delights and a client list that included Gandhi, Churchill and a galaxy of Hollywood stars. Stephen Ward he was, and his story came into the light just early enough in the swing of the decade that the old culture could bring its might crushing down on him in a mockery of a trial (the prosecutor: one Mervyn Griffith-Jones, the same chap who botched the *Chatterley* business) that drove him, eventually, to suicide—a fistful of Nembutals down the hatch while the jury still debated which of the trumped-up, unproved charges of pandering, soliciting and acquiring abortions for his young victims he would be scapegoated with. Ward was snuffed out but the taint of the business brought down the government; in October, Harold Macmillan—Super-Mac—resigned as prime minister, and the stripe of British propriety and pride his reign embodied was forever swept away. "A generation was fading before our eyes," remembered journalist Ray Connolly. "Within nine months, England had changed out of recognition."

With all this going on, it was no wonder that the Beat Boom seemed such a welcome respite, or that, with understandable shortsightedness, most grown-up observers in the media failed to distinguish between the Beatles, their Merseyside mates Gerry & the Pacemakers and Billy J. Kramer and the Dakotas and such second-tier hangers-on as Freddie & the Dreamers (from Manchester) or the Dave Clark Five, the North London group that had been assembled, it was whispered, by veteran Denmark Street moguls simultaneously frightened by the incoming wave of northern moneymakers and eager to mop up anything stirred up by them or left in their wake. So hot were record companies for the next thing that they signed and suited-up anything they could find that was young and rhythmic and, to their ears anyhow, poppy, even the

Rolling Stones, then steeped in as pure a brand of Chicago blues as you could put out if you were from a London suburb, and nobody's idea of a cuddly Beat Boom act.

In the course of their breakout year, the Beatles expanded their horizons with travel—not only to gigs in France and Sweden but on holiday to Spain, Greece, and, for George, the U.S.A. (where he visited a sister who'd emigrated to the Midwest). John became a daddy, however oafishly, and Paul turned twenty-one, and the two started their own songwriting company, Northern Songs, and invented a bit of stage business that became their signature, shaking their heads and *woooooooo*-ing into the same microphone. And Paul met a girl—Jane Asher, a gorgeous redhead from a well-to-do West End family then working as an actress, model and sometime journalist; before long, Paul moved into a spare bedroom in the attic of the Asher family's endearingly eccentric Wimpole Street menage and he and Jane would be one of London's top scene-making couples for another five years.

Everything any of the Beatles would ever do after 1963 would be news.

Hell, they'd even heard about them in America.

A BIT OF YANKOPHILIA

Talent was everywhere, spilling out of taxis; the streets teemed with it. You could bump one day into a random genius on a corner and get a hand in launching a forty-year career: serendipity.

Take itchy Andrew Loog Oldham, who had talked his way into jobs at the city's hottest boutique, nightclub and artist-management firm in just the most recent of his audacious nineteen years. In 1963, his latest adventure—embarked upon, as had been the others, with a characteristic melange of moxie, palaver and vim—was managing a rhythm and blues band that he was sure would rise above the sea of Beat Boom hopefuls who'd welled up in the wake of the Beatles' stunning success. Enamored of the flash style of American record producer and famed weirdo Phil Spector, Oldham, neither musically nor technologically literate, had anointed himself the band's producer; but, bottom line, the band's live sound—the frenetic, pulsing stuff on which they made their name—had eluded him on the first go, resulting in a tinny, limp single that had failed to crack the Top 20. (As another survivor of his studio ministrations, Small Faces keyboardist Ian McLagen, would one day declare, "This guy is not an engineer. He's an idiot. He has no idea about sound. He couldn't produce a burp after a glass of beer.")

One September afternoon, Oldham was fretting in a West End basement jazz club as his band rehearsed: Nothing in their current repertoire felt like the next single; the Beat Boom was happening without them. Discouraged, he decided to take a walk and come at things fresh. Out on Charing Cross Road, he struck gold: Emerging from a taxi were John Lennon and Paul McCartney, dressed for success, slightly tipsy, just after being feted at a Variety Club luncheon at the Savoy where the Beatles had been named Top Vocal Group of the Year.

Oldham knew them: He'd worked a few months earlier that year as a pavement-pounding press agent for Brian Epstein, who felt that EMI wasn't doing enough to promote the band. When John and Paul caught sight of Oldham's moue and asked what was wrong, he explained his dilemma: He needed a hit tune; had they any to spare; ha-ha-ha. Lennon and McCartney knew and liked Oldham's band and—hey, presto!—volunteered to help; they themselves were to resume recording their second album the very next day and had a song that they'd be willing to share; it just needed a little polishing; wouldn't take a minute.

Oldham thus returned to the dingy confines of the Studio 51 jazz club with England's hottest songwriting team in tow. Handshakes all 'round, and then John and Paul taught the band the parts of the song they'd already finished and worked out the incomplete passages in front of the startled onlookers: a two-man hit-making machine, even with a few pints in them, at the drop of a hat.

The next day, Lennon and McCartney recorded the song with their own group, giving the vocal part to dear Ringo—who sang braggily, jokily, nervily, a mark, perhaps, of how lightly the Beatles regarded the tune in the grand scheme of things. But the version by the other guys, recorded a month after that fateful afternoon encounter with two generous Beatles, turned into a number-twelve hit: "I Wanna Be Your Man," the first breakthrough record for the Rolling Stones.

When they finally cracked the Top 20 with that bit of Lennon/McCartney manna, the Rolling Stones were the most visible standard bearers of a new phenomenon in what had become a rapidly evolving music scene bubbling up in Soho—the rhythm and blues cult, a curious blend of the trad boom and the Beat Boom, paying fealty to American gods like Howling Wolf, Muddy Waters and John Lee Hooker, but infusing their worship with the youthful aspect and energy of the likes of Chuck Berry, Little Richard and Fats Domino. The movement had formed and risen in London clubs and suburban halls that had recently converted from temples of traditional jazz into meccas of R&B and the blues—places like the Flamingo, the Marquee, the Piccadilly, the Ealing Club and the Crawdaddy, where white boys like Alexis Korner, Graham Bond, Zoot Money, Chris Barber and the indefatigable Georgie Fame could be heard a-wailin' and a-moanin' and a-bangin' out imitations—often stirring—of American originals that only a handful of Brits had, prior to the early sixties, taken note of.

It was at the Crawdaddy—a makeshift venue in the back of the Station Hotel in the western London suburb of Richmond—that Oldham first beheld the Stones. The band had secured a regular Sunday booking at the club by happenstance: One snowy night, the regular headliners, the Dave Hunt R&B band (featuring Ray Davies on guitar), blew its gig by failing to make it to the show. The club manager remembered Brian Jones, who had presented himself as leader of the emerging Rollin' (no g) Stones; the moody, undeniably brilliant guitarist had been putting together the band over the past year and was offering its services to promoters for free, just to gain experience and exposure. The impresario rang up the Stones—to reach them, you had to call keyboardist Ian Stewart at the chemical firm where he worked as a shipping clerk—and told them they'd have their chance: February 24, a Sunday night.

The unknown Stones played to a nearly empty room, but they absolutely killed the couple dozen folks who were there. The subsequent weeks drew bigger and bigger crowds until the band became the unlikely center of a bona fide scene: The weekly sessions at the Crawdaddy were attracting Londoners who hadn't ever bothered to see the group play its semiregular dates at clubs in Soho and the West End. "We became sort of a cult," recalled Charlie Watts, the drummer who'd bolted Alexis Korner's Blues Incorporated to anchor the Stones. One April night, the Beatles themselves showed up, a quartet of world conquerors in matching leather jackets. It was, said Ian McLagen, who caught the band at the club, an unforgettable show: "Brian was doing all this flashy shit on the slide guitar. And everyone was on stools except Mick. And he'd reach out into the audience and touch people. Fucking great!"

Word of the goings-on in Richmond leaked to the London pop music press, which had traditionally expressed only the slightest interest in blues-related groups. Near the end of April, a middle-tier music trade paper was planning to run a feature exhorting the world to the Stones' greatnesses. The editor mentioned the article to Andrew Oldham, who was then working as a publicist and hustling him for some ink for his client list. Oldham figured what the hell and on April 28 took the train to Richmond to catch the act.

The surging crowd of scenesters, the heady secrecy of an out-of-the-way setting, the amazing trio of front men—Jones and Keith Richards twining their guitars into one sound, Jagger preening and mocking and inciting: Oldham experienced the same sort of epiphany that had struck Brian Epstein at Liverpool's Cavern Club the previous year. "I'd never seen anything like it," Oldham recalled years later. "Everything I'd done up until now was a preparation for this moment. I saw and heard what my life, thus far, had been for."

He had to be a part of it, but he was almost too overwhelmed by what he'd seen to comprehend taking the act on as a manager. The next morning he called Epstein and urged the band on him; but Epstein, with his stable packed with skyrocketing Scousers, demurred, suggesting that Oldham, who was two years too young to hold his own agent's license, ask the veteran Denmark Street hand Eric Easton to have a look at the group. Foxy Easton, who had played the organ on a holiday pier up north and had evolved to represent the sort of acts the Beatles and Stones were wiping off the face of showbiz, reluctantly accompanied Oldham to a show the following Sunday and was sufficiently impressed that he agreed to sign on to Oldham's plan: Oldham would be the de facto agent/manager, but paperwork, contracts and other legalities would flow through Easton.

Now only the band had to agree.

After the show, Oldham introduced himself and expressed his desire to manage them.

"Andrew is very young," remembered Richards, "he's even younger than we are, he's got nobody on his books, but he's an incredible bull-shitter, fantastic hustler, and he's also worked on the early Beatles publicity."

He also clearly understood the band—certainly better than Easton, who was among those retrogrades who felt that Jagger sounded too black and wouldn't be acceptable to mainstream showbiz bookers and promoters.

Oldham, in fact, had just the opposite idea. Though it was Brian Jones who stepped forward when Oldham had asked who was the band-leader, it was Mick around whom Oldham was fashioning his nascent vision of the band. Purists of R&B and the blues they may have valued themselves, but Oldham knew how little that mattered in the commercial world—and how much in the commercial world the frenzy into which Jagger could work a crowd could mean. The Stones were, in his mind, to be the anti-Beatles: Londoners as opposed to northerners, long-haired and dark-hearted as opposed to neat and sunny and, most of all, frankly sexual and predatory and indifferent as to who noticed. To this end in particular, and to the exclusion of the rest of the band—the soldierly rhythm section of Charlie Watts and Bill Wyman, the hollow-cheeked urchin Richards, the Renaissance decadent Jones—it was the taunting panther Jagger, the first white English performer he'd ever seen who embodied a sense of sexual threat, whom Oldham saw as the centerpiece.

Genetically, there may have been no less likely fellow for the part. Michael Phillip Jagger he was born, July 26, 1943, in Dartford, Kent, a mile or so west of the line that marks the eastern edge of greater London. Dad was Basil, known as Joe, a dapper, proper, secondary school fitness instructor from Lancashire; Mom, Eva, was an Aussie by birth—at a time when antipodean heritage wasn't nearly the badge of relaxed hip it would become. They each indulged a bit of yankophilia: He was one of the foremost English exponents of basketball; she was an Avon lady—two tics ironically revelatory of their son's essential character. Their house was neat and trim, as was the way they inhabited it: Eva kept up appearances scrupulously, presenting the most proper English face to the world with the fervor of a true arriviste; Joe, always fit, would insist that his sons (Christopher came along in 1947) maintain a scrupulous exercise regimen. It was a stereotypical to the point of banal suburban upbringing of the postwar era.

Indeed, grown-up Mick would claim to have found something of a challenge in the ordinariness of his childhood: "My mum was very working-class," he recalled, "my father bourgeois." In this status, quixotically, he discovered valor and hard knocks: "Part of the hero image is making it from the bottom. It's more of a hang-up making it if you're from the bourgeoisie, because if you're from the bottom you've got nothing to lose."

Badge of honor he may have conceived a bourgeois upbringing, but flaunt it he did not. In time he came to speak in an affected Cockney lilt that no one else ever born and bred in Dartford shared but which was the universal symbol in the so-called classless sixties of having risen from the depths. It came easily enough to him: "Michael could have been a very good impersonator if he wanted to," his mother declared. "He could probably have made a living at it" (a sentiment with which Bo Diddley and Tina Turner, among others, would no doubt have concurred). But it signaled, too, a divide in him: He was, in part, a suburban boy with a positive horror of bohemian excess and abandon and a thirst to blend in with the upper classes; in part, though, as well, he was a hedonist and rebel, one of the schooled and almost-privileged class who chose heedlessly to dive into the hellish and the sensual: the man who wrote "Lady Jane," on the one hand, and "Brown Sugar" on the other.

Of course, these tendencies would only emerge once he'd left Dartford and found himself fronting a meteoric rock band. Before that, he was just another kid—taller and thinner than his schoolmates, maybe—minding his mother's household edicts, dutifully carrying out his father's physical exercise program, making his way back and forth to Wentworth County primary school in the company of another lad from the neighborhood, a jug-eared slip of a boy a few months his junior named Keith Richards. In his teens, Mick did well enough in his exams to attend Dartford grammar school (Richards, having inherited a wild streak from a fiddling grandfather, had already acquired a guitar and a taste for teddy boy fashion and wound up at a technical school and then, fortunately for him, an art college).

But there was something new in the air that bit young Mick as it did boys in Liverpool, Manchester and various London suburbs: At the Stork Club on Regent Street, a revolution of sorts began in English popular music. A twenty-year-old Cockney merchant seaman named Tommy Hicks, who'd been singing in the new American style known as rock 'n' roll, was caught in his act by Larry Parnes, a club owner and sometime theatrical producer. It was pop history on a plate. The tousle-haired blond singer with the glad manner electrified Parnes, who, it must be said, was partial to handsome young men from tough neighborhoods. Parnes signed the kid to a management contract, renaming him Tommy Steele, teamed him with the aspiring young songwriter Lionel Bart to generate some tunes and launched a publicity blitz that would result in the birth of the first British rock star.

On the strength of Steele's breakthrough, Parnes started gobbling up lots of hot young boy singers, renaming them with his gaudy sense of showmanship: Marty Wilde, Vince Eager, Billy Fury and, most appallingly, Dickie Pride—they might've been porn stars. He never got his hands on Cliff Richard, who was to prove the only of the fifties pretty boy pop stars to have a really durable career, but he was the first great impresario of British rock, and his influence was absolute until the dawn of the Beat Boom in 1963.

At the same time that Parnes's pretty boys were dominating the scene, skiffle—a strange blend of American folk, blues, country & western and crude homemade British musicianship that had been bubbling under jazz circles since the start of the decade—emerged into the bright light of popularity. Lonnie Donegan, a singer and guitarist with Ken Colyer's revivalist jazz band, had made a specialty of raw, uptempo numbers by American composers such as Jimmy Rodgers, Huddy "Leadbelly" Ledbetter and Woody Guthrie: "Rock Island Line," "Mule Skinner Blues," "Midnight Special"—that sort of thing. As early as 1953, he was playing concerts on his own or doing small sets as entràctes during Colyer's shows, strumming out rhythmic lines and wailing in a Glaswegian approximation of an American field holler. By the end of the decade, alongside the showbiz stylings of Steele and company, Donegan became a chart sensation, scoring the first of thirty Top 30 records he'd release before the Beatles wiped all traces of him away.

The irony of that, of course, was that the Beatles themselves began as a skiffle group, the Quarrymen, learning their instruments out of a desire to emulate Donegan's raw, homey sound. All over England, in fact, teenage boys were learning to play the guitar, the bass, the washboard and the drums and taking up skiffle with a passion derived, in part, from the music's simplicity and, in part, from their lack of access to newer American music, which was still hard to come by as it was only available on imported discs. As the music grew in popularity, it coincided with the boy pop star phenomenon in one key way: Teenage skiffle players, unable to perform in places where alcohol was served, began performing in coffee bars. The 2 I's in Soho's Old Compton Street, the most famous of these venues, first began to offer live music after an impromptu skiffle concert during the 1956 Soho Fair brought in a lot of business. A potent combination was brewing: easy-to-play music, quick fame, a ready audience and lots of places to play: a formula that just about any earnest lad felt he could master.

Jagger, one such aspirant, took a fancy to singing—imitating things he heard on the radio, joining with some of his schoolmates in makeshift bands to do renditions of American tunes, mostly: folk and blues and country and R&B and early rock. (It's a measure of how unshaped and raw his talents were that his bandmates heard an improvement in his vocalizing after he bit off the tip of his tongue in a gymnastic mishap.) His fascination with American music led him to seek out and collect records; he bought discs straight from American labels via mail order.

But there was no thought of a career: He did well enough academically at Dartford Grammar to be admitted to the London School of Economics, pursuing a course in political science and economics with the vague notion that he might someday enter politics. Applying himself to schoolwork for which he didn't quite have sufficient mathematical aptitude, singing casually with chums in their ragtag little groups, he was an unexceptional lad, somewhat more ambitious than others, perhaps, maybe a mite stroppier, but living a life, by and large, as dully predictable as the trains that carted him back and forth between London and Dartford on school days.

It was on a commuter train, as it turned out, that something unforeseeable finally happened to him one October morning in 1961. Jagger was toting some records to London—Chuck Berry, Muddy Waters, stuff he'd grown fond of. Who did he bump into but Richards? They hadn't seen each other in a few years—the last time, Keith recalled, was when Mick had a part-time job selling ice cream at the park and he happened to stop by for a snack. Still, he said, "We recognized each other straight off." And when Richards saw what Jagger was carrying: lightning.

Richards, as it turned, had been playing in a pickup band that specialized in blues tunes and rock numbers with a blues feel—Chuck Berry was a special favorite. Encouraged by the coincidences, Jagger and Richards got together to listen to records and, eventually, to jam. Over the next few months, they grew serious enough to seek out other people playing the same music, real musicians, as it were, who were playing gigs in the handful of London clubs that were increasingly giving over to the raw American sounds. One spring afternoon they went clear across London to Ealing to hear Blues Incorporated play. Most of the band members were ancient by their standards—the leader, Alexis Korner, was over thirty—but on this particular date a guest guitarist of approximately their age took the stage halfway through the set. He called himself Elmo Lewis and he'd come from Cheltenham, Gloucestershire, but, Keith thought upon hearing him rip off blistering riffs on a bottle slide guitar, "It's Elmore James, this cat!" Knocked out by his version of "Dust My Broom," Mick and Keith went over to say hello. Elmo Lewis was, they learned, a stage name. The guy was really called Brian Jones, and he and the Dartford boys had a lot to talk about.

This is where the story becomes not about one guy but about a group. And in this, the pop star generation who came of age in London in the sixties were something new. Superstars in other fields—sports, movies, fashion, society—had always been one-offs; musical stars of previous generations had always been known in the singular. But with the coming of the second wave of rock 'n' roll—the British wave—it was the group, at least at first, that mattered most. No matter the magnitude of ambition and charisma and vanity that was growing inside Mick Jagger: He could only conceive of moving forward in a band, and it was indistinguishably as part of the band—sometimes to his real detriment—that he would make his name.

This wasn't necessarily apparent in the spring of 1962, when the Beatles were first making their way out of Liverpool under the aegis of Brian

Epstein. But within a year—and certainly by the time Andrew Oldham approached the Stones at the Crawdaddy—groups were it. The advantages of being in a group were obvious: Absent a genius of some sort up front—an Elvis Presley, a Buddy Holly, a Chuck Berry—a group represented a set of interchangeable parts, a package of like minds and talents contributing to a single thought. An individual performer would need to generate—or have generated for him—original material, whereas a group could dedicate itself to a sound and immerse itself in the repertoire. There were the benefits of moral support and other practical considerations: Four or five group members meant more hands to carry gear, more homes to rehearse or meet in, more distribution of labor, whether of the menial sort or the creative.

With the Beatles, groups became positively faddish: the names and the suits and the haircuts and the goonish, grinning photos. A group meant that many more faces for the girls to swoon over and the magazines and newspapers to write about. And it meant instant interest: Groups were the new thing, and the Beatles were so absolutely red hot that the new thing got more attention immediately than it might have ever before.

The flood of groups and the way in which the media characterized it was an industry unto itself. The Beatles; the Dave Clark Five; Gerry & the Pacemakers; Billy J. Kramer and the Dakotas; the Swinging Blue Jeans; the Searchers; the Hollies; the Animals: By the time the Rolling Stones began delivering hits, all of these had spent some time on the charts. It was an explosion of nonthreatening young manhood—squeaky clean, tuneful, smiley and skin deep—that swept the nation and, indeed, America, where the group concept was similarly novel outside of the arenas of black urban pop.

As Oldham and they themselves would have it, the Stones would come into focus as the antithesis of these other groups: uncooperative, antifashion, defiant. Bill Wyman remembered that the band's attitude occasioned a hellstorm of resistance, even from the people paid to photograph them: "They wanted you to throw up your arms and jump off walls and do all that and give the thumbs-up signs and do all those gimmicky things that those awful bands like Freddie & the Dreamers did and Herman's Hermits and the Dave Clark Five. The Stones never did anything like that. We really believed that that was the way that you should be allowed to behave. But the media didn't like it." (And they themselves weren't always orthodox in their iconoclasm: At the start, especially, they softened their stance enough to appear in *Queen* magazine in a photo spread promoting some of Mary Quant's designs: the Stones as fashion accessories!)

And, Wyman added, Oldham initially sided with the prigs: "We started off not wearing uniforms because we couldn't afford them—simple as that, otherwise we probably would have—and then we continued doing it. Andrew Oldham tried to change us and put us into uniforms. He always says he created our image but he did absolutely the opposite. He put us into uniforms and we lost them on our first package tour of England. Everyone conveniently lost a jacket or waistcoat or trousers and it became a hodgepodge of uniforms. We got out of it. Andrew said, 'You won't get on television unless you smarten up.' "

Among all the Stones, Brian Jones probably had the least beef with dressing up. A bit of a dandy by nature, older than Jagger and Richards, driven away from home, with illegitimate children here and there and a store of bravado Jagger and Richards couldn't begin to emulate, he was the one with the big plans, and he shared them with Mick and Keith at that very first meeting: He was going to start his own blues outfit, all professional like, and they could join if they were good enough. It's easy to imagine the two Dartford boys riding home after that chat with their heads spinning, scheming about how they could sign aboard this daring program.

As it was, they suited Jones fine, and they began jamming together in a room Jones rented in a Soho pub. With Brian and Keith on guitar, Mick taking vocal and Dick Taylor on bass, they sought out a drummer and keyboardist and any other hands they could acquire and started rehearsing. They advertised for additional players and turned up Ian Stewart, a rawboned pianist who worked days shipping explosives at a chemical factory and who, more importantly, owned his own van. The embryonic group began sitting in during the intervals of Blues Incorporated's gigs; now and again, Mick would sing a number with Korner's band during their regular set.

By the fall of 1962, they were ready to take on the world.

The world, however, had other plans. For a long, cold while, the only people who truly believed in the Stones were the Stones themselves.

If you were a scrappy young musician in London in the winter of 1962, you might be able to string together gigs and put food on the table—maybe—but a roof over the head was another matter. Jones, who was living in a seedy flat in Powis Square, Notting Hill, with a wife and child he didn't appreciate the burden of, suggested that Mick pool together with him on a flat on Edith Grove, in the western tip of Chelsea known as World's End. Jones had a little income from a string of small jobs, most of which he blew through eccentric and even petty-criminal behavior; Jagger had a bit of a scholastic stipend from university and collected a nominal fee for his singing with Blues Incorporated. They recruited a few more paying heads to make the rent—schoolmates of Jagger's from LSE, square as you like—but they managed it.

What they got for their money was a hovel of famously fetid squalor and chilly filth. "That revolting fried-up lino pisshole," as Oldham remembered it. And the inhabitants agreed: "It was disgusting," Richards recalled, "mold growing on the walls." Nonetheless, he began to crash there so regularly so as to avoid the long commute home that, eventually, he, his guitar and his fistful of spare clothes became permanent boarders. As they could barely afford the shillings necessary to keep the gas heater lit, the addition of even skinny Keith's body temperature was welcome; on the bitterest nights of that most frigid of English winters, the front line members of the Rolling Stones would share a single bed.

While enduring Edith Grove, Jagger scooted off dutifully to school, still uncertain enough about music as a career not to abandon the chimerical hope that he would become an economist. Jones and Richards, left in the cold and dirt of the flat, spent their days rehearsing until their guitar licks were impossible to distinguish by ear alone. "We used the kitchen to play in," Richards admitted, "and slowly the place got filthy and started to smell, so we bolted the doors and locked them all up, and the kitchen was condemned." Aside from the constant scraping for food and booze, a principal diversion was provided by Mick, who had acquired, somewhat alarmingly to flatmates who had to share his bed, a taste for dressing in hairnets and a pink housecoat and other campy signifiers—an affectation with which he was eventually to make both sexual and thespian hay.

It was a dulling pattern of life with little in the way of encouragement: Jagger continued on alternating studying economics with learning how to move and sing onstage; Richards and Jones attuned their playing to each other; the band gigged semiregularly at the Flamingo, the Ealing Blues Club, and the fabled Marquee, when it would have them.

Over these lean months, the three front men had acquired the rhythm section that was to prove so integral to the group's fortunes. Gone was the Dartford bassist Dick Taylor, replaced by a bloke nearly six years older than the oldest of them, married and with a kid and a band of his own, the Cliftons, who did quite nicely on the wedding circuit. He'd been born William Perks but he'd changed his name to Bill Wyman. A discharged conscript of the Royal Air Force, he was by profession a bookkeeper at an engineering firm in Lewisham, south of London, near where he made his home in Penge. When he showed up at the band's Soho rehearsal the first time, he struck them as disturbingly retro: "We can't believe him," Richards remembered, "a real London Ernie, Brylcreemed hair and eleven-inch cuffs on his pants and huge blue suede shoes with rubber soles." He could play, they discovered, and more impressively he had assets none of them could match—not one but *two* working amplifiers, one bigger than any the others had ever used. Fashion sense and cool they could teach him; those amps, on the other hand, were heaven-sent.

In time, too, the series of inadequate drummers who'd been sitting in with the band yielded up a keeper, another older guy with a job, Charlie Watts, who worked as a graphic artist with an advertising firm and who'd been with Blues Incorporated, which was how the Stones first became familiar with his dead-accurate—yet always swinging—beat.

They worked at blending their strengths together, and then came that snowy night, that no-show by the Dave Hunt R&B band, that first booking at the Crawdaddy.

Voilà: Beatles in the audience, slumming aristos and music journalists and aficionados of the latest thing taking the train to Richmond, and a stunned Andrew Oldham dreaming of how he could hitch on to the ride that he could see coming, the very rocket trip that would spirit Jagger forever out of Dartford and middle-class obscurity.

STRAW-BERRY BOB AND THE MODS

Save for the bohemian element that produced it in dingy studios and debated it in Soho pubs and clubs, British art had always been seen by the popular throng as a thoroughly toffee-nosed pursuit. Who but aristocrats and their idle children, after all, had the time to tromp off to museums or galleries or argue about whether this or that new canvas was revolutionary or just trash?

But one of the curious side effects of the shake-up in the class system in the early sixties was the spread of the esoteric concerns of the high-born among the common classes (and, to be fair, vice versa), so that at a given moment in 1964 you could see the latest innovations in modern art in one of two places—hanging smartly in an elegant Mayfair gallery or slapped onto a cheap shirt in a shop window less than a mile away in an obscure little street (an alley, nearly) of three short blocks: Carnaby Street, soon to be synonymous the world over with Swinging London.

That Carnaby Street came to be one of the symbols of the British invention of modern pop culture was, like so much of what blossomed in those heady days, a curious combination of history, prosperity and individual genius—or at least the knack for being in the right place at the right time and with the right taste.

And not only pop culture worked that way: More and more, as the sixties unfolded, high art was subject to the same serendipities of fortune.

Take Robert Fraser.

Few young Londoners were as successful as he in riding the current moods—indeed, in surfing just ahead of the mob—and bringing the high and the low together. A properly bred toff who ran a celebrated art gallery, he mounted important and sensational shows of pop (and, later, op) art by British, American and Continental artists and whose vision, sensibility and lifestyle gave him a unique place in the center of several swirling circles.

The sixties scene in London was far too diverse and divergent to have had a center, but if it could be said to have a central nervous system it might well have been the several hundred yards of Mayfair sidewalk between the Robert Fraser Gallery at 69 Duke Street ("I could always remember *that* address," cackled Dennis Hopper) and its owner's apartment at 20 Mount Street, a few blocks away. Fraser was one of those people who knew—you'd swear to it—everyone, and if you went to see him at the gallery and it was closed or he wasn't there, you simply went 'round to the flat.

"He was where you went to tell what was happening," recollected Marianne Faithfull, "or where you went to find out what was happening. Better than having or even being a copy of *Time Out*. Robert was a serious conductor of lightning."

The bolts you could be struck by in an evening's salon at chez Frazer were enormous and eclectic: Andy Warhol, Allen Ginsberg, William Burroughs, Dennis Hopper, Paul McCartney, John Lennon, Terry Southern, David Hockney, various Rolling Stones and Chelsea types, pretty Arab boys and lecherous old queens, star footballers, Maltese drug dealers, jet setters, models—you couldn't imagine. On a beach in Morocco once, he was walking along with a gaggle of Stones and Stones People and said hello to a pair of English gents he knew: Reg and Ron Kray, the East End thug kings. 'Round the flat you might bump into Sid Caesar, the American comic, acting a tad *altered* and in conversation with a lord or lady or other hyphenated British bigwig. Said the California painter Jim Dine, whose work Fraser showed to scandalous success, "Robert knew everyone in the world at one point."

And, of course, *they* knew *him*. With his stammer and sideburns and exquisitely daft clothes (shoes always militarily neat), with his upper-crust accent peppered with American slang, with his ease among his parents' courtly connections and his own acquaintances from the gay and drug demimondes and the gambling clubs near his home, he was as much a work of art as anything he displayed on the walls of his gallery.

Not that his work wasn't top-notch. He had a fabulous eye and a messianic zeal for the artists he represented: Fraser convinced Richard Hamilton to give up teaching school in Newcastle and make his living off his work, and he persuaded the Beatles to hire Peter Blake to design the cover photo for *Sgt. Pepper's Lonely Hearts Club Band*. When he saw that Bridget Riley was disappointed with his installation of a new show of her smaller works, he and his staff stayed up all night and painted the all-white gallery black so that the works positively popped off the walls for the next night's opening. He kept up with all the newest aesthetic developments in the States and the U.K. and on the Continent; he did a thriving business in stuff that he brokered but didn't show—Magrittes for McCartney, for instance, or the Balthus he once failed to convince Mick Jagger to buy. And at his opening night parties you might behold anyone from Marlon Brando to the Earl of Snowdon scoping out the new pieces and the young hotties.

For all that, though, Fraser's greatest artistic achievement was probably his invention of himself: The studied blend of Eton and Soho, the Savile Row polish in the gallery, offset by thick, black-framed groovy nerd specs, the *jellaba* and the Turkish slippers while entertaining at home. Keith Richards called him, affectionately, "Strawberry Bob," and the nickname captured both Fraser's preening presentation of himself and the puckish rebelliousness that was always—he couldn't help himself—his downfall.

Downfall, alas, may have been inevitable. Fraser's biography reads like a traditional résumé of English upper-class success perversely riddled with deflating holes.

He had all the tools: money, privilege, education, breeding, parental support, a lively and probing intelligence. But he nearly always thwarted what might have been expected of him, whether through his avowed homosexuality or his dalliance with drugs or his dandyish (though always fine) mode of dress or his lifelong refusal to conform to anything like the received social expectations of someone with his breeding or station. From early childhood in Knightsbridge through his schooling and military service and sensational rise in the world of art to the humiliations he suffered later in the decade, Fraser was a font of scandal and outrageousness, a living symbol of an era's restless excess.

His father, a City banker, had been knighted by King George VI in 1945. But *his* father had been a butler to Gordon Selfridge, the department store magnate.

He had had his name put down for Eton the day after he was born in August 1937, but he hadn't graduated; a bohemian rebelliousness that he'd evinced even earlier at prep school—where he was nearly expelled for writing an essay extolling the virtues of communism over capitalism—found him continually running contrary to authority; eventually, he was sent down, as it was phrased, for repeatedly being caught smoking cigarettes on school property.

He had served the Queen as a soldier, but failing to distinguish himself sufficiently in officers' school, he was denied admittance to the elite Brigade of Guards and sent instead to Uganda to fulfill his National Service as a subaltern in the King's African Rifles—"thirteen months," as he remembered it, "of purgatorial boredom," with yet another small trove of disgraces resulting from his reckless behavior. (Among the locals who served under him, there was a brutish sergeant major named Idi Amin—with whom Fraser later insinuated he'd had an affair.)

Fraser came from an artistically inclined family. He was given liberty to wander the Tate as a youth—his father served on the museum's board and his mother, after she was widowed, headed the Friends of the Tate Gallery—and he reciprocated with a genuine affection for both of his parents. (McCartney would recall a conversation with Fraser where, a couple of swinging hip cats, they both sheepishly admitted they loved their mums and dads.) Fraser's folks, in fact, encouraged his choice of profession. When he left the military, his parents, however concerned with his failings as scholar and soldier, thought enough of his potential that they encouraged him to spend a few years learning the art business in the U.S.

Fraser worked in Pittsburgh for the Carnegie Institute and spent time in New York and Los Angeles, meeting people and learning the ropes from the likes of dealers Sidney Janis and Leo Castelli, critic John Richardson and artists Ellsworth Kelly and Jim Dine. With some money from his father, he gradually acquired a small store of paintings and sculptures that formed the seeds of a gallery that would be to the stolid, draped, lugubrious art houses of London what the Vidal Sassoon salon was to the fussy old hairdressers' palaces.

When he returned to London in early 1962, Fraser took a lease on a Duke Street storefront and commissioned designer Cedric Price to redo it for him. Price removed all the wall trim and wainscoting and painted the place a bright white—a radical departure from the stultifying Victorian norm and a wonderful setting for the debut show: a collection of the first black-and-white works exhibited in the U.K. by Jean Dubuffet.

For several years, Fraser exhibited important works in modestly successful shows and made a place for himself in the homosexual night life of Soho and Chelsea. He often seemed precariously placed in all of his chosen worlds: Fraser was mortified one night when he and his Eton classmate Christopher Gibbs wandered into the Soho drinking room the Colony Club and were greeted by a sneering Francis Bacon with "Here come the Belgravia pansies!" But, as Gibbs saw it, Fraser gave as good as he got: "Robert always had a finely honed kind of snobbery . . . it was all-encompassing. It would cover musicians, politicians, bankers, athletes, bookbinders, criminals, etc. A sort of personal aristocracy."

The Robert Fraser Gallery didn't, of course, have a monopoly on representation of the important artistic innovators associated with pop art or any other avant garde movement. Mateus Grabowski had preceded Fraser into business by three years in a location on Sloane Street, and by the mid-sixties two other important rivals surfaced: John Kasmin's, a gallery similar to Fraser's in its modern emphasis and ability to draw stars to private viewing parties, and Indica, a space dedicated to conceptual works launched by Marianne Faithfull's husband John Dunbar and Barry Miles in early 1966, with the backing of Paul McCartney and his almost-brother-in-law, pop singer Peter Asher.

But none of these other gallerists had Fraser's ability to throw a sensational scene together, and none, to hear some tell, had his touch with the artists he represented. And, too, he had the gallery's reputation and successes to steady him. "There was a special communication between him and the artist that I didn't see with other dealers," remembered Ed Ruscha. "Robert wanted to break ground with his gallery and I don't think he had profit in mind."

Fraser's presentations were boldly conceived and far-reaching. A 1963 exhibit entitled "Obsession and Fantasy" mixed Continental greats like Balthus, Giacometti and Dubuffet with such English artists as the well-established Bacon and the emerging Peter Blake. He showed sculptures by Eduardo Paolozzi, films and assemblages by Bruce Conner, works by Andy Warhol, Claes Oldenburg, Derek Boshier and perhaps a dozen other artists who were actively reshaping the era's visual aesthetic.

Fraser might've been as successful and popular in New York or Paris, but time and circumstances made him a uniquely British character. The very movement with which his gallery was most commonly associated—pop art—had been invented in London by the Independent Group, a collective of theoretically oriented painters, sculptors and writers who popped out of the box in 1956 with a show called "This Is Tomorrow." In it, Richard Hamilton, then still working as a teacher to support his art-making, exhibited a collage entitled *Just What Is It That Makes Today's Homes So Different, So Appealing?* Composed of images nicked from the dream worlds of advertising, sexual fantasy and middle-class status-striving—a well-developed muscleman, a bosomy G-stringed woman, comic books, a canned ham, a cinema marquee, a Ford auto emblem, a Hoover ad—the piece helped define an aesthetic stressing the iconic nature of the ephemera of modern commercial culture. Along with fellow instructor (and future Fraser client) Eduardo Paolozzi, Hamilton influenced a new generation of students at the Royal College of Art—including Peter Blake, David Hockney, R. J. Kitaj and Derek Boshier—into seeking inspiration for their work in the popular culture that previous generations of fine artists had denigrated. And many of the works in which they did so first met public scrutiny on the walls of the Robert Fraser Gallery.

If it had been any other time, the novel ideas of Fraser and the artists he showed would've been known only to cultists, critics and the more daring of the wealthy patrons on whom the progress of art history depends. But postwar prosperity had produced a new breed of art lover: working-class lads who had been educated in, of all places, state-run art schools.

Art education had always been the province of the wealthy or intended as a kind of vocational schooling for young women entering the teaching field. But the Education Act of 1944 had expanded to include art school as an option alongside traditional trades, business education and professional or academic careers. By the mid-fifties, art colleges in most of the big cities—London, Liverpool, Manchester, Newcastle, Leicester—were flooded with young working-class men who were studying drawing, sculpture, drama, music, literature and other pursuits that had historically been the domains of the idle wealthy or the earnestly bohemian. Aside from any technique and attitude they might acquire passing through the institutions, this new bulge of working-class aesthetes were, anomalously, granted time, creative license and the opportunity for swell social lives. They could indulge in such trivialities as the polemic between traditional (or "trad") and modern (or "mod") jazz, or they could take up arms, in effect, and learn to play music themselves.

And a great many, famously, did: Among the art school students of the era were John Lennon, Keith Richards, Pete Townshend, Eric Clapton, Ray Davies, Jimmy Page, Eric Burdon and various members of the Pink Floyd, Roxy Music, Family, The Move and the Soft Machine. Said author, journalist and gallery owner Barry Miles, who himself attended art college, "You came out of it knowing a lot more about rock 'n' roll than you did about art." By accident, Britain had bred a class of young men from rough origins who had some simulacrum of the privileges previously enjoyed only by boys from old families.

So there were the toffs and eggheads with their pop art theories and hushed galleries and the young Turk musicmakers from dodgy parts of town with their taste for painting and fashion.

Robert Fraser couldn't have them all over to his flat, that was for sure. But they were all so right for one another: bright and young and lippy and cocky and keen. If only there was a place for them to meet. . . .

Two hundred fifty yards from stem to stern, with a name plucked out of nowhere and a history noteworthy for nothing, Carnaby Street was an unlikely center of a world youth movement. Prior to the sixties, it was a nondescript street of tradesman's shops and workrooms, an electricity station and, thanks to the Luftwaffe, which discovered the place incidentally in September 1940, a few bomb sites. At the dawn of the sixties, most Londoners didn't know it at all, even though it lay smack in the midst of seemingly everything, on the border of Mayfair, Piccadilly and Soho, between the London Palladium, Golden Square and the shopping hubs of Regent Street and Oxford Street. It had a decent pub—the Shakespeare—and a decent tobacconist—Inderwicks—and virtually nothing else to recommend it; that it was as far west of Regent Street as Savile Row—the traditional stronghold of bespoke menswear lay to the east—was an irony that would only become apparent after a few years had passed.

Over the centuries, though surrounded by history, Carnaby Street made none. It was named in the seventeenth century after Karnaby House, the first of many ramshackle housing blocks erected along it (there would be no reliable records of who or what Karnaby was). Its surroundings changed hands and character over the centuries: now part of the Abbot and Convent of Abingdon; now the property of the Crown, which used it as the location of a pesthouse after the twin scourges of the Great Plague and the Great Fire of the mid-1600s; now an open field used by a riding academy; now a tenement area filled with refugees, many of them French Huguenots. By the time Charles Dickens wrote about it in *Nicholas Nickleby,* it was "a bygone, faded, tumbledown street" that, truly, hadn't had very much to fade *from.*

How it came to be the locus of a boom in men's fashion—and, more particularly, *young* men's fashion—that echoed over the world is another of the improbable success stories of the times. John Stephen, a grocer's son from Glasgow, came to London in the mid-fifties with dreams of entering the haberdasher's trade. His first real job was as a clerk in a Covent Garden rentals shop, where he hired out military uniforms for fancy dress or film and theater work. After a year, he scored a much better position at Vince Man's Shop on Newburg Street—one block east of and parallel to Carnaby.

Vince was one of the very first places in all London where a man could buy clothes with color in them and made of material other than the dullest tweed, wool and gabardine. Not coincidentally, it catered largely to a clientele made up of gay men who frequented the public bathhouse around the corner on Marshall Street. Vince, pop critic and clotheshorse Nik Cohn would recall, "sold stuff that could once have been worn by no one but queers." (Indeed, according to the old joke as repeated by jazz singer and journalist George Melly, it was "the only shop where they measure your inside leg each time you buy a tie.") But in the late fifties, when Stephen was there, it started attracting a more varied clientele of pop stars, young actors and adventuresome sorts from Chelsea who'd shaken off the hangover of the war and felt like dandying themselves up a bit. (During this time, a young Sean Connery, no nancy boy he, modeled for the shop.)

Working days at Vince—as well as a few other men's shops in Notting Hill and Bond Street—and nights as a waiter in a Soho coffee bar, Stephen saved three hundred pounds to open his own workroom, booking a second-floor space on Beak Street, the southern end of Carnaby Street; his plan was to design clothes to sell to the shops he had worked in. One afternoon in 1957, while he was at lunch, an electric heater ignited some curtains and fire destroyed his work space. His landlord had another site to offer him, a spot on Carnaby Street that had, in the landlord's view, an advantage over Stephen's former digs.

"It's on the ground floor," he explained. "There's a shop window. People walking by will see your clothes."

Stephen knew the neighborhood. "Who walks by?" he asked, not meaning to be ironic.

The rent was a mere seven pounds and ten shillings a week, so, foot traffic or no, it was a bargain; Stephen moved in. Expanding on the palate of colors and fabrics that had been the hallmark of Vince (which closed when its owner went into the restaurant and catering business), Stephen's work began to attract some of the rising pop stars—the Cliff Richard and Adam Faith sort—who were emerging from Soho. The young men proved a remarkable sales force; in one of his awful films, Cliff wore a sweater Stephen had made out of some fleecy fabric, creating an instant demand for the remaining stock. Stephen had the unusual inspiration to use his profits to lease more storefronts on the street, going into business against himself in a sense, but also taking advantage of the window space the tiny shops all boasted and his own knack for turning out new styles and colors at a remarkable pace. "He changed styles monthly, weekly, even daily," recalled Nik Cohn. "Every time you walked past a John Stephen window there was something new and loud in it, and when you counted out your money, you found you could afford it."

By 1962, Stephen had four Carnaby Street shops and a patina of cool that had transcended the cult of gay men and pop stars who had been his initial customers: Boxer Billy Walker, as masculine a mixer as they came, who once fought Henry Cooper for the British and Empire Heavyweight Championship, modeled some of Stephen's tight jeans and a blazing pink sailor shirt. That sort of macho currency aside, the first Carnaby Street shops still retained a vaguely homosexual atmosphere: They came to be known as boutiques, a precious, campy touch, and their names were a little recherché—Stephen had His Clothes and Male West One, while others opened places with vaguely suggestive names like Adonis, Domino Male and Gear. "We thought Carnaby Street when it began was for poofs, it was nonsense," remembered Chris Stamp, the East End kid who would soon manage pop bands associated with the Carnaby Street scene but was back then just a hard case looking for a fight. "We liked to look slightly androgynous, but that was so geezers would think we were easy to take, then we'd kick 'em."

But if gay men and gay bashers had sussed out Carnaby Street, nobody in the fashion press had an inkling of what was going on. And then there was one of those awakenings so characteristic of the age.

Sometimes it seemed like the sixties started on a single day: Everybody woke up and the monochrome world was suddenly a riot of color. And color that not only women and children could indulge in but, for the first time, men. Before the sixties, only gay men, blacks, and entertainers dared to dress in pinks, purples, yellows, oranges or reds; but at roughly the time the Beatles were being put into smart collarless suits by Brian Epstein, young men in London began to feel comfortable in wild colors that would've made their dads and grampas blush in shame.

"Up until the sixties," remembered Ian McLagen, future keyboardist of the Small Faces, who would one day keep their offices on Carnaby Street, "you couldn't buy clothes other than your parents' clothes. I had a school uniform and I took my pants in to the tailor at the top of the road and without my parents' permission got him to taper my school pants. They were gray pants, and he tapered them—not too much, so that mom and dad wouldn't notice. Years later I bought my dad a couple of suits—when I hit the big money: ha! They were nice suits off the peg from Harrods. And he took them to that same tailor to have them adjusted and when he wrote his name down, the guy says, 'Oh, yeah:

Ian used to come in here all the time.' And my dad says, 'Did he?' Before that all you had was the same clothes your dad wore. Life suddenly was colorful.'"

It had started, as it would, among the upper-class bohemians around Chelsea, who began returning from hashish-addled trips to Morocco and Asia wearing bright native costumes or emerging from traditional public schools or the new art schools with their heads full of naughty notions and the need to show off and act out in front of adults. They wore tight pants and jackets made of exotic materials like silk and shantung and colored shoes with pointed toes; they performed wacky stunts like showing up at a restaurant in suits with neither shirts nor ties but rather buttons painted on their chests—as Alexander Plunket Greene, Mary Quant's husband, once did at Quaglino's in Soho. Their preferred tailor was John Michael Ingram, who opened a shop called John Michael on the King's Road to service a Chelsea clientele that was roughly his age and of a similar upper-class cool.

Soon enough, as these things do, this new sartorial sense dribbled down to other classes and out into less posh quarters of London. But being a rather underground taste, it popped up in the most particular way, among young men of a background and from neighborhoods which no one might have expected. Eventually, they became known as mods, but that label was itself a misnomer, borrowed from another subculture with a distinctly different aesthetic, agenda and outlook. The original mods were actually *modernists*, aficionados of bebop and cool jazz and other up-to-the-minute sounds that one could hear in certain Soho cellars—Chet Baker, Miles Davis, Gerry Mulligan, Thelonious Monk. They were the antitheses of the trads, who favored traditional jazz sounds like Dixieland and ragtime and comfortably sat alongside fans of folk music, skiffle and blues. Compared to trad fans, who aligned themselves with American beatniks and antinuclear CND demonstrators and adopted a generally shaggy, earnest appearance, mods were extremely particular about their clothing.

Like the upper-class Chelsea dandies, they wore tight pants and pointed winklepicker shoes and French-style "bumfreezer" jackets, so called because they were cut short above the posterior. Carefully maintained haircuts were very, very in with this set, as were sharp sunglasses and shirts and ties in colors that would startle your ordinary city gent—

or, probably more to the point, your typical working-class mom and pop. The influence of Continental kids was a keen component: French students hung out at central London clubs like La Poubelle and Le Kilt and were envied by a lot of hip-aspiring young English boys for their fashion sense. "The clothes the French guys wore were so well-cut," remembered one. "We weren't used to good casual clothes. They had hipster trousers and round-toed shoes, beautiful shoes. They had well-cut suits made from lightweight fabrics. The stuff used to look good for dancing. We used to get all our ideas for clothes from them." Tangentially, there developed among these London trendies an interest in existentialism—Camus and Sartre and the English equivalent, *The Outsider* by Colin Wilson; there was a gay element; there was a strain of conscious rebellion that was inherited from Beat culture but given a sleek French and Italianate finish; but mainly there was catching the latest Continental movies and hanging around coffee bars and jazz clubs in terrific togs wired up on amphetamines and trying terribly hard to look as if one weren't trying at all.

Inevitably, the swank, moody posture of these first mods caught the eye of forward-thinking young men elsewhere in town. Take Andrew Loog Oldham, for instance, at the end of the fifties just a public schoolboy longing to make a splash in the capital. He wasn't interested in existentialism or rebelling from society; he wanted *in*, and he knew that looking right was one way to get in. He may not have been as intellectually committed as those first mods, but he liked the same music, and he frequented the same coffee bars and jazz clubs and caught onto their sense of the importance of a style that could pass for proper yet signify, as well, both novelty and cool. Like many of the Soho mods—and unlike most of his public school classmates—he didn't have the money to get smart suits cut to fit, but he was clever enough to turn his minimal finances into the maximal wardrobe, even while at school. Consider his most brilliant scheme: Burton's, the great, dull equalizer of men's fashion ("They had three styles," remembered restaurateur Alvaro Maccioni: "small, medium and large"), had a long-standing offer of a made-to-order suit for about twelve pounds, for which customers could choose all the details; most men went along with the traditional English desire not to stand out or look ridiculous in any way and chose dull gray and black boxy numbers that palely imitated the bespoke suits their bosses wore (and which, presumably, Burton's tailors could—and, it often appeared, *did*—turn out in their sleep). Oldham, though, drove the firm crazy, memorably finagling out of their offer a dove gray mohair suit with a nipped waist, inverted vents and paisley lining to wear atop draped trousers with slanted pockets; he got approving looks around certain quarters of London, but when he showed up back at school in the getup, it was immediately confiscated by his housemaster. "I don't know why you bother," the man remonstrated. "You only wore it for one day." "Yeah," Oldham remembered, "but what a day!"

This was the face of the new mod: dandyism and preening and taking advantage of the system to look sharp, not trying to tear at the system with a dour-faced blend of Chet Baker and Samuel Beckett. Though it bore the same name—mod—it was like a new cult altogether: a breed of smart-styled young men hanging around Soho who favored rhythm and blues, amphetamines, motor scooters and, most crucially, fashion. It took hold not among an intellectual set but rather, oddly, Jewish schoolboys from such outlying areas as Stamford Hill, Shepherd's Bush, Ilford and Islington, as well as the East End. It began in Soho, once again, but this time it had evolved more in the direction fellows like Oldham were pointing—not a reaction to the unkempt aspect of trad jazz fans, not a vision of modernity that blended existentialism, jazz and sleek style, not a considered revolt at all, in fact, but a blossoming of dandification, a celebration of the new affluence, a new taste for pretty things for men. This, not the original, almost intellectual strain, was the mod that made Carnaby Street red hot, for one reason above all: Even compared to their finnicky forbears, the new mods were simply clothes-mad. All they seemed to care about was cutting an image, making the scene, scoring a cool scooter, pills and clothes and, holy of holies, becoming a Face.

"Face" was the name mods bestowed upon those rarest ones among them, the ones who most exemplified the aesthetic of male beauty bedecked in the most of-the-moment fashion. Faces were the most handsome mods, but they were also the ones who set the fashion agenda for the group, the first ones to score the latest style bearing the label of John Stephen, of Ben Sherman, the Brighton shirtmaker who had been imitating Italian designs, or of Fred Perry who, thrice a Wimbledon champion, was England's Rene Lacoste. As Richard Barnes, Pete Townshend's art school classmate and the man who came up with the band name The Who, recalls, "What the Faces were wearing in 1963, the others were wearing in 1964 and the Faces wouldn't be seen in."

It was the Faces who set the fetishistic plate, deciding what length of suit vent was to be worn, what color shirt was in, which haircut—the Perry Como, the French Crop, the College Boy or the French Crew—was to be worn (top mods might even go to ladies' hairdressers to have their coifs done and might even wear face powder and eye makeup). They were the ones that had the latest soul and R&B records from the States and who had found the newest English R&B bands and ferreted out the coolest R&B clubs. They were the first ones with the new dances—the Shake, the Block, the Bang, the French Blue. And they were surely among the first to get into the drugs that fueled the mod scene—amphetamines, mostly, known generically as leapers but specifically for their colors and shapes: purple hearts and French blues (the domestic and imported forms of Drynamil) and black bombers (Dexedrine). Wired on such stuff (which was legal until the Dangerous Drug Act was expanded to include them in 1964), the edge taken off, maybe, by a scotch and Coke or a vodka and lime, a mod Face could club hop, dance and pose all night, several nights a week if he had the stamina.

For all their drive and peacockery, though, most mods weren't, curiously, ladykillers: "It's your mate you want to impress, not particularly the girls," said a mod to a newspaperman, revealing the extent to which his was a boys' club. Some of it was the drugs, no doubt: All that speed shriveled both genitals and desire. But most of it was sheer narcissism of the sort that Oldham would've recognized and appreciated. Marc Feld, for instance, was a fifteen-year-old mod from Hackney, East London, who appeared in a 1962 article on mods in *Town* magazine. One day not far off he would metamorphose into Marc Bolan, the elfin pseudowizard folk-hippie protoglam pop star; but back then he was just a vain little lad preening over his clothes and "completely knocked out," he remembered later, "by my own image, by the idea of Marc Feld."

His self-adulation was typical of a cult whose members would never put a hand in a jacket pocket for fear that the line of the cut would be upset or who would insist on standing on even empty buses so as not to wrinkle the crease of a trouser leg. "It reached a stage," remembered one early mod, "where it took any one of us up to about three weeks to save up for a bit of gear that probably wouldn't have seen its way through a month of fashion." In other words, no true mod would have the money and, perhaps, the lack of self-awareness to chase girls: "It got to be a big deal to have a conversation with a guy," remembered a woman who'd hung around the mod scene in her youth. "We thought we were very lucky if one of these gorgeous creatures actually *danced* with us."

The idea of rebelling through one's clothes and paying fetishistic fealty to specific modes of fashion and styles of music hadn't originated with the mods. There had been the teddy boys, of course—the frightening guys in drape jackets, elaborate waistcoats, duck's-ass haircuts and crepe-soled shoes who represented the first spontaneous outburst of native youth culture in England after the war. But ted had a mean edge of violence and was limited to lower classes and outer edges of the city, unlike mod, which was quite smart and trendy and centrally located. Too, the teddy boy style bloomed early and quickly and disappeared into an extremely narrow niche soon after, more an eccentricity like trainspotting than a proper youth movement.

Tooling around Soho in their flash clothes on imported Vespa and Lambretta scooters, the mods were another thing altogether, a non-threatening spectacle for the popular press; that they kept real jobs to support their fashion habit—many mods were among the young clerical workers who filled the new office towers rising around the city—gave them a surface appeal in mainstream eyes. "It was acceptable—this was important," remembered Pete Townshend. "You could be a bank clerk and people would think, 'Well, there's a smart young lad,' but you could also be fashionable. That was the great thing about it." Indeed, mods were good for business. In an age when the average young person in London was earning ten pounds a week—as a group, twenty-five-and-unders were doing four times better than their parents had thirty years before—a Face might spend four pounds on a single shirt and put twenty pounds down on a scooter (three years of payments to follow).

On Carnaby Street, mod was a bonanza. By 1963, John Stephen had eighteen shops in London and was planning boutiques and shops in the States and on the Continent; Carnaby Street was attracting dozens of men's specialty retailers, including a pair of brothers who named their shop Lord John in an effort, probably, to confuse a public of noninsiders who were starting to show up on the little thoroughfare looking for Stephen's work.

And the mod musical taste—American R&B and some uptempo

Caribbean music—was catching on. Soho nightclubs that had previously featured jazz combos or even big bands were giving over to the new sound: the Flamingo and La Discotheque on Wardour Street and the Scene in Ham Yard, all near Piccadilly, and, above all the Marquee, a cavernous hall below a cinema on Oxford Street.

For two generations of struggling London musicians—the last trad acts and the nascent R&B bands—these venues, the Marquee particularly, were the beginning of the big time. The Marquee was unique among the important clubs: open-faced and accessible—no dark corners wherein lurked menacing West Indian dope peddlers or drunken U.S. servicemen—there were afternoon sessions with live music just like during the early postwar years, when there were big band dance fans at the Lyceum ballroom in the Strand. A band could leap from the Marquee to the really big time: a record deal, TV appearances, America. The Rollin' (no final g yet) Stones got their first important billed gigs there in January 1963; a year later, it was the Yardbirds who got their big break there, and ten months after that, The Who.

The band which, rightly or wrongly, came most to be associated with mod, The Who came from Shepherd's Bush and had already, by the time they took the Marquee stage, gone through personnel changes, several names (the Detours, the High Numbers and once and then again finally, The Who—although briefly, and surreally, just before that The Hair and The Who), various management schemes and even a few different playing styles. The mod thing wasn't really a natural fit for them— they weren't nearly as close to imitating American soul and R&B as, say, the Stones or the Yardbirds or even the Beatles, who covered well-known numbers like "Money (That's What I Want)" and "You've Really Got a Hold on Me." Rather, The Who were a nascent pop art band—the first anywhere, really; Pete Townshend was one of that generation of bright art college things who got a rush out of the sheer energetic drive of the modern world of sleek cars, French new wave films, steel-and-glass skyscrapers and paintings by Richard Hamilton and Peter Blake. Mod was part of it, sure, but it wasn't central to Townshend's vision, much less that of his bandmates.

But The Who were cast as top mods by Peter Meaden, a publicist who used to run with Andrew Loog Oldham and was himself something of a Face on the scene. Meaden heard something modern and sexy in

The Who's crisp line of attack and encouraged them to play to the hyped-up mod audience; he knew that, for all the specificity of their tastes, mods didn't really have a domestic pop group of their own. Townshend recalled that Meaden "had a hard time convincing the other three members of the band" to go mod. "Because of my art school exposure to pop," he continued, "I supported him." The band finally acceded and cut a record—written by Meaden, who nicked the melody outright from Slim Harpo—called "I'm the Face" and began dressing in Carnaby Street gear; one absurd PR balloon launched in the pop press claimed that Townshend spent one hundred pounds a week on clothes. But the record flopped, rightly, and Meaden, who made folks a tad nervous with his pillhead energy, all nervous tics and white powder at the corner of his mouth, found his role at the band's helm usurped by a new management team, the decadent aristo Kit Lambert and Chris Stamp, the rough-and-ready brother of a real Face, Terence Stamp.

The arrival of Lambert and Stamp coincided with Townshend's growing ability and confidence as a songwriter; the new guys had a much happier job on their hands promoting what turned out to be a rock classic and the band's breakthrough—"I Can't Explain," with its thundering opening riff and lyric that distilled the essence of teen angst. They were able, for instance, to score a gig for the band that Meaden, with all his connections and hustle, never could: a spot on *Ready, Steady, Go!*, TV's latest stairway to the stars.

Compared to the institutionalized London media, which moved glacially (when at all) to embrace youth culture, *RSG!* was a thrilling sprint through whatever was pop right then and there in a particular week: sounds, fashions, dance steps, slang, attitude, colors, the whole crazy teen shebang. *RSG!* was mutable, trendy and disposable in just the perfect pop way. After tuning in at 6:07 of a Friday night and rallying around the show's motto "The weekend starts here!," the *RSG!* audience could hit the hot spots that evening knowing whether or not their clothes, their lingo and their dance moves were sufficiently au courant. In a country where TV channels numbered a handful and the only decent sound on the radio emerged from American military networks on the Continent, *RSG!* became a vital lifeline, rallying point and object of fetish.

The show was created by Rediffusion, an independent TV production company; it was dreamed up by Elkan Allen, who was in his forties but canny enough to see the potential for a youth pop show with a youth sensibility. To that end, he hired young: Vicki Wickham, a former publishing and radio gal Friday, came on as booker-writer-editor; Michael Lindsay-Hogg, then working in Irish television, came on as one of the directors; and, most crucially, an easygoing, fashionable young presenter, Cathy McGowan—a nineteen-year-old secretary from Streatham who was making ten pounds a week—was discovered. Wickham and Lindsay-Hogg may have been the sensibility of the show—"We'd stick to a very rigid booking formula of only using artists we liked," Wickham remembered—but it was McGowan, with her trendy haircuts and clothes and her unironic use of terms like "fab" and "smashing," who was its plasma, the omnipresent transmitter of whatever was vital to the show's audience week in and week out.

And a stable presence was needed because Wickham and Lindsay-Hogg took pains to make the thing change as quickly and unpredictably as the emergent pop sensibility. They and their team scoured the trendiest clubs looking for good dancers and stylish dressers to showcase. They allowed their scenic designer Nicholas Ferguson to push edges by imitating in his sets the pop painters Robert Fraser showed in his gallery. They changed theme tunes regularly, now Manfred Mann's "5–4–3–2–1," now The Who's "Anyway, Anyhow, Anywhere," now "Three Hundred and Sixty-five Rolling Stones," an instrumental by (if you can imagine) the Andrew Oldham Orchestra. They did theme shows, like the April 1964 Mod Ball, which led them to the highest ratings they ever enjoyed. Most of all, they made their show the place to see the best bands, whether the hottest British stars, the most obscure groups from London clubs or visiting American acts: the Beatles, the Rolling Stones, The Who, the Kinks, the Small Faces, the Animals, Jimi Hendrix, Ike and Tina Turner, Otis Redding, John Lee Hooker and all of Motown. There were interviews with scenemakers and stars: Michael Caine, Terence Stamp, Muhammad Ali, David Bailey, Peter Cook, George Best, Twiggy, Phil Spector—"anyone interesting who had the look," according to Wickham.

The show's backstage green room—first at Television House near Waterloo Bridge and then at larger studios out in Wembley—was an essential oasis in the Friday night course of party-going and scene-making; you'd see anyone and everyone there, even if they had nothing to do with that night's show: Marianne Faithfull, Keith Moon, Andrew Old-ham, Kit Lambert, Hendrix, Nico, Barbara Hulanicki (whose Biba boutique was becoming a preferred shop of *RSG!* fans). The off-camera action was just like the stuff the kids tuned in for, an ever-changing parade of visual and audio wonders and cues that captured perfectly the present moment because it was always already in search of the next one.

Ready, Steady, Go! debuted on Friday, August 9, 1963, on ITV and was an immediate hit, spreading London's mood and look and beat throughout the country with unprecedented speed. The show, wrote George Melly, "made pop music work on a truly national scale . . . a tremor of pubescent excitement from Land's End to John o' Groats." And as it was itself a transitory object, dancing with the changes just like the kids to whom it proselytized, it helped institutionalize across Britain the idea that the new culture was disposable, mercurial and—in the best sense of the word—trashy. You could tell by watching the rag trade: On Carnaby Street, as the shops mushroomed, the clothes fell away from the standards of Vince and John Stephen's work; poorly tailored of indifferent material, they were true only to the very latest cut, color or sensibility, not intended to last any longer than the passing fashion that exalted it. "The kids want clothes to look terrific," Cathy McGowan announced. "And they don't wear them for very long so it doesn't matter if they fall to bits."

This view would have, of course, been anathema to the original mods, with their obsession with fine tailoring and aesthetic detail. But their small subcultural moment had been washed away by yet another iteration of mod—the second or third, depending on how you kept score, and the one that finally broke through to mass consciousness and emulation.

The new mod was chintzy, anti-intellectual and, unnervingly, violent. The first proper mass youth movement of the sixties, it contained the essence of everything that the decade was about to become: fashion, music, drugs, slang, sexuality, media attention, frightening incidents of unrest and a built-in expiration date. Unlike the Beat Boom, in which the bands themselves were the trendsetters and headline makers and their fans were observers, the new mod erased the line between the public and the star; a kid could aspire to Face-dom in the new mod without fear of flopping for insufficient talent; you had to have the look, the commitment and the means, and you were in.

This last incarnation of mod derived from the second generation just as that version had from the first—adhering to most of the superficial aspects while tossing aside anything that seemed complex or old-fashioned and adding a dimension that attracted wider attention. The second-generation mods, more affluent and consumerist than the original existential bunch, had discovered cheap and stylish transportation in the Italian motorscooter; the newest mods fetishized their scooters to an unprecedented degree, turning them into extensions of their stylized selves by tricking them out with souped-up motors, exotic paint jobs and seat-covers, huge, bug-eyed clusters of mirrors and reflectors and other inspirations of that guru of the scooter, Eddy Grimstead.

The favored music, too, changed with each successive generation of mod: The modern jazz from which the first mods had taken their name, for instance, had been replaced by R&B by their inheritors, but the new set went straight for pop—emerging groups like The Who, the Kinks, the Small Faces and the like. And where the first two generations of mods reveled in secrecy, the new lot were all about being known. Indeed, as the rise of new mod coincided with the rise of *Ready, Steady, Go!*, the show could be seen as the delivery system by which mod went everywhere, just as the Beatles had a year or two before. Mods, with their sharp, fashionable hair, clothes and dance steps, were perfect *RSG!* types, whether as hosts, dancers or bands. Thanks to the program, recalled Pete Townshend, "Mod fashions spread all through England overnight, and it wasn't the same anymore, because in the real mod scene no one would tell you. . . . It was incestuous, secretive. Difficult to be a real up-to-the-minute mod 'cause no cunt would tell you where to get the clothes."

The new mods were different in another crucial way that the country found out about one chilly spring weekend in 1964: They liked to fight. Starting on Friday, March 27, a pack of London mods assembled in Clacton-on-Sea, the Essex coastal town that had a long-standing name as a Cockney holiday spot, and got a little rowdy. They made the papers. The next day, their ranks had swelled—the newcomers no doubt drawn by the headlines in that day's papers reporting on the presence of "youth gangs" in the resort. On hand, too, were packs of local kids, decidedly non-mod, who still fancied Elvis Presley and the Marlon Brando of *The Wild One*, still sported leather jackets and still rode proper motorcycles.

Dubbed rockers, they resented the sudden appearance of a large number of outsiders in their clubs and pubs and they found themselves coming to blows over the following days with the mods, who, by virtue of their superior numbers (and, perhaps, the stimulation and artificial courage afforded them by amphetamines), more or less wiped the promenade with them in an honest-to-goodness teenage riot.

The London media, which had helped incite the fisticuffs to begin with, went to town on the incident: "Day of Terror by Scooter Groups," "Riot Police Fly to Seaside," and so on. Members of Parliament were alarmed by the news: "I am truly sorry for Clacton—a nice warm-hearted place," declared Lord Arran. "If some town had to cop it, I would have preferred Frinton. They are snooty around Frinton." Around Clacton, the reaction was much calmer: "The troubles," reported the *East Essex Gazette*, "were not so horrific as the flood of national press, television and radio publicity suggested."

But the die had been cast, and mod-rocker battles were suddenly fashionable. Over Whitsun weekend, May 15 to 18, members of the two groups squared off at seaside resorts in Brighton, Margate, Southend, Bournemouth and, once again, Clacton. In August, Hastings was the battleground. A year after the first incidents, Easter 1965, they were at it again in Brighton, Great Yarmouth and Weston-super-Mare: gang fighting had become a moveable feast for bored, angry kids and the tabloid media that fed off them. Around the country, the opprobrium for juvenile delinquents on either side of the battle lines was both predictable and tiresome: A Margate magistrate, sentencing some of the London dandies who'd come to his town armed with screwdrivers and little hammers, spat venom against what he called "long-haired, mentally unstable, petty little sawdust Caesars."

He'd pegged them just right: The mods fighting and fucking in the alleys of seaside resort towns were followers and parasites who'd merely adopted the poses of the first strains of mod without any agenda other than raw kicks. They'd seen the fashions, haircuts and dances on *Ready, Steady, Go!*, so they had a style to emulate. But they had nothing to do with the cultish London originals who had invented the scene. "True mods," after all, according to Richard Barnes, "were really too concerned with their clothes to want to ruin them by fighting with worthless rockers." By the time the bank holiday rioting petered out, the original mod scene was over. The fashionable young men who could curry favor with their elders a few years earlier by sporting neat clothes and carefully cropped hair were now lumped together with the snotty, trendy hooligans who were turning up in the headlines.

The Who were still playing to the mod audience—still appearing on *Ready, Steady, Go!*, still wearing T-shirts with pop-art targets and arrows imprinted on them, still writing mod anthems like the cataclysmic "My Generation," which debuted on Guy Fawkes Day, 1965, drawing a striking connection between the mastermind of the seventeenth-century Gunpowder Plot and the amphetamine-addled stutterer of Roger Daltry's vocal. But the end of the song—distortion, feedback and other aural equivalents of the band's new habit of destroying its gear as a finale to its stage act—made it seem as much a bomb dropping on mod as a rallying cry for the mod moment. Within months, pop would mutate away from mod and the pace of fashions in London would whisk the movement out of the limelight.

One could feel nostalgia for it; compared to what was coming, mod felt innocent, guileless and clean: "It was the first move toward unity I have ever seen," Townshend reflected years later. "I think of that fucking gesture that happened in England. It was the closest to patriotism that I've ever felt." He wasn't alone in that sentiment: Mod was uniquely, even exclusively British—Beatlemania and Beat bands gave Americans all the distraction they could ask for out of England—and the Union Jack itself became part of the palette of fashion designers and the makers of everything from lunchpails to scooters to boots. Even when it was bastardized, disseminated and diluted, it was always parochial in the best sense: organic and native and particular.

When you walked down Carnaby Street, jostled by dozens of faux mods and kids from around the world who'd been drawn to London to partake of the youthquake miracle, window-shopping outside boutiques with rents that had risen thirtyfold in the half-dozen years since John Stephen's Beak Street premises burned out, you were truly in the midst of something. Maybe not as authentic as the first generation of mod or even—in its way—its fucking-and-fighting-on-the-beach derivative, but something real nevertheless. The clothes may have grown shoddier, the fashions less tasteful, the customers less discerning, but the scale of it, the sheer tidal wave impact: The whole world was watching this obscure street in Soho where, a few years ago, a handful of gay weightlifters shopped for camp clobber. Sitting in his office above the bustle of the street, Stephen was, truly, Lord John, even if his competitors had, in fact, been the ones who invented that name and slapped it on their awning to fool the kids. He laughed over a drink while chatting with a journalist: "I can't think why I haven't got the OBE for services to export!"

He was only partly kidding.

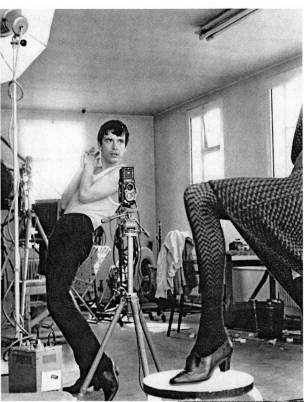

SARABANDE MAN:
DAVID BAILEY,
IN CUBAN BOOTS,
AT WORK.
(TERRY O'NEIL,
CAMERA PRESS)

JUST AN ORDINARY
ENGLISH COUNTRY GIRL:
JEAN SHRIMPTON
IN THE FAMILY BARN,
WITH THE FAMILY.
(TERRY O'NEIL,
CAMERA PRESS)

ALWAYS INVENTING:
MARY QUANT AND
ALEXANDER PLUNKET GREENE
WORK DURING A MEAL.
(REX FEATURES)

THE CUT: VIDAL SASSOON
ATTENDS TO THE DETAILS OF
MARY QUANT'S COIF.
(GETTY IMAGES)

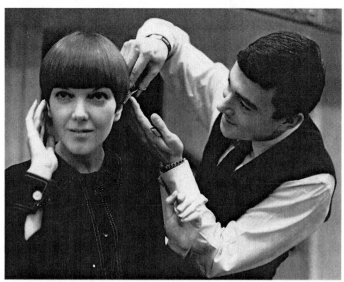

TUGBOAT TERRY:
THE DAY OF
THE BIG PRESS
CONFERENCE, WHEN
A BLEACHED-BLOND
TERENCE STAMP
MET THE WORLD.
(REX FEATURES)

NEMPEROR:
BRIAN EPSTEIN,
SMART YOUNG
ENTREPRENEUR
ABOUT TOWN.
(CAMERA PRESS)

THE DARTFORD BOYS:
KEITH RICHARDS AND
MICK JAGGER.
(REX FEATURES)

"THE STONES NEVER DID
ANYTHING LIKE THAT":
BILL WYMAN
(TOP LEFT) AND HIS
ROLLING STONES MATES
IN MATCHING SUITS AND
CAMERA-FRIENDLY GRINS,
MAYBE FOR THE LAST TIME.
(REX FEATURES)

MISS 1964:
CHRISSIE
SHRIMPTON
MODELING ON
CARNABY STREET.
(REX FEATURES)

THE BLUE BLOOD:
ROBERT FRASER
IN HIS GALLERY.
(GETTY IMAGES)

"A GENERATION WAS FADING BEFORE OUR EYES": STEPHEN WARD, PROFUMO SCANDAL MARTYR, SCHLEPPED COMATOSE TO A HOSPITAL WHILE A JURY DEBATES HIS FATE, JULY 31, 1963.
(GETTY IMAGES)

ALL THE YOUNG DUDES, PART I: A BRIGHT YOUNG THING CATCHES THE BIRDS' EYES ON CARNABY STREET.
(REX FEATURES)

A souvenir of Swinging London: A couple of likely lasses help themselves to a piece of Carnaby Street.

(Rex features)

Let's twist again: *Ready, Steady, Go!*'s Mod Ball, April 1964. (Getty Images)

STAMP AND SHRIMP—
TOO BEAUTIFUL
NOT TO BE TOGETHER.
(TERRY O'NEIL,
CAMERA PRESS)

BUT THE SNAPPER
SCORES ON THE REBOUND:
DAVID BAILEY
AND HIS SECOND WIFE,
CATHERINE DENEUVE,
ON THE SET OF
*LES DEMOISELLES
DE ROCHEFORT.*
(CAMERA PRESS)

PART
THREE

NEMPEROR

Whether it was because he had the eagle eye of a professional image maker or because he observed the scene from the cool, discerning remove of a resident alien, Richard Lester may have seen what the Beatles had done to traditional English mores and notions more incisively than any of the Britons whose world was being shattered by the band's ballistic rise.

The Liverpool pop stars, he reflected, "were the first to give a confidence to the youth of the country which led to the disappearance of the Angry Young Men with a defensive mien. The Beatles sent the class thing sky high: They laughed it out of existence and, I think, introduced a tone of equality more successfully than any other single factor."

American, intellectual, prematurely bald, a decade older than the Beatles, Lester had come to England in the mid-fifties after kicking around the Continent as a college-educated bum, stringing together a living as a journalist, piano tuner, minor-league smuggler (of flints into cigarette lighter-starved Spain), itinerant busker (piano and guitar specialities), aspiring songwriter and playwright and, finally, TV director—a line he'd entered into back home when he was a boy wonder just out of school but which he'd since abandoned for more romantic pursuits. After several years working in British television, he had become a rising screen director with two films to his credit: a short comic movie, *The Running Jumping & Standing Still Film*, featuring a pair of the Beatles' beloved Goons (Spike Milligan and Peter Sellers) and a modestly commercial film about trad jazz, *It's Trad, Dad!*, featuring the sorts of artistes the Beatles had all but run out of showbiz.

In one of the kooky strokes of fortune that dominated his early career, Lester was asked if he'd like to direct a Beatles movie by Walter Shenson, an American producer who'd acquired, almost by accident, the commission to make one. Sure, he said, and armed with a script by Alun Owen, a Liverpool playwright whom Shenson charged with imagining a day in the life of the insanely famous band, he created maybe the only pure instance of pop art in the cinema, a film part documentary, part slapstick comedy, part avant-garde technical spree, part musical—and only one of the greatest movies ever made: *A Hard Day's Night*.

The film was built on Owen's stroke of genius: using Beatlemania, the dumbfounding phenomenon of the band's success, as the focus of the screenplay. Rather than create a story about a band being discovered or working in other situations but harboring musical talents (as in so many lame Elvis Presley pictures or other of the earliest rock films), Owen presented a group so famous that its name was never mentioned aloud by anyone in the film. The picture opened with the Beatles fleeing enraptured waves of fans at a train station, traveled with them to a city where they appeared on TV, then picked them up (literally, in a helicopter) and whisked them away: no real story, no stock characters or plot tics, no fat.

There were set pieces that revealed who the Beatles were and what their impact on the world had been—a square off with a prim, old-school man in a railway car, a cocktail reception with the press, John's backstage encounter with a woman connected to the TV show, George's being mistaken by an advertising executive for an anonymous young hipster. But by and large the film is simply about being the Beatles for the span of a few hours: the ducking from the fans, the demands of publicity and management, the ogling of young ladies, the harassing of squares, the hurried meals and cups of tea and the sensual escapes into music.

And if Owen was inspired, Lester was perhaps even more so. The film was a virtual dictionary of techniques for shooting rock music.

Lester worked in a pseudodocumentary style—handheld cameras, jump cuts, faked accidents, blurs and wipes and quick pans—that matched the energy of his feisty young stars and allowed him to drop Owen's random inventions into the fabric of the film with harmonic ease. There were dozens of innovations that informed music videos for decades: aerial shots, slow motion, dissolves from one level of filmed "reality" into another, the final title sequence with its fetching flipbook of still photos of the band. The picture revolutionized moviemaking nearly as thoroughly as the Beatles themselves had pop.

A Hard Day's Night was made for about £180,000, shot between March 2 (three weeks precisely after the Beatles' epochal *Ed Sullivan Show* debut) and April 24 (the day after John Lennon was honored by Foyles bookstore for his bestselling book *In His Own Write*), and previewed, without a score or final edits, on May 7. On July 6, it premiered in London at a Royal Charity event that drew to Piccadilly Circus twelve thousand pilgrims hopeful merely of glimpses of their bright young gods. The reviews, from a film press that had every reason to expect *It's Trad, Dad 2: Mersey, Mersey Me,* were uniformly ecstatic: What had heretofore seemed an evanescent youth and media fad was now a certified cultural phenomenon, not to mention a moneymaker that would earn back its cost scores—maybe hundreds—of times.

But for all the grand tumult the film occasioned around the world, its most glowing reception was the July 10 special premiere held in dear, dirty Liverpool, the city that had birthed the Beatles, their manager, the screenwriter and, bizarrely, the newly emergent license Britons had to consider themselves the most switched-on people in the world. Already the band had conquered Scandinavia, the Continent, the Antipodes, Hong Kong and, most astoundingly, America, where, in a single week in April, the Beatles held the number-one, two, three, four, five, thirty-one, forty-one, forty-six, fifty-eight, sixty-five, sixty-eight and seventy-nine spots in the *Billboard* Hot 100. They were the foremost stars of record, television, radio, live performance and, presently, movies. They had sparked revolutions in show business, teen culture and, increasingly, the wider societies of England and America. And just eighteen months earlier they'd been nursing cups of tea in Lime Street station waiting for Brian Epstein to return from London, telling them that nobody wanted anything to do with them.

Now they flew in from the capital on their rare visits, such as the northern premiere of *A Hard Day's Night*, when their motorcade from Speke Airport into the city was greeted by 100,000, maybe 200,000 well-wishers. They were saluted by the city fathers, local royalty, peers, clergymen and a member of Parliament, then stepped out onto the Town Hall balcony where, to the sound of the city's police band playing "Can't Buy Me Love," they greeted the thousands of Scousers who were still rubbing their eyes at the spectacle of local boys having made it so good, so big, so fast. (One of the great endearing hometown celebrations of the Beatles' early triumph was captured on film—the toothless, cloth-capped soccer fans who inhabited the Kop End terrace at Liverpool's famed Anfield Stadium singing "She Loves You" instead of the usual litany of Manchester United–baiting songs.)

A year before, they had started, slowly and quietly, to cut their ties to the city. They played their last gig at the Cavern in August 1963, and a few weeks later took a flat in Green Street, Mayfair, a pied-à-terre to replace the hotels in which they'd been staying during their increasingly regular—and lengthy—trips to London. The four-Beatles/one-flat gig didn't last long: By the end of the year, Paul was living on Wimpole Street in an attic bedroom at the family home of his girlfriend, actress Jane Asher; John had moved with his wife, Cynthia, and baby son, Julian, to Emperor's Gate, Kensington; George and Ringo, both still nominally unattached, took a flat below Brian Epstein's in William Mews, near Hyde Park Corner, just after the new year. The summertime visit to Liverpool for the film premiere was just that—a visit: By mid-1964, the Beatles and Epstein were full-fledged Londoners. (Compare the fate of Gerry & the Pacemakers, nice enough chaps by any measure, who found themselves walking off the end of a gangplank into oblivion as the Beat Boom went bye-bye. Poignantly, they marked their retreat from fame with a hit ballad, "Ferry Cross the Mersey," in which, as they sang it, their fellow Liverpudlians declared, "We don't care what your name is, boy/We'll never turn you away.")

For centuries, London had been effervesced by the arrival of new provincial talents—poets and politicians from outlying shires, Oxbridgean scholars and the sons of noble families had "come down" to the capital to make their careers. More recently, a trickle of actors and writers from the north of England had followed suit, blending in with the culture of the city like assimilating immigrants. But the advent of the Beatles as conquering northern superstars ignited the city in a way that hadn't been seen since the coronation of Queen Elizabeth a decade earlier. By the time of the filming of *A Hard Day's Night*, London—with its adventurous fashions, new-style exotic restaurants, exclusive after-hours nightclubs and exciting young actors and models and pop stars from, seemingly, all classes and corners of England—was the coolest city in the world.

The Beatles, either solo or as what Mick Jagger called "the four-headed monster," were regulars of virtually every hot spot in town: the Saddle Room, one of London's first Paris-style discotheques; Les Ambassadeurs, site of the great nightclub scene in *A Hard Day's Night*; the Establishment Club, Peter Cook and Nicholas Luard's Soho satire emporium; old-style supper clubs like the Talk of the Town and the Blue Angel, where an off-duty pop star could get a decent late-night meal and maybe watch a bit of cabaret. In early 1964, the Ad Lib, the initial nucleus of Swinging London, became the clubhouse of the burgeoning popoisie: From its walls of floor-to-ceiling windows, the scenesters could look out with a usurper's sense of propriety on Piccadilly, Soho, Mayfair, even Buckingham Palace.

But Brian Epstein, the man who'd engineered the act that formed the crest of this wave, partook of a different sort of London. Where the Beatles were synonymous with the image of the new, arriviste swinging city, Brian sought to transform himself into a more refined, sophisticated, old-fashioned sort of man about town, the sort of London swell he had admired when, on leave from his duties as the Queen's worst soldier, his uncle treated him to dinner at the Savoy Grill and, reading the look on Brian's face, declared, "*This* is what you really enjoy."

So while his boys did the latest dances with long-lashed dolly birds in late-night clubs, Brian could be found instead rubbing elbows with lords and MPs and captains of industry in the city's most venerable, elegant restaurants, at chic theater openings, in various haunts of old showbiz such as Quaglino's and the Trattoria Terrazza, and, most frequently of all, in the elite gambling clubs that had sprouted around Mayfair and St. James in the wake of the Betting and Gaming Act of 1960.

Nicknamed the Vicars' Charter because it was formulated and passed by a Tory government that wanted to grant some uniformity to, among other things, church bingo nights, the Betting and Gaming Act had inadvertently given rise to a boom in casino gambling—which, through a loophole in the law, was permitted so long as there was no built-in advantage to the house in any game of chance. Of course, none of the traditional European casino games—roulette, vingt-et-un, chemin de fer, baccarat—was a break-even proposition; the house has the advantage by definition. To comply with the statute, casinos would therefore offer every player the opportunity to *be* the bank for a number of hands or turns of the wheel. In the long run, naturally, the house retained its edge: Most players shied from the risk associated with being the bank and so left it to the casino. But this little egalitarian quirk of British casino gambling strengthened the clubby atmosphere of the most exclusive of London's casinos—you and the others at the table were there, at least in theory, to compete against one another as gentlemen—and the city turned into what *Le Figaro* called "the European Las Vegas."

As in the American Las Vegas, there was a criminal element inherent in even the top-flight London casinos. Esmeralda's Barn in Knightsbridge, for one, was operated openly by the East End's notorious Kray brothers, who simply muscled their way into partnership with the founding owner. And the Colony Sporting Club in Berkeley Square, where George Raft was house shill and greeter, was so obviously mob-connected—on both sides of the Atlantic—that the place was kept under scrupulous watch by authorities and Raft himself was denied readmittance to the U.K. after he attempted to return from a trip home.

But Brian's tastes in gambling weren't so déclassé or dangerous. He played at the Curzon House off Park Lane, at Crockford's overlooking the Mall and, especially at John Aspinall's Clermont Club, also in Berkeley Square, above Annabel's nightclub. There, when not giving wide berth to Aspinall's pet tiger, which was from time to time allowed freedom of the building, Brian would win and lose thousands of pounds in an evening alongside the likes of Charles Churchill, son of the former prime minister, or he-man stars like Michael Caine and Roger Moore, or louche bastions of upper-class decadence such as Lord Lucan, nicknamed "Lucky," the society rake and sportsman who disappeared into mythology in the 1970s after murdering his children's nanny (whom he apparently mistook for his wife) and vanishing à la Jimmy Hoffa.

Brian's profligate way with money shocked some of the meat-and-potatoes members of his Liverpool talent stable. "I used to tell him he was stupid," remembered Gerry Marsden, "but it *was* his money." The somewhat more open-minded Paul McCartney would remember joining Brian on boys' nights at the gambling clubs, dining on fine food and wine (compliments of the house for such a regular high roller as Brian) and then hitting the tables, where Brian, fueled for a night's betting by amphetamines, would risk fortunes that none of them had been able to conceive of a year or so before.

"Brian would be, 'Ugghhh, the pills!'," McCartney recalled. "The jaw would be grinding away. I remember Brian putting his Dunhill lighter on a bet—'That's a hundred pounds'—and he'd lose it all. But he didn't mind, some people just like that bumpy ride."

He no doubt liked, too, the air his gambling club appearances gave him of being an important figure on the social scene—not the new scene that was being redefined with each new hit song or fashion show or club opening, but the old scene that he had fallen in love with as a soldier and RADA student first enjoying the liberty of the capital.

Even more than in Liverpool, Brian played the aristocrat in his new London environs. In his Belgravia flat, far more modern than the secretive trysting place he had kept for himself apart from Harry and Queenie's home in Liverpool, he was attended by a black American manservant, Lonnie Trimble, and hosted frequent parties attended by a mixture of young pop up-and-comers and old showbiz royalty like Judy Garland. He was as unnatural a driver as he had been an actor—it had taken him four goes to pass his driving test, and George Harrison was under the impression that Brian didn't know whether a green or red light meant stop—but he maintained three cars: a Bentley, a Roller and a Mini. He spoke proper, or at least in an approximation of upper-class public-school diction that sounded nice but which Scousers derided as "Liverpool posh." He clad and comported himself like a man of his father's day and was selected as one of the Ten Best Dressed Men in England in 1964, even though he confessed that he was an inveterate nail-biter. He served as the cool, suave English host of the American teeny-bopper musical showcase *Hullabaloo.* He even signed his name, somewhat grandly, given his age of thirty-two, to an autobiography ghostwritten by journalist and Beatle publicist Derek Taylor: *A Cellarful of Noise.* (There was even a Brian Epstein Fan Club, formed by some loons in America; appropriately, Brian kept his distance.)

He seemed of another age altogether, speaking to interviewers about what he called "my Victorian air." Observers concurred: "You never caught him out of it," said Terry O'Neill. "He was far more disciplined than they were. He was private." Marianne Faithfull said, "He was quite a lot in the grown-up world but also able to play with us." And, indeed, he often spoke as if he wanted nothing to do with the youthquake of which the Beatles were the most potent symbols. "All this finger snapping, hippie business is very contrived: so much nonsense in many ways," he declared. "There is a very grave danger of people deluding themselves into thinking this is some sort of artistic progress. I think this mod thing is awful. I haven't had much to do with it." And again, "I do believe too many people are confusing the social activity with artistic achievement. There is far too much self-indulgence and gluttony going on now. I find it horribly distasteful."

Unlike most of the people who came to fill the London scene, in fact, Brian bore an aura of gravity and import. That "Mr. Brian" business from NEMS Whitechapel Street had been translated down to London as a kind of gilded grandness. The London staff of NEMS—which had opened on Argyll Street next door to the London Palladium and were strictly managerial, selling no sofas, pianos or LPs—came to know a boss with a certain testiness who stood apart from his employees, even from old Liverpool intimates who'd made the trip down with him. They could be frozen or broiled by him, sometimes both in the same day, or they could find him the chummiest and most genteel of employers. Brian would now and again fire someone in a fit of pique and, minutes later, ask them about some detail of work as if nothing untoward had happened. "It was a bit of a seesaw ride," one would later admit.

And outsiders weren't spared his moods. When *A Hard Day's Night* was in production, film critic Alexander Walker did a five-part story about the making of the movie and chose to dedicate one day to Brian. From the moment they sat down together, Walker said, the atmosphere was strained: "He had been warned about me before the interview, and it was the most monosyllabic interview. It was 'yesses' and 'nos.' It was as if he was being cross-examined. He really didn't give very much away. And he showed much arrogance. He said, 'I am going to build these boys up to the point where they will be invulnerable.' I said, 'What do you mean?' And he said, 'To attack from people like you.' We ran the interview under the headline 'The Man Who Would Be Nemperor'; 'Nemperor' was his Telex address. And he didn't like it and threatened the lawyers, and they dismissed it. He was a curious blend of ancient and modern: a man who wanted to be the Fifth Beatle and yet wanted to look and dress like his father."

But surely such testiness was a result of his insecurity and the unprecedented pressures he was under. Unlike the Beatles, who thrived on sheer talent and cheek, Brian had to maintain an outward face that bespoke respectability while at the same time keeping up an agreeable affinity with the young people whose careers he oversaw. Paul McCartney understood that Brian's gentlemanliness was, at least in part, an act: "As the manager you have to deal with all these business people who he didn't want to look goofy in front of," he recalled, "but you would get back to the party and his 'Ohh!' would emerge again." And Brian himself admitted that his public persona didn't mesh with the inner man: "I don't often look ruffled," he told a reporter, "but by and large that is a facade."

But he was of a slightly older generation—not to mention more refined class—than the Beatles and the rest. And though he truly adored the stars of the emerging scene, he was most at home with an older breed of showfolk. He was matey, for instance, with Alma and Li—the Jewish Cockney songster Lionel (Li) Bart and his singing "girlfriend" (in an era when all gay celebrities had them), Alma Cogan. Alma and Li were a kind of golden couple of middlebrow British showbiz of the turn of the sixties. He had made smash hits with *Fings Ain't Wot They Used T'Be* and *Oliver!*; she was a much-loved pop singer known as "The Girl with the Giggle in Her Voice" who was as famed for her outrageously elaborate gowns, many of which she designed herself, as for her pedestrian way with novelty tunes and pappy American pop hits.

Li, who was an early (and uncredited) collaborator with Mick Jagger and Keith Richards as they taught themselves the craft of songwriting, was one of those sorts who seemed to be everywhere in London: chic restaurants and clubs, opening nights, private soirees, writing a little bit of something for this or that singer or movie or show. But he was emblematic of the old showbiz in that he never recovered from the jostling his career received from the advent of youth culture. His last unqualified success was *Oliver!*, which debuted to critical drubbings—and massive box office—in 1960. Two efforts to follow it up, complete with exclamation marks—*Blitz!*, about the Nazi's air war on Britain ("Twice as loud and twice as long as the real thing," per Noël Coward), and *Twang!!*, about Robin Hood and his Merry Men—bombed ingloriously as the taste for tuneful entertainments failed to hold the young.

Alma, too, was a sort of linchpin of the London scene, particularly in the smarter era before 1965, when older and newer pop cultures could more or less coexist. A popular but undistinguished vocalist, she compensated for what she lacked in raw talent and aesthetic style with plenty of gumption, showmanship and old-fashioned swank charm. She lived in a flat in Kensington High Street with her mother, Fay, and younger sister, and entertained the cream of London showbiz society and any visiting Americans virtually every night. Over cocktails, canapes and games of charades, a guest might encounter Bob Hope, Sammy Davis Jr., Danny Kaye, Laurence Olivier, Noël Coward, Stanley Baker, Tommy Steele, Sean Connery, Terence Stamp, Michael Caine, Cary Grant, Ethel Merman, Judy Garland and, eventually, the Beatles—all the swells.

The Beatles first visited Chez Cogan after appearing on the bill with the singer the night they debuted at the London Palladium. They, of course, knew who she was: John used to kill his coterie at art college with savage send-ups of Alma's voice and singing style. But they immediately felt at home in the flat, and after that first visit they would drop in, often unannounced, as if drawn to the sort of hearth-and-home scenes they'd left behind in Liverpool; they called Fay, for reasons no one but they understood, "Mrs. Macogie." In describing the evenings he spent at Alma's get-togethers, Paul McCartney declared, quoting John Betjeman, " 'There I learned to be a guest.' " (One time he came by to try out Alma's ear on a melody he was working on, just to find out if she recognized it, just to make sure he wasn't ripping anybody off; it turned out to be "Yesterday"—and he wasn't so fond a guest as to let her record it before he had.) John, in particular, was such a familiar of the household that his panty-sniffing biographer Albert Goldman investigated the possibility that he'd carried on an affair with Alma.

It's rather an ironic image to conceive: John Lennon dropping in on the Cogan ladies on a slow night at the Ad Lib and getting inveigled into a game of penny poker with Mel Tormé or Roger Moore over sandwiches and tea. In it, you could taste the seasoning with which Brian Epstein had imbued the Beatles. His affection and respect for the old show world ways had helped make the band palatable to the London powers who had initially balked at the notion of a Liverpool act. But at the same time it was that Liverpool act that wiped the boards clear of the sorts of music and showmanship that was the livelihood of Alma and Li and many of the other regular guests at the Cogan flat.

Still, their general respectfulness, coupled with international acclaim, was all part of the tenor, in the minds of most observers, that separated the Beatles from other acts. Charles Marowitz, an American drama critic and stage director who'd been living in London since 1956 and working in avant-garde theater, noted that, "There was a distinction made between what the Beatles were doing and the more rough trade kind of rock music. It was sometimes clear just by seeing where those bands played. The Beatles didn't play in clubs that were known for being druggy; they played more well-known venues. The only underground life the Beatles ever had was when they started in Liverpool. There was a period when there wasn't a distinction made between them and anybody else. But very quickly, because of their commercial success abroad and because they were very clean-cut seeming guys, they came to inhabit a different sphere."

Initially, the Beatles played in touring variety shows, with girl singers and comics and dance acts and other bands; under Brian's proctorship, they performed in such old-school fare as Christmas season pantomime, *Sunday Night at the London Palladium* and Royal Variety Performances. But few of the bands who surfaced after the Beatles broke through found it appealing—or even necessary—to pander in this way to an older audience or to London impresarios' antique ideas of what made a good show or career. As soon after the rise of the Beatles as the advent of the Rolling Stones, even the stodgiest hands in showbiz recognized that the kids who waited for hours to scream at pop bands didn't want to see dog acts, magicians or singers of novelty tunes, as well. The Beatles themselves soon found all the old trappings and methods onerous; before long, they were refusing to do any of it.

This put Brian in something of a pickle. Only a few months earlier, he'd been sincerely grateful to the likes of West End and variety tycoons Lew Grade and Bernard Delfont and to the producers of such middle-of-the-road pap as *Juke Box Jury* for their willingness to make a place for his boys. Presently, he found himself flattered with *their* attentions and requests. Finally, he was put in the unpleasant position of telling the Lords of Showbiz no: "Brian went through hell," Lennon remembered. "Brian was on his knees saying, 'Please do the Royal Variety Show,' after getting so much pressure from Lew [Grade] and the rest of them. We said, 'We've done them all.' We only did one of everything; once was enough."

In the end, Brian sided with the band against the powerful men he wished to join and emulate. In part it was because there was a side of him, stung by the many rebukes he received when he first tried to peddle the band, self-conscious of being an outsider (as a Liverpool merchant in this context, not as a gay man or a Jew, both of which were in ample supply in the upper reaches of showbiz management); in time, he relished delicately lording his guardianship of England's biggest act over the older crowd. He nearly admitted as much in his 1964 autobiography: "As time goes on my relationship with older elements in show business mellows. At first they thought of me as a young upstart, and one who would inevitably fall. I think a lot of them hoped I would, but I didn't, and now my acceptability is complete."

But there was also, foremost even, the fact that he was deeply loyal to—hell, *in love with*—the Beatles; if they said they didn't want to do something, he'd brave defying anyone to see that they got their wish. In McCartney's mind, Brian bore a paternal, or at least avuncular, bond with the group: "It's a great memory of mine: Brian in his polka-dot scarf at the back of the crowd, holding himself very proud, very proud of his boys." (Brian confessed, though, to Simon Napier-Bell, that he once allowed himself, standing in the back at one of the band's enormous American gigs, to scream along with the girls—something, Brian said, that "he'd always wanted to do from the first minute he'd ever seen them.")

He tried to keep in the background as much as possible, limiting his visits to the Abbey Road studios to the absolute minimum when the Beatles were recording, for example, and turning down all but the most dignified press opportunities for himself, insisting that the focus stay on the performers: all of them. McCartney remembered him looking after everyone in the band: During the early planning of the film *Magical Mystery Tour*, Brian spoke up to ensure that Ringo would get enough to do and that George would have a song included.

He was truly the Fifth Beatle—alongside the Cute One, the Clever One, the Funny One and the Quiet One—the Slightly Removed, Conscientious, Responsible One: a lonelier role than anyone might have imagined. Neil Aspinall, Beatles mate, roadie and confidant, and one of the very few people who could ken Brian's position exactly, mused that "the Beatles had each other. Brian was more like Elvis; he was out there by himself."

And outside he stayed—painfully—when, on June 11, 1965, it was announced that the Beatles, as part of the publicity courting of the recently elected Labour government, were to be awarded MBEs later that year by Queen Elizabeth. The 121st of the 126 honors with which the Crown, at the behest of the ruling government, may invest notable subjects, the Most Excellent Order of the British Empire had most often been awarded to military figures and had, in fact, been designed in 1917 specifically for the purpose of rewarding meritorious service in wartime. "I thought you had to drive tanks and win wars to win the MBE," said John Lennon, revealing a surprising knowledge of royal protocol. Actually, the citation was for the group's substantial contribution to the balance of trade; on the backs of the Beatles and the other groups that constituted the British Invasion had come an enormous flow of capital into the U.K. from America, the Continent and Asia, as well as increases in tourism and in those most ineffable resources of all, prestige and cachet.

The triumph in America was especially important. One of the very few important things that the old and new Englands had in common was a sense of awe with regard to the United States, a country that in the span of a generation or two had evolved from a backward, isolationist frontier to the dominant military, economic and cultural influence in the world. Movies, music, cars, teen fashions, TV shows, soft drinks, cigarettes, hairstyles, mores: If it was American, it seemed to British palates fresher, hipper, freer and more honest than the homegrown brand.

The Beatles were themselves proudly steeped in Americana: the music of, chiefly, Chuck Berry, Buddy Holly, Little Richard and Motown, plus the image of teenage freedom depicted in American movies such as *Rebel Without a Cause* and *The Blackboard Jungle*. Part of their surprise at the tumultuous welcome they received when they first arrived in New York was that they had reckoned they were doing little more than imitating their American idols, little knowing the low esteem in which the vast American mainstream then held roots rock 'n' roll.

To many Britons, however, the very thought of the rise of the Beatles had to cut through decades of inured cultural self-abnegation. Even a modern cat like Terence Stamp was subject to the syndrome. One night on TV he caught a film clip of chimpanzees frolicking in the grass with a bouncy soundtrack that was identified at the end as a tune called "Love Me Do" by some group called the Beatles. "Because we were so subjected to anything good being American," Stamp said, "I just assumed that it was American. I started telling people, 'There's this group, the

Beatles, and they're just fantastic.' And I went into a record shop and said, 'Do you have this American record "Love Me Do"?' And he said, 'That's an English record.' And I was floored."

You could understand his confusion. In head-to-head comparison between the two countries, England so rarely came off well. The British establishment liked to boast of England's "special relationship" with the U.S., but it was rather like a dotty great-uncle's relationship to a young playboy: The sense of privileged intimacy was distinctly one-sided.

In politics, England had the antiquated Macmillan, a walking exaggeration of such stereotypical national traits as reserve, sartorial conservatism and the stiff upper lip; the U.S. had John Kennedy, young and vital and sexy and just as popular in Britain as at home.

In boxing, England had Henry Cooper, the Battling Greengrocer, earnest and hardworking but apt to bleed from an eyebrow if a gnat lit upon it; America had Cassius Clay, brash and lithe and loud-mouthed and cat quick. The two met under the lights at Wembley Stadium in June of 1963, in front of a celebrity crowd that included Richard Burton, Elizabeth Taylor and Shirley Bassey, right at the height of the Profumo scandal (and the very night that, in an unscheduled undercard event, John Lennon was clocking Bob Wooler). Cooper initially seemed to have a shot, knocking the American Olympian onto his keister for the first time in his career. But the reliable tendency of the British heavyweight champ to gush blood like a garden hose—this time through a gash above his left eye that looked as though it had been opened by a serrated knife—ensured Clay's victory.

Typical, a lot of British minds sadly decided.

But the Beatles had overnight turned the world's biggest market into the playground of anything young, bright and British. All any English band with a working-class accent had to do was show up at the airport: nine different British singles claimed the top spot in the *Billboard* charts in 1964; twelve the following year. America's musical palate was completely reborn. And not necessarily for the better: As Bill Wyman remembered, "You started to have people going over there who were not very talented musically, but they were absolved because they were English and had English accents and wore funny clothes and boots. In the early to mid-sixties, you had groups who were inferior in England going over to America and becoming very popular for a year or so and then vanishing forever, after they'd already vanished in England—bands like the Dave Clark Five and Herman's Hermits and Freddie and the Dreamers and many other mediocre bands. Chad and Jeremy: They meant not a thing in England, but they were a great success in America."

It was a bonanza, and the Beatles had started it. Still, these economic and cultural arguments couldn't quell the inevitable outcry that resulted from the announcement of their royal honors, the sort of furor that you really had to be British to comprehend. Many veterans who'd earned their MBEs the hard way returned their medals in protest; one, a colonel, sent a total of twelve decorations back from whence they'd come. The press was filled with indignant commentary from retired soldiers and sailors: "The British House of Royalty has put me on the same level as a bunch of vulgar numbskulls," went a typical Blimpish outburst. It was the scene from the train carriage in *A Hard Day's Night* all over again: "I fought the war for your sort," said the City gent; "I bet you're sorry you won," Ringo countered.

The Beatles themselves, modestly flattered and a mite confused by both the medals and the backlash, said all the right, smart, clever, self-deprecating things, although they did voice one complaint: Brian had been excluded. It was because he was gay said some whispers, because he was Jewish said others. George Harrison, it's most reliably reported, said, "MBE really stands for 'Mister Brian Epstein.' " Brian, pleased to be noted at least by the Beatles, repeated the comment for weeks. But he was now open to a new kind of social slap: "Look at that poor boy over there," roared a drunken actor at the posh Mirabelle restaurant, baiting Brian. "He couldn't get an MBE!"

On the October day on which the Beatles arrived at Buckingham Palace for their investiture, among nearly two hundred other honorees, Brian was nowhere present; they'd been permitted only to bring family members as their guests. In time, the medals themselves seemed like props to them: Paul and George wore theirs for the *Sgt. Pepper's Lonely Hearts Club Band* cover shoot, and John famously returned his in 1969 to protest British support of the American war in Vietnam, British involvement in "the Nigeria-Biafra thing," and " 'Cold Turkey' slipping down the charts." George was equally cynical: "After all we did for Great Britain, selling all that corduroy and making it swing, they gave us that bloody old leather medal with wooden string through it."

But at the time it was a potent symbol in the algebra of English culture of how ascendant the new ways had become and how widely divergent the modern Britain was from the old. And it was a symbol, too, of how much outside of the center Brian Epstein really was. Never mind that he had given the band the public face that had made its successes happen in just the way they had, or that he had explained to them the significance of the honor and encouraged them to accept it. He would always be someone separate, ever more visibly now that the Beatles had risen to yet another unprecedented height. The band claimed he never complained to them that he'd felt snubbed, but the experience stung all the same: "I bet you're sorry you won" with a tint of rue.

I HADN'T THOUGHT IT OUT BEYOND THAT

If Terence Stamp wasn't, like his flatmate, Mike Caine, determined to be the busiest actor in showbiz, he was nevertheless set on enjoying his position near the top of the brilliant new zodiac of stars. He was still among the swingingest of young Londoners, after all—handsome, stylish and always up for some wild scene. In the mad way of the day, the press granted him authority with its liberal attentions and then called upon that authority to prove, via Stamp's imprimatur, that some nightclub or shop or haircut or pop act was cool.

In clothing, for instance, Stamp had some firm ideas: "I had been born into penury. So I knew all the things I wanted: I knew how I wanted to live, I knew the clothes I wanted to wear. So as fame and a certain amount of money happened to me, I was busy realizing my boyhood fantasy of dress, style, haircut. My style, the stuff I wanted to wear, wasn't Flower Children stuff. I liked wonderful materials that would age beautifully. I was never a slave to fashion. That was bullshit. My style was opposite. I went in for the really good clobber: shoes and things that would really last."

His favored source of such goods was Doug Hayward, a meat-and-potatoes chap who had learned the tailor's trade the old-fashioned way but made something modern out of it nonetheless. As he built his custom in the burgeoning sixties, Hayward didn't have a shop: You rang him up at a number in Fulham and he came by in his Alfa Romeo to see you for fittings and deliveries. His client list ran the gamut from old-line Hollywood stars like Frank Sinatra, Sammy Davis Jr., Tony Curtis and Peter Lawford to the new-school chaps he himself ran with like Stamp and Caine, for whom he cut their first bespoke morning coats and dinner jackets and the like. He did his chums' film wardrobes—nice, with-it but never trendy. "What I do mostly," he explained, "is based on a classic line with a modern look. I'm not a mod tailor." Times being what they were, however, he made occasional concessions. "I did some unusual suits," Hayward later confessed. "Not wild stuff. I used to make Polanski these funny jackets with velvet collars. But it wasn't that far off what I'd been doing. Style I know. Not fashion."

In the matters of dining and partying, Stamp was equally opinionated and equally switched-on. Like everyone in his echelon of the scene, he could be found invariably in two swinging spots: a Soho restaurant called the Trattoria Terrazza and a Leicester Square nightclub called the Ad Lib.

In the Positano Room of the Trattoria Terrazza, you would find a galaxy of the capital's brightest stars: film people, theater people, pop people, hot young journalists, gorgeous models, photographers, fashion designers: everyone. The Positano Room was more exclusive than any of the staid institutions of London's Clubland, more filled with famous flesh than even David Bailey's photo book *Box of Pin-Ups*. It was one of the first places where bright young Britons discovered the homey freshness of good Italian cooking. And it had arisen from a disused barroom and one man's puckish understanding of human vanity.

The Trattoria Terrazza started out in 1959 as a tiny, thirty-seat restaurant on a corner of Soho better known for bohemian pubs, private drinking clubs and coffee bars catering to teenage pop music hopefuls. Its founders were Mario Cassandro and Franco Lagattolla, the former wine captain and headwaiter, respectively, of the traditional French haute cuisine house La Mirabelle; they invested £1,800 in the operation—with Mario contributing a slightly higher sum, as wine captains were better tipped than waiters.

So beloved a couple of characters were the restaurateurs that their establishment became known as Mario and Franco's and immediately attracted the celebrity crowd who knew the two from their previous employ. As business at the Tratt, as habitues called it, increased, Mario and Franco took a lease on a downstairs space and opened an American-style bar, Il Gato Nero; when that proved a flop, they simply converted the room into a second dining room for the Tratt.

But compared to the upstairs room, with its windows onto Romilly Street, the downstairs felt like Siberia. Enter Alvaro Maccioni, who had waited tables at La Mirabelle and had come to work with his former colleagues as a waiter and, finally, headwaiter. He began to apply himself to solving the problem of having turnaway business upstairs and an empty dining room below. And he was inspired: "I said to Mario and Franco, 'We're using the wrong attitude. Leave it with me for one month and see what happens.' So when people rang and asked to reserve a table, I would tell them, 'I'm sorry, but I can only give you a table upstairs.' And you know, people are funny. They'd say, 'What? Why? Please try to get me a table down there!' "

As if he had planned it that way, the Positano Room, as the downstairs had been renamed, was suddenly the city's most exclusive dining spot. "If you weren't in the film industry or some sort of personality," Maccioni said, "I would not put you there. I ran it like a club. Within one month, we were arguing with people on the phone because they wanted to sit downstairs."

There were other nearby dining spots that catered to a similarly glittery array of clients—Quaglino's and Quo Vadis and, a little closer to Theatreland, the Pickwick Club. But the Terrazza became the standard for celebrity dining and elbow-rubbing throughout the decade. It launched the fashion for Italian food that seemingly never ended. And it was among the very first eateries whose owners themselves became part of the cast of famous faces.

"The sweet smell of success in the sixties," mused Mario, "started in our kitchens."

And after dinner, dancing.

In March 1963, just as the Beat Boom was climaxing and the young creative types around London started to recognize that one another existed, a new nightclub opened five stories above Leicester Place, a little walkway that connected Leicester Square to Lisle Street. Situated above the Prince Charles Theatre, it had fur on the walls, a large fish tank filled with piranhas, notoriously tiny stools and, according to one commentator, "an air of mild perversity." The club was the invention of Nicholas Luard, coowner of the famed Soho satirical night club the Establishment, and old Chelsea Set hand Lord Timothy Willoughby D'Eresby, and it was called WIP'S. Its arrival had been advertised in the smarter magazines for some months as a major social event with a decidedly jaded undertone: "WIP'S—piranhas—WIP'S—vodka—WIP'S—sharks and caviar and russian roulette—WIP'S—smoke and darkness—WIP'S—faces . . . WIP'S—piranhas in the darkness above london's skyline—WIP'S—black velvet and the new faces—WIP'S—music strong and hard and moody."

If the ads were bizarrely inspired, the timing and tone were off: Berliners of the thirties might've loved WIP'S, but the shiny, happy young movers and shakers of Swinging London were after something less sinister. Within eight months of opening, WIP'S was closed, a victim of Luard's financial woes, the failure to beat enough customers out of the bush willing to meet its expensive membership fees and a kitchen fire that necessitated costly repairs that broke the club's back. In stepped Al and Bob Burnett, a pair of brothers whose nightclubs included such old-time favorites as the Pigalle and the Stork Room in nearby Piccadilly. They put together an investment group including another night spot impresario, Oscar Lerman, and hired their own nephew, Brian Morris, who was then working at the elegant Mayfair club Les Ambassadeurs, as manager.

The new owners kept the fur and the fish but, closer in intent to the mood that they felt rising up around them, installed a booming new sound system, colored lights recessed in the ceiling, lower tables around the banquettes, a dance floor the size of a handkerchief, a lot of large mirrors and, most crucially, a large picture window facing out of the club across Soho, Mayfair, Piccadilly and Marylebone to Buckingham Palace and Regent's Park. They hired a DJ who wore a dinner jacket and stored his equipment in a piano, and they decided to serve drinks airline style—

in little bottles with ice and soda separate. On December 13, 1963, they reopened as the Ad Lib and waited to see who would turn up.

At first it was a trickle. Then, fate: Sandra Cogan, singer Alma's little sister and a performer herself at the Establishment, came by with one of her chums, George Harrison. As Morris recalled, "George loved it and a few nights later he brought Ringo. In 1964, to have one Beatle on the premises was something. To have two Beatles in one night was incredible. The news went through town like wildfire."

It wasn't long before all four Beatles—as well as the Rolling Stones, the Hollies and many of the hot young actors and models and photographers and business types—made the Ad Lib their clubhouse, as did seemingly every other dandy and dandisette in town.

Taking the tiny lift from the street, they were transported to another world where American R&B and soul were the staple sounds and the black chef named Teddy led a nightly conga line out into the street. The things that went on there! You could see David Bailey teaching Rudolph Nureyev how to do the Twist, or Nureyev crowing over the cheekbones of a fashion model—"I want cheekbones like that! They're Tartar's cheekbones!"—or John Lennon picking a fight with Alun Owen, screenwriter of *A Hard Day's Night*, or Ringo Starr proposing marriage to Maureen Cox, or Paul McCartney being propositioned by a transsexual or arguing with Bailey over the authenticity of "Michelle," or Jean Shrimpton sitting in a corner and . . . knitting: "People had once complained that I was awkward as a model. They should have seen me dancing!" she confessed. "I took my knitting to a lot of places. It used to drive Bailey mad."

The Ad Lib was the most obvious sign that England had changed utterly. American-born film agent Sandy Lieberson had all but given up on London as a place to live and work until he wandered into the place in 1965: "People were jammed in and dancing and all the music and sound! And you went out on the balcony and everybody had a joint, everybody was getting stoned. Rome in the early sixties had this strange element with discotheques and such. But I'd never seen it on such a scale as this. Everybody was pouring in and you could sit there and meet the Beatles or the Stones or The Who or whoever might be in town, and people would take drugs and pair off and go home and screw or have an orgy or fall in love. Drugs, sex, it was all hanging out. It was like coming to another country." Even the hippest cats had to strain to keep up with it: John Lennon was shocked when he saw art dealer John Dunbar smoking hash openly in the club, not realizing how absolutely safe they were in such an insulated environment.

"It was unique," remembered David Puttnam. "Like all good things, it wasn't created to be unique, it just happened. The guy who ran it, Brian Morris, had run a number of things in the past but nothing that had that sort of cachet. It was a society. It created its own society and it was a modern society. Prior to that there were always other London clubs. The Chelsea Arts Club was always there as a bohemian refuge. But it was the first time there was *our* club—my age group. We owned it. Prior to that, if you were in your early twenties, you were grafting onto something from an older generation. You felt alienated. You were dancing to an orchestra that your mum had danced to. But for the first time you owned the culture, and that was a terribly important thing."

It wasn't an expensive place to party—the first drink was twenty-five shillings, including cover charge, and they went down to ten shillings after that; and a dinner of steak or chicken was about a pound—but it was exclusive; you literally couldn't get in not only because it was so crowded (three hundred-plus customers a night) but because the company you would keep would be so incredibly desirable. The Ad Lib succeeded so well, said Paul McCartney's chum Barry Miles, because it was "the first place to play good music, stay open late and tolerate the antics that the groups got up to." It was a place small and inaccessible enough to make people comfortable who were overwhelmed elsewhere by the great public grabbing at their lapels.

The soul of the place was Morris, who made an effusive show of greeting regulars: "When you came in," recalled one, "he wrapped his arms 'round you. You cursed yourself that you hadn't been there the night before." But it also had the prettiest girls in town as if on tap: "They're such little dollies," enthused another habitué of the joint. "But where do they come from? You don't see them anywhere else."

The partying was nonstop—and immediately attracted unwanted attention from neighbors. Several Lisle Street residents began complaining about the loud music—which could run as late as 4:00 A.M.—within a few weeks of the club's opening. One fellow, a dairyman, complained to police and then a magistrate that the noise only stopped when it was time for him to get up for work; priests at the Church of Notre Dame, immediately adjacent to the club, concurred. A series of court orders to silence the noise was issued, and the club owners submitted to ten thousand pounds in repairs for acoustic muffling, double-glazing the windows and even offering to put the inconvenienced parties and their families up at hotels until an appropriate remedy could be instituted. Twice Brian Morris found himself in court defending himself against charges that he had ignored a judicial order to keep things quiet.

The noise issue never stopped hounding the club, but it never crippled it, either. The Ad Lib was too big for the neighbors or the law to slow down. The club even spawned a pop group—the Ad Libs, who served as a house band for a little while and released a sole single, ironically entitled "Neighbour, Neighbour," before splitting up in 1965. The whole thing was, wrote Francis Wyndham, "not so much a nightclub, more a happening; an unselfconscious, spontaneous celebration of the new classless affluence." George Melly called it "a triumph of style . . . chic, non-committed and amoral but . . . also cool, tolerant and physically beautiful."

It was also, like so much of its era, a will-o'-the-wisp. The accelerated change in fashionable taste caught up with the Ad Lib in early 1966 when another kitchen fire forced it to vacate the Leicester Place premises. The club briefly resurfaced in Leicester Square proper, at the former address of the 400 Club, an old-fashioned black-tie night spot, and then, when the fire damage was repaired, reopened in its original spot. For a while, the old habitués still made the pilgrimage, but the magic had disappeared.

By the spring of 1966, none of the original owners had anything to do with the new incarnation, and it was listed in *Queen* magazine as an *out* place to be seen. The very term "ad lib" was taken by some as a new way of saying "excessively trendy and pleased with itself for being so." But those, probably, were people who never actually got inside the place when it was at its height.

"It's just as well that it burned down," reflected David Puttnam. "It would've been sad to see it go into decline."

But who was thinking of decline? Take a look at the likes of Stamp and all you could think of was a helium-filled balloon rising and rising to impossible, enviable heights. The spectacle of his money and girls and fame helped encourage Stamp's younger brother, Chris, into a more creative frame of mind than their parents had ever bothered to; the kid wound up in rock management and even came to own a record label.

And the allure of him—his beauty and talent and glow—led him into one of the great romances of the era: a passionate, public love affair with, of all people, his dream girl.

As Stamp remembered, he first met Jean Shrimpton and her beau David Bailey at a January 1964 wedding. Shrimpton, however, said they'd all met before on a photo set; Bailey shot a dazzling dual portrait of the two beautiful young stars for *Vogue*: Stamp, dressed in black, smiled at Shrimpton with his arms cocked behind his head while she, in a striped frock and polka-dotted scarf, leaned backward in front of him, staring off into the distance. (It wouldn't be the last time they remembered events distinctly, either.)

At any rate, Stamp, who was seeing Caterine Milinaire but was attending the wedding stag that day, got a glimpse of Shrimpton at church. Later, at the reception at Quo Vadis on Dean Street, Stamp stood aloofly alongside the throng in that most demure of accoutrements, a Russian Cossack hat, sipping champagne. Bailey, who was shooting the party with Terence Donovan as a favor to the groom, came over to say hello.

Niceties were exchanged. The two East End lads had a lot in common and might've been competitive with each other, but Bailey, especially, was an easygoer, and it was he who invited Stamp for a drive out to Buckinghamshire, where he and Shrimpton were headed after the reception to visit her parents. The three of them piled into Bailey's Morgan—a two-seater; Shrimpton, with no other choice, sat in Stamp's lap. Stamp managed to control his delight, as did Shrimpton her discomfort at being squished into the car seat with a strange man. And yet, as she remembered later, "there was also the thought that I was locked in this intimacy with probably the two most attractive men in London."

They became a bit of a trio: Stamp tagging along for dinners at Bailey's favorite Chinese restaurant in East Ham or turning up with them at clubs or parties. Stamp was fond enough of Bailey, in fact, to sublimate his undiluted lust for Shrimpton: "I was increasingly taken by his charm," Stamp admitted, "and the friendship that developed was between Bailey and me."

In May, they all went to America: Stamp, after the barest minimum of location shooting in England on *The Collector*, had months of studio work in L.A. to look forward to; Shrimpton was doing shoots of her own in New York; Bailey came along to enjoy the city and, maybe, line up some work of his own. When Stamp had a hiatus in filming, he flew east to join them, and found things between Bailey and Shrimpton had grown a little uneasy. Stamp, mind you, had done nothing to violate the East End code against messing with your mate's bird. But Shrimpton was tiring of her time with Bailey: She was only twenty-one and they'd been together nearly three years. "It could have been anyone that caused me to break with Bailey," she remembered.

And then poor Bailey did something awfully dumb: "You don't want to get married, do you?" he asked. He might as well have inquired if she wanted to eat a bug.

She said no, of course, and he bolted back to England, where he made the even worse mistake of whining about the business to her mother. Meanwhile, she had a plan to help stave off the postrelationship blues: She was going to visit L.A.

When she got there, she found Stamp all deference and thoughtfulness. He put her up in the Beverly Hills house he was renting, he took her to quiet little restaurants—no Hollywood whirl for her—and then flew her to Vegas where they stayed two nights in separate rooms at Caesars Palace. A more cordial gent your mum couldn't imagine. She returned to New York untouched by him physically but entirely rapt in thought of him. A few weeks later she came back to California, this time with some modeling to do. They became lovers that very first night.

It was, by both of their accounts, blissful. They were young and beautiful and famous and, increasingly, rich, and very much in love. Together, they made a stunning couple, turning heads even at swank restaurants and night spots in L.A. where they were barely known. "I was in love with Terry, and that's all there was to it," recollected the down-to-earth Shrimpton, while Stamp, in retrospect, said, "I suppose that was the final fantasy realized. I had money, I became famous, and then I met the perfect sexual partner. I hadn't thought it out beyond that, not even in dreams."

Word of this divine liaison quickly, naturally, filtered back to London through a few ex-pat Brits in California and Bailey, well, you can imagine: Stamp and Shrimpton delayed as much as possible returning to England, taking a vacation in Nassau after his work on *The Collector* was completed. Shrimpton finally did a few sessions with Bailey (none of his loyal photographer mates would book her), but it was an ordeal that they both quickly chose sooner to do without.

At any rate, trouble with Bailey was something they'd reckoned on. Trouble with Michael Caine, that was another matter.

While Stamp was busy not working and chasing supermodel skirt, Caine (six-and-a-half years his elder, recall) was doggedly working on the acting career he'd been chasing for nearly a decade. Finally, at thirty-two, it was happening for him. In late 1963, he appeared in Cy Endfield's *Zulu* as the prim, public school–bred Lt. Gonville Bromhead, who turns into a ferocious fighting machine when his small platoon is attacked by Zulu warriors at Rourke's Drift. He'd had nice press notices before, but nothing to compare to the widespread attention his low-key approach here garnered. And while lightning didn't strike him instantly, it was a life-changing role. Caine was offered the lead in a new series of spy movies developed by Harry Saltzman, coproducer of the James Bond films. In search of a way to keep the spy picture money flowing, Saltzman, without his partner Cubby Broccoli, planned to adapt Len Deighton's novels about a distinctly unglamorous secret agent with none of Bond's polish, high manners or expensive tastes. Caine, drinking in the Pickwick Club one night and wondering if he would ever have a real career, was noticed by the effusive Saltzman and found himself, just-like-that, cast in the lead in *The Ipcress File* and any sequels that the film might spawn. He would be paid fifty thousand pounds—more than twelve times what he got for *Zulu*. He was made.

Among the first things that he did was look for a new place to live. He and Stamp both had enough money, he reckoned, to keep their own places: Why split rent? He found a flat in Albion Close, Bayswater, and set about renovating it before moving in, indulging various Cockney fantasies while furnishing the place, including filling the bathroom closet with piles of the best toilet products: shampoos, hairbrushes, aftershave lotions, towels and so on. Soon after he was installed, he was somewhat taken aback to find Stamp—and Shrimpton—expecting to share the small second bedroom. Caine felt he owed Stamp—the younger man had carried the financial burdens of their shared menage for years—and let them move in.

And here the stories diverge.

Stamp, according to Caine, said that they'd soon be living separately, indicated that he was looking for a place for himself and Shrimpton and wanted only to crash at Albion Close for a few days while he sorted something out. After a few *weeks,* Caine said, during which time Stamp disappeared mysteriously on both his mate and his bird for several days, the couple moved out.

Stamp claimed that, as far as he understood it, the flat was always meant to be shared by the two old chums, and although he was puzzled by the Spartan scale of his room—and the tiny twin bed it contained— he didn't reckon it so bad compared to the sorts of places they'd been sharing. "I'd still be sharing a flat with him now if it had been up to me," he would say decades later. By his account, he and Shrimpton settled in, if uncomfortably, and were getting along fine until Caine, without saying a word, had their newspaper subscriptions cancelled. They left, he remembered, that day.

And Shrimpton, though she had no recollections of the newspaper business, agreed with Stamp about where the blame for the tense, odd situation lay: "Michael Caine did not seem to want us around."

"Looking back on it," Stamp reflected, "there was an aspect of Mike that he played very close to the chest. He had a very, very tough time in the business and I think that during that time he must have been honing a dream about how it would be when he made it."

Whichever, the thing was done: The great team of Stamp and Caine was split. Aside from disagreeing in print over the years about how it all ended, there was just one more little item between them. In mid-1964, before *The Collector* appeared, Stamp was offered the title role in the American stage production of Bill Naughton's radio play *Alfie Elkins and His Little Life,* which had appeared on the London stage as *Alfie* with John Neville in the lead. After a brief warm-up run in Washington and New Haven, Stamp would make his Broadway debut that December.

It was a lot of role to learn—Alfie speaks directly to the audience throughout the play, narrating even as he takes part in scenes. And it was, like *The Collector,* quite a departure from *Billy Budd*: Alfie Elkins was a wisecracking Cockney lothario brimming with misogyny and macho confidence and, for all that, crippled by a pathetically underdeveloped sense of himself and the world; among his trespasses are stealing girls from other blokes, causing a mate's wife to have an abortion and, generally, treating women as sex toys to be collected, conquered and discarded.

It's a wonderful script and an acid etching of the sort of sexual relations that were becoming more and more typical in this new age of contraceptives and relaxed morals. But seduction and abortion on Broadway at Christmas? The play opened on December 18 to mixed reviews; Stamp, while generally recognized as doing terrific work, couldn't escape the generally dismissive light in which his character was seen: "Horribly well-played," said one review of his performance. It wasn't that it was new and British: *A Hard Day's Night*, which had opened in August, was still doing business; it was that it was so dark and frank and mean and true and generally disharmonious with the optimistic, uptempo tenor of the moment. It closed after twenty-one performances: a washout.

And so Stamp wanted to hear no more about it when director Lewis Gilbert, who'd been hired to do the film version, called to see if he was interested in reprising the role; in one of their last congenial conversations of the time, Mike Caine urged Stamp to reconsider. "I still wake up screaming in the middle of the night as Terry takes my advice and accepts the role," remembered Caine—who, of course, was soon offered the part himself and rode it to superstardom.

With Caine and Albion Close behind them, Stamp and Shrimpton set up first in Jimmy Woolf's suite at the Grosvenor House Hotel, then in a flat borrowed from Vidal Sassoon on Curzon Street and then, finally, in a place of their own on Mount Street facing the Connaught Hotel. If Shrimpton was expecting Stamp to get over the weird mood he acquired during those last weeks hanging around Caine's, she was to be disappointed. After playing a pair of heels in *The Collector* and *Alfie*, Stamp had grown taciturn, mercurial, odd. She wasn't given the key to the new flat, for one thing, and she could find herself simply shut out: He would disappear for days—off tomcatting, she surmised—or he would give her the silent treatment over some trespass she couldn't even recall. She all but caught him in flagrante in a dalliance with Candice Bergen, whom he met in L.A. while shooting *The Collector* and with whom, Shrimpton suspected, he trysted in the Bahamas during a trip he took to clear his head after his *Alfie* fiasco.

For all that, she was caught up still in his looks, his vitality, his talent, his enthusiasm. "Stamp's beauty was very powerful at that point in his life," she remembered. "He was more beautiful than me." Too, she said, he "was exceptionally generous with his support, his money and his advice." So she endured, if with a grimace, his odd enthusiasms, such as Royal Canadian Air Force exercises and a strict health food diet (well, there she drew the line: "I am not going to drink that muck," Shrimpton protested at being offered something terribly good for her). He may have been prone to weirdness, but they were still a couple.

Throughout 1965, in fact, they were *the* couple, trumping Paul and Jane, Mick and Chrissie, George and Patti, Ringo and Maureen: everyone. Shrimp and Stamp: They were photographed together at movie openings, swimming at beaches, shopping, riding, dining out. In May, when *The Collector* opened, Stamp won the Best Actor prize at Cannes and their inability to make it to France for the festivities was reckoned an international disappointment. In November, Shrimpton was hired to go to Melbourne for the horse racing season and model some Orlon outfits; Stamp offered to come along, and, as they habitually enjoyed each other's company better when away from London, she agreed.

If New York wasn't ready for *Alfie* the year before, Melbourne wasn't ready for any of the groovy new ways Stamp and Shrimpton brought with them. They were given a hard time about requesting to share a hotel room without being married. Then, on the day of the Melbourne Cup race—a capstone of the city's social calendar—disaster: Not only hadn't Shrimpton brought a hat and gloves, but she was wearing a skirt that was hemmed *above her knees—maybe by an inch or three!* The fault, she explained to her sponsors, was that Orlon hadn't provided her with enough material to make a longer dress (and, in fact, she herself had designed and created the outfit). But the outrage that followed was unimaginable: Shrimpton made her way through the crowd, which gaped and all but hissed aloud at her cheek; she was given an ultimatum by the Orlon folks that she must never dress in such a manner again (to which, good for her, she responded that she'd do as she pleased); she was photographed in what was, really, a very girlish and inoffensive dress and plastered all over Australian front pages—and, indeed, front pages all over the world.

The echoes were felt in London, where people mocked Australian provincialism and girls immediately began taking up their hemlines; in her studio in Chelsea, Mary Quant, who'd already been working on shortening skirts, went further than ever. It was, save for the hurt feelings at Orlon and Melbourne, a succès de scandale—but Stamp, not so much jealous of Shrimp as irritated by the priggish atmosphere, had already bolted for San Francisco, where she soon caught up with him.

Lately, in fact, Stamp had had quite his fill of the scenes caused by glamorous women. He had spent the summer and fall enduring the hellish shoot of *Modesty Blaise*, director Joseph Losey's adaptation of the campy comic strip spy adventures created by Peter O'Donnell for the *Evening Standard* in that most spy crazy of years, 1963. Shot in London, Amsterdam and Sicily, filled with op art decor and wardrobes, it was meant as an homage to and distillation of its moment: guns, a hot chick, an outrageous villain, a peppy soundtrack, the whole swinging deal.

It tanked, big time.

Stamp was cast as Willie Garvin, Modesty's Cockney henchman and not-quite lover; for the villain, the sexually ambiguous and frankly cracked Gabriel, Losey had hired Dirk Bogarde, whom he'd directed so successfully in *The Servant* in 1963; the lead would be played by a less likely candidate, Monica Vitti, muse to Michelangelo Antonioni, who had directed her into an international symbol of nervous sexuality and repressed angst in *L'Avventura, La Notte, L'Eclisse* and *Red Desert*. Vitti had never acted in English before, had never played in a comedy, had never demonstrated any of the physical spunk that her role would require. But she bore a strong resemblance to the comic strip Modesty (especially once her hair was dyed black) and, to be fair, Losey himself had never directed a comedy or action picture; they'd break the ice together, or so went the thinking.

In actuality, it was all they could do not to break each other's necks. From the very first day, when Vitti wouldn't report to the set because she was put out by her costumes, star and director were at odds. Stamp—who might have been making *Alfie* instead—felt as if he were merely along for the ride. As Stamp saw it, Vitti "was in a world of her own, playing in some kind of screwball comedy." He endured her vain refusal to be shot in profile, he watched in silence as Losey tried everything in his directorial bag of tricks to tame his obstinate star (even asking Stamp, who diplomatically demurred, to bed her), and he became the director's confidant, responding sympathetically when Losey pleaded with him, "Get that fat, lazy Italian cow off my back for five minutes, will you?" Long before the shoot was finished, Stamp knew that the picture would lay an egg.

But there was a benificent bit of fallout: During the making of *Modesty*, he had made the acquaintance of Michelangelo Antonioni, who had recently decided to shift the location of an upcoming movie about a fashion photographer from Milan to London. Would Stamp be interested in the part? Of course.

Months passed and Antonioni's intentions, still vague, were only gradually revealed to his putative star. The director asked Stamp for a list of his "swinging friends" and asked Shrimpton if she'd like to play a model in the film. But Stamp never got a good read of his director: "Antonioni was even more secretive than I was," he said. Stamp never got to see a script or hear the whole story of the film; he never even learned the title. But he put off other projects in favor of it: He was only interested, he explained, in working with such world-class figures as the Italian maestro. He traveled to Rome for conferences, still engaged in this odd courtship dance. His advisors—even Jimmy Woolf, who was always pushing him *away* from work—were eager that he get a contract, a letter of intent, *something* in writing indicating that he was to be hired, but Stamp was a sucker for Antonioni's aristocratic hauteur. "I went along with Antonioni's intrigue for eight months," he remembered. "It was my own fault. My snobbery provided the filmmaker with a button he could keep pushing." Finally, serious negotiations with MGM, the studio producing the picture, began. Stamp could begin the work of learning how to move like a photographer (Anthony Norris, at whose wedding he first spoke with Shrimpton, served as his tutor).

One night during his preparation period, Stamp got a phone call from an old friend who'd been hired onto the film as assistant director: Antonioni had cast somebody else in the lead, David Hemmings, whom he'd seen in a play at the Hampstead Theatre Club. Hemmings had been acting since he was a boy—he'd made ten films—but Stamp had never heard of him; few had, in fact. But that was that. At the urging of his advisors, Stamp sued and won half of the fee that his agents had been negotiating; he was also promised a plum role in a prestigious upcoming

MGM project, *Far from the Madding Crowd*, in which he'd be teamed with Peter Finch, Alan Bates and his old flame Julie Christie. But he was crushed all the same.

In fact, for a guy living his dream—doll and dough and fame and cool job and swell mates and good clobber and smart cars and all that— he seemed a bit low.

THE BOX

Every prom needs a king and a queen, and as 1963, that sprawling party of a year wound down, the reigning couple of the London scene was David Bailey and Jean Shrimpton. They were everywhere—working and dining and dancing and partying and embodying everything that was good and cool and chic and sexy in the emerging new world. He was the envy of every man, and she the ideal of all girls: strictly fairy-tale stuff but very modern.

Pity he was still married.

At the end of that year, Rosemary Bailey, the photographer's forgotten wife, finally filed for a divorce, which her husband, who'd been living openly with another woman for some eighteen months, didn't contest. The next weeks found the papers and the gossips wondering when Bailey and the Shrimp would tie the knot: a royal wedding of the cool new sort.

But nobody reckoned on Shrimpton's growing weary of Bailey's constant presence and his controlling ways. Now nearing twenty-two, Shrimpton was looking at the world a little differently than she had when Bailey discovered her and turned her into an icon. "Bailey made me as he wanted me to be," Shrimpton reflected. "That was why in the end I had to go."

Go: to Terence Stamp: a sensational story: the sexy photographer dumped by the gorgeous model he'd invented.

Bailey was knocked for a loop that affected his sleep, his appetite, even his work. "I filmed Bailey on a beach somewhere where he was doing a photo shoot down in Kent, I think," remembered Dick Fontaine. "A beautiful location, quite barren. Perfect for the subject: Svengali has been abandoned. And he was on the beach with his camera."

Coinciding with his split with Shrimpton, Bailey began a series of experiments with framing and lighting; he started to tilt his camera, pose subjects in outdoor settings that he washed out with extreme flashes of light, capture models in midflight in the studio. He visited movie sets—he photographed the stars and director of *Alphaville* and briefly entertained Richard Lester's offer to work as cinematographer of *The Knack . . . and How to Get It*.

And he started to work on the portraits for an idea he had that would capture the sense of glamor, exclusivity and intermingling that was the essence of the world in which he lived.

In 1965, if you were at all anybody who made things move or groove or swing in London, you could be found in one of a handful of select boutiques, restaurants or nightclubs.

But if you were *really* somebody special, you appeared, thanks to Bailey, in a box.

In December of that year, the box showed up in bookstores around London—slightly larger than one a laundry might use for a man's shirt, and a bit thinner. It cost sixty-three shillings. Inside were thirty-six stiff, slick leaves of paper—small posters, really—bearing black-and-white photographs on one side and captions, some amounting to short interviews, some little more than labels, on the reverse. They were portraits of thirty-one men and four women of widely varied identity: photographer, pop star, actor, model, club owner, advertising executive, hairdresser, interior decorator, criminal. It was a somewhat jaded slice of the London scene—media stars and the people who hovered comfortably among them shot plainly against white backgrounds and cooed over in sometimes preciously voluptuous prose. And, uncannily, it froze a time that otherwise never stood still.

David Bailey's Box of Pin-Ups it was called, and while it wasn't any kind of runaway hit—indeed, a mere single edition was published—it was an apt and sharp portrait of its moment, the height of the Ad Lib, the dolly birds, the sharply elegant pop stars, the youthful achievers in fields dominated for centuries by tired old blood (or in fields that hadn't even existed a decade or three ago), the absolute peak of London's evanescent global cachet—as well as some of the behind-the-scenes tacticians and manipulators who engineered it all.

Turning the pages of the *Box*—lifting them up, fondling them, sticking them to the wall, perhaps, like icons—the lucky few who happened to get a copy encountered some likely, famous faces: Beatles John and Paul (and manager Brian), the Rolling Stones (and *their* manager, Andrew Oldham), Rudolph Nureyev, Cecil Beaton, Lord Snowdon, David Hockney, Vidal Sassoon, Terence Stamp and Michael Caine. There was the luminescent Jean Shrimpton (Bailey was always able to stay close to ex-wives and former lovers) and her sister Chrissie and a couple other women famous from magazines: Sue Murray, Celia Hammond. There were people who ran in Bailey's circle but were largely unknown too far beyond: ad executive David Puttnam, magazine art director Max Maxwell, milliner James Wedge, fashion designer Gerald McCann, Ad Lib manager Brian Morris, interior decorator David Hicks, photographers Michael Cooper and Terence Donovan. And there was, near the bottom of the *Box*, a stunning three-shot of the Kray brothers of Bethnal Green: the twins Reggie and Ronnie and the older (and softer) Charlie—known gangsters who'd only just that spring endured a sensational trial for demanding money with menaces from a baronet's son.

The text for the images was provided by journalist Francis Wyndham, who had recently profiled Bailey for a magazine (as, over time, he had many of the photo subjects), and it was, in the fashion of the day, excitable and overheated and dismissable and convincing all at once. Wyndham wrote of Bailey's fascination with "tinsel—a bright, brittle quality, the more appealing because it tarnishes so soon," and of his "private vision" of his subjects as sharing "the throwaway elegance . . . of Fred Astaire," who is dubbed Bailey's idol. "Glamour dates fast," the introductory material reads, and Bailey "has tried to capture it on the wing."

A lot of the sitters for the *Box* were obvious choices—colleagues, acquaintances from the Tratt and the Ad Lib, models, celebrities and behind-the-scenesters happy, presumably, to find themselves included in such select company.

But the gangsters—the Krays—they were another matter. Wyndham took credit for coming up with the idea of photographing them. "I had a very naive idea for doing something about gangsters," he remembered, "so I wrote 'round to them all and only the Krays replied. They'd just successfully sued the *Mirror* for libel and had just got off some charges so they felt on top of the world. . . . Bailey was their ideal person. They really respected him because he was from the same place as them but had won his success and fame legally."

Such was their rapport, in fact, that Bailey served as the official photographer when Reggie Kray married Frances McShea in April 1965, at St. James' Church in Bethnal Green. Bailey pulled up in a blue Rolls-Royce and a blue velvet suit and took portraits and candids of the ceremony and festivities. He did it, he said later, as a favor, and also because he felt a certain kinship with the notorious groom: "I know people will hate me for this, but I like him. I suppose that's like saying I like Hitler."

Well, maybe not Hitler, but certainly Al Capone. In the mold of the infamous Scarface, Reggie Kray and his twin brother Ron had for the preceding decade exerted their will over the East End of London—and a few select footholds up West—with mailed fists and carnivorous single-mindedness. A pair of thick-witted goons whose empire of extortion, gambling, blackmail, vice and theft was built on the ability to take a punch and return it twice as hard, they operated with impunity in a criminal milieu in which police tolerated a certain amount of larceny so long as it went hand in hand with a kind of peacekeeping civic-mindedness and a patina of respect for church, Queen and mother. The Krays did the crime business the old-fashioned way—beating their opponents silly, maintaining order in their Bethnal Green neighborhood, cooperating with the cops when something really untoward—a child murder, say—happened.

But the Krays were newfangled bad guys, too. They liked publicity, and rarely missed a chance to be photographed with the likes of Judy Garland, Sonny Liston, George Raft, singer Billy Daniels, actress Barbara Windsor or various prize fighters, variety performers and low-level media celebrities. Dick Fontaine, invited by the twins to discuss a possible documentary about them, went to their Kentucky Club in Stepney and saw a wall of photos of the Krays with various swells: "That's my movie," he thought. When theatrical doyenne Joan Littlewood made a film about life in the East End, *Sparrers Can't Sing*, the Krays hosted the premiere party at their Kentucky Club and nearly had Princess Margaret as a guest; she was too ill to attend the film, however, and thus missed the party, perhaps pointedly. The Krays courted power—particularly power that was handicapped by vice, such as gambling, drug addiction or a penchant for young boys, which Ronnie shared; one of the more sordid episodes they engaged in during the sixties was their association with Lord Boothby, a degenerate peer who was photographed with Ronnie (and won a libel suit when a newspaper published insinuations about the nature of their relationship) and who scandalously spoke out for the Krays in Parliament when the police had finally managed to bring charges against them. And they gained a toehold in the posh end of town when they took control of Esmeralda's Barn, a Knightsbridge casino with a clientele that included aristocrats, celebrities and wealthy businessmen.

For all that, the Krays were never exactly with-it. "They were absolutely on the periphery," remembered David Puttnam, who ran into them once or twice. "The clubs that they ran were very unhip. They were just those few years older. They would be into Alma Cogan or Gerry Mulligan. Those few years' difference were a world." But they were always visible, and, when Bailey chose to include them in the *Box*, their status as minor celebrities was certified.

There was, in fact, a brief heyday of criminal celebrity in London during the sixties. The Krays and their South London rivals, the Richardson brothers, had style and liked to flaunt it, and in the increasingly blurred social lines of the new London it was easy for them to blend in with a crowd that could include high and low life, old money and new, the famous, the infamous, the worthy and the worth knowing. And it wasn't just jaded hipsters who had a fondness for bad men: In August 1963, a dozen highly organized bandits waylaid a postal train in a midlands field and made off with £2.5 million in worn-out bank notes, and many in the media and the general public regarded them as loveable Robin Hood figures, fancifully dubbing them the Great Train Robbers. A good part of the nation perversely reveled in the escapades of a dashing pair of them—Cockney flower peddler Buster Edwards and high-living mastermind Bruce Reynolds—who managed both to elude capture for several years, and a third, Ronnie Biggs, who broke out of

Wandsworth Prison and spent decades thumbing his nose at authority from the safe harbor of Brazil.

In some circles, Bailey's photographs of the Krays and the implicit glorification of their way of life was enough to make the entire project of the *Box* irredeemable. The censorious buzz that circulated probably raised the estimation of the project among those whose opinions Bailey would've reckoned worth swaying. But there was at least one bit of genuinely hurtful fallout: Lord Snowdon, the Queen's brother-in-law and one of the faces in the *Box*, revoked permission for Bailey to use his portrait further; as a result, no American version was ever published, nor were subsequent editions printed in England.

For some who beheld the *Box*, it was an outrage, a cheeky and superficial testimony to a cheeky and superficial time. One critic spoke of the subjects of Bailey's portraits as "all narcissistically self-conscious, yet each dependent on the others to prevent him in isolation from looking ridiculous." Others found the collection precisely right for its age: George Melly called Bailey "the openly sardonic historian of his time, elevating a narrow circle of his own friends and acquaintances into a chic but deliberately frivolous pantheon."

Ironically, while several of the subjects' careers in the limelight barely lasted long enough for them to be admitted to the publication party without producing an invitation, many of the pictures themselves have remained iconic: Michael Caine staring impertinently from behind his Harry Palmer glasses, a Gitane dangling unlit from his lips; Mick Jagger peering out of the fur-lined hood of an overcoat, a pouty mix of animal innocence and sexuality; Lennon and McCartney standing nearly shoulder to shoulder and looking out in opposite directions like Wyatt Earp and Doc Holiday expecting an ambush; Jean Shrimpton, seen from the breastbone up, for once not modeling some frock, dissolving, gorgeously, into an all-white heaven; the trinity of Krays, impeccably neat and shot from below, imposing as Easter Island monoliths.

If these images were to remain startling, almost tactile reminders of the carnival of their famous subjects' mid-sixties ascent, it was fitting, too, that other of the photos—shots of P. J. Proby, Max Maxwell, Gordon Waller, Sue Murray and Bongo Wolf, say—should outlast the renown of the sitters. Bailey, after all, the most celebrated and sensational of the East End fashion photographers whose appearance kicked off the decade, had preceded any of them up the golden ladder of pop stardom:

It was only apt that he should serve as the gatekeeper to their exclusive little kingdom. Even more, he had portrayed his age in as succinct and neat a manner as possible, creating a constellation of his own designation, gathering together an impressive array of portraits and proving, per his famous phrase, that "the fifties were gray, the sixties were black and white."

During the time he was working on the *Box*, Bailey had chased the pain of losing Shrimpton by carrying on with another girl whom he groomed into stardom as a model: Sue Murray, a completely new face whom Bailey nevertheless felt worthy of entree to the *Box*.

But soon enough, Bailey dumped Murray—he unambiguously told a newspaper that while Jean Shrimpton had "brains and a body, Sue has the brains but not the body"—and rebounded spectacularly as one of London's sexiest figures: He was getting hitched.

In August 1965, at the St. Pancras Registry Office, Bailey married the French actress Catherine Deneuve in a wedding sensationalized in the press for the lack of ceremony accorded it by the bride and groom: Bailey wore his trademark Cuban-heeled boots, a pale sweater and green corduroy pants, the bride dressed in black and smoked right up until the brief nuptials, and the best man, Mick Jagger, sported a denim suit and an open-necked shirt.

Bailey and Deneuve had met a mere eight weeks earlier, when he had flown to Paris to photograph her for the publicity campaign for Roman Polanski's *Repulsion*. It was Polanski's idea: "He kept saying, 'You've got to meet Catherine; you're going to be crazy about her,' " Bailey remembered. "And I kept saying, 'No, she's not my type. She's too short.' " (The photos, however, were for *Playboy*, so there was plenty of incentive.) Deneuve, a mere twenty-one and already the mother of a two-year-old boy fathered by director Roger Vadim, protested when Bailey locked the door of the photo studio, but he mollified her with the lie that he was gay, and the shoot—and the subsequent romance—commenced.

The very prevalence around London of sexy figures such as Bailey and Shrimpton and Jagger and Polanski and Deneuve had become such a commonplace that it had overspilled the extant media and come to seem a suitable subject for a magazine of its own. *London Life*, as it was called, was staffed by remarkable talents—Marc Boxer, formerly of *Queen* and the *Sunday Times* color supplement, was editor; young advertising hot shot David Puttnam was managing editor; the masthead listed such contributors as Brian Duffy, Francis Wyndham and Jean Shrimpton; V. S. Naipaul, Mordechai Richler and Patricia Highsmith wrote commissioned stories; and Bailey violated his exclusive deals with other publications by shooting under the *nom de camera* Daniel Boom. It had listings of events, show times and the like, news of new restaurants, boutiques and galleries, even expository journalism about financial matters and the advent of LSD. It played host to cool promotional events and swinging parties. It was a raw and guileless celebration of the scene.

It lasted all of fourteen months.

Financial ineptitude, sabotage by management, rumors of mental imbalance high up the masthead: Take your pick—all these excuses were proferred.

But it may simply have been the case that the ideal format for parsing Swinging London wasn't journalism but, maybe, film. Certainly that was the thinking of Michelangelo Antonioni, the Italian writer-director who had become world famous for his bleak, still, strangely vibrating films about anomie, ennui and despair amid the sleek textures of modern life.

Antonioni arrived in London in the winter of 1965–66 with the intention of sniffing around the scene, or at least the scene that he had seen portrayed in the popular media: the parties, the photographers' studios, the nightclubs, the trattorias, the boutiques, the drug-and-sex orgies. He had been lured by producer Carlo Ponti, who, looking for a new subject for a film a year or so earlier, had come across Francis Wyndham's May 1964 article about the East End photographers, "The Model-Makers," in the *Sunday Times.* That portrait of Bailey, Donovan and Duffy had impelled Ponti to approach Bailey and ask him if he'd like to be involved in a film project entitled *The Photographer,* a short documentary about his life and work. Scheduling made it impossible, but Ponti didn't let the idea die, and when he heard that Antonioni was adapting a Julio Cortazar story about a photographer and planning to shoot it in Milan, he suggested the auteur visit London.

For the next year, Antonioni and his muse, Monica Vitti, were everywhere in London: dining at the Trattoria Terrazza and the Osteria

San Lorenzo restaurants; dropping in at Robert Fraser's apartment to watch Paul McCartney's experimental movies; attending the wild opening gala for the *International Times* newspaper; and hosting a number of parties in his suite at the Savoy in an effort to get a sense of the city and its young lovelies. "I *hate* parties," Antonioni told a reporter. "I only go for the film."

While Antonioni absorbed the visuals of the scene (his English was sketchy at best), he developed a novel method of discerning the details of the life of a London fashion photographer. He had Wyndham produce a lengthy precis of his research for the *Times* article, a document that eventually came to two hundred pages and included a mountain of details about the scene and the working and private lives of the photographers. Then Antonioni himself developed a six-page questionnaire that was distributed to several photographers and people who knew them. The amount of detail he sought was staggering:

> Are fashion photographers requested to stress the sexual angle or merely to concentrate on the clothes? . . . Do they drink? How do they spend their days? Evenings? Weekends? What is really "fun" for them? . . . Some have Rolls-Royces: Have they personal drivers? Or do they drive themselves? What is, broadly speaking, their social background? How do they speak? Have they a particular way of expressing themselves, some professional slang, or anything of this kind? . . . Do they eat at home, in their studios, or in restaurants? Do they go to pubs? . . . How do they spend the money they make? Do they think about the future? Do they endeavor to make money outside their profession? . . . Do they worry about themselves, life, death? Are they religious? If not, is it a matter of unconcern about such ethical codes of behavior, or is it deliberate rejection? . . . What is their relation with their wives? As a rule, are their marriages happy? If not, what is the reason? Have they steady mistresses, or only occasional pickups? . . .

Bailey found himself once again contacted by people associated with the film, but not in the fashion he might have anticipated. "I thought they wanted me to direct," he remembered. "Then they started talking about the way I dressed. I said, 'What's that got to do with it?' They were asking me if I was interested in being in it. Then I wouldn't talk to Antonioni because he thought I was trying to shag Monica Vitti. It wasn't me, it was Terence Stamp!"

In the coming months, a script took shape, first under the title *The Story of a Man and a Woman on a Beautiful Afternoon*, then as *A Girl, a Photographer and a Beautiful April Morning* and finally, sensibly, as *The Antonioni Picture*. Cortazar's story about a mysterious pickup that an amateur photographer unintentionally interrupts had become a story about a dynamic but hollow London fashion photographer who thinks he may have photographed a murder in a park and then tries to convince others—and, indeed, himself—that he's right. The script was a mere thirty-two pages long and had been scrupulously stripped of slang expressions and anything else that might specifically date it. ("This meant," said the star, David Hemmings, "getting rid of the 'supers' and the 'fabs'.")

The shoot began in late April 1966. Wherever the filmmakers went, they left a subtle imprint on the landscape. A park in Woolwich acquired an ambiguous neon billboard; streets were painted true black and pigeons were dyed; fire hydrants and doorways and the fronts of houses were repainted into bold primary hues. "He literally painted the town his colors," reflected film critic Alexander Walker. "And he found a metaphor for the way people were exchanging reality for playtime."

Vanessa Redgrave was cast as the ambiguous object of the photographer's obsession, Sara Miles as the wife of his artist chum, the model Veruschka as a model to whom the photographer figuratively makes love with his camera and nineteen-year-old Jane Birkin (then married to composer John Barry) as a dolly bird willing to screw a photographer to break into modeling.

There was a fair amount of Bailey in the trappings and work habits of the protagonist. Asked if his photo sessions ever got as sexy as the one between Hemmings and Veruschka, Bailey replied, "When I was lucky," and Birkin confirmed that the real Bailey was, like the screen character, apt to say things to his models like "Stick your tits out." What's more, some details of the fictional photographer's life were absolutely stolen from Bailey's: When he caught up with the film with Deneuve at a New York cinema, Bailey was stunned to see the character walk, as he had, into a London antique shop and buy an airplane propeller: "I never understood how they knew that I'd paid eight pounds for that propeller," he remarked, ignorant of Wyndham's role in advising the production.

Other pieces of the film were cobbled together from various parts around London: The photojournalistic shots that the photographer produces were, in fact, the work of Don McCullin, who was paid a comfortable five hundred pounds—"a lot of money to me at the time"—by a troupe of Italians who pulled up outside his studio in two limousines. And the notorious pot party near the end of the film was shot over the span of five days in Christopher Gibbs's opulently decorated Thames-side house and cast with various students and scenesters from around town.

Antonioni made sure that he would have plenty of fodder for his camera by literally paying people—thirty pounds, nearly triple the national weekly wage—to come to Gibbs's house and get stoned. "I remember the word around town was, 'There's this guy who's paying money for people to come and get stoned at some place in Chelsea,'" said Paul McCartney. "And of course in our crowd that spread like wildfire. . . . Everyone was being paid, like blood donors, to smoke pot."

"I lived on Cheyne Walk opposite the houseboats," Gibbs recalled, "in a beautiful apartment on the first floor, which belonged to the National Trust. It had great big paneled rooms, which I rented for this modest sum. There's this bend in the river, so you get a mile of water, and you get these amazing light effects over what they call Turner's Reach. I was staying up all night taking acid, and entertaining expansively, having twenty-five people I'd never seen before. There were piles of Moroccan things, ancient Persian carpets, tapestries on the wall and more or less no furniture. It was very beautiful, like hippies in Venice in the seventeenth century: great dishes of fruit and incense burning, very glamorous heterosexual boys hanging around waiting to be goosed. Then I had my own gang of friends who they liked, too: Some of whom could be described as aristocratic, some of them were just straight bohemian, some were just loons, but generally relaxed people."

As on all movie shoots, there were stresses: The English weather was uncooperatively fair that summer, foiling Antonioni's desire to shoot in gloom; the Italian crew whom he'd brought with him would insist on breaking to play games of football and on flying to Rome whenever they could—even for haircuts. Ronan O'Casey, a Canadian-Irish actor who played Redgrave's lover—and the corpse that the photographer may or may not have seen—found the director a somewhat infernally conceited presence: "During our scene in the park, he spoke to Vanessa in Italian and to me in French, and I called him 'Signore Antonioni,' and he said, 'Don't call me Signore. Call me Michelangelo.' And he meant it!"

According to O'Casey, the plot of the film was supposed to recount an actual murder story, but much of it was cut when Carlo Ponti declared that Antonioni couldn't have any more time to shoot; traces of that storyline could be detected in an otherwise inexplicable scene involving a young man (actor Jeremy Glover) spying on the photographer as he lunched with his agent in a pub. But even if Antonioni *was* forced to hack away at his script during the shoot or the edit, the finished film still formed a beguiling critique of a culture that had come to confuse mirages with realities. And he got the picture into the can—over budget but not unreasonably.

When it opened, finally entitled *Blow-Up*, the following year, the British press was harsh on it, feeling that Antonioni had turned their pulsing, vibrant world into another of his enervated tableaux of unresolved longing and meaningless enigmas. "It comes close in its effect," wrote critic Penelope Gilliatt in a typical reaction, "to one of those shiny magazine features about this month's swinging depravity. You look at the pictures, admire the eye, sense not much reality and recoil."

Alexander Walker was one of the few critics who defended the film upon its release. "There was an underlying resentment at an Italian coming over and making a film that was going to be the iconic view of Britain," he recalled. "Some of the objections to it were petty: 'We've never seen black nuns in white habits in Regent Street'—that sort of thing." He went to see Antonioni the day of the film's debut. "He was sitting in the Savoy Hotel, he'd had the papers translated for him and he looked the picture of misery. The reaction to the film had corresponded with a grave doubt in Antonioni's mind. The doubt was, 'Was what he was seeing what he thought he was looking at?' Which of course was also the theme of the film."

Outside of the catty London reception, *Blow-Up* was a sensation—in part because of the nudity, frames of which were trimmed out by projectionists not so much out of Puritanism as to augment their private collections of occasional porn. David Bailey—the man who had inspired the film, the man who had referred to his camera and tripod as a "three-legged phallus," the man who had created fantasy girls of Jean Shrimpton and Sue Murray, among others—had inadvertently given the world another sexy chimera to spend money on.

MICK DOESN'T LIKE WOMEN. HE NEVER HAS.

Two weeks they'd been on the road and they were tired.

Manchester, Liverpool, Yorkshire, Durham, Leicester, Warwickshire, Kent, Middlesex and, finally, Essex.

No nights off, cheap railway station hotels, egg-and-chip suppers, booze (of course), birds (of course, of course) and driving through ancient farming towns from tumultuous gig to tumultuous gig.

They were nearly home—West Ham, the eastern edges of metropolitan London—and they needed petrol and to take a piss.

For more than a year they'd been making headlines for behavior that no respectable English adult would abide: near-riots at their concerts and around their hotels, rudenesses toward stage managers and security men and fellow acts on the tour. They had become notorious—and recognizable.

On the night of April 18, 1965, they pulled their Daimler into a filling station on the Romford Road and one of them asked if he could use the toilet. The mechanic on duty must have known who they were, or at least caught the scent of trouble off them: He said no.

By this time, a handful of them (including—oh, horror!—some girls) had emerged from the car and began to make a scene in front of the garage. One of them sneered at the mechanic and brushed past him with "We will piss anywhere, man." Others began dancing in the driveway, repeating this challenge as a kind of singsong. Finally, three of them unzipped and let flow on the side of the garage, in plain view of anyone who might have been driving by. Then they all fell back into their car laughing and signaling their parting affections to the mechanic with a one-fingered salute.

The next day, three of them were arrested for public indecency and insulting behavior.

In July, the case came to court and the magistrate let them have it: "Just because you have reached an exalted height in your profession, it does not mean you can behave in this manner."

To prove his point, he gave them a real firm slap on the wrist: a fine of five pounds each, and a warning to keep up a better moral standard for their fans.

Oh, those Rolling Stones . . .

If Andrew Oldham was dumb-lucky in bumping into a couple of tipsy Beatles when he needed a song for the Stones' second record, if he was in way over his head as a producer of their first singles and albums, he was a master—a genius, even—when it came to creating an image for the Stones that would set them apart from all the young pop acts that had crowded the public consciousness since the Annus Beatleus of 1963.

He had enjoyed a front-row seat to the spectacle of Brian Epstein, with his immaculate manners and silk scarves, orchestrating the rise of the Beatles; his backstage access to that group had ensured, as well, that he learned just how surprisingly real the gap was between the Beatles' public image of chipper, pleasant boyishness and their native Scouse irony, cynicism and rascality.

With his group of blues-mad Londoners who refused matching suits and haircuts, Oldham had decided to go the other way, turning the Rolling Stones into a threat to the nation's prosperity, good feeling, proper mores and—especially—virgins. The Beatles were the avatars of a reemergent England—sleek and triumphant and safe for the kiddies and grandmum; the Stones, in Oldham's arithmetic, would be the Beatles' dark doppelgangers, a threat to common decency and the commonwealth itself. As the brilliant catchphrase that Oldham dreamt up and the media dutifully disseminated asked, "Would you let your daughter go with a Rolling Stone?"

Epstein had built a great career for his group but had defined them narrowly and it would be a few years before they could spread out and be themselves publicly; Oldham watched the Beatles bowing smartly and being polite and funny and obliging old showbiz lights and even royals and decided, in the words of one journalist who was on the scene, "Fuck that, the Stones don't do that." (John Lennon, this same observer noted, "always believed the Stones had hijacked the Beatles 'original' image," that Liverpudlian-Hamburgian melange of leather-clad insolence, booze, drugs and quick, rough sex.) So if the public's first vision of the Beatles was four smart lads always ready with a felicity or a tune, Oldham would go 'round to his guys' flat, rouse them and bring them right down to meet photographers in hopes of catching "that 'just-out-of-bed-and-fuck-you' look."

Truth be told, Oldham wasn't pulling this stuff out of thin air: "They were all bad boys when I found them," he said of the band. "I just brought out the worst in them." If the Beatles were a quartet of agreeable northerners charmingly taking a seat at the adult table, the Stones were the suburban middle-class kids knocking over the establishment's lunch cart, the nearest thing English music had produced to James Dean or the Elvis Presley who caused southern preachers so much alarm. The Beatles, dressed for an earlier world's notion of success, had opened up a space in which anything young and lively would at least get a hearing; Oldham ensured that what the public heard about the Stones was all rotten and sinister and frightening.

At first, it was almost too strong for even a media culture emboldened by the Profumo scandal and the Argyll divorce to swallow. Terry O'Neill was shooting photos for the *Daily Sketch* when he learned how differently the Stones appeared to the larger world, his editors, say:

I took their first pictures of the Beatles, and it took them three months to publish 'em, and when they did, they got so much fan mail that they sent me out to discover the next group. Well, being a musician I'd been watching the Stones for a while. They were more bluesy. So I went and took their pictures, and I brought them back, and they said, "These look like prehistoric monsters!" The Beatles looked odd to them, and that's why they didn't publish the pictures, but when they saw the Stones, they thought they were horrendous. So they sent me out to find another group. And the Jewish mafia on Denmark Street had put together the Dave Clark Five, and they were very good-looking, very showbizzy, although nowhere near the same musicians. And I did that lot, and they did a double-page spread: "Beauties and the Beasts."

Even outside the sensations they created in the press, the Stones managed to drag insults out of the very sorts of old-time showbiz folks with whom the Beatles made nice. Twice they traveled to America in 1964; twice American showbiz spat them back.

In April, they appeared on the *Hollywood Palace* TV variety show and were brutally insulted by host Dean Martin: "Aren't they great?" he asked with rolling eyes after their performance, adding, "Their hair isn't long. It's just smaller foreheads and higher eyebrows." (Later, after a trampolinist performed, Martin added, "He's the father of the Rolling Stones. He's been trying to kill himself ever since.")

In October, they were booked as the latest English discovery of Ed Sullivan, on whose show the Beatles had completely reversed the hip-to-square current of Anglo-American cultural relations earlier in the year; after their performance, phones at the network offices blazed with protests at the Stones' physical appearance; Sullivan told reporters the next day, "I didn't see the group until the day before the broadcast. They were recommended to me by my agents in England. I was shocked when I saw them. I promise you they'll never be back on the show." (A promise, by the way, he failed to keep.)

Bill Wyman remembered other painful instances: "We did a live interview on radio in Chicago in 1964, and when we left, as we were listening to the radio in the car, the guy completely abused us and insulted us, saying, 'I could see the fleas jumping off of their heads,' and that kind of thing. You just learned to live with that. Dean Martin on the *Hollywood Palace* show holding his nose and saying he wouldn't be left backstage with those people. It just went on and on. It became part of life:

You were insulted. Three in the morning at Grand Central Station, we would get off the train after coming from some gig and be walking up the platform to the hotel, and the people cleaning the platform would be yelling at us: 'Are you for real?' 'Are you goils?' All day long."

It was equally bad at home, Wyman continued: "We were insulted daily, all the time. You could not go in a shop and buy a pack of cigarettes. You'd go in a cigarette shop to buy a pack of cigarettes, and the guy'd say, 'I'm not serving the likes of you, get out of my shop.' We'd go in pubs where everyone goes for a drink; the moment we walked up to the bar, this buzzing pub with loads of things going on and people talking and singing and dancing, they'd say, 'We're closed. Out.' We got refused hotels. All because of hair and attitude. It was nothing to do with our behavior."

But the behavior changed, or at least catalyzed change. Their concerts, frantic little rave-ups at first, became full-blown horror shows as their reputation spread. There were fistfights in the audiences, screaming mobs of hysterical fans outside hotels and stage doors, policemen attacking concertgoers in vain, angry efforts to stem the craziness. They weren't so much rock shows as, in Wyman's phrase, "riots and near-riots."

Oldham had a field day with this sort of thing, billing the Stones as the Ugliest Group in Britain and reveling in each appalled and snooty headline. As the Stones graduated from the Crawdaddy to Decca Records (where Oldham brilliantly manipulated executive Dick Rowe, who'd famously passed on the Beatles, into signing the band) to national tours of Britain with, first, the Everly Brothers, Bo Diddley and Little Richard and then the Ronettes, the band's reputation for awful behavior, hygiene and influence spiraled as surely as their records kept selling: Their third single, "Not Fade Away," went to number three; the follow-ups "It's All Over Now," "Little Red Rooster" and "The Last Time" all hit number one; and their debut album, which showed the five of them glaring out sullenly from the shadows and bore no identifying text (a record with no name—how cool was that?) knocked the Beatles out of the top spot for the first time in a year. The Stones were *in*, filthy or not.

But, in fact, Eva Jagger's son *wasn't* filthy (nor, in fact, were the other Stones, though Keith and Brian, apparently, had their ripe moments).

Rather, as with his affectations to black vocalizing and dance moves, his flirtations with women's clothing and his campy comic voice, he reveled in the image of the Stones as guttersnipes besmirching the table linen of polite society. He could dive fecklessly into this persona when he so desired: "Marriage?" he once told a journalist who asked him for his thoughts, "It's alright for those that wash." In truth, he was far more careful and scrupulous than he let on.

Take school, for instance: Jagger only left LSE just as the Stones began their first U.K. tour, writing to the registrar that "I have been offered a really excellent opportunity in the entertainment world" and making certain that he could return to his studies if the band didn't prove a going proposition. Later, as the band's success grew, he would admit to interviewers that he didn't reckon the band would last very long and that he was banking all his royalty checks as security against becoming unfashionable.

Socially, too, he was more conservative than his seedy image allowed. In late 1963, he began a steady relationship—the first in the string of such involvements that would form a foundation for the thousands of briefer liaisons in his life—with Chrissie Shrimpton, an early Stones fan and younger sister of Jean, the very face of the sexy new Britain. Compared to her sister, with her doe eyes, bold, pert face and air of voluptuousness atop rustic propriety, pretty Chrissie seemed relatively familiar, almost a neighborhood girl, really. She had been raised largely in farmlike comfort in Burnham, Buckinghamshire, not far from Windsor Castle, and had grown up a kind of hellion beside her older sister's correct young lady: Jean was obedient and internalized frustrations and even anger; Chrissie, Jean recalled, "quite enjoys a good dustup" and "was truly naughty and rebellious at school."

Chrissie had seen the Stones at Ealing a few times but finally worked up the nerve to talk to Jagger at one of the gigs the band played at the Star & Garter pub in Windsor in early 1963. Presently, they dated, and by the time the Crawdaddy Club scene exploded, they were an item; Andrew Oldham remembered seeing the two of them in an alley beside the Richmond Station Hotel before the first show he saw the Stones play. More precisely, Oldham remembered that the two lovebirds were engaged in a full-on row that night, a scene that became as emblematic of their relationship as their ascent as a beautiful couple of the first wave of the Swinging Sixties.

"She shouts at me all the time, Andrew," Jagger moaned to his manager one night as the two walked and talked after the singer endured yet another spat with Chrissie.

"They all do," Oldham noted.

"But she hits me!" Mick rejoined.

(On occasion, she alleged, he hit back.)

Their fights were legendary—"plate-throwing, Hollywood-style rows," said a friend—and often public. The first time Marianne Faithfull met Jagger, he and Chrissie had what Faithfull recalled as "a flaming row . . . she was crying and shouting at him, and in the heat of the argument her false eyelashes were peeling off."

But there was a core domesticity to their relationship, as well. They were to share two flats, both in Marylebone—the first on Bryanston Mews, just around the corner from a place Ringo Starr lived in (and later sublet to the likes of Jimi Hendrix and John Lennon and Yoko Ono), the next in Harley House on the Marylebone Road; as befit a couple of kids, their smallish bed was graced with a teddy bear. Chrissie, who, like her older sister, attended secretarial college, had jobs—cool ones at Radio Caroline and Decca Records and, finally, in the Stones' own offices on Oxford Street. (She also "wrote" a monthly my-life-as-a-pop-star's-girlfriend column entitled "From London with Luv" for *Mod* magazine.) She had charge accounts at Harrods and Fortnum & Mason and had a hot dinner waiting for Jagger when he was in town. They visited each other's families (Mick once got busted by Mr. Shrimpton in Chrissie's bed, but Chrissie, as luck would have it, was sleeping in Jean's room). He wrote her love letters when they were apart, and they talked about marriage as early as late 1963.

She was, in many ways, the perfect Miss Pop Star's Consort of the moment—big hair, eyelashes, lots of makeup, short skirts and genuinely pretty beneath it all. But Jagger wasn't sure that it was good press to *have* a girlfriend at the time (the marriages of Charlie Watts, Bill Wyman and John Lennon were hushed up by press agents for the Stones and Beatles). He had a habit that infuriated her of pretending not to be with her when he was recognized in the street by fans. He refused to allow her to attend the Stones' recording sessions. And, as his circles expanded from groupies and little knots of rising stars in trendy night spots to bona fide celebrities and genuine aristocrats, he began to ignore her more significantly: In the summer of '65, for instance, they were guests at the sixteenth birthday party of Lady Victoria Ormsby-Gore, one of the daughters of the former British ambassador to the U.S. William David Ormsby-Gore; Jagger spent the night laughing and chatting in a posh accent with Princess Margaret (quick becoming a fast friend, inciting all the likely rumors), and Chrissie stormed out in a huff.

She knew how to get back at him: When his attentions strayed more than she liked, she would simply go on a date (there was perhaps something more to her relationship with the bombastic American pop singer P. J. Proby). Inevitably, whether out of pride, jealousy or something more tender, Jagger came back.

Clever Chrissie would later brag about this strategy, declaring, with premature, ironic accuracy, "He would never let the woman be the one to call things off." And her insights into her man's character ran even darker when the romance was over: "Mick doesn't really respect women," she groused, and, again, "Mick doesn't like women. He never has."

For all the aggravation they caused each other, whether it was true love or no, Mick did accrue one tangible advantage from his affair with Chrissie: As a blossoming songwriter, he was given some delicious subject matter to write about. By the time the couple split, Jagger, with Keith Richards, had written such classic portraits of macho predation and female pettiness as "Heart of Stone," "The Last Time," "Play with Fire," "Satisfaction," "The Spider and the Fly," "Stupid Girl," "19th Nervous Breakdown," "Under My Thumb," "Surprise, Surprise," "Out of Time"—blistering, acidic and irresistible numbers that sputtered with anger and contempt and sexual frustration and satiety and which established the songwriting team of Jagger and Richards as, if not nearly the equals of Lennon and McCartney, then certainly estimable peers.

Songwriting hadn't come naturally to the two—indeed, the idea of original blues and R&B tunes written by white Britons seemed almost a violation of the Stones' original conception of fidelity to American roots music. But Andrew Oldham, ever on the prowl, had sussed out that the surest way for artists to make money wasn't in recording or touring but in song publishing: You could have other musicians perform your compositions and still earn royalties, for instance, and you could keep the fingers of record company and promoters out of the pie, or at least farther from it. What was more, after Lennon and McCartney and Dylan, it was something of a necessity for pop musicians to try to get a few songs written—something unheard of in the pre-Beatle era, when Denmark Street and the Brill Building were anonymous tune factories for manufactured stars.

Of course, there were those in the Stones who didn't think that they were pop musicians at all. Group founder Brian Jones, pointedly, thought that blues purism was the thing—particularly at the beginning. But Brian was as enamored of fame as of flatted sevenths—maybe even more. One night before Oldham popped into their lives, the Stones went to see the Beatles perform at the Royal Albert Hall and helped the band's crew lug their gear into the vans; Brian, mistaken by fans for one of the Beatles, was briefly mobbed. All the way home, he cooed, "That's what I want!" So long as their records and performances left room for a bit of blues and authentic R&B, he could live with the commercial stuff.

When it came time to find songwriters in the band, though, Oldham, a nasty politicker if ever there was one, hit upon the tandem of Jagger and Richards. In part it was because Jones, although an ingenious native musician who could teach himself virtually any instrument and do exciting things with it, didn't have the discipline to sit and write. In part, too, it was because Oldham had fallen under the spell of Jagger's sexual charisma (with all the likely rumors) and sought to make it the centerpiece of the band; in order to do that, he'd have to trump Jones's position, and the best way was to divide the tag team of guitarists, pairing Richards with Jagger and leaving Jones out in the cold.

Jagger, not remotely the musician Jones was, welcomed the opportunity, understanding the financial benefits of being a songwriter ("As far back as I can remember," his younger brother Chris said, "he said the thing he wanted most was to be rich"). Even more, perhaps, he was coming to see himself as a superstar; Chrissie Shrimpton remembered him around this time spending long spells staring into the mirror at his own reflection, trying out postures and facial expressions and gestures as if willing himself to develop magnetism; when he met black American female dancers—Tina Turner and the Ikettes, in particular—he frankly asked to learn their moves. In the developing formula of the day, it only made sense for him to try to equal the success of Lennon and McCartney by writing his own songs to sing. (Besides, no one was ever going to mistake him for an authentic Chicago bluesman, no matter how he learned to prance or pout or slur his words.) And it would certainly eliminate any questions about what other than singing and strutting he provided to the band.

And yet, with all that motivation, Jagger and Richards required some coaxing from Oldham to get to it. He literally locked them up together and told them that they had to come up with a song before he'd let them out and feed them. They earned their release, but not with anything they ever bothered to record. Still, they had started, and in time they would develop technically and artistically so that they actually produced songs not only for the Stones but for some of the other artists who'd fallen into Oldham's orbit.

But the big success of this first flush of songwriting was to come with Oldham's discovery of a new girl on the London scene who wasn't a singer but whom he was convinced he could craft into a star. She was a former convent schoolgirl and a direct descendent, through her mother, of the Viennese writer Leopold Baron von Sacher-Masoch—yes, *that* Sacher-Masoch, the author of *Venus in Furs* and eponym of masochism. Oldham beheld her at a party—unadorned beauty, ripe bosom, big eyes, long blonde hair—and immediately saw how he could package and sell her: "She had this fantastic virginal look," he remembered. "At a time when most chicks were shaking ass and coming on strong, here was this pale, blonde, retiring chaste teenager looking like a Mona Lisa, except with a great body." Haunted by his vision, he gave Mick and Keith a songwriting commission: "I want a song with brick walls all around it and high windows and no sex."

They came up with just the thing (with a bit of help from Lionel Bart): "As Tears Go By."

In August 1964, it would be the debut hit—at number nine—of Marianne Faithfull.

If Mick and Keith had entered into the music racket in imitation of Americans whose lives they couldn't possibly emulate, by becoming songwriting popsters they were attempting to follow in footsteps from another direction. The American original may have lit the fuse of British rock 'n' roll, but the idea that young Brits could write songs just as good as Buddy Holly's or Chuck Berry's was the real explosion—and, like so much of what set off the sixties, it was imported to London from the North.

The whole topsy-turvy new London that nobody could rein in or fathom had, in fact, first intimated itself in unlikely provincial removes, with actors out of Leeds and Manchester and pop bands out of Liverpool. They kept their accents and their rude provincial ways—the first generation to do so en masse—but just the same they all came down to London to rattle the windows and make their names just as centuries of practice had required. As it ever had for blue-blooded Oxbridgeans and uppity bucolics both, for the hotshots of the youthquake, London was the place to prove one's self.

And they did, the Beatles and the Hollies and the Animals and Albert Finneys and Sean Connerys and Rita Tushinghams and Peter O'Tooles. They took over the capital's most visible industries, these unlikely northerners, the ushers-in of what amounted to a full-on revolution in England's—and then the world's—tastes and bents and habits.

But London, too, could issue forth talent just as raw and hungry and willing to dash custom for the sake of the new. And by the mid-sixties, the Londoners had moved aside the northerners and come to stand boldly in the center of the picture.

In the movies, it was Michael Caine and Terence Stamp who were the hot ones, O'Toole having ascended to Hollywood, Finney having taken a curious sabbatical.

And in pop music, London bands were virtually all that mattered anymore, with an enormous exception that none of them could disallow: London acts like the Rolling Stones, the Kinks and The Who might've ruled the world in 1966, but for the colossal fact of the Beatles.

That spring, for instance, the Stones released an album that felt, like *Rubber Soul*, of a piece: *Aftermath*, unlike the three Stones studio albums that preceded it, wasn't a hodgepodge of nifty tracks but a through-and-through conception, with songs strung together one after another in a purposeful pattern and a real sense that a coherent vision was at work. The textures and tones were varied—there was room for sitar and harpsichord, for instance, as well as for the enormously varied lyrics of such songs of diverse temper as "Stupid Girl" and "Lady Jane."

But then a few months later, *Revolver* appeared and made the whole thing seem limp, tame, dated.

Time and again, musically, the Beatles trumped the Stones. There was the night in the summer of '68 that a party was held to mark the opening of a new club (with Stones money behind it) on the Tottenham Court Road, and the soundtrack for the evening was *Beggar's Banquet*, which hadn't yet been released. The crowd was stunned, as well they should have been, by what turned out to be the band's first true cut-to-cut classic. But then Paul McCartney showed up with an acetate of *his* group's latest—a single of "Hey, Jude" with "Revolution" on the back. One spin on the turntable, and the Stones were back in the caboose with everyone else. (Stones' agent, Sandy Lieberson, recalled that the night ended in a really dark, druggy mess, with people being accidentally dosed with acid and Paul McCartney walking out muttering, "The Stones are *evil*.")

And yet, for all these setbacks, the Stones had clearly outclassed the Beatles in one key area: More than any other band, the Stones were the essence of the spirit of mid-sixties London. The Beatles were bigger and more famous and sold many more records and had two hit movies and broke far more new ground, but the Stones were much more implicated in the white-hot center of the goings-on.

In part, it was because the Beatles were too famous: When the Stones were still trying to figure out whether they were a pop or blues act, the Beatles were running for their lives from fans on four continents. Mc-Cartney couldn't walk to the store in London, but rather took taxis for two-block shopping trips and even then was mobbed; ditto George Harrison, who would take two cabs to visit Andrew Oldham, who only lived just across the road. When they wanted to shop for Mary Quant gear for their wives or girlfriends, the designer let them come to her studio: "They couldn't come into the shop," she remembered. "They'd be mobbed." When they wanted to go to a movie, they had to rent out a private screening room and orchestrate their coming and going like a military maneuver. A *Vogue* editor was visiting the Asher household with some photos of Jane when McCartney asked her if she wanted to come to Soho to see *The Great Escape* with the band. As she recalled,

> They had to call the police about five minutes before they were ready to leave the house, and then two minutes before they were ready to leave, they called the driver. And the driver pulled up to the front door, and her parents did a countdown, like, "Five, four, three, two, one," opened the door and we rushed across the pavement. The girls were packed on the pavement outside, the doors to

the limousine were opened and Paul pushed Jane Asher into the back of the car and pulled me in at the same time, and the driver slammed the door and pulled away with three or four girls on top of the car already. We almost got our clothes ripped off, and the driver had to go through three red lights to get rid of the girls who were chasing us down the street.

But the Beatles were distinct from the other acts, too, because they were very quickly domesticated and rich: By mid-'65, all four were publicly attached and John and Ringo were married and living in suburban mansions. (And not only married, mind you, but to the sort of Liverpool lasses that other northern boys fled to London to escape. Cynthia Lennon and Maureen Starkey were and are, by all accounts, attractive and delightful women and good mothers and wives, but they weren't the sort of catches that sixties stardom was meant to confer upon its chosen. Compare Jane Asher, Paul's beautiful, town-bred actress girlfriend or, even more to the point, Patti Boyd, the gorgeous young model who became the first Mrs. George Harrison: *That* was why a provincial boy learned how to play bar chords and sing harmony and hitchhiked down the Great Northern Road to the capital!)

Still, even if the Beatles hadn't ascended to an unprecedented sphere of pop glory, it might still have been the case that a London act would have risen to a station just beneath them as the city itself became the focus of so much energy and creativity. Surely the Stones' increasingly iconic status grew importantly out of the fact that they were true Londoners—or at least as true as any other band out there, having played their first gigs, flopped in their first dingy flats, screwed their first women, taken their first drugs, bought their first flash suits and so forth in the city. Their songs spoke directly about their town: rich girls whose mothers slummed in Stepney, strange characters who hung around the Chelsea Drugstore, rent boys in Trafalgar Square. The Beatles, who sang of their Liverpool boyhoods in comparatively mystical tones, weren't the kings so much as the deities of the scene; they created it and steered it and never gave the sense of looking back but always forward; they changed their hairstyles or the cut of their clothes and the world took note; the mere fact that one of them was attending a lecture or a restaurant opening or a movie premiere made that event a top news story.

The Stones, on the other hand, were able to shuffle along, relatively, more or less, in the groove of things. They didn't create the times so much as they reflected then exemplarily. And that, ironically, allowed them to seem rather more imitable and real: royalty, if you will, to the Beatles' divinity.

Mick, for one, certainly comported himself with a regal air. By dint of application, talent and historical good fortune, he had turned his native narcissism into external adulation and his love of imposture into a chameleonic ability to ride just ahead of the crest of fashion. Although Brian Jones, principally of his bandmates, was perhaps even quicker to haunt the latest chic club or dress in the most outrageous new getups, Jagger, as Oldham's anointed focal point for the group, was inevitably more visible. (John Lennon, half teasing, called Mick "the king of the scene.")

Jagger's rise as a symbol of his age coincided with his assumption, abetted by Keith Richards and plotted by Andrew Oldham, of the most prominent position in the Stones. Oldham had reckoned Mick for the top spot from his first glimpse of the band at the Crawdaddy, but Brian Jones's legitimate claim to having founded the group—and the intimacy of the guitar duets played by Jones and Richards, so essential a part of the Stones' sound—had always been an obstacle. After a few years of songwriting, however, Mick and Keith had become important—if nevertheless distant—rivals to Lennon and McCartney. This innovation, coupled with Brian's increasing drug abuse and always suspect ability to control his tempers and moods, created a not-too-subtle shift in the group dynamics. By the mid-sixties, Jones was being mocked openly by his bandmates for pettiness, unreliability and vanity; "Miss Amanda Jones," a nasty little tune from *Between the Buttons*, was said not to be another Jagger-Richards potshot at some haughty dolly bird, but a slap at Brian!

If Mick was becoming more and more proprietary toward the band, you couldn't blame him. He had, more obviously than the others, transformed and grown in his art, evolving from an ordinary, ambitious boy singer into the premiere vocal talent of his time. It was partly a learned thing, part mimicry, part effort, part sham, but Jagger had become the best blues singer—or, more precisely, bluesy pop singer—in England. He had begun in apery and found himself unique, perfecting a kind of sleepy-sexy drawl that implied decadence, spite, cockiness, frustration, drollery and even, when he felt the urge, hope and yearning. If the thought of an eighteen-year-old, skinny white boy from suburban London trying to belt out an old Slim Harpo sexual boast like "I'm a King Bee" was ridiculous, within a few years Jagger *was* a King Bee, and by decade's end, still only twenty-six, he could sing "Love in Vain"—a song made famous by *Robert fucking Johnson*—and not embarrass himself. Moreover, he and his bandmates had credibly merged their blues and R&B influences with their pop instincts so that their own material—all those great singles—were *really* authoritative. No singer anywhere, by the end of the sixties, could touch him for incendiary power.

Socially, too, he had come to occupy a place that was uniquely his. More than any of his fellow Stones or, really, any of the other important rock personalities of the time, he had the arriviste's thirst to mingle with aristocracy and be flattered by its passing attentions. He turned up at posh parties and fetes, properly dressed, and would slightly alter his affected Cockney accent upward (while, in the manner of the day, his high-bred new friends ratcheted theirs down a class or two). More than any Beatle or, indeed, any of the young film stars, Jagger was a familiar figure on the aristocratic social circuit. "He would attend dinners given by any silly thing with a title and a castle," recalled Marianne Faithfull. "He was as smitten as any American millionaire in the movies."

Ah, Marianne Faithfull: She, too, was part of the evolution of Mick Jagger, one of the trophies he acquired, part of his ever-changing public persona.

In that it's-all-happening-right-now year of 1966, Faithfull was still lolling about London, recovering from having had a hit single of "As Tears Go By" in 1964 but having no substantial musical career (or, indeed, really, the desire for one) to follow it. Having been vaulted from nowhere to stardom but lacking a true calling to either pop music or fame, Faithfull became a fixture of the scene—the girl all the boys (and some of the other girls) went crazy for. "We hadn't seen a girl like her," remembered Terry O'Neill, who took stunning photos of her in black lace lingerie. "She shows up with that natural look and a really good body and a beautiful face. But she didn't have the look of a model, all made up."

Faithfull still made the odd record, but mostly she just turned up in groovy new outfits and her otherworldly demeanor at this or that incredible going-on. She had spent a lot of time, for instance, hanging around with Bob Dylan at the Savoy Hotel the previous summer when the American superstar was touring the country. She'd been reckoned his likeliest English match but he turned on her when she told him about her relationship with John Dunbar. Faithfull's boyfriend had become a mainstay of the London avant-garde with his Indica art gallery, his friendships with beatniks and Beatles and, increasingly, his involvement in the world of drugs, up to and including the hard stuff. Dylan warned her off: "Hell," he sneered, "he ain't nothing but a goddamn *student!*" Maybe, but that summer Dunbar and Faithfull wed, and in November she bore him a son, Nicholas.

By the spring of '66, a wife and mother at eighteen, Faithfull grew restless and, caught up in the tide of the times, began hanging out with Brian Jones and his witchy German girlfriend Anita Pallenberg, a model-actress-whatever with decadence running thick in her blood, at their elaborately decorated flat—a lush mix of Moroccan and Olde English details—on Courtfield Road, South Kensington. Faithfull had been "discovered" and Svengalied by Andrew Oldham nearly two years earlier, she'd had her big hit with a Jagger-Richards song and she'd caught Mick's eye and lusted vaguely after Keith all this while. But this was her first true immersion in the world of the Stones and Stones People, a demimonde that more and more had become the center of sixties London. Chelsea aristocrats, Soho decadents, actors, musicians, artists, models, photographers—all the high life and low life the city and the times could belch up, simmering together in a druggy, misty, merry pudding of hedonism, bohemia, the underworld and jeunesse dorée. It was the first great flush of hippie, and the Stones, with their deep ties to the city, were, more even than the Beatles, at its core.

With her exotic lineage, captivating beauty and questing nature, Faithfull was a natural fit in this piquant new milieu, and she dove in avidly: drugs, a little sex, shopping, chattering, running around at all hours. She dropped acid with Brian, Keith and the ill-fated Guinness heir Tara Browne; she dallied sexually with Brian and Keith; she smoked hash with all of them (Dunbar, priggishly, wouldn't let her do it at home, though he used every drug he could get his hands on).

Finally, inevitably, Mick: Invited to watch the Stones play in Bristol in October '66, she hung around his hotel room after the show, smoking dope, watching a brand-new print of *Repulsion,* Roman Polanski's new antisex, antidrug, anti-Swinging London horror show, and, finally, going to bed with him. Then she went off to Italy for a vacation without Mick or her husband. Nevertheless, the seed had been sown: Jagger wrote her constantly while she was gone and, soon after her return to London, they let the world see them together. They were, in her phrase, "*the* couple"—or, at least, *the latest* one.

For John Dunbar it was an unpleasant reality but one he'd created: "It was over before she left me for Mick," he said of his marriage, and he equanimously stayed friendly with his wife (they didn't divorce until the seventies) and even worked as a technician on the Stones' 1967 European tour.

For Mick's girlfriend, Chrissie Shrimpton, however, this new affair was a massive, disorienting shock. She had put up with Mick's dalliances—hundreds of them, more than she knew, and not always one-nighters with casual acquaintances but some real amours. But in Faithfull she was faced with another sort of threat: a woman just as beautiful as she (if not, indeed, more) with an independent spirit, mind and (more or less) career and, what's worse, one steeped in the new vogues that seemed, cruelly, to be passing Chrissie by.

The drugs, for instance: Chrissie was dragged unwillingly into hash and pot; Mick had warned her not to use them and had told her that he wouldn't, either, and for a long time, incredibly, she believed him, finally seeing the truth when he couldn't be bothered with hiding his increasingly frequent use of them from her. Once psychedelics were around, Mick once again tried to steer Chrissie away, but when she caught a whiff of what he and his mates were up to, she wanted to have a go. At Tara Browne's acid-laced twenty-first birthday party at an estate in Ireland in April 1966, Mick and Chrissie took LSD together; given their volatile history and the fissures that were developing, it ought to have been no surprise that they had an awful experience—the inspiration it was said—*wrongly,* as it happened—for his wicked "19th Nervous Breakdown."

Worse, Chrissie was so . . . *1964.* Her look—sleek and pampered and bewigged and mascara-ed and punctilious and exact—was out of tenor with the hedonic casualness that had entered the scene with the advent of hallucinogenic drugs. Faithfull was like a Renaissance maiden or gypsy princess, comfortable in loose, sheer, ethnically inspired garments and a relaxed style of living, able to float with whatever the day or night brought along. Chrissie, on the other hand, was, in Faithfull's view, "very put together. . . . It took her simply ages to get ready. She could never spend the night anywhere because she might fall apart." For that first smart era of the sixties, to frug in the Ad Lib or dine out among the movie stars at Quaglino's, Chrissie had been the perfect fit for Jagger and his ambition. But now, as songs like "Under My Thumb" and, especially, "Out of Time" signaled, she and her high-strung dolly bird act were toast.

In September 1966, Mick and Chrissie survived a fender bender near their house—Mick's nearly new Aston Martin was winged in the passenger side; people who knew them wondered if they weren't spatting when it happened. The final coup came in December 1966: Chrissie showed up at the airport expecting to fly to Jamaica for a Christmas holiday with Mick that had been in the planning for months; he never showed. For a few days she tried to reach him; he didn't respond. On December 18, she attempted suicide: pills, of course. Mick came by the hospital in Hampstead, finally, to drop the bomb that he was leaving her and who for. In succession, he told the hospital he wouldn't be paying her bills, he had his office cut off her various credit lines and, on Christmas Eve, he had a hired crew remove her belongings from the flat they shared in Harley House.

"Mick completely broke me in the end," is how she managed to put it when she'd recovered and had time to reflect.

She had no way of understanding, poor thing, that she'd merely been another of the skins he'd so eagerly shed as he kept ahead of the times.

ALL THE YOUNG STONED HARLEQUINS

As Mary Quant's Bazaar had grown and came to dominate young British women's sense of what clothes ought to be like, the designer continued to knock herself out in small Chelsea workrooms, dreaming up one novel design after another and then supervising the creation of them hands-on. But as demand came to outpace her capacity—several important department stores had opened Bazaar-like misses boutiques and were eager to stock her work—she had thought about mass production: designing and manufacturing reasonable facsimiles of her costlier inspirations for a broader and less pricey market. She finally confronted the reality of this idea during a trip to America to meet fashion editors of influential publications and visit some tony department stores to solicit orders. While there, she was approached by a representative of JC Penney, the gigantic midpriced department store chain: Could these clothes be mass-produced and sold in America?

It was a completely preposterous marriage: Penney was dowdy

and lowbrow and conservative, and Quant was the most exciting new designer in the world. But the store had been trying to hit on ways to update its image and had sent a scout to Europe to find the hot new thing; he had found Quant. And the call happened to come just when Quant felt that her business was outgrowing her ability to oversee it like a mom-and-pop shop. Details were worked out, cultures reconciled and Ginger Group, Quant's mass-market label, was born, first in America, where the line of young women's dresses was a smash hit, and then in Britain, where the success was just as complete.

Inevitably, perhaps, Quant was followed to the U.S. and the mass market by Vidal Sassoon. In 1964, he was approached by investors who hoped to find an operating partner for French hairdresser Charles of the Ritz in a salon on New York's Madison Avenue. It took some time to get it started—you can neither mass produce haircuts nor blanket the nation with them in a single television broadcast. But eventually, Sassoon had as powerful an impact on the American notion of coiffure as he had on London's. "Everybody got a kick out of whatever came out of London, whoever did it," he remembered, "and the whole world was looking at us."

America, the font of the cool and the chic for so many years, was suddenly switching on to British clothes and manners. It was a stunning reversal, remembered journalist Ray Connolly: "In 1963, I went to the States, and we were quaint. The Beatles hadn't been there yet. And then I came back to England. And at the end of that spring, I remember a girl said to me, 'Don't the Americans seem old-fashioned now?' And I said, 'Yeah, they do.' The change had come that quickly."

It wasn't long before all of America realized what Connolly had: The coolest clothes and hair and movies and music, the most modern manners and mores and modes of speech and social intercourse—all of it was coming out of London.

By the end of 1965—the season Sassoon always thought of as New York's "English winter"—if you were American and at all with it, you danced to British music in British clothes and, if you were lucky enough to get an appointment, with a British hairdo.

And, if you were a with-it young woman, you showed some thigh.

After Jean Shrimpton made scandalous headlines in Australia with her above-the-knee hemline, skirts all over London seemed to rise with the spirits. Mary Quant was given credit widely for inventing what came to be called the miniskirt, and while she never expressly declared as much herself, she was perfectly willing to be associated with the look and to produce it in shorter and shorter versions as the seasons rolled out. "The Chelsea girls had really terrific legs," Quant remembered. "If I didn't make the clothes short enough, they would shorten them more."

But the look wasn't exclusive to the model girl sorts for whom Quant designed. Lynn Redgrave, for instance, who never felt a fashion plate because of her height and full figure, adored the new look. "For the first time, I appreciated being tall," she said, "because it became quite the thing for the first time to put on a pair of *really* high heels and a *really* short skirt, even if it didn't suit you that well. It felt very freeing, especially as I felt so shy and insecure about my body and my look. It gave you something to hang on to, something to transform yourself with."

And, naturally, the men agreed. "The miniskirt was a piece of magic," sighed journalist Peter Evans. "Suddenly all women were attractive. The first thing you noticed about them were their legs. Then you looked at the boat (Cockney slang: boat race = face) and said, 'Well, you know . . .' But by then you were hooked."

In the rag trade, a game of chicken began with designers testing one another to see who would raise hemlines highest. "Brevity," *Vogue* declared, "is the soul of fashion." When Quant showed a collection of miniskirts in Paris, remembered nightclub owner John Gold, who was married to the designer's favored model, Jan de Souza, the fashion press reacted with outrage: "You would've thought there was a football match going on in that room!" Later, the models, still wearing the designs they'd showed, went with Quant to Maxim's for dinner and created the opposite effect: "All you could hear," Gold said, "was the clatter of knives and forks."

And that was *France*. In America, well: Lynn Redgrave got a vivid taste of just how far behind the States were when it came to showing off your legs. "I went to New York in 1966 for a week to publicize *Georgy Girl*," she remembered, "and I got *really* stared at. Now, I did not wear my skirt that short by London standards, but by New York standards, which were way behind in '66 . . . ! I remember going into Bonwit

Teller's and standing in the elevator and everyone staring at me. And my skirt wasn't really that short: I have very long legs, so midway between hips and knees for me is still very covering. But, oh, did I get stares! It was kind of fun!"

The opprobrium wasn't limited to old ladies in polite shops, either. Rita Tushingham recalled catching an earful from, of all people, Joan Crawford, when she and Redgrave went to a film festival in Mexico to promote *The Girl with Green Eyes*. "Joan Crawford was very upset with us," Tushingham said. "We were a 'terrible representation for the film industry' because of our short dresses. And we didn't have long dresses, apart from one we might have worn to a Royal Film Performance. And she thought we were a disgrace."

And while British politicians might have agreed with Mommy Dearest on that point, they had a concern regarding the miniskirt that no one might have anticipated. By the end of 1965, the fear was spoken that the miniskirts being exported to America were so short that manufacturers could declare them as children's clothes and pay a less substantial export tax.

Another curious sidelight to the raising of the hemlines was the fascination with boots—really, really *high* boots made out of space-age materials, often white or silver or some other bright hue. André Courreges, who, along with Quant, came to be most frequently associated with the miniskirt, made a specialty of the long, lean footwear; even Quant wore Courreges: "I'd have no handbag," she recalled, "and I'd keep my door key inside my thigh-length boots. I'd have to dig into them for money and pencils and such"—a victim of her own fashion genius.

And after liberating women's thighs, Quant went about liberating their faces. Just as she abhorred the clothes that had been foisted upon women in her youth, Quant could never abide the choices in cosmetics: "The manufacturers were all huge international companies," she recalled, "and they had a very lacquered, hard approach to the thing, and they had a very limited idea of what sort of colors to use: pink, orange and red. From my art student days on, I'd been experimenting with tins of crayons and paint boxes and brushes, bringing in those sort of fashion colors and using color in a different way."

Setting her head to rethinking the field of cosmetics, she applied the same sort of sensibility that she brought to her clothing lines: color, fun, sexiness, girlishness.

It was a new concept and approach based on color and applying it with brushes and using your face as a canvas and having much more fun with makeup—greens and blues and browns and purples and whites. Because prior to that there simply wasn't white nail polish or other colors. And we spent eighteen months working on it and launched in '65. And it was the most dynamic success! It went worldwide. We did our own false eyelashes, which we sold in a small coil, and the marvelous art director whom we were working with came up with the ad, "Bring back the lash!" I wanted waterproof mascara, which didn't exist at that time, and that was a hell of a battle technically, and the men who ran these companies said, "Well, why do you want waterproof mascara? Women don't put their heads in the water when they swim." And I would say, "Well, that's why we don't!" And we got it, and in fact it was so waterproof that it was a deuce of a job to get it off, and people often kept it for a week. For that the ad was "Crybaby," with a picture of tears running down but the mascara not smudging. We had huge posters in the underground and in the King's Road. The first one I saw, I was so excited: I was driving, and I bumped into the car in front of me!

The Quant line of makeup included Jeepers Peepers for the eyes, Blush-Baby powders and rouges, and a foundation called Starkers. Just as Quant's clothing ideas had swept away decades of weary practice, so did her cosmetics revolutionize the way women prettied themselves. "I had a rather round face," remembered Lynn Redgrave, "and I bought her makeup and put a big dark thing in the eye socket and I would highlight with silver—in daytime! And I had no cheekbones, they were hidden at that point, and I put the dark Mary Quant shader on. She kind of began this whole thing of shaping your face; you didn't just put on lipstick and blue eye shadow, which our mothers would have done. You shaped your face and made it look modern and exciting."

Vidal Sassoon, too, continued to innovate after the boom he ignited with his Bob and Five-Point Cuts. He was a confessed workaholic—"I remember leaving parties at eleven o'clock, and they looked at me like

I was crazy and I'd say, 'No, no, I've got one heck of a day tomorrow.' You had to be a professional"—and was inspired by his early successes to keep innovating. He designed a couturish look involving large, square curls; he experimented with asymmetric designs; he and his team developed a technique to give hair multicolored highlights; and he managed to combine his short, cropped style with a permanent, creating a look he called the Greek Goddess cut, a bob adorned with ringlets—an exotic, casual style that suited the oncoming rush of hippie fashion splendidly. At the same time, he busily expanded his empire of salons, opening in Sloan Square, in Toronto, Canada, in Beverly Hills; he introduced a line of high-end wigs in classic Sassoon shapes; he undertook promotional and educational tours of the U.K., Japan and North America. By 1968, he had begun to market the proprietary shampoos and conditioners he used in his salons under the Vidal Sassoon label and was exploring doing the same with professional hair care products for the consumer market. And plans were in the works for an actual haircutting academy—"the Harvard of hair," as it would be known—to take the place of the apprentice-style tutelage new employees received from old before they could work in his salons.

Sassoon became what no haircutter before him ever was: a star. He rubbed elbows with his movie star and socialite clientele, of course, but he published an autobiography (*Sorry I Kept You Waiting, Madam*) and appeared on TV talk shows. In one of the most celebrated publicity stunts of its type, he was flown to Hollywood specifically to cut Mia Farrow's hair for *Rosemary's Baby* (the film's director, Roman Polanski, had shot his film *Repulsion* for a solid week in Sassoon's Bond Street salon); earning a fee of five thousand dollars, Sassoon appeared on a soundstage on the Paramount back lot in front of scores of reporters and photographers. He had an American wife, Beverly, and more and more an American reputation; before long, he would leave England altogether for the States and a new life—a rising, smiling balloon, practicing yoga and making people look wonderful in the California sun.

Like Sassoon, Quant was successful enough to relax by the middle of the decade: Her companies were grossing upward of $12 million a year; she even published an autobiography, *Quant by Quant*. But she continued to innovate in ways that made her stand out: She began to sell raincoats, dresses and even hats made out of PVC, the waterproof substance that had been used to date to dress fishermen and firefighters and which she infused with bold, cheerful colors and smartly tailored lines. Soon after, she was making clothes with intricate black-and-white and primary color patterns that reflected the influence of the op art canvasses being shown in daring Mayfair art galleries.

Her ascent was capped, Beatlishly, by royal decree: In June 1966, in recognition of her contribution to export and the British economy, she was invested by the Queen with the OBE, an honor higher than even the one accorded the Beatles the previous year. Upon being told of her pending award, she joked, "What's it going to be like curtsying in a miniskirt?" But, in fact, she accepted the medal in a conservative suit of her own design with a respectable—if still fashionable—hemline.

Yet money and regal recognition couldn't insulate Quant from some realities. At the same time she was being singled out by the Queen, she was in a business that was growing more competitive than ever, the grand dame—at barely thirty—of a real explosion in women's fashion right there on the King's Road.

The King's Road in which Quant and Alexander Plunket Greene opened Bazaar in 1955 was such a quaint throwback that it seemed more like a village thoroughfare than a big city street. "The King's Road was our high street," remembered David Puttnam, who lived in the area. "That's where we bought our television set and our groceries. In 1963, it had bakers and shops." The King's Road was home to greengrocers and butchers and fishmongers and all the amenities you'd expect to find in a central location if you were in a small town or a London suburb. The proximity of these shops—and the general lack of commercial premises in the area's other avenues—meant that Chelsea dwellers tended to run into one another in the King's Road routinely while doing their marketing or running errands. There was nothing rustic about the sort of people one ran into. Chelsea was a bohemia of long standing, and the men and women were quicker than just about anyone else in London to adopt new fashions or habits or mores. It was only the surroundings that seemed quaint.

Through the early sixties, the West End and Soho had been the most obvious sites of novel activities—the largest concentration of chic clubs, restaurants and performance spaces such as theaters, cinemas and music venues. But the hot young things didn't *live* in those neighborhoods; they merely played there. They tended to live southwest of the center: Brompton, Knightsbridge, Kensington and, especially, Chelsea, where the longtime residents—whether artists, blue bloods or pensioners from the riverside Royal Hospital for aged servicemen—tended not to stare or point at famous people or eccentrics. There was a superior trendy men's shop, John Michael, and a few hot night spots nearby—Blaise's in Queen's Gate, the Cromwellian in the Cromwell Road—and, of course, Quant and Plunket Greene's two-plex of Bazaar and Alexander's for shopping and congenial dining. But in the main it was a district given over to leisurely living within easy commute of the bustle of the West End.

That began to change, however, in late 1965, most pronouncedly with the opening of two boutiques with names that brashly signaled the coming of a new era: Granny Takes a Trip and Hung on You.

Granny was opened in the World's End portion of King's Road by the tailor John Pearse and the graphic artists Michael English and Nigel Waymouth. The name was pure psychedelia, derived in part from the fact that the shop, very proto-hippie, sold antique clothes that Pearse fixed up with a slightly modern feel. The shop was outrageously deco- rated and done over as the fancy struck its owners: Now a big grinning sun as the front window, now the cartoon image of a flapper, now a fifteen-foot-high Sitting Bull, now elaborate marbling painted on the walls, now purple *everything,* even the telephone. The proprietors changed the decor, Pearse explained, "through the night sometimes. It could be anything that we were dealing with at that time. The last one, which was really a monument to my demise, was my Dodge car that we'd sawn in half and welded to the front, simply because the car had broken down and it was such a beautiful object that we decided to do it. I think it was based on a Claes Oldenburg piece. Before that, we actu- ally had a glass window. But it was smashed by the football crowd going to Stamford Bridge. Chelsea must have lost or won. So we dispensed with the glass after that."

As you entered, you passed under lettering which read "One should either be a work of art or wear a work of art"—a purely King's Road sentiment that harmonized, Waymouth explained, with the store's philosophy of "playing out fantasies in real life. It's a romantic dream world we're catering for."

Granny's catered to both men and women and included plenty of wild items designed by the owners: miniskirts, op art shirts, garments in loud florals and paisleys, the whole hippie closet. It stood out even on garish King's Road, explained Pearse, because, "We were taking things even further. There was some sort of radical stuff that we could single-handedly take credit for: certain designs and cuts. And we were also the first multisex boutique." And, too, unlike many King's Road shops, Granny's sold stuff that was well-made. "That's really because of our up-bringing and our knowledge of the craft of tailoring," Pearse said. "I always had style and flair, but I did know how things were put together. It gave me a sixth sense: I could look at something from one hundred paces and know if it was well-produced or not."

Still, the real novelty was the Sargasso Sea of discarded fashions up for sale: flapper dresses, Victorian bustles, Boer War helmets, antique military jackets, Chicago gangster suits, fezzes, turbans and all manner of what a contemporary travel guide called "cleaned and darned exotica." Granny Takes a Trip, along with Ian Fisk's Portobello Road shop with the equally outrageous name I Was Lord Kitchener's Valet, had pio-neered the idea of cultural regurgitation as fashion. Simply by putting on a bit of clothing that screamed out Empire, a long-haired, dope-smoking scenester of the mid-sixties could both declare alienation from the es-tablishment and look darned smart: All the important English pop bands—the Beatles, the Stones, The Who—had a moment in old-time military togs. The trend took off so steeply that Fisk opened an outlet on the King's Road—I Was Lord Kitchener's Thing, he called it—helping fuel a high season of silly, campy and status-conferring dressing up.

Hung On You, which was located on Cale Street, just off the King's Road, was similarly steeped in modish moods but had a slightly different ambition—a blend, as it were, of traditional English fine menswear with the groovy new trends of the day. At a time when Carnaby Street was overrun with weekend mods looking for bargains on something they'd seen on *Ready, Steady, Go!*, Hung On You was promoting a wild new aesthetic of op art fancies, faux Victoriana and the sort of cheek that re-sulted from public schoolboys coming into contact with hallucinogenic drugs. The very sight of the place from the street was arresting, and the interior decor, constantly updated, ranged from the playful to the plain weird: During one phase, not a stitch of clothes was on display in the main premises; attuned shoppers who noticed a hole in the floor and descended à la Lewis Carroll's Alice down a narrow staircase entered *another* showroom where sales staff awaited—with, again, no merchandise on display. You had to know enough to ask for what you wanted: retail as a giggling insider's game.

If Hung On You sounded impossibly fey, it was generally more grounded than that. Hung On You's wares followed the spirited lead of John Stephen's earliest Carnaby Street creations: clothes with a sense of fun and sex and the slightest edge of daring, albeit of a later phase in the evolution of dandyish men's fashion. Stephen had opened the door for trendy young men to wear color and sensual fabrics and form-fitting cuts; at Hung On You, the imagination ran toward floral prints, mad artistic designs that covered whole garments, intimations of a bygone England in wide velvet collars and hand-embroidered jackets and clashes of stripes and polka dots and geometric patterns.

The genius of the enterprise was Michael Rainey, a latecomer to the Chelsea Set—chummy with the likes of Christopher Gibbs, the clotheshorse and gentlemanly rogue now doing business as an antiques dealer, and Tara Browne, the young heir to the Guinness fortune. Among his pals, according to fashion designer Ossie Clark, it was conceded that Rainey "had all the style." "Michael was just so wonderful and so handsome," concurred Anita Pallenberg. "I think everybody I knew had a crush on him in those days." He was a terrifically fashionable figure, both in the new sense and the old; in 1966, just nine months after opening his shop, he would marry Lady Jane Ormsby-Gore, one of the daughters of William David Ormsby-Gore, the fifth Baron Harlech: real aristocracy, flavored with a soupçon of Kennedy fairydust. "The Ormsby-Gores were exceptional," remembered Barry Miles of the family. "Lord Harlech was a chum of the Kennedys, and everyone thought he was going to marry Jackie Kennedy at one point. He was very Americanized, and they had become Americanized living in D.C. That experience certainly changed them."

Beatles and Stones and Donovan and The Who and that lot all shopped at Hung On You, and what they got when they did was, remembered Nik Cohn, an even more expanded sense of their selves: "When you shopped at Hung On You, you felt like both Oscar Wilde and Captain Marvel, locked up inside one body." It wasn't a cheap experience. A typical made-to-order suit ran upward of forty pounds—more than triple the average weekly wage. Michael Hollingshead, the man who might very well have been the first to bring LSD to London, was encouraged by friends to discard his bohemian graduate student wardrobe of jeans and sweatshirts for something more fashionable when he arrived in Chelsea to give people a taste of trips. Accordingly, he sent 'round to Hung On You for some clothes; he received a "huge pile" of fashionable togs, he recalled, plus a bill for six hundred pounds—more than the cost of a Mini Cooper automobile.

Such prices helped further distinguish the Carnaby Street shopper from the King's Road shopper. According to one guidebook of the time, "Carnaby Street's customers are (to use an unfashionable expression) working class. While they think nothing of spending a week's wages on a complete outfit, the class that shops on the King's Road will spend that sort of money on a *shirt*."

It had always been that way, at least as far as modish fashion went. Mary Quant's clothes were never very cheap. And the clothes by the important designers who followed her in Chelsea were similarly exclusive, none more so than the work of the enigmatic, bisexual gadabout named Ossie Clark. Clark specifically rebelled against the playful, puckish, geometric stuff that was Quant's metier by looking into fashion's past—the thirties and forties, especially—layered, floaty, romantic, wrapped designs made in bold colors out of such materials as chiffon and snakeskin and silk and marocain. Clark's stuff was fluid and drapey and revealing all at once—in key places it fit so exactly that you couldn't wear a bra or panties: "You're meant to be able to lift your dress up and pull down the top and have sex anywhere," he told Marianne Faithfull when she questioned him on one of his designs. And he had other little modern touches, too, such as discreet little pockets intended for the hiding of joints.

Clark began designing at Quorum in 1965 and hit his stride a few years later. His stuff wasn't cheap—his clientele included pop star's wives and girlfriends and actresses and aristocrats. And, like Quant, he ran socially with the people he dressed. But he was just as influential out in the wider world as Quant had been, pioneering a new look and inspiring others to copy it.

There wasn't a name for it yet, perhaps because there was such an eclectic look to the various designs. "They were lovely," remembered *Vogue* editor Marit Allen. "They weren't tacky. They were quite luscious. They were like the Matisse paintings of women wearing Moroccan things. Things that are draped and eclectic necklaces from different cultures—jewelry and great big chunks of African beads. It was part of a big opening up to the whole world." Eventually, it came to be called flower power and then just hippie, a completely new sensibility yet again from the smart, sexy things with which Quant had created her revolution, yet for sale right there on the very same street.

By 1966, the King's Road was a nest of Clarkish designs just as it had earlier been filled with Quant imitations. Wherever an empty storefront became available, another boutique with a titillating sobriquet seemed to mushroom up: Forbidden Fruit, Mr. Freedom, Gloryhole, Dandie Fashions, Just Men, Through the Looking Glass, Mitsukiku, Mexicana, Ad Hoc, Hem and Fringe, Just Looking, Skin, Clobber, Blast Off: It never seemed to end. "Shops came and went so fast you never remembered their names," said Alexandra Pringle, a literary agent and book publisher then growing up in the area; by 1967, nearly two thousand "boutiques" were listed in London's telephone directory.

The single most important of them all, you would get no argument, was Biba, which had four locations in its existence, none of which were on the King's Road but all of which were within a reasonable trot. At the dawn of 1966, Biba was still lodged in a two-room storefront on Abingdon Road, nearly Earl's Court, nowhere special but, increasingly, a vitally necessary weekly destination for young women who wanted to swing but had only a few pounds with which to propel themselves. "There should be a plaque on 87 Abingdon Road," declared one famous habitué of the shop. "It transformed the way the ordinary girl in the street dressed."

On Saturdays, teenage girls from all over the London area would race over to Abingdon Road and the piles of new, inexpensive clothes that awaited them. "Every girl in London would take their pay packet and spend what they could possibly afford," remembered Marit Allen. Jostling one another in the communal dressing room (the first in the city), the little London dollies might rub up against Cilla Black or Julie Christie or Chrissie Shrimpton, Cher, Barbra Streisand, Brigitte Bardot,

Samantha Eggar, Princess Anne: More than Quant's Bazaar, Biba was a truly egalitarian haven of the new and now. "In 1966," remembered *Vogue* editor Georgina Howell, "for fifteen pounds, the price of a Mary Quant party dress, you could walk out of Biba in a new coat, dress, shoes, petticoat and hat."

The secret, of course, was volume. Biba was said at one point to have the highest turnover per square foot of any store anywhere. Hulanicki would dream up designs, shoot them into a very quick production process and wait for the trucks to pull up at the store with the goods. Girls would hover around outside the front door waiting for deliveries, then set upon them like fashion-mad locusts. "The clothes changed all the time," remembered one of the clutching girls who made the weekly pilgrimage. "If you didn't buy what you wanted then and there, it wasn't worth coming back next week and hoping it would still be there."

In addition to its excitingly ephemeral stock, Biba was unique in its decor, a blend of art nouveau and Victorian with smatterings of tsarist Russia, the colonial Middle East and art deco. It was reflected in the dark, woody feel of the showroom, the antique hatstands that served instead of clothes racks, the selections of accessories—beads and floppy hats and scarves—and the colors that Hulanicki favored: not the bright, bold Day-Glo look that was so common in other shops' stock, but plum and chocolate and slate and other muted, saturated colors which, she felt, were favored by the English weather. "Luscious, bright colors were meant for sunny climates," she explained.

The first really important customer to favor Biba was Cathy Mc-Gowan, the *Ready, Steady, Go!* presenter, who had noticed a magazine spread about the shop and quickly made a new Biba dress a staple of her weekly wardrobe for the show. That meant that every Friday, tens of thousands of girls saw on TV what the week's stock looked like, and the queues began hours before the shop opened the next morning. "We had to go out with a damp cloth," Hulanicki remembered, "to wipe the nose marks off the window." Biba was a hit, too, with shoplifters (including one very famous movie actress): Hulanicki was always trying to devise new ways to keep the young trendies from waltzing off with the goods, but, she acknowledged, "When people are stealing, you're doing the right thing. It's when they stop stealing that you have to worry."

By March 1966, the business had outgrown the Abingdon Road location, and Hulanicki had found an empty grocery store on Kensington Church Street—four times the size of the first shop. Terrified that nobody would follow her there, she devised a gigantic moving party: McGowan, Cilla Black and all the attractive shop employees, the famed Biba Girls, hung off the back of a moving van as it wended its way a half mile to the new location, where a pop group was playing and champagne bottles were being uncorked.

In time, Biba constituted an empire. Hulanicki had put in an entire line of children's clothes, as well as shoes, cosmetics and household products like sheets and towels: Even more than Mary Quant's vision, Biba constituted a complete aesthetic a decade before Laura Ashley or Ralph Lauren tried the same trick. But it was a strange success: Unlike some other celebrated designers and boutique operators, Hulanicki felt herself scorned by the fashion press. "We were just a gimmick," she reckoned they thought. "The fact that we sold to real people and not just jet setters made them ignore us. The popular press, however, seemed to love us." The snobbery of fashion writers and magazines bled into the sort of society that Hulanicki began to frequent: In social settings, she would find herself being subtly insulted and fielding complaints about her store and its customers. "We'd never go out to parties when Biba was really popular," she said, "because the English like to go for your throat when you're a success." But, like John Stephen on Carnaby Street nearly a decade earlier, Hulanicki and Biba made a mark that couldn't be erased. Flowing, lithesome dresses in your grandmother's style for three pounds; miniskirts and ribbed T-shirts and fanciful blouses for two pounds; maxicoats that cost eight pounds and scarves and belts and fun jewelry that went for next to nothing: The Biba look was the look of the ordinary mid-to-late-sixties London girl. Gilded in Hulanicki's designs, the young chicks and dollies were ready for anything.

A good walk, say.

Once a hip young Brit of '66 was bedecked in some Chelsea finery—whether the disposable chic of Biba or the near-couture of Bazaar or Hung On You or the ironic outrageousness of Granny's or Lord Kitchener's, and boots, naturally, from the Chelsea Cobbler—he or she simply *had* to promenade. King's Road, once a place where people marketed and talked about the weather with neighbors and shopkeepers, became a parading ground for the city's young loons. On any given day, the free spirits could be seen darting in and out of boutiques or the handful of coffee bars and pubs along the street. Saturdays, however, was a holiday of nonconformity. From Sloane Square to World's End and back, the young scenesters flaunted themselves in a game of sartorial oneupsmanship and sexual provocation, the boys in whatever queer gear they could lay their mitts on—Arabian, Chinese, American Indian—the girls in skirts that seemed to rise and rise with each step: "All the young stoned harlequins," as John Pearse put it.

It became the world's most colorful and outrageous pageant—and it wasn't only fashionistas out to impress one another or get laid. Along with the boutiques there came restaurants and clubs catering to the celebrity crowd who were living and shopping in the area. Among the hippest was Alvaro, the restaurant opened in April 1966 by Alvaro Maccioni, the former headwaiter of the Trattoria Terrazza; so chic and exclusive was the new place, Maccioni explained, that "I had a telephone ex-directory. The visiting cards and matches had a picture of me with my finger up to my lips—'Sshhh!'—and it said, 'If you know who I am, don't say where I am.' And there was no address, no telephone number, no name, nothing."

With novelties like that making it a cultish destination, it could be argued that the King's Road had come full circle—hosting the full bloom of the revolution that it had been inspiring for a decade or so. But to old Chelsea hands—natives or longtime transplants—the transformations of the street were nightmarish. Some, like Alexandra Pringle (whose brother caught impetigo from an old army coat he'd bought in some trendy shop), pined for the village of their youth: "One could not even buy the ordinary stuff of life in the King's Road. There was no grocer anymore, no fishmonger or butcher," she explained. Worse, she said, the quality of the silly shops that had driven out the mainstays had itself declined: "There was no glamor now, only tat." "It had ceased to be any kind of a neighborhood," agreed David Puttnam. "It was kind of a social gathering point with little or nothing to do with satisfying local neighborhood needs."

For Christopher Gibbs, one of the first men to saunter down the street in bell bottoms, a floral shirt or something pink, the crowds marked the passing from an age of secretive conspiracy to one of mass market dullness. "I remember that you could walk down the King's Road and you could see six or seven people who had long hair and cool clothes and they looked like creatures from another planet, but you always knew all of them," he remembered. "And then suddenly you turned around and everyone was dressed like that—if they weren't wearing abandoned army uniforms from I Was Lord Kitchener's Valet. They were everywhere, perfect strangers, and one felt they were taking over."

If this was the attitude in open-minded Chelsea, just imagine how awful old-timers on Carnaby Street felt—or would've felt, if there'd been any old-timers there. That little dogleg throughway that even cab drivers might've had trouble finding readily a decade earlier had become a popular Saturday gathering place, fair enough. But now it was choked on almost a daily basis, especially in the warm months, and not necessarily with provincial pop bands looking for cool stage gear or suburban London kids who wanted to scope out the latest mod clobber and one another, but with tourists and journalists and camera crews and middle-aged neck craners, none of them fashionable. "Like any elitist club," reflected David Bailey, "once it became popular—once Sammy Davis Jr. started coming over to shop—you knew it was over." It had transformed from a scene into a spectacle.

The thing was most pronouncedly damned in "Dedicated Follower of Fashion," a blistering single by the Kinks, virtually the only English group that, owing to some bad breaks on an early tour of America, didn't have as large a following in the States as at home. Combining a singsong music hall melody and archly stilted diction (the "square" in "Leicester Square" was pronounced "skwah" in a perfect send-up of posh speech), it only just fell short of calling out by name the male peacocks who'd emerged in the Carnaby Street era—"the Carnabitian army" in singer-writer Ray Davies's saucy phrase. With damning descriptions of clothing trends—the stripes, the polka dots, the "frilly nylon panties"—and the self-satisfied, well-off fashionistas who pursued them, it was as acerbic as any English pop tune before the rise of punk—and as precisely aimed at its own audience as any gob of Johnny Rotten's spit.

Davies had captured the new London dandy in the net of his art, pinned him, framed him and, amazingly, sold him to himself and his friends; the song reached number four in the charts in early 1966, and surely some of the people who put it there were the very sorts out of whom the song was taking the piss. Pete Townshend, for instance, only a year or so removed from the days when he bragged—falsely, probably—of spending a hundred pounds weekly on Carnaby Street clobber, spoke of admiration for Davies's broadside: "I think 'Dedicated Followers of Fashion' are great." But then, Townshend had used clothes as a means to an end: He was trying to gain attention for his band, and the pop/mod thing was the pry bar that opened up their success. Davies, never so trendy, was calling a false spade for what it was—and he didn't care if it made him seem sour.

But maybe the joke was on him. Shopping on Carnaby Street was no longer a truly groovy experience but an exercise akin to that afforded by any tourist trap anywhere: The reputation of the street had grown so far beyond its origins that the spectacle of it consisted largely of the spectators themselves, strolling back and forth, thumbing through shabby merchandise, with less cool in the lot of them combined than in any single one of the street's first cultish customers.

Coming to Carnaby Street to see an authentic mod or swinger or, glory be, Beatle was as useless as going to Montmartre to see a real-life avant-garde painter; run out by tourists, high prices and the media, the coolest cats had moved on. Carnaby Street had long been mocked by the fashion establishment: The Menswear Association of Great Britain had lambasted its products as "the codswallop fashions of perverted peacocks." But now even those purported to be associated with the street's aesthetic—pop stars, hip aristocrats, gay men—had turned away. "The 'in' group wouldn't be seen dead in Carnaby Street by 1966," reflected George Melly, while *Design* magazine noted, " 'Carnaby Street' has turned into one of those phrases that sets the adrenaline pumping into your bloodstream"—not in a good way, it was clear. "Only suckers remained," sneered Nik Cohn.

And yet, business on Carnaby Street boomed: £5 million-plus in turnover in 1966 alone. Little of that was coming from the headline makers who were shopping for clothes on the King's Road or patronizing youthful bespoke tailors in Mayfair, such as Doug Hayward, Michael Fish and Rupert Lycett-Green. So if no well-known or fashion-conscious Londoners were shopping in Carnaby Street any longer, who was? "They're nobody in particular," said John Stephen, the king of the street. "They're Mister Average."

But, really, he might have more properly said Mister Average *Ameri-*

can. Thanks to a cover article in *Time* in April 1966, Americans had come to think of London as "the Swinging City" and were visiting the place in record numbers, transforming Carnaby Street into a stop on a sightseeing route and turning, in the way American enthusiasm has of doing, cultish modes of speech and fashion and sexuality into worldwide emblems of mass-market cool: bell bottoms and put-on accents and Union Jacks plastered all over everything.

The *Time* story was unique in a number of ways, not least of which being that the cover subject was not, as usual, an individual but a place or, more precisely, the *mood* of a place; rather than light on, oh, the Beatles, Prime Minister Harold Wilson, Oscar-winner Julie Christie or Mary Quant as a focus, the editors chose a zeitgeist approach. It was also, according to its writer, Piri Halasz, the first *Time* cover story ever written by a woman—and one sitting at a typewriter some three thousand miles from the city in question.

Halasz had first visited London as a schoolgirl in 1949 and then again in 1965, when she had been working at *Time* for nine years and was trying to acquire sufficient expertise in some subject that would allow her to write a cover story. During that visit, she remembered, "People in the bureau had taken the time to show me what Swinging London was. It was kind of irritating to me at the time, because I wanted to be taken seriously and wanted to be exposed to politics and the stories that there were. And instead I was taken to the Ad Lib. Murray Gart, the bureau chief, had just recently been transferred from the Chicago bureau, and his wife was still home in Chicago finishing out the school year with the kids, and Barry Farrell, the Paris correspondent, was in love with a researcher in the New York office and had just recently been transferred to Europe. So here were the three of us sitting in a row, and we were watching the dance floor, which was a little handkerchief with red, white and blue lights flying around it, and there were these beautiful young ladies in short skirts dancing, and on my right hand was Murray saying that his wife could still get into her wedding dress, and on my left hand was Barry saying he wished Marcia were there."

The concept of a cover story on London and its social revolution wasn't hers, Halasz revealed: "The story had originally been dreamed up in January 1966, as I understood, when a senior editor from the New York office had visited the London bureau. And everyone was talking about what a great party town London was. And somebody said, Wouldn't this make a great travel story for the 'Modern Living' section? The idea was always that it would be done in the spring because the spring was the beginning of the travel season and Americans would be going to Europe and they would want a travel story telling them where to go."

Halasz, however, worked in the far more serious "World" section of the magazine, where she was trying to convince editors to let her do a cover story on political situations in Germany, Greece or Indonesia. But news events put the damper on each of those pieces, she said, and "I was suddenly told that as a consolation prize I would get to write a cover story on London.

It was like the last week of March that I was told that we would do it the following week. I sat down and wrote what are known as queries: The process is group journalism and everyone gets into the act. I had all these little rat scraps of notes: pretty girls and short skirts and good times. The most substantial contribution was from a correspondent named Peter Forbath. His idea was that London was the city of the sixties and had replaced Rome, which was the city of the fifties. And that was my lead, and it was his idea.

The queries went out on Saturday; the files came back on Tuesday and Wednesday. We sent queries out to other capitals in Europe to find out if other people thought that London was such a big deal and various bureaus in the United States to find out if American teenagers thought England was the be-all and end-all. Simultaneously, our photographers were taking pictures all over London.

The piece Halasz put together was part social analysis, part cultural exposé, part travelogue; along with a portfolio of color photos, the magazine printed a map of central London indicating where the most fashionable shops, restaurants, clubs, galleries and casinos could be found. "It was packaged for the American market and it was designed to appeal to American tourists," Halasz explained. "Half of it is written about what England was and half was kind of written for a tourist who would want to take it along and read it."

The story was given a fair going-over by editors, Halasz said, and it was finally given a headline by managing editor Otto Fuerbringer: "You Can Walk Across It on the Grass." The title referred to the chain of parks that allowed pedestrians to make a trip across central London into a veritable country ramble. But it had another obvious meaning: London was a cool place to wander around stoned. Amazingly, neither Fuerbringer nor anyone on his staff heard the pun on marijuana in the phrase: "There were only two things that Fuerbringer did to that story," said Halasz. "One was to change the title, and the other was to delete a reference to pot parties in Chelsea. It could have been an unconscious slip on his part."

When the story hit the streets in mid-April, Halasz recollected, "The readers of *Time* were mostly horrified. They were conservative for the most part and it struck them as sinful and decadent, and they loved the old England of tea and scones and lavender and half-timbered houses. And they were upset by what was happening to their beloved country. And then there were people who thought it was perfectly marvelous and loved every bit of it."

Reaction, Halasz learned, was similarly mixed on both sides of the Atlantic.

Jane Ormsby-Gore was interviewed, and there was a quote in the story that was really suggestive. It sounded as though she was sleeping with her boyfriend and she didn't care who knew it. And I was concerned about that, because I didn't know what kind of young lady she was. In '66 there were young ladies who wanted their private lives to be kept private, and there were young ladies who didn't care. And when the story finished, I sent a checking query to London, and I said, "Are you sure this quote is okay to use?" Because I didn't know. Forbath, the correspondent who had interviewed her, was recently divorced and not very high on womanhood in general, and I was afraid that he had taken her out to lunch and maybe they'd had a little too much to drink and she had said this and hadn't realized how it would look to print. Anyway, the answer came back, "Okay to use," and we used it. And it wasn't okay. She was furious. When I got over there I called her up to invite her to lunch to try to make it up to her. And she said, "Uncles understand about these things, but I have aunts. And the aunts didn't understand." I'm sure she didn't mind her friends knowing, but *Time* magazine had like sixteen million readers at that point.

Halasz was hardly the first writer to attempt to capture the wild variety of novel goings-on that had enlivened London in the previous half decade: From the newly launched color supplements in the major Sunday newspapers to the revivals of such long-standing consumer magazines as *Queen* and *Man About Town* (known also as *Town*) to the invention of *London Life,* British journalists were making a healthy cottage industry out of that, thank you.

Halasz wasn't, either, the first writer to speak of "Swinging London" or even the first American: A year earlier, almost to the day, John Crosby, an American writing in the *Weekend Telegraph,* wrote a similar paean to the city's remarkable metamorphosis, "London, The Most Exciting City In the World." Structured similarly to Halasz's article, flitting about from scene to scene and hep cat to hep cat, Crosby's piece was both more blatant in its lecherous voyeurism ("Young English girls take to sex as if it's candy and it's delicious . . . English girls walk like huntresses, like Dianas . . .") and more unlikely in its claims for an overall renaissance in British culture (in a paragraph near the end, it even proffers a new theory of the cosmos by a Cambridge physicist as evidence of the boom).

And after Crosby but before Halasz there had been Roger Miller, the easy-on-the-ears, quasicountry American pop singer, and his "England Swings," an insipid little ditty about "bobbies on bicycles," "dapper men with derby hats and canes" and "the rosy red cheeks of the little children." Bouncy and vacant with its emblematic chorus—"England swings like a pendulum do"—it was a Top 20 hit in both the U.S. and England (where it was released twice).

Such was the reputation of the city's energies—its swing—that no less a curmudgeon than V. S. Naipaul was called upon in the first issue of *London Life* in October 1965 to, predictably, cast a pall over the party. "I can see that there are many young singers about," he admitted, "and that their foreign tours have replaced those of royalty as a cause for national cheering. . . . I can see that there are interesting designers of clothes and other things and photographers and models influencing the taste of millions." But, finally, he had his dig: "This great, swinging city always remains something out there, to which other people have access."

But none of these other advertisements for (or screeds against) Swinging London had anything like the impact of the *Time* cover—on either side of the Atlantic. In London, the *Time* piece was taken by just about everybody who'd been early onto the scene or prominent in it as its death knell, even as it was published at what could rightly be considered the height of the city's cool cachet. *Queen,* that regular barometer of what was cool and worthy on the scene, soon after whined, "London? No, not more about London!" and ran a tirade by Anthony Blond entitled "Swingers: I Hate You," which specifically charged that *Time's* Swinging London was a fantasy world far beyond the means of most Londoners: "A few people *can* afford this kind of life in London and writer Halasz only met and only quotes these few."

What had been going on had hardly been a secret—or as exclusive as some might have liked—but people who were being held up as Eminent Swingers (or, in the title phrase of a journalistic book being written at the time, Young Meteors) were suddenly and loudly disparaging the scene they were being taken to exemplify. When someone in a shop where Terence Stamp was browsing called some item "swinging," the actor muttered, "that bloody expression." A theater director, when asked if London was swinging, told a reporter, "If you mean jazzing away the evening, then I suppose it does. But swinging means being with it on all points. California swings: that's the place." Pop critic Nik Cohn, turning his wrath from Carnaby Street tourists to the In Crowd proper, spoke of "a period of great flamboyance and smugness and decadence, during which nothing seemed to exist beyond sitting in Italian restaurants and buying clothes and getting stoned." (Later, he would similarly brand Swinging London "a media myth, a couple hundred people who propped each other up while the rest of London went about its drab way.")

For decades, Swinging Londoners pointed fingers at *Time* for ruining through publicity something for which, in truth, publicity was mother's milk. And considering what it wrought, they couldn't be blamed.

Initially, there was a flurry of imitative articles in *Esquire, Life* and various other American publications. A brilliant parody of these appeared in *London Life*, which tried—with a lack of success so complete that it *had* to be predetermined—to follow Halasz's lead by seeking evidence of swing in pubs, clubs, theaters, boutiques and art galleries. The story was illustrated with photos of American humorist Allan Sherman running about to both famous new hot spots and typical old English settings with a copy of the Swinging London issue of *Time* in hand, trying to get with it; he didn't. Another send-up aired on Peter Cook and Dudley Moore's *Not Only . . . But Also* TV series; John Lennon played the liveried doorman to a Swinging London club called the "Ad Lav"—actually a public men's room—while Cook portrayed an American TV commentator, Hiram J. Pipesucker Jr., who hands Lennon a five-pound note to gain entry. The joke was that the club, clearly labeled "Gentlemen," is in fact a public toilet.

Soon enough, visiting Yanks in search of swing wouldn't even need that copy of *Time*, either. Within a year of Halasz's article, no fewer than four books propounding to offer the inside skinny to the world's coolest city appeared: *Len Deighton's London Dossier*, an omnibus edited by the spy novelist and gourmet columnist; *The New London Spy: A Discreet Guide to the City's Pleasures*, edited by journalist Hunter Davies; *Swinging London: A Guide to Where the Action Is* by Karl Dallas; and *A Swinger's Guide to London* by Halasz herself.

Of course, the very coolest Americans had been making their way to London for several years, drawn by the Beatles and the Stones, the clothes, the rumors of sexual liberty and the work and play opportunities for people doing new and exciting things.

In January of 1966, the Robert Fraser Gallery hung "Los Angeles Now," a show of new young painters and photographers from California, among them Dennis Hopper, the wild Method actor and lifestyle experimentalist who'd taken up art collecting and photography during the first of the forced hiatuses from the movie business his hot head had earned him. "London was such a concentrated thing," Hopper remembered. "In America, you were in New York or L.A. and it wasn't just one place. In London if you went to hear music in a club, you'd see everybody: musicians, actors. You'd go into Annabel's and you'd see musicians, actors, lords and ladies. I remember seeing Peter O'Toole and Richard Burton trying to drink each other under the bar. But that was the high end. You'd go into the funkiest clubs and it was the same. I remember going to see Georgie Fame and the Blue Flames, he was so hot, and wherever he was playing everybody seemed to end up at one point or another."

There were others: Lenny Bruce for his appearances at the Establishment Club; Andy Warhol, to dig the scene, show some work and stir things up; Allen Ginsberg as a sometime regular on the London party and literary scenes. William Burroughs lived now and then in St. James and Earl's Court; socialite Baby Jane Holzer gushed about the Ad Lib in the pages of *New York* magazine to writer Tom Wolfe, who did several London stories during the period.

Cassius Clay returned in 1966, as undisputed heavyweight champion of the world and renamed Muhammad Ali, drawn not by magazine writings or tour guides but the prospect of two paydays: a May rematch with Henry Cooper at Highbury Stadium (once again, the ref stopped the fight after Cooper's left eye opened like a burst dam, this time in the sixth round, and this time Ali wasn't knocked down) and an August bout against a pug named, of all things, Brian London at Earl's Court. That fight lasted only to the third round; *The Times* called it "a public execution"; afterward, at the Trattoria Terrazza, Terence Stamp talked it over with actor Laurence Harvey, who'd been there: "Did you get excited, Larry?" "I simply called for the ref to stop the fight." "When that flurry came in the third?" "Actually, no: when Mr. Brian London removed his dressing gown."

If Ali was knocking London out, both literally and figuratively, Bob Dylan, another key figure in this American Invasion, was blowing it up. Dylan liked the new London and its stars: he was fond of the Beatles—he turned them, famously, onto pot—and he sang mischievously in 1964's "I Shall Be Free Number 10" about the strange new things going on in the city: "It's nothin'," he says about some mysterious "thing" he reckons his listeners are curious about, "It's somethin' I learned over in England!"

In 1965, Dylan had come through town with his air of smoke and mystery and vituperation, a folk-singing poet and sneering whelp with his own entourage, including a muse (Joan Baez) and a filmmaker (D. A. Pennebaker, whose magnificent *Don't Look Back* resulted). He'd partied with the Beatles, Ginsberg and Marianne Faithfull and made a mockery of poor Donovan, just a kid really, barely eighteen, whom the British papers insisted on comparing to Dylan. When they finally got together at the nonstop party Dylan was hosting at the Savoy Hotel, Donovan played his fey little Dylanesque tune "To Sing for You" to the modest approval of the assembled, even Dylan, who said, "Hey, that's a good song, man"; then Dylan took the guitar and played the first two verses of *his* new song, the classic kiss-off "It's All Over Now, Baby Blue," pointedly singing the title phrase right at Donovan, who sat fetally, smiling and smoking and watching the chord changes and working his jaw and looking like a man resigning himself to the fatal tug of a riptide.

On his spring of 1966 trip, Dylan picked on someone more his own size: namely, his big English audience, who were just as earnest about folk purity as the Americans who booed him in recent concerts in New York when he'd made the leap from solo acoustic performance to fronting an electric band. Once again, he partied with his mates—he and John Lennon took a boozy drive one afternoon, with Lennon mercilessly baiting the carsick Dylan—and once again he brought along a film crew led by D. A. Pennebaker. But when he played, he evoked not the swoony, attentive passion of the previous tour but opposing waves of anger and adoration. In Swinging Manchester, Dylan was derided by one zealot as a "Judas," but the London crowd, if it included some dissenters, was cooler, and to many at the concert the event was electrifying and uniting. The folkies who attended the Royal Albert Hall gig seemed determined to make a spectacle of exiting when Dylan and The Band started their electric set, but the more with-it people who stayed—longhairs in wild clothes—seemed suddenly to realize how many they'd become: "All these fuckers who looked like us!" remembered editor and musician Mick Farren.

And just a few weeks after Dylan, another American outrage exploded off of Hyde Park with the opening of the London Playboy Club, a £1.6 million celebration of female pulchritude and high living complete with restaurants, nightclub, a casino and members' flats and suites available for rent by the day, week and month. The Playboy Club was the pride of Victor Aubrey Lownes III, an educated Chicagoan who had moved to London at the end of 1963 to supervise the establishment of the growing Playboy empire's first international operation. Lownes had joined Hugh Hefner's organization nearly eight years earlier, when he'd left his wife and children to seek out hedonistic pleasure in life. With Playboy he found that and more—namely, a chance to exercise entrepreneurial instincts that he'd never had sufficient capital of his own to follow. He had helped build both the Chicago and the New York Playboy Clubs, and he was thus a natural to head the London outfit.

In London, Lownes lived in pharaonic splendor in a mansion in Montpelier Square that doubled as Playboy's base of operations. He entertained such visiting Americans as Woody Allen, Warren Beatty, Telly Savalas and Judy Garland and such locals as Michael Caine, Laurence Harvey, Terence Stamp and the odd Beatle. He ran wildly and with a wild crowd: An early sampler of some of the first stash of LSD to enter the U.K., he turned Roman Polanski onto the drug at a party and shared some with his dentist, who, in turn, dosed John Lennon and George Harrison with it. There were women—*many* women—and there was the business of opening the club, which, with his right-hand man Tony Roma (who would become famous in his own right as the founder of a chain of rib joints), he did.

The London Playboy Club opened in 1966 to sold-out membership and a star-studded gala. "I opened the Playboy Club," remembered Woody Allen. "I did the opening night party as a favor to Hefner, the opening night show." The place became something of a clubhouse for visiting Yanks in the coming years, Allen recalled: "I spent a lot of time in London because I was working on *Casino Royale* as an actor, and it was such a screwed-up production that I was there for months and months and months, getting paid good money and high per diem and they didn't even get to my part for months. So I was gambling and playing poker games all night with the cast of *The Dirty Dozen* that was there: Telly Savalas, John Cassavetes, Charlie Bronson and Lee Marvin. It was the most swinging place."

There were plenty of Brits in residence at the Playboy Club, too, especially in the casino, which was one of the most lucrative in London. In its best years, it returned more than 900 percent on its overhead, posting multimillion-dollar gains and drawing the scrutiny of English gaming authorities—who came away declaring that the operation was completely clean and that the complaints against it were likely fabricated by a jealous competitor who, in the midst of this remarkable British boom, was obviously galled to see Americans doing better at anything.

Playboy's claim to the scene may have been hard for some to swallow, but that was nothing compared to the next American sensation to hit London. On September 25, in front of a very lucky few scenesters assembled at the Scotch of St. James, the pop world's favorite intimate gathering spot, a black guitarist, who looked, in the words of one witness, "like the wild man of Borneo," took the stage and jammed. It wasn't a scheduled gig—he only had a seven-day visa that banned him from work, even unpaid work—and his clothes weren't especially outrageous, as he hadn't yet had a chance to hit the boutiques. But there was the sort of hush in the air that night that might greet the long-awaited appearance of a famous recluse. Jimi Hendrix, with his penumbra of hair, his left-handed guitar and his stupefying talent, had arrived.

Over the coming weeks, while Hendrix and his manager, Chas Chandler, bassist of the recently disbanded Newcastle R&B group the Animals, fleshed out a backing band, Hendrix sat in for a few numbers with several acts at the Scotch, Blaise's and other venues. Like the LSD that was spreading through the city, he blew people's minds, and not just with his unimaginable virtuosity: Hendrix adorned his lithe form in the wildest outfits he could find—skin-tight pants in sensual textures and flamboyant colors, shirts in the most fanciful patterns, headbands and scarves and, famously, a military jacket from Portobello Road. Women went crazy for him—he was slender and soulful and soft-spoken and an experienced and uninhibited lover. He looked like nobody else, he sure as hell *played* like nobody else and he frankly made the most important guitarists in London—Eric Clapton, Jeff Beck and Pete Townshend among them—piss their pants.

For a decade, these suburban white English boys had immersed themselves in the music of impoverished black Americans: blues, R&B, jazz. They had learned the craft well enough that they'd been able to emulate it and turn back and peddle it in the States, never failing to credit their inspirations but not exactly looking to share their royalties, fame or women with, oh, Son House. And now along came this guy who not only had an authentic claim to the musical and cultural heritage they emulated but who could play like a god in both the original idiom and in their version of it—and who seemed freer and wilder and cooler—and they were just stunned.

Beck got a load of Hendrix jamming one night and, so he claims, went home to tell his wife he would have to find a new line of work. Townshend and Clapton, though their rivalrous friendship was still very new and fragile, made a date to go to the movies together so they could talk privately about how they might respond to this extraordinary challenge. Members of the Beatles and the Rolling Stones, bands with enormous followings who had already carved out territories of their own, could afford to be magnanimous toward this new genius, but even they suffered by comparison: Hendrix "made Jagger look like Shirley Temple," wrote George Melly.

By the end of 1966, Hendrix and his English bandmates, drummer Mitch Mitchell and bassist Noël Redding, had coalesced as the Jimi Hendrix Experience, played small tours in France and Germany, dominated the club scene in London and recorded their first Top 10 hit, a slow, sexy version of the Leaves' "Hey Joe." At the start of the new year, they began recording an LP, *Are You Experienced?*, which would yield two more Top 10 singles and spend thirty-three weeks on the album charts alongside *Sgt. Pepper's Lonely Hearts Club Band*.

Various American acts had managed to make their presence felt on the London music scene throughout the first half of the sixties: Dylan, the Beach Boys, a number of soul and R&B performers from the Motown, Stax and Atlantic stables and, most recently and perversely, the Monkees, mocked openly as the Pre-Fab Four. But Hendrix, it seemed, might very possibly be enough to turn back single-handedly the assembled force of the entire British Invasion. He was as modern as anyone in London, he was more rooted in the blues than any Englishman could hope to be and he had populist instincts that he somehow managed to blend with a genuine avant-garde sound.

The irony was, of course, that Hendrix couldn't have done it in the States. In America, he was a struggling session guitarist from Seattle who'd moved to New York to be around the folk rock scene and play at some of the more daring clubs in Greenwich Village. It was a Brit who found him there, it was Brits in a British club who recognized his brilliance the moment they beheld it, it was Brits who dressed him and joined him in his band and recorded him and sent him out into the world an instant superstar. They had to: His realness, his awesomeness, his blackness overwhelmed them. He would destroy them and they would respect him for it, the prophet of their downfall, the first American to outplay them at their own game, celebrated by them as he conquered them and yet entirely needful of their blessing to get so much as even noticed back at home.

On the other hand, London could still pump out the sensations as quick as the world could shift gears to ogle them.

And in 1966, nobody there was a greater sensation than an eighty-seven-pound sixteen year old from Neasden, northwest London, born Lesley Hornby but known to a world she'd hit like a red-hot meteorite as Twiggy.

Twiggy was the anti-Hendrix: childlike, sexless, domestic, familiar, painfully ordinary and very, very white. She didn't, like Jean Shrimpton, seem an epitome of wholesome English girlitude, nor, like Marianne Faithfull, did she mix a sense of the angelic with a lusty body: At the fullness of her fame, her bust measured thirty inches, her waist twenty-two, her hips thirty-two. She presented, rather, to the untrained eye, the most quotidian of images, the sort of schoolgirl who fainted at Beatle shows, devoured *Rave* and *Fab* magazine, shopped on Carnaby Street—*still*—and swelled the lesser dance palaces.

Just the previous year, little Lesley had been just another skinny little mod girl freezing in a plastic mac and Hush Puppies in the rain outside a North London music hall, screaming as the Beatles or the Kinks or the Dave Clark Five drove up. She was attending Brondesbury and Kilburn School for Girls and working as a Saturday girl at a Queensway hair salon for two and a half pounds. She had a little more style than some of her peers—she used to sew her own outfits and augment those with cheap goodies she bought at Biba, and she had this thing she did with her eyes, an elaborate treatment she'd devised that made her eye socket look deep and her lashes take on the texture of caterpillar legs. But in the main she was as ordinary as could be.

One day in early 1965, she met the older brother of one of her coworkers at the salon. He was pure shady rake: ten years older than her, separated from his wife and daughter, running a stall at the Chelsea Antiques Market after flopping as a hairdresser, bouncer, boxer, debt collector, softcore porn merchant, shill to a auctioneer and so forth. He dressed flash and drove a Triumph Spitfire (not his own) and he called himself Justin de Villeneuve (JayDeeVee to chums), though he was none other than the same cheeky Nigel Davies who'd gotten himself fired from Vidal Sassoon's first salon years before for brazenness and playing hooky.

"She had the loveliest face I'd ever seen," Justin remembered. So even though he kept a string of women handy, he began seeing a lot of the girl in the coming months, picking her up after school in his car, visiting the family home (where he got the pointedly cold shoulder from Lesley's dad) and, finally, the first kiss: love, requited, for both of them.

He was convinced that Lesley could do some modeling, but no one else was: An editor he knew at *Queen* simply brushed her off—she wasn't a professional, and they only worked with girls from agencies; another, at the *Women's Mirror*, decided that she was too tiny to do real modeling but she might be pretty enough to do head-and-hair work. They offered her a year's contract at nine pounds a week for one day a week.

She would need her hair done, though, and by a professional. They booked her into one of the poshest salons in town: Leonard of Mayfair, Upper Grosvenor Street. Lesley was totally cowed—"People like me didn't go to places like that"—but after a few minutes, Justin was running the place: Leonard of Mayfair turned out to be the very same Leonard Lewis he'd been matey with at Sassoon's. Leonard, curious about whether the girl would be suited for a new cut he had in mind, asked if they wouldn't mind visiting a photographer he knew 'round the corner named Barry Lategan. A few days later they returned, after Leonard had done the exciting new cut he'd envisioned for her, and Lategan took some shots to hang on the salon wall.

And so it was that a few days after *that* that Deirdre McSharry, fashion editor of the *Daily Express*, sat in Leonard's salon, having her hair done and looking at the picture.

"I don't know that girl. Who is she?"

Leonard told her how to contact Lesley, and she called and asked if she and Justin would come to Fleet Street to meet and talk. Twiggy wore a pair of bell bottoms she'd made and a ribbed polo shirt; the newspaper took a few pictures, and she and McSharry talked about her family, her daily life, her likes and dislikes, her ambitions. Then Twiggy and Justin went back home.

Back in Neasden, Twiggy woke up and scoured the *Daily Express*, looking for a little line or two about her conversation with McSharry. On the morning of February 23, her father came bursting into her bedroom with the paper. Opening it to the center spread, Twiggy received the shock of her life: There were two huge photos of her—one of Lategan's head shots, one from the day she visited the newspaper. There was a sizeable and full-of-praise article. And there was a banner headline: "I NAME THIS GIRL THE FACE OF '66."

"I went," Twiggy recalled, "from total obscurity to full-time working model in a matter of days."

She did dozens of shoots, learning on the job from photographers, editors and other models. She became a sensation. Fashion writers were inspired into purple paroxysms: One said she bore "the strange appraisal of a Martian"; another described her as "one half orphan of the storm, the other purely aesthetic"; said society photographer Cecil Beaton, "She's a fairy! She's Ariel! She doesn't belong on the Earth." The *Daily Sketch* sent her to Paris to review the new couture season in the form of letters home to her mom, and her published reaction to the first clothes she saw—that they were okay for middle-aged women but too old-fashioned for her—got her banned from the rest of the shows. There were Twiggy jokes: She had to pass a place twice to cast a shadow on it, it was said; "Forget Oxfam: Feed Twiggy" read a semi-popular button.

The fashion world's highest nabobs weren't ready for her: *Vogue* hired her only to shoot her feet—so much smaller than the other girls'; Irving Penn refused to shoot her at all—"When you get a little more experience, I'll see you again"; and she became the subject of an explicit boycott by the Terrible Three of London fashion photography—David Bailey, Terence Donovan and Brian Duffy.

This last ruckus began when David Montgomery refused to shoot Twiggy if Justin insisted on being in the room. Twiggy had already been shot by Donovan, but he and the others now lined up in pronouncing the model an unfit subject: "Twiggy is too amateur in her approach," Bailey was quoted as saying. "Grossly unprofessional."

It was easy to see what it was really about: To date, the most important models—Jean Shrimpton, Celia Hammond, Sue Murray—had been discovered by the photographers themselves and were often romantically involved with them. Even with that sort of support, it might be years before they became top models. Here, however, was a new girl with a Svengali already on her arm—and not only that but an East End boy with gumption just like the original lads. They didn't like the cut of him, plain and simple, and he would have to go before they allowed Twiggy into their world.

Before long, Twiggy commanded as much as eight hundred pounds a day for modeling. She was able to sell the clothes she made, developing a line of dresses to go along with the hip-hugging trousers that she'd worn in the *Daily Express*. Together with Justin she began a business, Twiggy Enterprises, and entertained all sorts of new offers for licensed merchandise: wigs and makeup and T-shirts and stockings and hand bags and lunch boxes and Thermoses and board games and dress-up kits for little girls and life-size mannequins with her face for store windows. (Actually, these clothes dummies were more than life-size, as the manufacturers and their customers agreed that Twiggy's figure—which she herself derided as "not really what you'd call a figure, is it?"—needed augmenting about the bosom to make a proper clothing display.) She got fifty thousand pounds from Monsanto to model their new synthetic fabrics. She had a deal with Yardley for a new line of eye makeup. She cut a record (!), "I Need Your Hand in Mine," that did nothing in the U.K. but was a number-one hit in Japan, where at one point she appeared on twelve magazine covers at the same time. The American toy manufacturer Mattel gave her $40,000 as a down payment on a line of Twiggy dolls, then only made a sample run of them, preferring to eat the money than launch a competitor to its lifeblood of Barbie dolls.

All of this money, just like the few pounds a week they'd made on her pants at the Chelsea Antiques Market, was split fifty–fifty by Twiggy and Justin—although she never really received an accounting. They did everything first class, and she got cash and clothes and whatever else she wanted whenever she asked, but Justin had a line of fabulous cars and watches and suits that got people talking. In *Private Eye* he was belittled as "Justinit for the Money" and "Justin de Vilepoove." He laughed all the way to the bank.

And they both laughed all the way to America. For not only was

ALL THE YOUNG
DUDES, PART II:
MAKING THE SCENE
ON THE KING'S ROAD
IN FUR, SILK AND VELVET.
(REX FEATURES)

PRETTY THINGS:
THE PRIVATE PARTY
OPENING SIBYLLA'S,
JUNE 22, 1966.
AMONG THE DANCERS,
MICHAEL RAINEY AND
JANE ORMSBY-GORE.
(GETTY IMAGES)

THE $5,000 TRIM:
VIDAL SASSOON
ON A
HOLLYWOOD
SOUNDSTAGE
WITH
MIA FARROW.
(CAMERA PRESS)

NOWHERE MAN:
BRIAN EPSTEIN,
NOT LONG
BEFORE THE END.
(CAMERA PRESS)

HI, MOM!
ROBERT FRASER
(NEAR WINDOW)
AND MICK JAGGER
LEAVE COURT,
JUNE 29, 1967.
(GETTY IMAGES)

DANDIES ON TRIAL: MICK AND KEITH, MAY 10, 1967. (GETTY IMAGES)

THE WAY ONE LIVED
IN CHELSEA,
CIRCA HIGH '60s:
SIR MARK PALMER
AT HOME.

(GETTY IMAGES)

IF ONLY BRITAIN *HAD*
A DRAFT...: A CURIOUSLY
ILL-INSPIRED WHITEHALL
PROTEST MARCH.

(CAMERA PRESS)

SORT OF
BAUDELAIRE-ISH:
JAMES FOX AND
MICK JAGGER
PHOTOGRAPHED
BY CECIL BEATON
ON THE SET OF
PERFORMANCE.
(CECIL BEATON,
CAMERA PRESS)

THIS YEAR'S MODEL:
DAVID BAILEY AT THE NOVEMBER 1969 CLUB DELL'ARETHUSA PARTY FOR
GOODBYE BABY & AMEN WITH, FROM LEFT, MISS 1963, CHRISTINE KEELER;
MISS 1969, PENELOPE TREE; AND MISS 1966, MARIANNE FAITHFULL. (GETTY IMAGES)

Little girl lost: Marianne Faithfull, just days after the death of Brian Jones and days before her suicide attempt in Australia, sits with son, Nicholas, on her shoulders as Mick Jagger performs at the Stones' Hyde Park concert. (Getty Images)

Stoned: Terence Stamp on the Arizona set of *Blue*.

(Lawrence Schiller, Camera Press)

Twiggy the first instant supermodel and the first girl superstar of the sixties, she was the last great British export to the States, the final swell of the British Invasion, yet another novelty—a skinny Union Jill—which everybody in American had to have a piece of. In early 1967, barely a year after she'd sat for those first photos by Barry Lategan, Twiggy had amassed sufficient offers from American magazines, businesses and photographers to accept an invitation to come to New York.

She made only a slightly smaller splash than the Beatles had three years before.

After initially being denied a passport by the Foreign Office—who feared she might be a pawn in some sort of white slavery ring (!) and needed coaxing from not only Twiggy's parents but Prince Phillip (!!), who published a letter in the *Daily Sketch* agreeing that so valuable an export as she deserved better treatment—she and Justin and his old mate Teddy the Monk, who served as bodyguard and factotum, landed at Kennedy Airport to a mob of reporters and photographers and a helicopter waiting to take them directly to Manhattan.

If the press conference caught them aback—"What do you think of America, Twiggy?" "What do you eat?" "What do you have that all the other models in the world don't have?" "Do you think you're a typical English girl?" "Are you beautiful?"—then the helicopter ride was stunning: Photographer Bert Stern had been inspired in advance to have a number of headshots of Twiggy made into cardboard masks mounted atop little sticks that could be held at chin height; the helicopter pilot had one, as did the helipad crew, as would, in the coming days, crowds that Stern posed around Twiggy in an Automat, at the Central Park Zoo, on Fifth Avenue, in a staged ticker tape parade, all over town—Twiggys everywhere. The resultant shots of the real Twiggy standing amid crowds of bemasked pseudo-Twiggys brilliantly reflected both her wildfire fame and the instant commodification of her image.

As part of a documentary Stern was shooting for NBC television, Twiggy was interviewed by Woody Allen (whom she felt tried to belittle her) and had her hair cut by Leonard, who flew over separately for the big event. She appeared on Johnny Carson's *Tonight* show and was followed around town by a reporter from *The New Yorker*. She was shot by Richard Avedon for *Vogue* and nearly gobbled up in a riot when she went shopping at B. Altman's and emerged into a mob that wanted a piece of her; a quick-thinking security man lifted her up and plunked her to safety through the window of her limousine.

For much of the rest of their visit, Twiggy, Justin and Teddy the Monk lay low in an empty apartment that Bert Stern had lent them. They did, however, make it over to Arthur, the New York nightclub acclaimed by Manhattanites to be the Big Apple's answer to a Swinging London hot spot.

Justin wasn't impressed: "Such a draggy place," he pronounced. "The dancers were so far behind. Arthur is four or five years behind clubs in England. You could go to Herefordshire and see clubs more swinging than that."

Ouch.

Actually, Justin was right: There *were* no clubs in America to compete with the new London clubs. In fact, at the way things were progressing in 1966, there were no clubs in *London* to compete with the new London clubs. The scene was spiraling into hysteria, each new club trumping the last.

Dolly's opened on Jermyn Street in the wake of the Ad Lib, attracting a crowd as fabulous and trendy as the Ad Lib ever had. The Speakeasy, with an Al Capone theme, opened above Oxford Street and catered to a more raucous crowd of rock journalists, groupies, rising bands and all-round rowdies: "A roadie's heaven," as one of its habitués remembered with a sneer. The Scotch of St. James held a unique spot in the firmament of post-Ad Lib night spots, partly because of its location just across Mason's Yard from the trendy Indica Gallery, partly because it was as exclusive as the Ad Lib had been; its management thought nothing of barring millionaires from the joint or tossing out a customer who was so uncool as to ask George Harrison for an autograph. But even at its acme it wasn't as beloved as the Ad Lib: "It's like a rhythm and blues Angus Steak House," groused David Hockney. "The chairs are so small it's like an organized children's tea party. I object to paying a pound for a drink at that kind of place. These places are my pet hates."

Out on the King's Road, Alvaro Maccioni, who had virtually been running his restaurant as a members-only club, finally went the full distance and opened Club dell'Arethusa, a proper club with a discotheque, an American bar, a restaurant and a desk that provided member services such as flat hunting and message taking: "the Che Guevara of restaurants," as he termed it. It was much loved by the pop stars in the King's Road scene for the superior sound in its discotheque. The reason, Maccioni explained, was that "it was *built* to be a discotheque. The dance floor was built separate from the rest of the building, with the bass underneath it buried in sand so that the floor had a vibration. And the walls were soft and didn't disturb the sound. It was so perfect that the Beatles and the Rolling Stones, when they wanted to hear their records, they tested acetates there."

But giddy and sensational as all these clubs may have been, none quite seemed so symptomatic of how self-reflective the London scene had become as Sibylla's, which opened in June 1966, just east of Piccadilly Circus on Swallow Street.

The premiere of the club was preceded by months of publicity, rumor and—the word wasn't in use then, but it would've been apt—hype. Part of this was due, undoubtedly, to George Harrison's small percentage of the business: a Beatle-owned discotheque! And part was due to a list of members and potential members so filled with great and trendy names that the club owners were offered a thousand pounds just for a copy of it (they refused—but told the press so, thus turning their discretion into a form of show-and-tell). But part was due, too, to the ripeness of the moment—the swingingness of the scene, its self-celebration, its self-awareness. Sibylla's was planned, built and launched as what one of its owners called "the first Classic London Discotheque." And the highwater mark of the whole shebang might've been the night the joint opened its doors.

Sibylla's got its start in March 1965 when three young men—ad copywriters Terence Howard and Kevin MacDonald and property dealer Bruce Higham—realized among themselves that they had a lot of strong opinions about what would constitute an ideal nightclub. They got to thinking that they might as well do it themselves—with the major obstacle being their lack of capital: "club-building green," as Howard termed it. They tried to raise it at first by calling on some rich friends—including Harrison—and managed to get about a third of what they thought they would need.

Their next inspiration was probably the one that made the club a hit even before it opened: They put together a list of people they knew who might want to invest in and/or join their club, a group that Howard called "the new boy network." "We discovered," MacDonald recalled, "that we knew a hell of a lot of people, people who were doing things in finance, architecture, press, pop and films."

Who were they? In the days when the club was still a notion, the owners wouldn't say exactly—"the kind of people the color supplements write about," Higham declared. He added that he imagined the club as a place "like the Ad Lib used to be. Everybody was there. I don't really know who Everybody is, but it was a very swinging clubby scene."

Actually, he *did* know who Everybody was: "Sometimes you go into a club, and everyone is swinging, and over in a corner you see three or four people looking at everyone else but who are somehow not part of the scene. Well, *they're* not Everybody. Everybody is the talented people, people who are good at something. It doesn't really matter *what* they're good at—photography, or modeling, or making love fantastically well three times a night. What they have is a kind of self-confidence, an awareness, which they transpose to their environment."

This was certainly not going to be the same happy accident that made the Ad Lib into the spontaneous orgy of mutual good feeling of just a few years earlier. Higham and company had identified an elite and were appealing to its sense of self-worth. Amid all the talk of classlessness and broken boundaries and such, a certain strain of hip had come to replace breeding, schooling and wealth as a means of separating one set of people from another. If the Chelsea scene of exaggerated fashions and experimental drug use exemplified one sense of the word "decadence," this was surely another: a self-congratulatory and exclusionary sect of insiders who doomed outsiders with a damning glance at their haircuts, wardrobes or bankbooks.

Of course, it worked. Of the two to three thousand names Higham, Howard and MacDonald collected, approximately one third—eight hundred—agreed to join for about eight pounds a year. The trio found a disc jockey who agreed with their conception of the mood, Alan Freeman ("Baby, if it's a palace you're building, then I'm there," he told them), and they came up with a muse after whom they would name the place, Sibylla Edmonstone, the twenty-two-year-old distant heiress to the fortune of Chicago department store magnate Marshall Field who spent her days working with handicapped children. All they required now was, um, a premises: Six months into the PR campaign, they still hadn't found a suitable location. And when they did, in November 1965, they were still short of money. Then somebody passed word to a chum, the young steeplechaser (and skirt-chaser) Sir William Pigott-Brown, and, voilà: In exchange for 25 percent of the business, he gave them what they needed.

Finally, after more than a year of clucking, a private party was held to open the club on June 22, 1966, followed by an official debut the following night. For the invitation-only party, the guest list consisted of owners, the people who helped build the club and the elite of the elite, including all four Beatles (with wives and dates); Mick, Brian and Keith of the Stones; photographers David Bailey and Terence Donovan; boutique owner Michael Rainey and various Ormsby-Gores; Julie Christie; Mary Quant and Alexander Plunket Greene; interior decorator David Mlinaric, who designed the place; Tara Browne; Celia Hammond; Mark Palmer; Jacqueline Bisset; Michael Caine; Sue Murray; John Barry; Andrew Oldham; Leslie Caron; Cathy McGowan and Roman Polanski. Several hundred of the paid-up members weren't invited: "I should think," Higham replied, when asked about this, "that they will say to each other, 'If *I* wasn't asked, *then who was?*' "

This exclusivity became a mark of Sibylla's. "It only needs a dozen idiots to ruin a club," Higham pronounced. Potential members were vetted by several layers of screening, the most important being that they would already be known to the owners and other members. "How many potential members whom we might want *are* there in London," asked Howard. The point was to keep people out so they'd be hungry for the experience: "What good is a discotheque?" asked Higham. "It's only successful if you can't get in." And to a large extent, it worked: In her *Swinger's Guide to London*, Piri Halasz said of Sibylla's: "At the moment, frightfully exclusive. If you're Sammy Davis Jr., they might let you in, but only if you book in advance."

At first, like so many other things that sprang up in the decade, Sibylla's boomed: The initial expenditures of £50,000 were justified after just a few months, when the owners turned down an offer of four times that for the joint. And a New York branch—watch out, Arthur!—

was planned. That never materialized and, in fact, Sibylla's barely managed to stay open for two years, such were the vagaries of fashion among its In Crowd membership. But for a moment, it was the place to see and be seen and prove yourself a qualified member of the swinging set. It was the tiny little central node of the nervous system of the elite stratum of the chic-oisie, the drawing room of Swinging London.

When he was researching the new London scene for a book in the summer of '66, journalist Jonathan Aitken wandered into the club to speak with Kevin MacDonald, and was given this astounding earful for his efforts:

> This club exists for people who can communicate with each other. A lot of people ring me up and say, "How do you become a member of Sibylla's?" Well, of course, anyone who had to ask how to get into Sibylla's wouldn't be a member. I mean, it's logical. If you were going to be a member here, you'd know how to be one. It's all communications. . . .
>
> This is Psychedelphia, man. It's all happening. Can you read me? No, well, I'll try and explain. You see, it's a dreamland, and to enjoy it you have to be dreaming. Everyone here's in touch. Sibylla's is the meeting ground for the new aristocracy, and by the new aristocracy I mean the current young meritocracy of style, taste and sensitivity. We've got everyone here (he clicked his fingers to emphasize the point), the top creative people (click), the top exporters (click), the top artists (click), the top social people (click) and the best of the PYPs (swingingese for Pretty Young People). We're completely classless. We're completely integrated. We dig the spades, man. Relationships here go off like firecrackers. Everyone here's got the message (click). Can you read it, man? Sibylla's is the message. We've married up the hairy brigade—that's the East End kids like photographers and artists—with the smooth brigade, the debs, the aristos, the Guards officers. The result is just fantastic. It's the greatest, happiest, most swinging ball of the century, and I started it!

What's as stunning as this paisley rhetoric—pure essence of blather, rancid as a vintage container of yogurt—is how hollow it turned out to be. On October 15, less than four months after his triumphant opening,

MacDonald hurled himself from a Chelsea rooftop to his death, leaving no note, no clue, no hints to friends that something was wrong. Just like that: 'bye. If he was King of the World, he sure had a funny way of showing it.

That wasn't the only death among the swinging set that year—less than two months after MacDonald's suicide, Tara Browne would wreck his car in South Kensington and pass from this life into immortality as the man who "blew his mind out in a car" in a Beatle song. But nobody paid too terribly much mind: The whole thing was too big to allow for even a friend's bizarre passing to intrude.

There were other signs, of course. In July, English outcry against America's military efforts in Vietnam exploded into violent protest outside the U.S. embassy in Grosvenor Square, the first of what would become a series of demonstrations against the war. More pointedly, the English economy was staggering: A seaman's strike had crippled international trade in the spring, and in July the Labour government tried to stall the choking effects of inflation by declaring a freeze on wages, prices and dividends.

Indeed, if you wanted to, you could make the case that 1966 was one of the *worst* years for Britons since the war. In the spring in a courtroom in Chester, south of Liverpool, a pair of young lovers were tried and convicted for the torture and killing of three children—the infamous Moors murders; in August, three policemen were gunned down in the street in Shepherd's Bush by an ex-soldier who had turned to robbery; in October, in Aberfan in the south of Wales, 144 people—116 of them children attending school—were killed by a sliding mountain of mining waste that came crashing into the village.

In many ways, England was a mess: Assessing the situation from the cool remove of the U.S., *The New York Times* said, "The atmosphere in London can almost be eerie in its quality of relentless frivolity. There can rarely have been a greater contrast between a country's objective situation and the mood of its people." A commentator in London looked around and saw "England sinking giggling into the sea."

And what seemed even worse was that the people on the scene itself knew quite well what they had done. The media attention, the international visitors, the new drugs—all of it conspired to give the scene a patina of lurid self-consciousness that went against the spontaneity of the initial era of Swinging London and made for something more cynical and sad.

"The hairdressers moved in," said journalist Peter Evans. "Instead of it being a pure, kind of small group, you'd go to your favorite place once it was exposed to the light, and it had kind of been fucked up. It was the beginning of the look-at-me restaurants where anybody went in who knew it was the place to be. Whereas before people didn't know where anyone was supposed to be except for a small nucleus of people. I suppose we're talking about a hundred, maybe several hundred people—but in a big town that's not many. That's all it came down to, but they fed off each other in a wonderful way."

Even Piri Halasz, who had inadvertently abetted the decline with her *Time* cover story, rued the changes. Visiting London some months after her cover story appeared, she said, "I was horrified at how the whole phenomenon of Swinging London had been cheapened and vulgarized. There were people selling guidebooks to Swinging London in Piccadilly Circus. It was really depressing. It was a kind of private thing, and the cover kind of publicized it and let tourists in on the phenomenon. It had been an insider thing and tourists were by definition excluded; and our cover was written for tourists and it invited tourists in by the mob."

But in the middle of the summer of '66, those sorts of qualms seemed absurd. History was simply too much on the side of the sunshine and the grooving and the fun.

One afternoon, for instance, with the help of a ball that bounced impossibly in the mouth of a soccer goal and a Soviet linesman who may have been handicapped in eyesight or political objectivity or both, England won the World Cup on the turf at Wembley against Germany— the Jerries pantsed in front of the whole world.

The Beatles and the Rolling Stones had new records in the shops. The girls were on the Pill and wearing their skirts shorter than ever. LSD was still legal. The weather was bright and clear—a mild summer for a welcome change. And now the sons of the men who had tried to bomb the city into the stone age just a generation before had been bested at England's national game.

You could look around with rose-colored granny glasses—bought, naturally, on Carnaby Street or at a King's Road boutique—and mistake what you saw for Paradise, Arcadia reborn, the point to which all civilization and history and culture had happily wended.

There had never, ever been a moment so sweet.

And nothing—nothing—could possibly happen to ruin it.

PART FOUR

WE ARE NOT WORRIED ABOUT PETTY MORALS

Along with the groupies, the big cars, the model girlfriends and the invitations to every hot shindig in town, the most visible perk of pop superstardom—the thing that separated the millionaire big boys from the blokes driving their own vans to their gigs—was the country house.

Long a standard of English aristocratic life—indeed, in many ways, the very basis of the class system, wherein serfs worked the estates of landlords—the grand manor with the high-flying name on splendid grounds was a sign of arrival that very, very few from the underclasses—or, in fact, from the worlds of art and culture—could aspire to. But with the advent of young men who wrote songs that sold millions of copies and who thus accumulated massive piles of royalty checks, young men whose city homes were besieged, literally, by adoring fans who deprived their heroes of even the pretense of privacy, estate agents of the bedroom communities in

Surrey, Kent, Essex, Buckinghamshire and Sussex found themselves showing historic properties to loons in outrageous costumes—and making sales.

The Beatles, naturally, were first: John and Ringo, the marrieds-with-children, moved into big suburban palaces among City gents and solicitors and their families near Weybridge, Surrey; George and Patti Boyd (later Harrison) took up residence at a cottage called Kinfauns in Esher; and Brian Epstein bought Kingsley Hill, a house near the sea in East Sussex. (Paul McCartney alone stayed in town, walled within the parklike atmosphere of his Cavendish Avenue digs in St. John's Wood.) They were followed, naturally, by the Rolling Stones: The ultradomestic Charlie Watts settled at Peckhams, a thirteenth-century home near Lewes on the Sussex coast; Bill Wyman bought Gedding Hall, way out in Suffolk, a property that entitled him to call himself Lord of the Manor of Gedding and Thormwoods; and Keith Richards, of all rootless people, found his own Sussex cottage near the sea in West Wittering, a house known as Redlands.

Of course, by "cottage," what was understood was a large home—many bedrooms, expansive grounds, some history. Parts of Redlands dated back to the twelfth century, and with its thatched roof, peekaboo upstairs windows, exterior half beams and honest-to-God moat, complete with ravenous families of rats, it seemed more like the seat of a grand Tudor family than the weekend retreat of a suburban boy who grew up to be a filthy rich guitar player—but, hey, such were the times. Inside, too, Redlands was not what it appeared at first view. With a nod toward the blended aesthetic of North African, medieval and pre-Raphaelite touches, it was a prime instance of mid-sixties London decadence: mauves and blacks and tapestries and fur rugs and priceless tables and elaborate hookahs and wall hangings and precious gewgaws and who knew what else.

"Redlands gave us a bit of a shock," remembered Police Constable Don Rambridge. "From the outside it's a really beautiful house. . . . It turned out to be a typical ravers' place. It really hurt looking at the inside."

How PC Rambridge came to be looking at the inside at all was one of the more sensational and scandalous stories of the day, a cataclysmic clash of Olde England and new, a test of democracy, liberalism and decency, a career-making and -destroying fiasco—and a wicked good tabloid yarn, complete with nude girls, corrupt cops, dissolute aristocrats, unrepentant celebrities, mean old judges, snitches, payoffs, a briefcase full of LSD and rumors of a chocolate bar being consumed in a fashion never dreamt of in its manufacturer's test kitchens.

The whole business began on February 5, 1967, when Mick Jagger and Marianne Faithfull were indulging in that most indulgent of London Sunday morning rituals: waking to breakfast in bed—croissants and coffee—and a big pile of newspapers, including the ne plus ultra of trashmongering scandal sheets, the *News of the World*.

No worries at all, a pure sycophantic lull, and then Jagger spat café au lait all over the sheets.

Splashed across a multipage spread was the latest installment of a multipart series entitled "The Secrets of the Pop Stars' Hideaway," an account of "Mick Jagger's" licentious, drug-fueled binge at Blaise's, the Kensington nightclub, during which he popped Benzedrine tablets like peanuts, bragged about using LSD with the Moody Blues at a house party in Roehampton and seduced two girls back to his flat with promises of hashish and other delights.

Jagger, who would sooner reenroll at the LSE to complete his economics degree than confide so frankly to a journalist, was sputtering mad. The whole thing was made up, he declared: a total fiction. Faithfull, though, sussed out the situation right away: "It's Brian," she told him, referring to Jagger's dissolute bandmate Brian Jones, whom they could both easily imagine acting so foolishly in front of a reporter with an open mike. "They've confused you with Brian. He's always going around telling everyone he's the leader of the Rolling Stones."

Jagger had for several years kept a scolding eye trained on Jones, a musical genius and insecure creep who couldn't be counted on but to stir up shit, threatening the band's ascendancy and too often stealing the spotlight as much with outré offstage behavior as with his virtuosic instrumental versatility and dashing fashion sense. If Faithfull's guess was right, and Jagger quickly considered that it was, then Jones had once again stepped in it. But he would be dealt with in private—there was a plan afoot to wrest him out of the band altogether; the *News of the World* would need to be taught a more public lesson.

That night, Jagger and the Stones performed on *The Eamonn Andrews*

Show, and Mick sat and talked with the host and another guest, the Conservative politician Lord Hailsham, Quintin Hogg. Hogg seemed ready to dismiss Jagger until the singer caught him off guard with the information that he had been an LSE student—and then Jagger surprised everyone with his declared intent to sue the *News of the World* for libel, a serious matter in the Queen's courts. "I am quite shocked," he pronounced in his best posh manner, "that a responsible newspaper can publish such a defamatory article about me." Two days later, his lawyers served the paper with a writ—and opened an abyss beneath their client that it would take many grim months for him to escape.

The week that followed was devoted to fairly ordinary matters. The Stones' most recent LP, *Between the Buttons*, hadn't made a splash equal to that of their previous, *Aftermath*, and while sales of the album and its first single, "Let's Spend the Night Together," were hale, neither would reach number one; plans were hatching for the band to tour the Continent to promote sales there. On Friday, Mick, Marianne, Keith and the elfin folksinger Donovan were among the throng who watched on at Abbey Road Studios as the Beatles and George Martin put a roomful of classical musicians through a series of unlikely paces as part of the composition of "A Day in the Life": impressive.

And the next day they all got out of town. Keith was throwing a bank holiday house party at Redlands, and simply everybody would be there: Mick and Marianne, Brian and Anita, George and Patti, Chelsea folks like Christopher Gibbs, photographer Michael Cooper, flower child Nicky Cramer, art dealer Robert Fraser and his Moroccan manservant Mohammad Jajaj and a new guy—in ways the most important guest—David Schneiderman, a Californian unfamiliar to the gang but welcome for reasons which his nickname made clear: the Acid King.

Brian and Anita didn't materialize: fighting again, apparently, back home in London. And on Sunday morning, George and Patti, not digging the vibes, said their good-byes. That left nine of them. As they awoke, Schneiderman went around the house and ceremoniously dosed them each with a cup of LSD-laced tea. Then they made plans: It was a mild February day; a drive to the ocean, perhaps, or a visit to the nearby estate of Edward James, an eccentric patron of the Surrealists whose home was filled with all sorts of follies and strange works of art. It was the time, Richards later recalled, of "Visiting Famous Places While Whacked Out." But, too, according to Faithfull, it was the age of "Plans

That Go Awry on Acid." In their wild getups—Keith wore a wooly white afghan coat with a hood and bug-eyed reflecting sunglasses, for instance—they were denied admittance to the James estate, and they soon wearied of banging about country roads in the van they'd driven down for the purpose. They slithered back to Redlands to sit out their trip in more comfortable circumstances.

Dim lights. Soft pillows. Hash pipes. Cups of tea. Incense. A blazing fireplace. The Who on the stereo. *Pete Kelly's Blues* (with Jack Webb, of all people, as a Prohibition-era jazzbo) on TV with the sound turned down. Marianne, after bathing the beach off herself, wearing only a big fur bedspread and snuggling with Mick on a sofa.

Quiet. Peace. Dreamy vibes. Something like bliss.

And then, faces at a window; knocks at the door.

Keith, thinking it was fans, went to answer.

Cops, nineteen of 'em, with a warrant: A fucking raid.

Quickly, the group of partiers was divided: The three policewomen took charge of Marianne; the couple of respectable-seeming types— Gibbs and Fraser—were dealt with by senior officers; Mick and Keith and the other assorted odd numbers were taken in hand by the rest of the police. One of the suspects—Cramer? Gibbs?—was initially mistaken by the cops for a woman: "He had long fairish hair," reported a female officer who searched him, "and was dressed in what would best be described as a pair of red-and-green silk 'pyjamas.' I searched him and this was all he was wearing. I formed the opinion he, too [along with Jagger], was wearing makeup."

Everyone was frisked, including Marianne, who was naked under the rug; she let the thing fall a bit, giggling at the idea that they thought she might be hiding something, affording the cops a cheap thrill and a basis for all sorts of lurid fabrications about the scene.

The house was searched up and down: drawers and cupboards and the pockets of pants and coats. Upstairs, a number of books on witchcraft and the occult and "a large hold-all which contained two or three dagger-type weapons" were found; Marianne's clothes were discovered amid a pile of pink ostrich feathers. Keith had taken to collecting little bars of soap from the various hotels he'd stayed in around the world, and these were all unwrapped and examined. The police confiscated incense, ashtrays, odd little tchotchkes. In a green velvet jacket they found four pills—pharmaceutical amphetamines that Marianne had bought from a disc jockey in Italy, where they were available over the counter as an air-sickness remedy; when the cops asked whose they were, Jagger chivalrously declared they were his and that they'd been prescribed by his Harley Street physician.

The cops must've expected great things: an orgy, a massive pile of drugs sitting on the coffee table and certainly more women, which is why there were three female officers—one each for Faithfull, Anita Pallenberg and Patti Boyd Harrison. The numbers, in fact, would disprove the long-held supposition that the cops had waited for the Harrisons—members of that nice band, the Beatles—to leave the party before swooping in; George himself believed that to be the case, declaring, "They were waiting till I had gone because they were still climbing the ladder, working their way up. They didn't want to get the Fabs yet." But it would be likelier that the police got their tip-off about the party before the Harrisons decamped and were prepared to arrest everyone.

For all the thoroughness of their search, however, the cops never, amazingly, found the treasure trove of acid—hundreds of hits and Lord knew what else—that Schneiderman had in his attaché case; claiming that the bag was filled with exposed film, he kept the cops from opening it. Indeed, save for the little stash of pills in Mick's jacket and a pinch of hash residue they found in Schneiderman's clothing, the cops were crapping out.

All, that is, except for PC Rambridge, the man assigned to search Robert Fraser.

Fraser had, by all accounts, managed to maintain his equilibrium despite the LSD (and the other substances he'd ingested) and tried to put an end to the raid with a display of aristocratic manners. "You can't really do this sort of thing," and so on, as if he were dealing, patiently, with idiot househelp.

The policeman didn't feel bullied: "Robert was a very affable guy, good as gold," Rambridge said years later. "I didn't feel he was arrogant."

But when he turned up a stash of two dozen pills—which Fraser claimed had been prescribed by his doctor to treat some ailment (some accounts say he claimed stomach trouble, some diabetes)—PC Rambridge stood by his duty: Declaring that he believed Fraser's protests, he nevertheless held on to a few pills for testing.

After maybe an hour, the little army of police officers split with their soap and knickknacks and their little cache of confiscated pills. "They took away all our incense and left most of the drugs," Richards laughed.

The mood inside the house had been irrevocably altered—just try dealing with a police raid while on acid!—but only Fraser knew how bad it was going to get.

Those little white pills?

Pure heroin.

In the years since he had established his business and begun championing both native avant-garde talents and international art superstars, Fraser was the most important art dealer in London, always a step ahead of even the trendiest of his rivals and usually as good a judge of quality as he was of what was à la mode. In 1966, he impressed London with a ground-breaking show—"Los Angeles Now"—featuring works in a variety of media by Ed Ruscha, Bruce Conner and others, including Dennis Hopper, who was emerging as a collector and photographer with his acting career half in the tank.

"Robert had come to California probably in '62 or something like that," Hopper remembered, "and stayed with Brooke Hayward and me, and I got him very interested in Mexico. I told him the folk art of Mexico was influencing our artists the same way that African art had influenced the Cubists. And he got very interested and I took him around the various galleries and took home a lot of work from Los Angeles and really got us started there. His show in London was the first time that L.A. art had gotten any kind of international recognition."

Hopper made the London scene during the show, checking out the bands and the women and meeting various of his artistic heroes—not always in the way he had planned. "Robert and I had David Hockney bring all the artists together," Hopper said. "Francis Bacon, Peter Blake, all these guys came to Hockney's apartment. It was a Sunday afternoon, and I was going to photograph them, and I didn't have any film. So David and I went all over town, and nothing was open on Sunday in London. We couldn't find anybody who would sell us film. And he said, 'Look, you cannot embarrass me. You must go ahead and photograph these people as if you had film.' So I spent the whole afternoon photographing these people without film."

No one but Fraser could have been at the center of that fiasco, and no one but he could have put together that Los Angeles show; indeed, only half a handful of London galleries could compete with him in any fashion: Fraser's Duke Street space made an appearance in the famous *Time* magazine cover story in April 1966, and was singled out as the city's "most dashing" art shop in Piri Halasz's subsequent *Swinger's Guide to London*.

But at around the time his own name was becoming internationally known, Fraser showed signs of slipping—most obviously in the way he handled money. He was never exactly a good businessman or even a reliable one: Even given the long-standing traditions of shadiness in the art business, Fraser had an ambivalent reputation. "He was a very contained and enigmatic person," remembered Bill Bowen, a young American sculptor who worked for the gallery doing odd jobs. "He played his cards close to his vest." He could be quarrelsome about trifles, stiff and awkward with his employees and positively diabolical when it came to money, alienating artists, clients and rich friends alike. He would blithely borrow cash or a work of art to sell, and the party he'd availed himself of would have a hellish time getting him to pay it back: "Anything that was to do with money, you'd be screaming and biting your lip and rolling about on the floor and saying, 'I'm never going to see this creep again,' " recalled a much-touched Gibbs. "And he would look at you, if you asked him to pay, look at you very startled and outraged."

Artists would recall Fraser standing in their flats and studios pleading poverty and unable to pay them while taxis idled outside waiting to take him to elegant parties; Richard Hamilton told a reporter, "A number of artists have suffered materially at his hands." Fraser bragged about bouncing an entire book of checks and was once chased down a Soho street with a cleaver by a restaurateur with whom he had an outstanding tab. Spanish Tony Sanchez, who served as Fraser's drug connection until he went to work in that capacity for Keith Richards, once had to talk the Kray brothers into being satisfied with only a partial payment for a gambling debt Fraser had run up in their Knightsbridge gambling club Esmeralda's Barn: "It's a bad business," said Reggie Kray in despair, "when a gentleman like him has no honor."

To some, Fraser's behavior seemed purely pathological: "I liked Robert very much," Mick Jagger said, "but he was obviously a tremendous sharpie." But very few people realized that a lot of Fraser's money, especially as the sixties wore on, was going not to line his pockets or finance his lavish tastes but to satisfy an increasing drug habit. "About 1965 it moved, as far as Robert was concerned, from faggy to druggy," recollected Gibbs. (It might be noted, too, and not necessarily unrelatedly, that his beloved father, Lionel, died at the age of sixty-nine in January of that year.)

Like everyone on the scene, even people who didn't share his predilection for North African culture, Fraser was into the hash and the pot; the rituals of smoking, including the opportunity to use fascinating little pipes, appealed to both the aesthete and the collector in him. Then came the acid: Like so many of the early experimenters in LSD, Robert proselytized the drug to friends such as Gibbs, Brian Jones and Anita Pallenberg. Then there was cocaine sniffing—Fraser turned on both Mc-Cartney and Marianne Faithfull—and then, inevitably, probably, the heroin, snorted off lovely antique mirrors through rolled-up American currency.

The sheer decadence of that image—the cost and the finickiness and the indulgence of it—perfectly harmonized with the mood of the city in 1966. Fraser could authentically claim a place in every sphere—high and low—that was starting to combine in the new social fluidity, and his ability to introduce people to one another and to daring new ways of life made him a keystone figure, even if he was one whom most of the public wouldn't recognize.

Anita Pallenberg recalled the first load she got of Fraser at a posh party soon after she arrived in London: "Bright green suit, green shirt, green tie, green shoes, and his fly open. That's someone I've got to meet!, I thought." They knew people in common—J. Paul Getty, Tara Browne, Michael Rainey, Mark Palmer and various Ormsby-Gores and other European and English notables, whom Anita had met through her relationship with the Italian photographer Mario Schifano: the well-heeled hedonists who were then starting to hang around with pop stars, particularly with the Stones.

According to Anita, it was a case of mutual attraction and symbiosis: "Mick and Keith pretty quickly realized that those people all had something that the Stones wanted, and the Stones had what all of these kind of decadent aristocrats wanted—all these girls and that kind of action and singing and playing music. It seemed to them so romantic at the time, and so it kind of fell together—they both had what the other one wanted—so it was very compatible because of that and quite exciting, really, and very nice, too. And it was a crash course in good manners for the Stones, as well. Not that they became 'well-behaved' or anything like that—I mean, they were still outrageous—but they could see that there was a different background, and some of the courtesies, for instance, were actually rather charming. It also made the Stones wiser much more quickly."

As Faithfull recalled, "The Stones came away with a patina of aristocratic decadence that served as a perfect counterfoil to the raw roots blues of their music." They were already mimicking the nobles of bygone eras with their increasingly outlandish wardrobes; now they were partying, fucking and getting zonked with their descendants. "There's always been an aristocracy in Britain who've been interested in the counterculture," reflected Barry Miles. "To some extent they were the black sheep of the family." And blacker you couldn't get than dallying with Mick and the boys.

It was a truly lunatic world the Stones, Fraser and the new young Chelsea people inhabited: They attended parties with members of the royal family at which such powerful hash brownies were served that people had to have their stomachs pumped; they cavorted in Tangiers with Cecil Beaton, who came back to London so enthused about the bright new people he'd met that he was snickered at behind his back as Rip Van With-It.

Some of the most high-born among the Stones' new pals would soon take on new lives as caravaners, traveling through the countryside in horse-drawn carts, dressed in hippie-gypsy gear, smoking dope, practicing free love in the fields, attempting to make contact with UFOs, which they believed still followed ancient ley lines—magnetic landing strips, in effect, built into the landscape but lost to centuries of ignorant civilization. The youthful Sir Mark Palmer, who attended Eton and Oxford and served as a page at Queen Elizabeth's 1953 coronation (his mother was a lady-in-waiting) was the most celebrated of the lot. Although he ran a modeling agency—English Boy Ltd.—out of his home in Radnor Walk, Chelsea, he joined up with a posse of itinerant rich folks who eschewed baths and roofs and responsibility for a life of giddy freedom, carvaning about the countryside in a moveable commune of like-minded spirits. When he was arrested for possession of cannabis a few years later, Palmer left the courthouse in a horse-drawn cart bedecked in chrysanthemums;

"The metamorphosis," said somebody who knew him as a somewhat straighter fellow, "was so complete as to transcend mere affectation."

"They were into ley lines and flying saucers," remembered Barry Miles, "and that sort of cuts across all sorts of class barriers. When Jane [Ormsby-Gore] and Michael [Rainey] left London they went in a sort of gypsy caravan traveling along ley lines to Wales with motorcycle out-riders. This is a sort of eccentricity you've always had among English aristocrats. They're famous for being very cuckoo, a lot of them. Because they don't have anything to prove. They don't need to keep up appearances. And that's the great side of them. That's what made them great to be around, the Ormsby-Gores: very nice people."

The Chelsea scene was a general, if benign, madness, a kind of communicable derangement of the senses, and if Robert Fraser wasn't Patient X, the ur-carrier, he was happy to be Typhoid Mary.

But for all the eyebrows raised by their behavior, the Chelsea types who carried on like merry, trippy nuts never drew the official opprobrium that seemed Fraser's doom to endure. In September 1966, he mounted an exhibit of new works by Jim Dine entitled "London 1966," which consisted of drawings, abstract paintings and sculptures of male and female genitalia—social commentary of a sort about how randy the town had become. Like everything else that ever hung in the gallery, you could see Dine's works from the street, and somebody—either a retired general from Weybridge or a greasy young man from the Lord's Day Observance Society; history isn't clear on which, but either would do nicely—got a glimpse of a sculpture of a penis in wrapping paper from Selfridges and called the cops. They shut down the exhibit, confiscated the offending artworks and brought charges against the gallery under not the Obscene Publications Act of 1959 but the Vagrancy Act of 1838—which was designed to keep beggars from displaying war wounds for pity and included under its rubric any and all explicit displays of the body.

It was just the sort of scandal that Fraser gobbled up. When a police artist was sent to sketch the offending pictures, Fraser insisted that he take photographs: "At least let's have it accurate." Later, when another policeman declared that he found the pictures objectionable, Fraser sneered, in pure Eton, "I am certainly not bothered by the opinion of a tuppenny-ha'penny policeman. I consider these pictures to be as pornographic as Cézanne." Bill Bowen, who found the Dine show "all in all pretty boring," was enlisted to plaster the city with posters showing images of the exhibit with BANNED splashed across them; Fraser quickly came up with the felicitous phrase "Regina versus Vagina" and used it practically as an advertising slogan. In November, when it came time to defend Dine's works in court, Fraser told the magistrate, "The one thing that stands out among them is their humor and their optimism." He didn't win—the gallery was fined twenty pounds plus an equal amount in court costs; Fraser would probably have paid ten times that for the attendant publicity and the rallying of the right-thinking people with whom he did business.

So as he stood being frisked by PC Rambridge at Redlands, Fraser knew from courts and barristers and even from police. Indeed, he was sufficiently comfortable around cops that he used to buy his hash from the Savile Row police station. Still, an absurd obscenity charge was one thing; possession of heroin was another altogether. He had to suspect the worst was coming, but, like the others, he could only wait.

For a few days after the Redlands arrest, it seemed as though nothing might happen: So little contraband had been found, after all, and the papers had said not a word—not even the tabloids—about what ought to have been a sensational story. The Stones camp quickly suspected that the silence indicated a desire on the behalf of the cops for a bribe that would make the whole thing go away. Fraser put Spanish Tony onto the case to see if a greasing was in order and was told that £8,000 would make the charges disappear. Well, the money disappeared, anyhow: Spanish Tony took it to a pub in Kilburn and handed it over to someone, he said, and presently the whole thing splashed into the papers and the courts.

A week after the bust, a story appeared in the *News of the World* detailing the event but not naming names—adding to the speculation that the newspaper had tipped off the cops and maybe even set the Stones up with an agent provocateur as a way of deflecting Jagger's threatened libel suit. The only candidates for the role of rat were Nicky Cramer, a featherweight King's Road flower child who was eliminated as a witness after he withstood a near-crippling beating from David Litvinoff, a tough guy and thief known to the Stones crowd, and the Acid King himself, David Schneiderman, who had already conveniently left England and didn't surface again for decades.

Eventually, the more respectable newspapers began to report the Redlands bust, naming names and getting specific about what substances the police recovered. And rumors began flying about what had been going on that night in West Wittering when the police came knocking—the sort of things the cops *expected* to find but didn't: raving LSD heads, unthinkable drug-and-sex behavior and, most notoriously, Mick Jagger eating a Mars Bar out of Marianne Faithfull's vagina.

Seriously.

It was actually some time before Mick and Marianne got wind of this particularly insane canard—the Stones and their chums had decamped to Morocco on a holiday soon after the bust, and then the band went on a tumultuous tour of the Continent. The Mars Bar story took on a life on the street, in pubs, even in Her Majesty's prisons. Other mistruths about the raid abounded: Fraser was said to have been tackled on the lawn by police as he fled the scene (try *that* on an acid-and-heroin cocktail!), and Gibbs was said to have been dressed in full drag. But none of these became as famous as the notorious Mars Bar.

"There was no Mars Bar," Gibbs declared emphatically later on. But, as it turned out, Keith was fond of Mars Bars, and there *were* some on hand at Redlands that weekend—not only did the cops take note of them but so did Richards's legal team when they examined the house later on. But the idea that they'd been used as sex toys was patently absurd. For Marianne, it was proof that the authorities were willing to do *anything* to ruin the Stones and their circle: "It was far too jaded for any of us even to have conceived of," she reflected. "It's a dirty old man's fantasy—some old fart who goes to a dominatrix every Thursday afternoon to get spanked. A *cop's* idea of what people do on acid!"

The very notion that a Sussex policeman should, in early 1967, even *have* an idea of what people do on acid was extraordinary. Two years earlier, maybe a dozen people in all the British Isles would have heard of LSD, let alone used it. By the time of the raid on Redlands, however, it was one of the most widely discussed novelties of an increasingly novelty-mad age, to some minds a radically liberating and self-expanding elixir, to others a dangerous threat to the very fabric of society.

How did it happen? How did acid spread so fast and come to mean so much to so many people? You could amass data and dates and set up chronologies and weigh the critical mass to pin down the moment when it all changed from smart to groovy, from fresh-scrubbed to burnt, from outgoing to inward, from glad-handing, bright-eyed and inclusive to confrontational, dilated and obscure.

Or, as ever, you could simply watch the Beatles.

The Beatles weren't always the first to embody all the changes of the time, but they were almost always among the eagerest and most earnest and absolutely the most visible. To a world far removed from the little founts of coolness from which they sipped, the band came to look as prophets, always somehow around that curve just up ahead, particularly as things got more esoteric and freakish and people found themselves more in need of guides. Others in London were psychedelic sooner— the underground types around Notting Hill, maybe, or some of the more louche aristos of Chelsea—but the Beatles were the ones in the middle of the picture, the ones whom everyone watched and learned from.

And so it was that in a virtually daily process during the span of five months—November '65 to April '66—that the Beatles became the first stars of any medium to metamorphose fully and obviously from perky and aboveboard to mysterious and covert, from good-time boys to heralds of a new consciousness, from wholesome lads your mom could enjoy to dangerous subversives speaking liberation to like-minded deviants. They became, in short, the world's first household psychedelics, avatars of something wilder and more revolutionary than anything pop culture had ever delivered before.

Something had been going on with them as early as *Rubber Soul*, the December '65 release that followed the Fab-fun *Help!* by a mere four months. A lot of folks, though, didn't know even to look for—much less how to identify—the gene-level change that the band was undergoing, and so they were left merely with the queer vibe that things were a smidgen amiss: the spacey gazes of the lads on the album cover (their hair, once moppish, now downright foppish); the strange, breathy, submarine textures of "You Won't See Me" and "Girl"; the allegorical weirdness of "Norwegian Wood" ("This bird has flown . . . ."), complete with—Rama help us!—sitar. For all that, though, and despite the jaded lyrical insinuations of "Drive My Car" and "Run for Your Life," the record was not all *that* dissimilar to *Help!*—a tad more esoteric and smoky, certainly, but tuneful and straightforward all the same.

But if there were vague skews to *that* record, *Revolver*, well, was so genuinely—how to put it?—*weird*. The gnarled mutterings, throat clearings and recording studio noises at the start of "Taxman"; the frankly subcontinental idiom of "Love You To" and, most of all, John Lennon's trio of tuned-in, blissed-out, spiked and spaced tunes: "I'm Only Sleeping," "She Said, She Said" and "Tomorrow Never Knows." This was pop music? These were Beatles?

Something deep inside the band had changed and they seemed giddy to be rid of their old selves. On the ultra-groovy album cover, their old Hamburg chum Klaus Voorman drew portraits of them with hair like cartoon spaghetti, snaking around and strangling images of themselves from their moptop past, a past that had receded all the more since the Cavern Club shut its doors, a fallout of bankruptcy, in February 1966.

But in the place of the smiles, the matching suits and the jokey affability, the new Beatles bore something there was no widely known name for. They had discovered some other sort of reality, and it had changed them: *Revolver*, their account of what they'd learned, was indolent, experimental, hedonistic, cryptic save to those who had some special knowledge. McCartney's melodic impulses notwithstanding (he wrote "Eleanor Rigby," "Here, There and Everywhere," "Good Day Sunshine" and "Got to Get You into My Life," among others, for the album), *Revolver* was just plain strange—strange enough, in fact, to make virtually everybody look deeper into it and follow the Beatles' lead.

The first inkling of something going on had been "Rain," the B-side of "Paperback Writer," which appeared June 10, 1966, the very day Mary Quant was awarded her OBE by the Queen. "Rain," a Lennon number, wasn't perky and aggressive like the A-side, which was McCartney's. It contained stuff nobody had ever heard: snippets of backward-recorded singing and guitar work and Ringo's brilliant reverse rolls on the drum kit ("It's out of left field," he said later, "I know me and I know my playing, and then there's 'Rain' "). Its lyrics were allusive and cryptic, evoking a distinct class of outsiders—a "they"—and boasting of some arcane knowledge the singer could share with his audience. That knowledge, it so happened, was a doorway: *Revolver*, which followed "Rain" into stores by two months, was the first true drug album, not a pop record with some druggy insinuations, but an honest-to-heaven, steeped-in-the-out-there trip from the here and now into who knew where.

It's a completely brilliant album—first note to last, probably their best—not least because it showed the band taking hold of its image and shaking it into something distinctly uncuddly. This may have been a gambit: Older folks who had been frightened by Elvis Presley's frank sexuality had been ameliorated by Brian Epstein's managerial choices, which had plastered onto the Beatles a wholesome mien that more resembled Tommy Steele or Cliff Richard; such nice boys, the thinking went, couldn't *really* be after our daughters. But now the Beatles were declaring themselves Pied Pipers of another sort of license: not fornication but intoxication and, with it, liberation. You'd have to have been a cultist to get the marijuana jokes on *Rubber Soul*—dig the hissy little joint tokes on "Girl"!—but you'd have to be thick not to notice that *Revolver* was, most loudly in Lennon's contributions, an homage to the wonders of *something*: a something that turned out to be LSD.

LSD changed everything. If amphetamines were the pharmaceutical fuel that amplified natural teen exuberance (not to mention a tonic to musicians who needed to go as hard as their all-night audiences), if marijuana and hashish were covert larks that involved passing joints and wandering off into obscure corners of Notting Hill to meet up with dealers, LSD was the first indigenous manna of the drug culture, not a mother's little helper or an ancient herb of medicine and holiness, but a manufactured and completely nontherapeutic substance that marked those who took it as distinctly and permanently as the loss of virginity or a first visit to a foreign land. LSD users—and not only wild-eyed advocates like Timothy Leary, but virtually the lot of 'em—spoke of personal transformation and loss of ego and glimpses of alternate realities and truths discovered and beauties revealed. It was a psychic rocket ship, no argument; pot, in comparison, was a Skateboard.

But there was a price to the interstellar internal journey that LSD afforded. If pot smokers were silly and clannish and prone to be nervously alert about being caught out, acid heads were fragile, brittle even, in danger of confusing their visions with the concrete world around them, of making awful mistakes of judgment, of freaking out, breaking down, going frankly gaga. The potheads at the party would sneak out in little groups and come back in a minute all knowing and giggly; the acidheads needed minders and Turkish pillows to recline upon and maybe didn't make it to the party at all but stayed in the wombs of their flats or went out wandering in the countryside—a tribe unto themselves, complete with initiation rituals and revered elders.

LSD was brand new to London in '65, but hallucinatory dabbling had a long and distinguished history in English culture. From the hashish smokers and opium eaters who flourished in various colonial outposts of Africa and Asia to depraved domestics like Thomas De Quincey and genteel mystics like Aldous Huxley, the exploration of inner space by Englishmen of the educated classes was nearly as common a calling as the exploration of outer. Huxley, in fact, was one of the first Englishmen to try LSD, which had been invented in a Swiss laboratory in 1943, tripping for intellectual inquiry and hedonistic pleasure in the early sixties in Los Angeles.

At around the same time, across the U.S. in New York, an employee at the British Cultural Exchange, one Michael Hollingshead, got his mitts on some acid and stunned himself with his first trip. He contacted Huxley and asked him what he should do with the rest of his stash—approximately two thousand trips worth, which he had mixed into a cake frostinglike goo that he carried about in a disused mayonnaise jar. Huxley had heard of a Harvard researcher who was proselytizing for psilocybin, a chemical derivative of magic mushrooms extracted from natural sources and synthesized by, once again, Albert Hoffman; he suggested Hollingshead look him up—fellow by the name of Timothy Leary.

When Hollingshead showed up on his doorstep, Leary was welcoming but wary: He had heard of LSD but wasn't interested. He let Hollingshead crash in a spare bedroom in his house and offered to help him find some work, but that was the extent of it. One night, jazz trumpeter Maynard Ferguson dropped by the house and Hollingshead told him about his wonder drug. The musician asked to try some and Hollingshead obliged, offering some to Leary, as well; the professor demurred, saying he had some student papers to grade. But the party got so inviting that Leary gave in and dipped into the stash.

Zowie.

Once Leary got a hold of LSD, that was that. He became a spittle-chinned, hoop-eyed zealot scaring the wits out of anyone who stopped long enough to hear him and making instant converts of plenty of those whom he could turn on to the drug. His advocacy got him booted from Harvard, but he was such a convincing preacher that he got financial backing to help him spread the word of the new miracle potion across the world. In October 1965, he dispatched Hollingshead to London with another two thousand trips of acid—purchased and imported legally from a government laboratory in Prague. Hollingshead opened up the London offices of the World Psychedelic Centre in Pont Street, Brompton—skipping distance from the King's Road—and London was soon off to the races.

Particularly among the burgeoning English underground, LSD spread quickly. Hollingshead's arrival and the search for alternative consciousness were the chicken and the egg of the high sixties: Did LSD instigate the coming changes, or were the impulses already there just waiting for something to rally around? Within months, the chic bohemian druggy set around Chelsea was grooving on Hollingshead's stash: blue bloods like Tara Browne and Julian and Victoria Ormsby-Gore; artistic types like Roman Polanski, William S. Burroughs, poet Alexander Trocchi and Christopher Gibbs; the odd hedonist such as Victor Lownes, the American businessman in town to set up the Playboy Club on Park Lane, or Sir Roland Penrose of the Tate Gallery and the Institute of Contemporary Art.

When they came to the WPC, Hollingshead's converts found a solemn invocation of an Eastern mystical shrine: incense, candles, tapestries, pillows, the works. In the Hollingshead scheme, adopted from Leary, LSD was a spiritual elixir that demanded a certain cool reverence and, funnily enough, sobriety. There were specific steps to a "proper" trip and following them appropriately led the user to a state akin to the Zen satori: a lifetime of meditation, devotion and study boiled down to a sugar cube and a few hours.

But the stuff was just too much fun, too perfectly suited to the cultural moment, to stay so precious and solemn for so long. John Esam, a vagabonding type from New Zealand who had been active on the London underground scene for about a year, got hold of a portion of Hollingshead's acid and began circulating it in far less pompous and portentous situations—like at parties and rock shows, out of a medicine dropper. It caught on like a merry virus.

The tabloid media started reporting on the "Heaven and Hell drug" that was sweeping the city—"Just half an ounce could knock out London," screamed one article. And the more responsible press was only slightly better: *London Life* ran a multipart exposé in which it reported,

"If anyone wanted to, they could take control of London, and Britain, in under eight hours" by use of acid. Talk like this naturally caught the attention of the police: The 1920 Dangerous Drug Act was amended—for the second time in two years—to include LSD on the roster of banned substances.

By then, of course, the genie was out of the bottle. LSD was just the thing everyone seemed to be waiting for: Pop stars and painters, scenesters and revolutionaries, philosophers and journalists and members of Parliament, everywhere people were turning on and reacting with welcoming astonishment at what they experienced. "Great!," thought that exemplary barometer of the moment, Marianne Faithfull, when the fireworks began on her first-ever trip. "It's something I'd always hoped I'd be granted: second sight."

Faithfull and her fellow trippers reveled in the sheer strangeness of the drug's effect—the visual and auditory hallucinations, the giddy rush of interconnected thoughts, the way the colors and textures that had become chic in the period's clothing and furniture seemed to take on organic life, the way music sounded and could be made to sound. Introduced, at least by Hollingshead, an adjunct to a form of Eastern mysticism, LSD had its users convinced that their experiences were a version of ultimate truth, that it had helped them break from the shackles of quotidian perception and come to see themselves within the context of divine, eternal energies. (Others, make no mistake, just liked to get all fucked up and numb.)

Mick Jagger, though he turned on to acid plenty, never really allowed himself to become beholden to any drug, and he would come eventually to give up LSD and dismiss the Stones' effort at replicating *Revolver*—*Between the Buttons*, with its trippy signature the pseudo-psychedelic ditty "Something Happened to Me Yesterday"—as "rubbish." But acid turned plenty of its earliest users into advocates—some prescribing it as a means for humanity to achieve a new stage of evolution, some seeing it as a tool for bringing down a corrupt society ("Spike the reservoirs, lads!"), others believing it was a means to make the to-now impossible move backward toward the innocence of childhood or some prelapsarian Eden.

This last thought connected LSD, curiously but comfortably, with the Arcadian strain of English thought, the sense that decadence, foppishness, hedonism and even infantilism were part of a privileged, lost history of the island nation, a golden past that could best be apprehended by children, artistic geniuses, the mad, the sainted and—mirabile *triptu*—the acid-fueled. Thus the conflation of English psychedelia and the Arthurian legend, the works of William Blake, Lewis Carroll and J.R.R. Tolkien, even such Empire artifacts as Victorian military uniforms, flapper dresses and clothing and decor from colonial outposts of Africa, Asia and the Indian subcontinent.

As in America, LSD brought with it an explosion of sight and sound, wild hippie behavior, renewed reverence for the natural and the aboriginal and a widespread evocation of the spirit of love—physical, spiritual, altruistic. But there was a gnomish quality to psychedelic London that wasn't echoed in New York or San Francisco. If American psychedelia was a burning fuse, entwined vitally with the antiwar movement, the student rights movement and the widespread sense that the existing structures of society needed to come crashing down, English psychedelia was precious, arcane, hermetic, linked more to the Epicurean than the apocalyptic. "It's very different from American psychedelia," reflected Barry Miles. "If you combine a lot of English fairy stories and English children's stories with enough LSD, then you get a very different underground scene than you've got in San Francisco. It does lock into a notion of England as a sacred place criss-crossed by ley lines and all the rest of it."

Like miniature Learys, scores of acidheads became advocates of their newly found elixir, urging it on friends and, in a common and astoundingly reckless practice, surreptitiously dosing the ones who were reluctant to tamper with the chemistry of their own brains.

John Lennon and George Harrison were dosed, very early on in the acid game, sometime in the spring of 1965, by a Bayswater dentist who'd acquired some acid from Victor Lownes (even before Hollingshead entered the country) and was hoping to involve the two Beatles and their wives in an orgy. Angered at their host for suggesting something so tasteless, the Beatle couples left the party and headed for the Ad Lib which, to their amazement, seemed to be consumed in flames: the entryway, the elevator, the dance floor, the lot of it. (Prophetic that, as the club would be shut by a literal fire six or so months later.) They somehow escaped Leicester Square for the pastoral comforts of George's estate in Esher, George driving his Mini at "ten miles an hour, but it seemed like a thousand," as John later told Marianne Faithfull. Once they arrived, Paul Mc-

Cartney reported, "These huge, big friendly trees were waving at them," and they were safe once again.

John claimed he stayed stoned for months after that trip; when the effect wore off, he tried it again. In August '65, John and George dropped acid, voluntarily this time, with the Byrds in L.A., and Ringo joined in; Peter Fonda came by and freaked John out with his tale of having been clinically dead on the operating table when he was an adolescent. "Everybody but Paul was on acid," Fonda remembered, "and George was getting a bit upset. He thought he was gonna die. And I said, 'Well, that's just what it's all about, don't worry about it, it's okay, because I've been dead and there's nothing to worry about.' John was pissed that I was there; he didn't want any attention going around. But I was there at the invitation of the lads and David Crosby and Roger McGuinn. I had no idea he was so filled with invective." (Fonda's comments wound up appearing, suitably altered, in John's *Revolver* number "She Said, She Said," a marvy early acid tune; later that same night in Hollywood, the Beatles, still buzzing, turned up at a party along with the likes of Jack Benny, Groucho Marx, Hayley and Juliette Mills, Dean Martin and Edward G. Robinson—none of whom was to make an appearance on the album.)

Back in London, acid was spreading—willing or not—through the popoisie, at first with a slow fizz and then with a roar. Pete Townshend was dosed by a stranger—in a plate of food, no less—and soon evolved into a devotee of and advocate for the drug. Brian Jones dove, as he would, feet first into it on the Stones' late '65 tour of the U.S.; his playing got so sloppy that Ian Stewart tried shaking sense into him—physically, by the lapels—after a set. Syd Barrett—whose group Pink Floyd hadn't even cut a record yet—became so enamored of acid that he was giving the stuff to his cat and locking himself in his flat, all wired up, for days on end; he and a mate were so notorious for surreptitiously spreading trips that people who visited them wouldn't dare drink or eat anything or even touch a doorknob with bare skin for fear of being dosed.

Ironically, given the early experiences of his bandmates and his own reputation as an inquisitive cat, Paul McCartney was the last Beatle to try LSD. In late '65, maybe early '66, he was turned on by Tara Browne at a late-night, after-the-clubs-closed get-together in London. Browne, who would also be present at Marianne Faithfull's first trip, was one of those fabulous aristocrats who were turning on to the pop-and-glitter scene. His father was Lord Aranmore-and-Browne; his mother was Oonagh Guinness, a young beauty who was heiress to the brewery fortune. Tara had a couple of kids by an Irish farmer's daughter he had married secretly in France in 1963; she was slightly older than him and didn't exactly appreciate being left behind when he began showing up in swinging night spots with rock stars. Browne owned some automobile garages and was dabbling in the boutique business. By later 1965, he had become matey enough with McCartney that he had joined the Beatle on a Christmastide trip to Liverpool; they larked about on minibikes and McCartney crashed and busted up his lip and a tooth. A year later, separated from his wife (who was engaged in a struggle with Browne's mother for custody of her young children), living at the Ritz with fashion model Suki Poitier, Browne had an accident of his own, smashing his blue Lotus Elan into a parked car in Redcliffe Gardens, Chelsea; a woman who lived at the crash site came out from her house with blankets to cover him but he died soon after arriving at the hospital. Rumor among Browne's set had it he was tripping at the time of the accident, but Poitier told police a fairly mundane car wreck story.

Browne was only twenty-one at the time and left an estate of £28,272—far short of the one million pounds he would have inherited on his twenty-fifth birthday; his death—with a model and a custody battle and an unclaimed fortune embedded in the tale—became a tabloid sensation. When John Lennon read about the coroner's inquest into the accident in a newspaper the following year, he turned Browne into a centerpiece of the Beatles' great '67 acid-inspired mini rock opera, "A Day in the Life," the masterwork of that beloved centerpiece of psychedelia, *Sgt. Pepper's Lonely Hearts Club Band*.

If Browne's fate seemed cautionary, nobody in the hip sets seemed to mind; people embraced LSD as avidly as any advent of the age. Beatles press agent Derek Taylor, for one, was dosed by his bosses at a housewarming party for Brian Epstein's estate in Sussex on a sunny Sunday in May '67 and never looked back: "I had already been prepared to examine life through a prism of cannabis cigarettes," he wrote later. "That had been good, but this new lark was ridiculous. How could a poor man stand such times and *live*?" Taylor took after his employers, particularly Lennon, in dosing himself a *lot*: whole weekends tripping and weekdays at the Apple press office, until he harassed some poor woman who said she "needed" to speak to Mary Hopkin and Paul, who overheard Taylor's resulting tirade, insisted that he not use any more hard stuff at work. Taylor complied but remained jealous of Lennon, who had the unique liberty to take the drug as often as he liked: "He had a lot of leisure," Taylor recalled. "He had that pop star—it wasn't rock star, then—that pop star space which was very conducive to acid. If he was up all night he could go to sleep all day. He didn't have any of those conventional things to deal with."

Right there was the cold hard truth that made LSD—and a few other harder drugs like heroin—a wall between one sort of hipness and another. You had a job, you had a place to be in the morning, you had lines of a script to memorize or a fashion collection to debut or a set of photos to shoot or hair—just imagine it!—to cut, you didn't make acid a habit. You tried it, sure: *Cary Grant* tried it, for Pete's sake. But as a lifestyle, it was limited to those rich enough—or, ironically, poor enough—not to care about where their next rent payment was coming from.

To the more solidly grounded people from the earlier London scene, the new lot were a little frightening, or at the very least a nuisance. As tailor Doug Hayward remembered, "They'd come into the shop and say, 'You see that tree out there? How beautiful it is?' I'd say, 'I've been looking at it for three years.' 'Yeah, it's beautiful, man.' And I'd say, 'You mind coming back later? I've got work to do here.' When that crowd was running around I thought, No one's ever going to wear a suit again. Funny outfits they wore. There was nothing really solid being done. Most of it was very frivolous. But it made for excitement."

Unlike the swingers of '63 to '65, who were united by youth, charm, ambition, style and that dubious classlessness, the new scenesters were classifiable by the adherence to a drug and a way of life that separated them entirely from the middle. There had always, for instance, been an underground of drug users, political dissidents, sexual adventurers, artistic pioneers and social malcontents in London—how else could it call itself a world-class city? But with the rise of psychedelia, the underground came out into the light, uniting with the highest fliers and challenging in their very combined ascendancy the sort of wide acceptability enjoyed by the Beatles when they were named MBEs. Smart young men in Pierre Cardin suits dancing to peppy tunes in a Leicester Square discotheque were one sort of hot new class; people who dressed in afghan jackets and paisley shirts and sandals and spent days on end staring wide-eyed at the wallpaper were another. With the spread of LSD, the Swinging London of boutiques, trendy restaurants and a new, sharp British self-image began to disappear into a blur. And in its place was something revolutionary, yes, and maybe even *necessary*—but also alienating, secretive, dangerous and strange, not to mention imported from the USA, which was regaining the upper hand in the transatlantic race for cultural cool. LSD may have been the fuel that stoked the second act of Swinging London, but it was also the stuff that burned it down.

Certainly officialdom wasn't going to give England over to a bunch of loons in fancy dress with their minds melted by some ghastly new drug. There would be a crackdown before tradition utterly surrendered, and the ideal place to start, it was widely agreed, would be with the Rolling Stones, who had for years, it would've been argued in high places, been asking for as much. Indeed, when Mick, Keith and Fraser were actually called down to court in Chichester in May to plead to charges of possession of amphetamines, allowing his home to be used for consumption of cannabis and possession of heroin, respectively, you couldn't ignore the fact that the cops were targeting the Stones: While his bandmates stood "Yes, sir-ing" a judge, Brian Jones was busted at his Courtfield Road flat, along with his Eurotrashy good-time playmate Stash de Rolla (actually Prince Stanislaw Klossowski de Rola, Baron de Watterville, son of the painter Balthus), for possession of cocaine, methedrine and cannabis resin. For the next few years, barely six months would go by without a Rolling Stone being arrested or tried on a drug charge.

The trial began at the West Sussex courthouse in Chichester on June 27. Predictably, it was a circus, with teenage girls lining up outside for a glimpse of their idols, hippies massing to protest the drug laws and newspapermen and photographers everywhere, shooting dozens of snaps and telling an eager world what the Stones smoked, drank and, most importantly, wore. (The record showed that Mick went with a green blazer, ruffled shirt and striped tie, while Keith sported a devastating pinstripe suit on the first day and a black silk suit with white cravat the next.) For Faithfull, the peacockery seemed to soften public opinion in favor of the defendants: "They seemed more like fragile aristocrats being bullied by beefy cops than the sinister types the prosecution were trying to foist on the court."

At the bar, Mick and Keith had been advised to contest the very basis of the charges against them: The pills that Mick had claimed as his own were frequently prescribed in England, and his physician was ready to testify that he had given Jagger an oral prescription for such medication. As for Keith's allowing his premises to be used for cannabis consumption, the police couldn't really prove that anyone there had *done* any such thing: They had no corroborating witnesses and, more damningly, no cannabis or cannabis-smoking paraphernalia to back up their claim, save the minute bits they'd found on Schneiderman—and he'd already bolted back to America.

In theory, a cakewalk. But they hadn't counted on the severe approbation of Judge Leslie Block, a formal naval officer and staunch provincial moralist. The first shock the Stones received was when the case against Jagger was heard: Judge Block declared that since the singer's physician hadn't *specifically* prescribed the *specific* pills in question, that his willingness to do so was immaterial; as the doctor was the only witness for the defense, the judge directed the jury that they should consider the charge uncontested. Deliberations lasted six minutes: guilty. Jagger's lawyer was so taken aback by the speed of this reversal that he had no appeal ready; when he asked for bail and it was refused, the lead singer of the Rolling Stones was taken to Her Majesty's prison in Lewes to spend the night.

Then it was Fraser's turn. There wasn't much that could be done to quash the charges: He had the heroin on his person, after all, and admitted to the officers at Redlands that it was his. But his lawyer pled the quality of his character, his stint in the National Service, his breeding and what was characterized as a tragic tumble into drug addiction that he was now bravely fighting. Again, with so unsympathetic a judge and such cut-and-dried facts, Fraser's case was doomed: guilty.

The following day brought Richards's trial. That morning, a police car pulled up at the courthouse with a stunning cargo: Jagger and Fraser, whose presence would be necessary in case their sentences were to be delivered, handcuffed together in the rear seat, a sensational spectacle that revealed the extreme length authorities were willing to go to make examples of the Stones and their set. The handcuffs were that one irresistible bit too much, however: a pair of educated young men with no previous police records and who posed no threat of violence manacled like hardened criminals. The photos of the two men, with sheepish grins, trying to hide from the cameras or wave them away, became totems of the ascendant prodrug underground. The *Evening Standard* spoke out against the show of repression, calling it "an unnecessary humiliation"; elsewhere in London, trendy shops began selling "Jagger Links"—handcuffs meant to be worn as jewelry, some encrusted with real gems, others painted in psychedelic hues.

At Richards's trial, the deep division between the old culture and the new was most fully bared. Whereas Jagger and Fraser were caught in possession of controlled substances, Richards was being charged with hosting a party at which cannabis was consumed—or, rather, *was likely to have been consumed*. Richards's attorney suggested, with good reason, that the disappeared David Schneiderman—the one on whom the traces of hashish had been found—had been an agent provocateur, planting drugs and telling the cops when to show up. The prosecution, meanwhile, absent hard evidence of dope-smoking, resorted to defaming Richards and his guests as dissolute, deviant, decadent, depraved—and, by insinuation, drugged. Police witnesses described the strange music, the TV with its sound turned down, the unusual smells throughout the house, the "merry mood" and peekaboo striptease of Marianne Faithfull (anonymous in court and in most of the press coverage, but known to everyone as the "Miss X" of the trial transcripts).

Badgered by the prosecutor about the condition in which this young woman was found, Keith delivered the classic line of the case:

> PROSECUTOR: Would you agree, in the ordinary course of events, you would expect a young woman to be embarrassed if she had nothing on but a rug in the presence of eight men, two of whom were hangers-on and the third a Moroccan servant?
> RICHARDS: Not at all.
> PROSECUTOR: You regard that, do you, as quite normal?
> RICHARDS: We are not old men. We are not worried about petty morals.

Well, that may have rung true in certain neighborhoods of London or among the people with whom Richards associated, but Judge Block and the good people and true of West Sussex certainly *were* worried about "petty morals," and Richards, like his friends, was convicted. The three guilty men were carted off again to return the following day for sentencing.

Throughout the two days of the trial, Marianne—still only eighteen years old!—had been looning about London in denial, effectively, about the seriousness of her boyfriend's situation or that of her mates. She dropped acid with the Small Faces at Steve Marriott's house and then made her way down to Redlands, nearer the courthouse, where she slept with photographer Michael Cooper. She finally visited the trio of convicts in jail, bearing salutary gifts of books and cigarettes. Fraser, the former soldier, was playing it stoical, and Richards seemed actually to be relishing the whole outlaw thing. But Jagger was in a state: wringing his hands, sobbing, "What am I gonna do? What in *hell* am I gonna do?" Marianne upbraided him: "God, Mick! Pull yourself together!" But how could he—suburban lad, chosen by the Fates to be a rock god—faced with this?

The next day, his worst fears were confirmed. Judge Block handed down stunning sentences: Jagger, three months imprisonment and £100 in fines; Fraser, six months and £200; and Richards, who dared to speak out, one year and £500. The money, obviously, was meaningless: At the end of the year, it would be reported that Rolling Stones records had earned more than £42 million worldwide in the four years since their first disc. But the prison terms: These were all first-time offenders, after all, and no one claimed they posed a threat to anyone but themselves; you couldn't blame the Stones' camp for crying conspiracy. Some months later, in fact, Judge Block spoke to a dinner of the Horsham Plowing and Agricultural Society and confessed, "We did our best, your fellow countrymen and I, and my fellow magistrates, to cut these Stones down to size." With Mick being carted off to prison in Brixton and Keith and Fraser headed to Wormwood Scrubs, he looked to have achieved his aim.

The following days were tumultuous: Michael Havers, counsel to Jagger and Richards, managed to get bail for his clients and see them freed, if temporarily; Mick spoke briefly to the press at a pub near his solicitor's offices, sipping a vodka and lime and wearing a button that declared "Mick Is Sex" (surely he hadn't had the guts to sport it in prison!). Fraser, however, convicted of the most serious offense, was denied release. In the *Evening Standard* and a few other right-thinking papers, The

Who took out ads supporting the Stones against the lunatic sentences and announcing their intention to release a series of recordings of Stones songs as a form of protest; the first, covers of the pointedly chosen "Under My Thumb" and "The Last Time," appeared that very day. That night, at the underground UFO club, an agitated crowd of several hundred was encouraged to march down to the offices of the *News of the World* and protest the paper's involvement with the trial; they then moved on to Piccadilly Circus, where some among them began discussing the possibility of more tangible means of countering such disproportionately punitive sentences for minor drug crimes.

As if these musings magically bore fruit, the next day's edition of *The Times* carried the most unlikely and stirring defense any of them could have imagined of their case. Written by *Times* editor William Rees-Mogg and entitled "Who Breaks a Butterfly on a Wheel?" the several-thousand-word editorial spoke only of Jagger's sentence, arguing that his crime, if it was one at all, was so minor as to amount merely to one judge's unusually strict interpretation of a technicality of the law. The piece invoked the martyrdom of Profumo scandal scapegoat Stephen Ward explicitly and argued against the sense, presumably current among many nonswinging Britons, that Jagger " 'got what was coming to him.' " Further, it came just short of declaring outright that the heavy-handed sentence Jagger received resulted from official (if not personal) distaste for the man, his music and his way of life. "There must remain a suspicion in this case," it concluded, "that Mr. Jagger received a more severe sentence than would have been thought proper for any purely anonymous young man."

A stunning validation, and from the least likely of sources. It was followed presently by a similar piece in the *Sunday Express*; by public disapproval of the smear tactics (if not worse) of the *News of the World* by the likes of playwright John Osborne and Viscount Lambton, a Conservative MP; and by a speech in the House of Commons by Labour MP Tom Driberg, who would one day try to persuade Jagger to run for Parliament—really. Suddenly, the whole sordid thing seemed to have taken on for many observers the aspect it had always had for the Stones themselves and the people among whom they lived and worked: They were being persecuted.

Though it was originally thought that the three men's appeals wouldn't be heard until October, the case was hustled through the system and the verdict of the High Court was presented on July 31, less than five weeks after the sentencing in Chichester. Mick was exonerated, mostly: The judges found the willingness of his doctor to prescribe the sorts of pills he'd been caught with to be a strongly mitigating factor and converted his sentence to a year's conditional release. Stay out of trouble for twelve months, he was told, and it would be like nothing ever happened. But a stern warning was attached: "You are, whether you like it or not," declared the judge, Lord Parker, "the idol of a large number of the young in this country. . . . If you do come to be punished, it is only natural that those responsibilities should carry higher penalties."

Richards, who had been excused from court because of a case of chicken pox, had his conviction utterly quashed, the judges declaring that the jury ought to have been instructed that there was only the merest circumstantial evidence that anyone had smoked dope at the house, much less that Richards knew of it. Indeed, it was insinuated that no case had been made that cannabis had been consumed at Redlands at all.

But Robert Fraser, well, that was another story altogether.

During the previous month, when the Stones were being defended in *The Times* and valorized among the emerging underground, not many voices could be heard supporting Fraser. He was less well known, of course, and his conviction was more defensible. There had been some rallying 'round him: Richard Hamilton curated a tribute at the Robert Fraser Gallery, with every important new English artist and many of the international art figures whom Fraser represented contributing pieces. The centerpiece was Hamilton's series of prints about the Redlands arrests and trials; entitled "Swingeing London," the works were built out of torn-out newspaper articles, photos and headlines—"Naked Girl at Stones' Party," "Stones: 'A Strong, Sweet Smell of Incense' "—along with random bric-a-brac of the era. The single most famous piece was an image of Jagger and Fraser shackled together, tinted by Hamilton so that the handcuffs stood out prominently while the two men appeared in a kind of lurid blur.

But if Jagger and Fraser were linked in the public mind for decades to come through Hamilton's canvas, the appellate court made it clear that their cases were entirely different. Declaring an important distinction between the pills Jagger was convicted over and the heroin capsules in Fraser's possession, the judge pronounced, "Where heroin is concerned . . . the public interest demands that some form of detention should be imposed." Furthermore, he made it clear that Fraser's background, upbringing and military record made him a uniquely appropriate subject for punishment in this case: "If anything, those privileges raise greater responsibilities and would tempt the court to give more rather than less by way of sentence than to a person whom I will deem the man in the street." Fraser, in Keith Richards's words, "was caught between two bits of England"—and rather than find himself transformed by this alchemy, he would be crushed.

When the dust settled that day, it was as if the world had been shaken and turned on its head. Jagger was flown by helicopter to a stately mansion in Finching Field where he appeared live on the television news program *World in Action* to discuss the case and his views on the current affairs with the editor of *The Times*, the Bishop of Woolwich, a Jesuit priest and a former Home secretary and attorney general. The Rolling Stones had faced down the black heart of the establishment and had triumphed; indeed, the establishment had made a place at the table for Mick Jagger. "In the end," reflected Marianne Faithfull, "the assault on the Stones backfired because it hugely empowered the Stones. . . . Before Redlands, the Stones weren't perceived all that differently from a number of other groups—The Who, the Yardbirds, the Kinks—but subsequently they were on another level entirely. The only other group in that category was the Beatles."

The Stones marked the closure of the case with the release of a single—"We Love You"—that opened with the sound of jail doors being slammed. They made a short promotional movie for the song—an early rock video—that showed Mick standing in the dock as Oscar Wilde, Keith as the Marquis of Queensberry and Marianne in drag as Wilde's lover Lord Alfred Douglas. Despite the pockets of support for the Stones in the media, the BBC banned the film.

Robert Fraser, though, didn't fare as well as his friends. Six months in Wormwood Scrubs didn't literally kill him, as it might have Jagger—he reveled in the rough sex and, ex-soldier, dealt well with the discipline and the spartan conditions. But his gallery was placed in receivership, and when he emerged, despite such flashes of his old panache as being driven home from jail in a Daimler limousine, he had changed—almost entirely for the bad. "He came out with a black vengeance in his heart," remembered Faithfull, "but he turned it all against himself."

The drugs, for instance: He was back into that soon enough after his release. And, formerly affable and excitable, he was notably grouchier and moodier in social settings. He went to India for a spell—simply *everybody* did India in 1968—and when he came back, he still seemed addled. That fall, he did a show of conceptual works by John and Yoko—it was the last big boom the Robert Fraser Gallery would make. The following summer, he closed up shop and then he pretty much vanished: India again and then a string of small jobs, culminating in a second, short-lived gallery that had none of the resonant impact of the first.

Booze: debt: drugs: AIDS: one of the first cases to strike a celebrity—or even near-celebrity—in England. He was dead by 1986. Old friends grieved, vexed friends forgave, a legend bubbled in select circles; but the world at large remembered Fraser only as that fellow cuffed to Mick Jagger in that old picture. He was the ideal emblem of his moment in the sun in that he was just as fleeting, inconclusive and disharmonious as it had been.

"He was," said Jim Dine in tribute, "an amazing survivor, except he didn't survive."

THE ROAD TO NOWHERE

On June 4, 1967, Paul McCartney took his new romantic interest, New York photographer Linda Eastman, on a double date with George and Patti Harrison to see the Jimi Hendrix Experience in concert at the Saville Theatre on Shaftsbury Avenue. Only three days earlier, the Beatles had released *Sgt. Pepper's Lonely Hearts Club Band* to a stunned world which, seemingly, hadn't yet taken it off the turntable; everywhere in Europe and North America, young people about to embark upon the giddy, trippy Summer of Love sat red-eyed and wide-pupiled listening to a wholly conceived album of music, the likes of which they'd never heard before. It was an instant global cultural event—maybe the first—and it had simply reinforced the universal impression that the Beatles were the most important musical group in the world.

But the Experience were, arguably, the hippest band in London that spring, riding their own brilliant LP release of just three weeks earlier—*Are You Experienced?*—and headlining their last U.K. concert before traveling to California to play at the Monterey International Pop Festival two weeks hence. That night, after sets by Procol Harum, the Chiffons, Denny Laine and His Electric String Band and the Stormsville Shakers, the Experience opened their performance not with one of their Top 10 singles of the previous months—"Hey Joe," "Purple Haze" or "The Wind Cries Mary"—but, rather, with the title track of the new Beatles album.

In the audience, McCartney sat flabbergasted, working out the logistics of the Experience's hearing, learning, rehearsing and then deciding to perform a number that they only could've become aware of a few days earlier. It was one of his first inklings of what *Sgt. Pepper* would come to mean to people in the next months. Hendrix was obviously a very cool cat with a knack for keeping a jump or three ahead of the others who played the game of street cred; it's no wonder, in that light, that he got to *Pepper* early and continued to play the tune in his stage act for the rest of his life. So, yeah, he was the first person anywhere, in all likelihood, to stop playing the record long enough to learn one of the songs and then perform it.

But if McCartney thought that it was some sort of tribute to him and George in the audience, he might have thought again. Hendrix, after all, may or may not have known that any of the Beatles would be catching his gig. But he *did* know, for sure, that the Saville Theatre, which he played in January and May, was owned by Brian Epstein, who had expanded his management empire beyond the discovery and promotion of Liverpool Beat Boom bands.

Owning a West End theater was one of the more ambitious enterprises in which Brian had involved himself in his bid to become a pillar of traditional English showbiz. He had grand plans, and many of them involved the legitimate stage that had seemed forever closed to him the day he decided to leave RADA. "I intend to buy a wonderful American musical for one of my artists," he boasted. "I should also like to direct or play in a straight drama without the slightest interest in profit."

Good job he wasn't worried about the money: He had begun renting out London theaters as early as 1964, when he hired the Prince of Wales in Piccadilly for a series of pop concerts that resulted in a financial soaking. Then he entered into a partnership with a disc jockey named Brian Matthew to build and operate a theater in Bromley, south of Greenwich, pouring thirty-eight thousand pounds into that prospect bootlessly. Finally, in April 1965, he joined into the partnership group that owned and operated the Saville, buying a 60 percent interest and taking a two-year lease for his experiment.

The booking policy at the Saville was erratic. In its first eighteen months under Epstein's hand, the theater hosted the London run of a new musical with book by James Baldwin, a season of the D'Oyly Carte Opera doing Gilbert and Sullivan, a series of concerts by the Four Tops and a play produced by Brian himself, *A Smashing Day* (future Oscar-winner Ben Kingsley had a small part). Reviews for all were generally favorable, but box office was tepid—and, compared to the millions the Beatles were bringing in, piddling. Brian's connections in the music world ensured the Saville a steady diet of weekly pops concerts, multi-act showcases modeled after revues at the Apollo Theater in Harlem and the Olympia Theatre in Paris. The talent he booked was eclectic—The Who, Chuck Berry, Cream, Fats Domino, the Jimi Hendrix Experience—and a tier of London's popoisie made it the place to be seen of a Sunday night; Brian was often on hand himself, watching the shows from the royal box with the occasional Beatle along. But after a while, savvy old showbiz hands realized that the writing on the wall was in permanent marker: the Saville had become a white elephant.

Brian's failure to expand his success significantly beyond the Beatles had been whispered about derisively for some time, and well-intentioned fiascoes like the Saville only fueled the gossip. By 1967, Gerry & the Pacemakers and Billy J. Kramer and the Dakotas were virtually oldies acts; and other NEMS signees such as the Fourmost, Tommy Quickly, the Silkie, the Cyrkle, Sounds Incorporated, Michael Haslam and the Ruskies had never made any real impression; of the NEMS stable, only Cilla Black, the former Cavern Club hat check girl and one of the original Beatlemaniacs, had something like a career, and that was as much to do with her willingness to go along with Brian's avuncular ministrations and traditional showbiz schtick as with her way with light pop tunes.

The whispers that Brian had merely lucked into the Beatles were underscored in late 1965 when a dispute arose between NEMS and a pair of companies that had been contracted to oversee all licensing agreements for official Beatles merchandise. The companies—Seltaeb (Beatles spelled backward) in the U.S. and Stramsact in Britain—were formed at the suggestion of Brian's legal advisor David Jacobs, whom Brian consulted when NEMS found itself overwhelmed by entrepreneurs who wanted to market Beatle wigs, guitars, badges, chewing gum, dolls, sweaters, record cabinets, candy, shirts, pillows, boots, towels, ottomans, baked goods, wallpaper, caps, drums and whatnot. Some licensing was already being done on an ad hoc basis out of the NEMS office, but it had become clear that a whole new continent of opportunity (and attendant hassle) had been discovered; in 1964, American sales alone of Beatle-related tchotchkes came to more than $50 million. Seltaeb and Stramsact, which were only owned in part by NEMS, were meant to relieve the strain and, of course, turn a few bucks for Brian and the band.

The international segregation of the two licensing outfits worked better on paper than in reality, and the amount of money that was at stake only accentuated the resentment the two firms felt toward each other. When various manufacturers started to complain that somebody else was making and marketing a product that they believed they'd purchased an exclusive license for, Seltaeb and Stramsact came to a series of conflicts and impasses. The men who ran Seltaeb finally brought suit against NEMS, the Beatles and Brian for upward of five million dollars, charging them with violating their contractual right to exclusivity in licensing. After a painful series of depositions in which Seltaeb's lawyers ridiculed and baited Brian, the savvy New York attorney Louis Nizer helped Brian and his opponents reach a settlement of $90,000—plus $85,000 in legal costs—in early 1967.

That was bad enough, but when the Beatles toured the States for the last time in 1966, they heard for the first time about the suit—and, worse, about the vast ocean of money that their likenesses and logo were drawing, none of which was flowing to them. To their horror, they were told that Brian and NEMS had signed away all of the rights to the Beatles' name to Seltaeb for just 10 percent of the net; even putting aside the legal problems, they'd been screwed. Tens of millions had been granted to leeches who had nothing to do with the band—and then tens of thousands had been paid on top of *that* to keep those same leeches at bay.

Their initial reaction was, naturally, to get angry at Brian: "You're supposed to be a manager!"—that sort of thing. But years later, the situation became clearer to them: No one, least of all a Liverpool record store manager, could've foreseen the vast oceans of income the Beatles would produce or the impossible rapids that had to be run to get to them. It was learned, eventually, that the ruthless Colonel Tom Parker hadn't done much better with licensing Elvis Presley's image and name, for instance. "I think the rest of the time Brian did good deals," reflected an older (and richer) Paul McCartney. "I think that for what he knew and what he could bring us he was really excellent."

So he was forgiven, eventually, but there were those qualifiers: ". . . *for what he knew and what he could bring us. . . .*" The truth was, by 1967, Brian had become far less important to the Beatles than he had been five years earlier. Part of it was their decision to stop touring the previous year; booking halls, arranging tours, seeing to specifics on the road—Brian was aces at all that; absent another global tour or even a barnstorming series of shows around England, he had less to do. Plus there was the new reality that the band had grown up: In their mid-twenties and men of the world (and not just any world but one, in large part, of their creation), they felt capable of making their own decisions and dealing with the consequences of their own actions. They relied upon Brian to pull them out of a scrape now and then: He was John's official voice of apology during the absurd "bigger than Jesus" debacle of 1966, for instance. But for the most part they had stopped conferring with him about things like where they should live, how they should dress, whether they should marry and so on—let alone what they should play or record. Even on paper their relationship was in doubt: At the end of 1967, Brian's contract with the band, finalized in 1962, was to expire, and there were hints in the wind that they might not wish to renew it.

Brian felt the need to feel useful to his boys once again, though, and he devised a scheme wherein he would call in somebody else to run the rest of the NEMS empire and leave him to concentrate on the Beatles exclusively. To this end, he had come to a joint operating agreement with Robert Stigwood, the Australian impresario who'd bounced into town a few years earlier and bounded into note as manager of a motley grab-bag of singers, comedians, screenwriters and whoever else happened along; by 1967, Stigwood had such acts as The Who, Cream and the as-yet-unknown Bee Gees in his stable. Brian met Stigwood socially and saw in him, apparently, someone with the energy to run NEMS as well as his own Robert Stigwood Organization. With no counsel from his colleagues at NEMS and no input from the Beatles, Epstein entered into an agreement with Stigwood whereby NEMS acquired RSO and Stigwood was given the option to purchase 50 percent of NEMS for the appallingly low sum of £500,000.

A few years earlier, Brian had shocked the Beatles when he'd asked them if they would agree to his selling them to show mogul Bernard Delfont, who had offered £150,000 for the band outright. Brian had considered it a good deal and asked the band: "They said they would rather break up than leave me," he said afterward. "John told me to fuck off, which was *very* moving." Now they had a similar reaction, declaring that they wouldn't be managed by Stigwood or anyone else other than Brian. "We told Brian that if he sold us to Stigwood, we would only ever record out-of-tune versions of 'God Save the Queen,' " McCartney reported.

But the fact was that, Stigwood or Delfont or no, Brian was losing touch with the band, partly through their transformation and partly through his own. Like the Beatles—indeed, like everyone in the music business and everyone in London connected in some way to the new pop world they'd all created—he was using drugs: pot, LSD, a little heroin even and, most ruinously, pills: ups and downs, the usual mother's little helpers that he relied on to adjust his mood or energy as needed. His mother, Queenie, had been a pillhead of the lace-curtain, dieting-and-then-needing-to-get-some-sleep sort, and the Beatles themselves had dabbled in speed and sleeping pills in Germany, so it was natural that Brian should slip into using pharmaceutical drugs, as well. ("I introduced Brian to pills," John Lennon one day confessed, "to make him talk, to find out what he was like.")

Brian had turned on to pot the same evening the Beatles did—at a New York hotel with Bob Dylan, who had assumed, after mishearing the lyric "I can't hide" in "I Wanna Hold Your Hand" as "I get high," that the Brits were well-steeped in cannabis. Among the evening's ripped hijinks, McCartney recalled, was a very stoned Brian pointing at himself and shouting "Jew!" while laughing hysterically. A few years later, along with the rest of Swinging London, Brian dropped acid, staying at home for the duration of his first trip with friend and employee Pete Brown; in all, he probably tripped about six or so times (compared to, say, Lennon, a true acidhead, who confessed to "hundreds" of LSD doses).

The messy little rituals of using drugs neither appealed to nor suited Brian. He couldn't roll his own joints, for instance, and McCartney would laugh at the recollection of this very grand man holding forth with a scraggly little doobie in his fingertips. But he more and more immersed himself in drug use, taking chauffeured drives through New

York's Central Park while he smoked dope or holing up in a marijuana-scented bungalow at the Beverly Hills Hotel. When the drug use of the Beatles became public—largely on the strength of Paul's admissions to it in *Life* magazine in June 1967—Brian tried to calm the ensuing storm by admitting to the press that he, too, had taken LSD and smoked marijuana. Like many of the young acolytes who were speaking out in favor of psychedelic drugs, he averred that they weren't nearly so harmful as, say, alcohol, and that he had accrued some real benefits—relaxation, awareness and the classic: reduction of ego.

But what was good for a pop star or other type of artist wasn't necessarily a tonic for a businessman. As Brian became freer and more open-minded, he also became less reliable at the office. He was hardly around at all, according to McCartney, during the conception or recording of *Sgt. Pepper* and wasn't able to offer the band much help when they needed to negotiate the complex matter of obtaining permission to use the famous faces they wanted to have on the album cover. He would retreat from the main NEMS office to a private office he maintained near Piccadilly, separate from the Argyll Street headquarters, and then he would find himself unable to make it over to *that* location, locking himself up in his bedroom and insisting that he not be disturbed by anyone for any reason. He was increasingly erratic when he did appear, losing his train of thought, shunting meetings onto profitless and insignificant sidebars, becoming more temper-prone than ever before.

He even had trouble keeping up a public facade. He was quite obviously zonked on the air in a radio interview with New York disc jockey Murray the K, for instance, and he was seen by old chum Lionel Bart shopping in the King's Road boutique Granny Takes a Trip in what can only be charitably described as a state of disrepair. Bart, too, had succumbed to the drug culture (and, more, booze), and it was a fleeting and not very happy reunion. "It was the first time I'd ever seen him without a tie in the city," Bart recalled. "We did not talk; we both knew we were both wrecked and on the road to nowhere."

On May 17, 1967, Brian's road finally found a destination: the Priory Hospital, a private rehabilitation clinic in Roehampton, a green southwest London suburb, where he would take a much-needed rest and, hopefully, learn to live without relying so heavily on drugs. Brian had visited the clinic once before for a rest and checkup; this time, he was rushed there by friends after collapsing into unconsciousness after what at least one of them claimed was a suicide attempt—and maybe not the first. He stayed at the facility on and off for a while; as a voluntary patient, he was able to come and go as he pleased, allowing him to see to such duties as the press party for the launch of *Sgt. Pepper*, which he held at his discreetly elegant Chapel Street, Belgravia, home on May 19 (meeting number two, as it happened, of Paul McCartney and Linda Eastman, who were photographed in conversation).

Brian's health crisis—coming as it did when the Beatles were searching for new avenues of expression, had come to rely less upon his day-to-day administration and were even questioning his judgment—might have given the band reason to seek another manager outright. But it occasioned, rather, another fraternal outpouring toward him: John, of all people, sent a floral bouquet to the hospital with a note attached: "I love you and you know I mean it."

A heartening gesture, obviously, but one tinged with bittersweet irony. John had made a point for years of teasing Brian openly and somewhat caustically. When Brian asked the published author Lennon what he should call his ghostwritten biography, John suggested "Queer Jew"; when it appeared as *A Cellarful of Noise*, John was among the mocking throngs who persisted in calling it "A Cellarful of Boys." He loudly asked publicist Tony Barrow, "If you're not queer and you're not Jewish, what are you doing coming to work for NEMS?" Once when Brian made a suggestion from the control booth at a recording session, John (who, like George Harrison, seemed always keenly aware of the fact that Epstein and NEMS had a 25 percent cut of the Beatles—more, in effect, than any single band member) shut him down with, "Stick to your percentages. We'll make the music."

If the sting of all that was lessened by Brian's knowledge that John didn't half mean the cruel things he said, his personal life nevertheless offered him little in the way of comforting balm. Though his wealth and celebrity might have allowed him at least an introduction to any number of likely lovers and potential partners, his taste for lower-class, rough sorts remained—and remained problematic.

"Brian was always attracted to a crass and macho man," said Nat Weiss, the New York impresario with whom Epstein formed a transatlantic business alliance and who spent many nights catting about Manhattan with Brian at such notorious gay haunts as Kelly's bar and the Wagon Wheel. Simon Napier-Bell, himself a focus of Brian's attentions, recalled Brian's eye being caught by what Epstein called "a Greek god"—who was, in fact, merely an Irish navvy with a pneumatic drill engaged in roadwork.

As per his account of that awful arrest in Swiss Cottage back in his RADA days, Brian wasn't a very straightforward suitor of men he fancied. "He was like the girl that drops the handkerchief," said Weiss. " 'I'm available but you come after me.' " Of course, given his wealth and, even more, his fame and association with the Beatles, many prospects were enticed to take the initiative. And, naturally, some were rapacious.

In late 1964, Brian became involved with a young American hustler named John Gillespie, who bore the nickname Dizz. Dizz was the longest-lasting and most visible attachment Brian ever had, and he was as awful as anyone might have feared. After moving him from New York to London, Brian put Dizz on the NEMS payroll for fifty pounds a week in exchange for no discernable work. He introduced Dizz to the Beatles (who couldn't stand him) and even to his parents; Dizz would often be a dinner guest at Brian's home when Harry and Queenie were down from Liverpool. But Dizz was a piece of work—stealing from Brian, sleeping around on him, throwing temper tantrums in front of whomever. When he couldn't behave himself respectfully while accompanying Brian and the Beatles on a 1965 tour of America, Brian had Weiss pay him to get lost.

The following year, the very night the Beatles were playing their last proper concert, in San Francisco, Brian, who had stayed in Los Angeles on business, was contacted by Dizz. Gullible as ever, he allowed the guy to visit him at his bungalow at the Beverly Hills Hotel, then excused himself while he and Weiss went to dinner; when they returned, Dizz was gone and so were their briefcases. Brian was missing money, contracts, pills; while the two men argued about what to do—Weiss wanted to call the cops—a note arrived: Dizz wanted $10,000 or he would go to the police with Brian's stash of contraband drugs. Something was arranged and Brian recovered the papers, but not the drugs nor all the money. Weiss, too familiar with Dizz's type to share Brian's romantic chimera about the boy, wound up bringing in the cops.

Maybe the aftertaste of that experience was enough to turn Brian, the following year, to pursuit of not another mean little rent boy but

Napier-Bell, a classic fallen public schoolboy who had essayed careers in jazz trumpeting and filmmaking before stumbling into the pop management gig. Napier-Bell was introduced to Brian in August 1967 by Robert Stigwood; Brian, having finished his rehabilitation at the Priory, was back in the swing of life, inviting Napier-Bell to dinner and then, after a deluxe French meal, back to his Chapel Street house; Napier-Bell spent the rest of the evening fending off advances. Brian, switching tactics, suggested next that Napier-Bell pass the upcoming bank holiday weekend with him at his five-acre Queen Anne country home, Kingsley Hill, in East Sussex, which he'd purchased earlier in the year for £25,000 and where he had hosted a grand, acid-drenched hippie house party on May 28. Again, Napier-Bell, who'd already made plans to traipse through Ireland with rock journalist Nik Cohn, declined—some other time, perhaps.

There would be no other invitations—at least not as such. Brian went to Kingsley Hill with a group of friends, throwing together a ragtag weekend party. It was a dull, foggy get-together and Brian was restless. He drove back to London on Friday night and, over the next twenty-eight hours or so, left a series of strange messages on Napier-Bell's answering machine: cajoling, pleading, spitting spite, babbling. Sometime during the earliest hours of August 27, inside his locked Chapel Street bedroom suite, his bloodstream full of the sedative Carbrital, which he'd been using for months and had built up a constitutional tolerance for, Brian died.

It had been, especially for Brian, a death-soaked season: In October 1966, Alma Cogan, barely thirty-three, had succumbed to cancer, a tragedy made more bitter to Brian, no doubt, as it preceded a posthumous hit LP, *Alma*, which included several Beatles covers including, finally, "Yesterday." The following February, on the exact anniversary of the death of his beloved hero Buddy Holly, Joe Meek, England's Phil Spector, a genuine loon who recorded acts in his bathroom for the acoustics, killed his landlady with a shotgun blast and then turned the weapon on himself; the fashions of music had passed him by—his last really big hit had been "Telstar" in 1962—but his death still created a chill ripple around town. In June 1967, six months after a massive heart attack, Brian's father, Harry, had died in Liverpool. A mere handful of weeks later, Joe Orton, the hot young playwright (and bit of rough) who had been commissioned by Brian to write the next Beatles movie (unsatisfactorily, as it turned out), was murdered by his lover. ("A Day in the Life," then banned by the BBC, was played at the funeral.)

But none of those passings had quite the impact of Brian's. This was the Fifth Beatle, after all, the well-spoken, dapper, thoughtful young man who'd managed, by popular myth, to create the biggest act showbiz had ever known. Yes, he'd admitted to drug use, and, yes, everyone had heard by now of one or two tragic drug casualties. But Brian was as near to a star as pop management had ever produced; people like him were supposed to be immune.

Perhaps that's why, inevitably, rumors about the circumstances of his death spread so quickly: It was suicide; it was murder; he'd been smothered; he'd used a pharmacopoeia of drugs; he'd had company—a Coldstream Guardsman, one nitwit swore—throughout the weekend. Lord knew there was plenty of reason to assume the worst: After breaking in on his death scene, his house staff and a NEMS employee discovered a total of twenty-eight bottles of prescription medication in his bedroom and bathroom, as well as some marijuana. On top of that, any wild theory, it seems, could stand. But so, too, could the most sad and squalid: drugged and boozed, lonely, depressed, a man who'd always been careless with medicine took one, two, six pills too many and died in his sleep, never realizing his mistake.

The Beatles got the news in Bangor, North Wales, of all places, where they'd gone to study at the feet of the Maharishi Mahesh Yogi, George's guru and the band's newfound spiritual leader. In a sense, it was the ideal setting in which to hear of such a devastating event: tranquility, privacy and the instruction and example of a man with, one would think, a deep understanding of the cycles of human life to convey. Predictably, then, the first public responses that the band made to Brian's death were infused with the calm, accepting grace of Eastern mysticism: There's no such thing as death; Brian has simply moved to another level of Being; grief is a selfish emotion; forget it; be happy; blah blah blah.

On October 17, 1967, the Beatles, who'd avoided the Liverpool funeral to keep the attendant media uproar to a minimum, gathered at the New London Synagogue in St. John's Wood for Brian's memorial service. They sat in suits and paper yarmulkes, for one afternoon, in that most psychedelic of years, abandoning the hippie gear they'd all adopted. Just down the road stood the Abbey Road Studios where they'd recently finished work on the tracks for *Magical Mystery Tour*. And three blocks away was the St. John's Wood tube station via which Brian had cabled them in Hamburg to let them know that EMI wanted to give them a recording test.

In the wake of Brian's passing, according to at least one account, the Maharishi volunteered to be the new father to the band; they went so far as to make a pilgrimage to his home base in Rishikesh, India, in early 1968 to study further with him. But John, maybe because he felt closer to Brian than the others, maybe because he was just being John, quickly turned aside any notion that Brian could be replaced; "fucking idiot" he was said to have responded at the giggling little holy man's suggestion that the Beatles shouldn't mourn their friend; years later he claimed that he knew the band was finished the day Brian died.

In the spring of 1968, while developing the songs that would comprise what came to be called The White Album, John revealed where his alliances truly lay: The Indian guru was scalded in a song about duplicity, "Sexy Sadie," which was originally called "Maharishi," while the Beatles manager was the subject of an improvised blues. Ebullient, raucous and irreverent, it made reference to Queenie and mocked Clive Epstein, Brian's brother, as a "dirty old man"—and, curiously, pronounced Brian's surname as "Ep*stine*" when, in fact, the family always pronounced it "Ep*steen*" (polite Brian rarely corrected people who used the wrong form).

The tune was a trifle, a throwaway, nothing Brian would have allowed the band to record when he had a say. But it was exuberant and joyous, irreverent and danceable, just the sort of thing he'd fallen in love with at the Cavern a mere six years earlier—an ironically fitting tribute from Lennon to the man who helped pull him and his mates up from the cellar.

God knew they would miss him—even his dodgy business sense. Unmoored after his death and searching, ever searching for new ways of being and expressing themselves, they fell into a financial miasma of comically grotesque proportions.

In December 1967, they opened a clothes boutique called Apple in a four-story building they owned on the corner of Baker and Paddington streets, a bland commercial district between Marylebone and Soho. The name was inspired by a Magritte that Paul McCartney had purchased through Robert Fraser, one of those stunning depictions of large, round green apples that the artist produced toward the end of his life.

The idea of the shop was, in part, inspired by The Fool, an artistic collective consisting of three Dutch hippies and a Brit. The Fool had been kept busy by the Beatles throughout 1967: They'd been commissioned to design a discarded cover concept for *Sgt. Pepper's Lonely Hearts Club Band*; they'd done the costumes and sets for the global satellite transmission of "All You Need Is Love"; they'd been hired for some graphics work for the Saville Theatre; and they'd painted a piano for John Lennon and built a fireplace and chimney for George Harrison's Esher home.

At the same time, they ran their own little boutique off New Cavendish Street, not far from the Baker Street location. It was Lennon who discovered them there, remembered Simon Posthuma, one of the principals: "John walked into our place and saw our stuff—furniture and posters as well as clothes—and he said, 'This is where I want to live.' "

John had, in fact, been discovering all sorts of new people and bringing them into the Beatles' orbit: Yoko Ono, of course, whom he met in late 1966 and for whom he would leave his wife and with whom he would attempt to challenge everyone's ideas about fame and love and peace and art; and Magic Alex, a Greek TV repairman born Yannis Alexis Mardas, who did a better job scamming the Beatles out of good money than any Denmark Street song publisher, showbiz lawyer or corporate pillager they ever came across.

Mardas came to the band looking for investments in "inventions" he'd "dreamed up"—some quite practical (and, in fact, already in the works in the labs of legitimate scientists) like a telephone that responded to voice commands or displayed the number of incoming callers, and some plainly the work of a drugged-up madman: electric wallpaper that would light up or serve as stereo speakers ("loudpaper," he called it); a hovering house; an X-ray camera that could reveal the goings-on inside a building; force fields to protect the privacy of your home or the rear bumper of your car. Mardas had put together a light show for some Rolling Stones concerts, but those savvy fellows didn't go for his bigger schemes (nor, truly, did they have the money to fund them). But the Beatles set him up in an electronics studio—Apple Electronics—and commissioned all sorts of goodies from him, everything from flying saucers to recording studios. He even got them to buy a Greek island, Leslo, with the plan of having them build a communal house there for themselves, their wives and girlfriends and select chums.

Compared to Magic Alex and his vaporware, The Fool were for real.

Given £100,000 by the Beatles in September 1967 to start the Apple boutique, they designed some truly wild hippie gear, some suitably outrageous furnishings for the store and, most audaciously, a gigantic psychedelic mural for both street fronts of the building—fully forty feet high on either side, a magnificent, rainbow-hued godlike figure with hints of Hindu, Buddhist, American Indian, Taoist, Incan and Egyptian gods as well as infernal flames and space travel. There was an opening bash on December 5, and then the place unlocked its doors to the public two days later. It was a success in the sheer volume of noise it invoked in the press, bodies clocked through the doorway and consternation provoked in neighbors, whose objections to the lovely mural got the thing whitewashed by legal order. The expensively manufactured clothes (The Fool were permitted to mark the shirts they designed with silk labels that cost more than the garments themselves), the stoned accounting practices and the unreliable shop staff that would pilfer more merchandise than it ever sold led to astounding losses: £200,000 in a little more than half a year.

But it wasn't what was happening on the street level or on the outside brickwork that was truly amazing. It was inside, upstairs, where the Beatles were—at the advice of their financial advisors—endeavoring to lower their increasingly outrageous tax burden by creating companies that would, in essence, give away their money in worthy fashion. There was already Apple Electronics and Apple Retail (with a second location—Apple Tailoring—opening on the King's Road), and soon there would be Apple Records (with the subsidiary label, Zapple, devoted to the spoken word), Apple Films and Apple Publishing.

By the end of the year, the group announced that Beatles Ltd., the company they owned along with Brian Epstein's NEMS, had been yoked together with all the new Apple companies as Apple Corps. "The idea is to have an 'underground' company above ground," explained McCartney, "but with no profit motive." And then they all flew off to India to learn how to meditate while the lawyers, leeches and functionaries in their wake set about seeing to it that Apple never did turn a penny of profit.

Some of the people involved with Apple were legitimate, like Derek Taylor, the former newsman who'd worked in publicity for Brian Epstein and gone on to be a principal creator of the Monterey International Pop Festival. Hired to run the Apple publicity department, Taylor helped steer such events as the May press conference in New York where John and Paul declared their intentions—very vague ones at that—for the new company (after which they sailed in circles around the Statue of Liberty in a Chinese junk, trying to figure out just what it was they really meant to do). And he was on hand for the grand opening, in July 1968, of the Apple headquarters at 3 Savile Row, a splendid Georgian townhouse in which Admiral Nelson had kept Lady Hamilton and which most recently served as the headquarters of former bandleader Jack Hylton's theatrical management firm.

But Taylor, for all his savoir faire, cunning and wit, had gone hippie with the times, and while he was able to create fabulous PR events for Apple products and launches, he was also at the center of the chaos that ensued at Savile Row. It wasn't all his fault—the Beatles had literally encouraged the world to come to them with its daffiest ideas and its hands out. They put out fliers asking people to send demo tapes and unpublished manuscripts and experimental films; they entertained such insane prospects as opening a children's school and establishing a park where the police wouldn't be allowed to enforce laws about public nudity, intoxication or vagrancy; they kept an astrologer on hand to toss the I-Ching for them and a house hippie whose paid work involved rolling joints and mixing drinks. Out on the street congregated the masses the band called Apple Scruffs, girls swoony just to be in the proximity of their idols; inside, you could find almost anyone who was anyone in London—and a fair number of people who'd come to London just to mooch off the Beatles. Among the throngs were the Doors, the Mamas and the Papas, the Jefferson Airplane, Hare Krishnas, Hell's Angels, the Diggers, the Merry Pranksters, Peter Sellers, Lauren Bacall, Dean Stockwell, Diana Rigg and Terence Stamp, who lived just across the road—as well as countless girls and Fleet Street journalists and a shifting cast of international oddballs, including a homeless family from California who actually took up residence in the visitors' room. In the famous Apple press offices, guests could always count on a whiskey and Coke—or three or four—and a joint and maybe a trip and some shapely legged girls to ogle and maybe even, on those odd occasions when any of them bothered to drop in, a peek at a Beatle.

There was real business to attend to: Apple Records signed, among others, James Taylor, Mary Hopkin, Liverpool rocker (and old Beatle mate) Jackie Lomax, the Modern Jazz Quartet and Billy Preston. Zapple released recordings of poet Charles Olson and made others of

Richard Brautigan, Allen Ginsberg and Lawrence Ferlinghetti, which appeared elsewhere later on. And the Beatles recorded a lot of *Let It Be* in the basement studio that had been built for them—after torturous labors—by Magic Alex, who was so ill-informed about his own professed specialty that he initially built a sixteen-track stereo recording system with sixteen separate loudspeakers for playback.

By the time of those sessions, however, and the group's famous January 1969 rooftop concert, much of the Apple dream had dissolved. The Baker Street boutique had been closed after less than eight months of operation, the Beatles allowing people to come in and take whatever they wanted out of the place for free (after picking the cream themselves); the King's Road premises barely outlasted it.

And in the ensuing bickering—legal, financial and personal—that ended in the demise of the group, most of Apple's employees, legit and not, were given the boot from Savile Row. The company, which had been designed to lose *some* money, had succeeded too well: It nearly bankrupted its four principals. "Apple wasn't being run," said Ringo Starr. "It was being run into the ground."

THIS EGO I HAD NURTURED WAS CRUSHED

Albany is among the most handsome and storied addresses in Piccadilly, a block of apartments built in the 1770s for the first Viscount Melbourne along the lines of a Parisian mansion. In the early nineteenth century, the property was acquired by a builder who had it broken into sixty bachelor flats—places in town in which rich young men from the provinces could hang their hats and get laid. With gates onto Piccadilly and Vigo Street, it sits smack across the road from Fortnum & Mason on one side and Savile Row on the other and has the Royal Academy of Arts and Burlington Gardens on its western border. The interior seems transported from Italy or France: The apartments (or "sets," as Albany residents call them) look out on an immaculate garden divided by a paved, colonnaded walkway with rope railings. Lord Byron lived there, dallying with Lady Caroline Lamb, and in his wake Albany (never "*the*

Albany") was home to scores of distinguished men—Macauley, Gladstone, Bulwer-Lytton, T. S. Eliot, J. B. Priestley, Graham Greene, Terence Rattigan, Sir Thomas Beecham, Edward Heath—and, after the doors were opened to women, Margaret Leighton and Dame Edith Evans.

The first time Terence Stamp got a gander at the place, he was working as a messenger boy and thought he'd stumbled upon Shangri-la. It was years before he learned its name and more years still before he first entered to have tea and cakes with Jean Shrimpton, their mutual pal antique dealer Geoffrey Bennison and their host, art critic John Richardson. Stamp tried to hide his awe at the surroundings, sinking into his thickest East End dialect (a sure sign, Shrimpton knew, that he was nervous), but he brightened up when he heard that one could actually acquire a residence at Albany through the usual sorts of means: newspaper ads, sublets, even long-term leases. Stamp tried to act nonchalant and, casual like, asked Richardson to contact him if he knew of a set coming available. A month later, through Bennison, he did: Stamp made arrangements for a two-year lease on an eight-room set, which Bennison decorated for him ("I won't make your pad too camp," he promised"). In the spring of 1966, Stamp moved in, a tugboat pilot's son claiming a slice of aristocratic history as his own.

Like other East End boys who made good, Stamp was always loyal to his roots, and used them as a measuring rod as he went on to fame and fortune in the world. "All the East End boys loved their families in the way I never saw middle-class people love their families," reflected Patsy Puttnam, wife of David Puttnam. "All the boys I knew, as soon as they made a bit of money, saw that their families were taken care of, bought them a house. Stamp, until the day his mom died, was there every Sunday he was in England. There was never any feeling of, 'Oh my God: I can't show people where I came from.' Terence, sometimes when he was talking about some of his girlfriends, said, 'I sometimes want to say to them, "You wanna have met my mom. You wanna have seen what my mom did." ' He said, 'I see these girls: They can't even make a flipping cup of tea!' "

But for all that, moving into Albany put Stamp beside himself with pleasure. "It knocks me out, I'm so happy with it," he said. "I wake up in the morning and think of all the great men who have lived here." He made sure that he obeyed all the ancient rules of the house:

Shrimpton, much to her annoyance, was announced each time she arrived; he kept his household decorously quiet and clean, relying on a cook and maid to see to details and promising the press, "I will not bring in floozies and give all-night parties." Yes, he spoke to the press about his new home. Sniffed one cold-eyed observer: "He lived in Albany, but he *talked about* living in Albany, and one doesn't talk about living in Albany." Perhaps such gauche touches were inevitable given Stamp's youth and his line of work; for the most part, he fit in (he would stay for decades); as he explained, "It's not a question of money. It's a question of the type of person you are. I was the right type for the [sic] Albany."

He was certainly sufficiently on top of the world: *Modesty Blaise* hadn't yet opened to the first indifferent reviews of his young career, he was involved with the most desirable woman he could imagine, he had money and fame and status. "I often used to think that if I died today, this moment, I would have had more than my fair share," he remembered. "No man could have asked for more."

But there were unexpected blows ahead. That spring, in a bungalow at the Beverly Hills Hotel, Jimmy Woolf died of an overdose of sleeping pills, a copy of *Valley of the Dolls* open upon his chest. Stamp tried not to let anyone—not even Shrimpton—see how hurt he was, but he was unmoored; Woolf was a paternal figure for him, a daily presence in his life, a touchstone for all career and personal decisions of any magnitude. He tried to make light of his loss—"Jimmy taught me to be an honest bastard," he told the press—but Shrimpton knew "he could not fail to miss this friend who had taken such a close interest in his career."

In fact, as she was to discover to her shock, Stamp had learned from Woolf more than just directness. Just as Woolf had shepherded Stamp's career into what many of the actor's friends felt was too rarefied and anemic a mode, Stamp was trying to steer Shrimpton's career—both as a model and as an aspiring actress—in ways that she neither approved of nor even knew about. A variation on the classic he said, she said situation, it was enough to fracture the dream.

When Shrimpton found herself increasingly requested for work other than modeling, Stamp suggested she get herself a proper agent and, at Woolf's suggestion, went to see John Heyman, who was still working as an actor's representative but branching out slowly into producing.

Heyman agreed to help Shrimpton in all but her modeling work and she signed over 25 percent of whatever he booked for her as his fee; in a gesture of magnanimity to Stamp, Heyman offered him ten points of his twenty-five—a finder's fee. Stamp declared that he wanted nothing to do with it, that he wasn't looking to make money off his girlfriend. But Heyman insisted, and Woolf said there was nothing wrong with it. And then Stamp did something very foolish: He decided he would surprise Shrimpton by keeping the money for her in a dedicated account and later handing it over to her in one lavish lump; "I've always been a sucker for surprising people," he gushed.

But it all got prickly when Shrimpton was finally offered real film work. Peter Watkins, who'd created a sensation with two films for the BBC, was looking to break into features with a story about a decadent rock star. In the lead, he'd already cast Paul Jones, lead singer of the Manfred Mann group; he wanted Shrimpton to play opposite. Stamp thought it was a bad move: unproven director, unproven leading man, enormous role—a rotten situation for a first-time actress. But Shrimpton didn't like being told no. And Heyman—who was counting on the film to be his first theatrical production credit—was able to show her his signed agreement with Stamp for that 10 percent as a means of making her doubtful of her boyfriend's advice.

Learning that Stamp owned, in effect, a piece of her, Shrimpton was furious. It didn't matter that Stamp had never been paid a penny—she hadn't done any work through Heyman yet, after all—or, as she admitted later, that "I never really made any money until I was with Terence Stamp." She felt tricked and used—even if, as she was eventually to acknowledge, that he hadn't profited at all. She would go ahead and make the film just to spite him.

It was their first serious row—or at least the first time she had responded to some off-putting behavior of his with real pique and resentment. And as she went off to make the film, she was astounded to read a newspaper account of Stamp's estimation of her chances. "When Jean announced to me that she was going to do the film, I felt a sense of loss," he said. And then it got worse:

> You don't have to climb into bed with a man to be unfaithful. I felt Jean had cheated me. It hurt. . . . She's very much an amateur as an actress, and I'm dead against amateurs being used when profes-

sionals are available. Jean announcing that she was playing a lead in a film would be like me announcing that I'm going to perform a rather complicated brain surgery tomorrow afternoon. Crazy, man. I mean, that's it. That's the strength of it. For her to feel she can cope with a big part in a feature film must take a great deal of conceit or a genuine unawareness of the bloody pressures you're under when you're making a film. . . . It must change it. It'll never be the same again, that's for sure. Good or bad, it'll never be quite the same. . . . If Peter Watkins is supposed to be such a dedicated cat, what's his excuse for using a model with no acting experience at all? There's no excuse, except he's jumping on the Shrimpton bandwagon. It would be like casting Mick Jagger to play Hamlet . . . a cheap stunt.

(This was the same Stamp, mind you, who was to declare of Shrimpton, "She was always supportive of me in public." How was *that* for reciprocation?)

It was too much for her, and she briefly left him. But not altogether—she truly was so ill at ease making the film that she felt it necessary to have as much stability in her life as possible, even if it was tinged with hurt. At Christmas, in fact, she gave him a horse as a gift—part of his preparation for *Far from the Madding Crowd* would be learning to ride. But when he went to Dorset to make the film, she never once visited: Not even the threat of his old flame Julie Christie playing opposite him could lure her to the set.

(There were even rumors that Stamp and Christie were back together, and the lilt of their names in the tabloids—Terry and Julie—inspired, said Stamp, Ray Davies of the Kinks in his remarkably wistful single "Waterloo Sunset." "He told my brother he thought of Julie Christie and me when he wrote it," Stamp declared. But Davies later on said that he was writing about his nephew and the girl he was seeing, who happened to have the same names. Whichever: It was still a great song.)

His private life aside, Stamp wasn't enjoying the work on the film. Although he relished the chance—his first—to play a real romantic lead in the dashing cavalry officer Troy, he was told by director John Schlesinger to ditch the Dorset accent he'd worked so hard to master.

And he felt decidedly a second-class passenger compared to Christie, whom Schlesinger had directed to a Best Actress Oscar in *Darling*.

"I didn't have a good time with Schlesinger," Stamp admitted later. "He was the first director that I worked with that didn't think I was the greatest thing since sliced loaf. I think that he genuinely saw the character differently, and I think that the producer had sort of foisted me on the director. So I can't really lay the blame at Schlesinger's feet. I'd just had this love from Ustinov and Wyler. But [Schlesinger] wouldn't have known also how tender I was. I was like Jack the Lad, you know, at this great critical moment of my life."

And the film didn't work out all that well, either. The idea of Swinging Londoners like Stamp, Christie and Bates struggling within the moral straightjackets worn by Thomas Hardy's nineteenth-century provincials wasn't so much provocative as risible. The film was well played—and beautifully photographed by Nicolas Roeg—but critics attacked it and audiences were bored. "The critics pissed on us," Stamp said. "You could have run a shy horse through that *Far from the Madding Crowd* first-night party, you know. There was Julie Christie and me and a few people there for the beer."

Yet Stamp made a convincing romantic lead—part diabolical sex, part chivalrous heroism—continuing to display a bracing range in his ability. His next picture was small but pivotal in that he was playing the nearest he had up to that point to the sort of fellow he really was—or might have been had he listened to his dad and stayed out of acting. Ken Loach's *Poor Cow* was the story of an unwed London mother's struggle to make a life for herself as various men drift through it. Stamp was cast as Dave, a young thief who romances her and then winds up in prison. The role, though hardly as celebrated as the others he'd done, was liberating for him. "With my London accent," he explained, "I would've had a career playing lorry drivers or the domestics in *A Midsummer Night's Dream*. You had to speak properly, you had to have this kind of sophistication. So all of my early films were almost played as a dialect. *Poor Cow* was the first part where I was asked to play a Cockney. And I was able to revert back not to what I was, but to young spivs and yobbos that I had grown up with."

If such a choice of roles hadn't made it clear that Jimmy Woolf was no longer steering him, his next project would be the clincher. Silvio

Narizzano, who had nearly cast Stamp in *Georgy Girl*, had been given the chance by Paramount Pictures to direct Robert Redford in a western (somebody must have been drunk on the sixties notion that Italians had revitalized the cowboy movie but failed to discover that Narizzano was, in fact, Canadian); when Redford bowed out, he asked Stamp if he'd like to play the role—of a half-Mexican criminal.

A Cockney bandito? Jimmy Woolf would have pissed himself laughing. And Stamp would've eventually seen the joke and joined in. Instead, making his own decisions—idiot!—he said yes.

Off he went to L.A. while Shrimpton went to New York to work on a campaign for Yardley, the London cosmetics company that had penetrated the American market more deeply even than Mary Quant. Stamp didn't think the company had offered Shrimpton quite a good enough deal—he wanted her to have a signature line of products, for instance, not to mention more money—but as the contracts had been worked out by John Heyman's office, he wasn't exactly eager to point out their flaws to her.

Worse, while she was in Manhattan working on the ad campaign, she met someone—a photographer's assistant—and she went out on a date with him. When they got to the restaurant, whom did they run into but Chris Stamp, in New York on record business. Shrimpton always liked Chris—she described him as "attractive and far less complicated than his big brother"—but a brother's a brother, right? A few days later, when Chris passed through L.A. en route to the Monterey International Pop Festival with The Who, he stayed with his brother in a house above the Sunset Strip and told him what he'd seen. And then Shrimpton herself came west.

Maybe Stamp just didn't want to admit what was happening. Maybe he really did love her as much as he says and was blinded. Maybe he was just an obstinate, egoistic Cockney boy who couldn't imagine that his bird would leave him. Or maybe he was just stoned. He had discovered marijuana on this particular trip and was getting into the habit of smoking it all day—just as eager to dive into the drug culture, Shrimpton recalled, as he had been to get into physical fitness and health foods. "The house stank of the stuff," she said of the dope.

On her second morning in L.A., they sat out by the pool smoking a joint—her first—and making small talk: a terrific strain by her account; ecstasy by his: sun, water, weed, a gorgeous woman.

And then she dropped the bomb: It was over.

He paled. He stared. He spoke, more calmly than she feared he might and just as pathetically, in the end, as David Bailey had just a few years before: "But I was going to marry you. . . ." (The last words, it would appear, of every Cockney Romeo standing on the edge of getting dumped.)

They talked and cried and never quite rowed, but it was clear somebody had to go. Such was the stress of the moment that they didn't agree, in retrospect, who left the house: He said she did; she said it was him. Whichever, his account of the final moments of the morning is the more poignant:

"I'd like to make love to you, before you go."

"Oh, just do it, then."

Ouch. (For the record, her retort, he said, "rendered me instantly desireless.")

Within a few days, a parting dinner, and she was back in New York with her new man.

And Stamp was left to fall into a whirlpool.

Just as it had three years earlier when Shrimpton had left Bailey for Stamp, London was now buzzing with word that she'd left Stamp for somebody whom nobody knew. Stamp actually got a transatlantic telephone call early one morning from some full-of-gall reporter: "I hear Shrimpton's given you the elbow."

The first face he put on was, naturally, brave: "There comes a point in every relationship when two people who have been going together for a long time either get married or go their separate ways. Well, we separated because even after all this time we weren't sure about each other. Our relationship wasn't going anywhere."

But it was far, far worse to live through it than to act the stoic. "It was terrible," he admitted later on. "Not only was it somebody I really loved, but this ego I had nurtured was crushed—and publicly."

And: "The trauma was so deep that I thought, well, nothing helps me now. Not the Roller [Rolls-Royce], not the money, not the travel."

And: "I was under the impression that I was Errol Flynn. Whereas in fact I was Freddie Bartholemew."

Luckily, there was still the western to make in the Utah desert. He bought a shoebox full of pot—Acapulco gold, "the heads' equivalent of 1906 cognac," he remembered, barely—and lost himself in the rocks and the smoke and the roadside pool halls and the companionship of his costar, Joanna Pettet. When the shoot ended, he visited Haight-Ashbury, spent time learning how to grow pot on a sinsemilla orchard and made a pilgrimage to an Indian medicine man out near Joshua Tree. Tooling around the Malibu Mountains in a sports car with his brother and a journalist, he got busted by the cops on a pot beef: "Policemen claimed," said a newspaper account, "that they detected a strong smell of burning marijuana when they drew alongside the actor's car at a (stop) sign. They also said that they found a small glass tube full of marijuana in the pocket of Terence Stamp's blue jeans and that his brother . . . dropped a half-smoked marijuana cigarette."

Eventually he couldn't keep running: He had to attend a press premiere of *Far from the Madding Crowd* in Bath; he would have to return to England.

It was awful: He lay in his bed at Albany cuddling one of Shrimpton's old sweaters. He went to a party on Cheyne Walk and smoked so much hash that he could barely walk out of the door. He contemplated suicide. Then, a miraculous lifeline: his agent on the phone: "Fellini's sent to London for the most decadent young actors we've got. He wants you to go to Rome."

Perfect. Federico Fellini was making a short film as part of a trilogy of Edgar Allan Poe stories; he had chosen "Never Bet the Devil Your Head," a story about Toby Dammit, a reprobate who tempts an ill fate by continually invoking the Dark One, and transposed it into the story of a debauched, effete English actor who comes to Italy to accept an award and make a western, only to spend a fatal night racing around Rome in a Ferrari. The part had been written with Peter O'Toole in mind, but he had pulled out at the last minute, and Fellini needed a replacement pronto. Stamp jetted to Rome. The driver, who had just escorted James Fox to an unsuccessful meeting for the role, knew right away when he got a look at Stamp that the director had found his man: "Theees other, hee too much *inglese*, too gentleman for Federico. You, 'ee like; *decadente*, yes?"

Yes, indeed. Physically, Stamp was ideal for the part—he'd become gaunt and bedraggled and was obviously deeply unhappy. The self-loathing that practically dripped from his skin meshed perfectly with the character of Toby Dammit. Fellini exaggerated the actor's condition with makeup and wardrobe, but Stamp projected such sad, wasted energy that it was almost unnecessary.

Even still, when he arrived on the set the first day to shoot Toby Dammit's arrival at the Rome airport, he asked Fellini for just a little bit of direction. He got everything he needed in one go: "This night, last night, you was at a party. Big party, but really an h'orgy. You come late after your show. You drunk. You drink more, anything, but much whiskey, lotta whiskey. Also smoke hashish, marijuana, sniff cocaine and fuck, much fucking all night. Big woman with big breasts, you fucking her, somebody come fuck you. All night like this. This morning a *macchina* come take you to airport, put you on plane to Rome. But before you get on airplane your chauffeur drop a big tab of LSD into your mouth. Now you here." (Compare the character motivation he got from Pier Paolo Pasolini, for whom he acted in *Teorema* later that same year: "He is a boy." The only other specific direction Pasolini offered was, "Open your legs more"; the finished picture would, in fact, be filled with shots of Stamp's crotch.)

Stamp and Fellini got along well: They shared secrets, such as Stamp's resentment of the ill treatment he had received from Antonioni. (Fellini avenged his new friend, running into Antonioni in a barbershop and ex-tolling Stamp's work: "Theese actor, this *Francobollo*, 'ee is incredible. I think this artist's a *genio*. *Fine del mondo*.") Stamp found moviemaking in Italy congenial and life there even more so: "Rome became his citywide Albany," reflected film critic Alexander Walker. "He had been a fashion-able boy but never iconic. Then he was the English actor who discov-ered he was really an Italian."

Beyond his acting career, Stamp was led by Fellini to explore a side of himself he had never known, a latent spirituality that jibed with Stamp's habit of diving into the trendy fascinations of the times. Through Fellini, Stamp met an astrologer who advised him to give up meat and dairy—a resolve which became lifelong; through her, he met Jiddu Krishnamurti, the Theosophist holy man who was delivering a series of lectures in Rome.

The idea of spiritual restoration hit him at just the right time: The end of his romance with Shrimpton had left him searching, ironically, for other types of fulfillment. "It took the failure of that love affair," he said. "That's what turned me inward. If I'd just been a little more dumb, I would have chased after the next supermodel and then I might have still been riding the tiger."

There were still painful hitches. When he returned to London after working for Fellini, he was so wretched a sight that his mother cried to see him—and she actually got him at his best: His regular Sunday dinner visits to her home were about the only occasions for which he bothered to shave and dress properly. News that Shrimpton was seen around town with yet another new beau didn't help. "I stopped going out," he confessed. "I retreated into my chambers like a badger to his set in winter; some days I lit my fire in the morning and stayed close to it all day. By night, unable to sleep, I would put on old gear and roam the streets, taking late buses to the East End to buy cups of tea at the stalls I'd frequented as a youth. Having schizophrenic chats with myself, falling asleep fully dressed on the sofa in the early hours": Pathetic.

While Stamp floundered, his estranged mate, Michael Caine, soared to the heights he'd always plotted for himself: His *Ipcress File* persona, Harry Palmer, became iconic (and the film spawned two sequels that proved very lucrative for their star); *Alfie* won him international fame and an Oscar nomination; he worked with the likes of Shirley MacLaine, Otto Preminger and Anthony Quinn; and he starred in two of the great crime films of the age, *The Italian Job* and *Get Carter*, capping the first act of a four-decade career as leading man.

Stamp, meanwhile, mooned and moped and, as if he resented his success, didn't work. He was never exactly prolific—he made nine films between 1962 and 1968, one of them a short—but now he seemed not even to be trying. In the coming two years, he made only two films: In one, another Italian picture, unreleased in England or the States, he played Arthur Rimbaud; in the other, *The Mind of Mr. Soames*, he was cast as a man who awakes at age thirty having been in a coma since birth: Somewhere in between was the real Stamp.

And he determined to find it. On January 30, 1969, he stood outside the northern entrance to Albany waiting for a taxicab to take him to Heathrow. He was off to India, to follow up those first inklings of spiritual awakening with a real investigation of his inner world. As he got into the cab, a tremendous noise emerged from just up Savile Row: the Beatles had emerged onto the roof of the Apple offices to play an impromptu selection of new material.

The last thing Stamp remembered of London in the sixties: John Lennon pleading to the sky, "Don't Let Me Down."

SORT OF BAUDELAIRE -ISH

After the death of Brian Epstein and the dissolution of John Lennon's marriage and the introduction of heroin, lawyers, opinionated women and wayward avant-gardism into the perfect pop frappé that was the Beatles, a strange cloud seemed to hover where the band had once stood inimitable and alone. The Beatles still mattered vitally, but they didn't seem to matter so exclusively; they had followed the psychedelic road toward some place that the entire world wasn't as eager to follow as it had been a few years before. There was suddenly space around them for another band: voilà, the Rolling Stones.

As recently as 1967, the idea that the Beatles could be rivalled, much less superceded, seemed impossible. *Sgt. Pepper*, for instance, seemed to put an end to any group's hopes of ever topping them for creativity, inspiration, novelty and pioneering genius. But, perversely, its excessive craft, heavily overlaid textures and unnatural mix of musical genres (music hall meets raga meets pop meets cabaret meets circus air meets acid rock) had boxed in the Beatles, as well: How do you follow up a record that everyone in the world hailed instantly as an unmatchable masterpiece? They took a few stabs at re-creating that stunning success—*Magical Mystery Tour*, the so-called White Album, *Abbey Road, Let It Be*—and, though each was filled with treasures, none out-Peppered *Pepper*, at least in the contemporary view. *Pepper*, appearing at the cusp of the Summer of Love of '67, the ultimate tripping album, the most blatantly out-there music (and package—artwork and all) ever released by a major act, became a standard, yes, but one that no one could adequately fulfill.

The Stones, foolishly, tried: Their uninspiring late '67 release, *Their Satanic Majesties Request*, was an obvious knockoff of *Pepper*, from the Michael Cooper photo on the jacket to the inorganically dense material—head-fake fade-outs, found sound effects, synthesized, multitracked vocals and instrumentation—inside. (Jagger, who wrote the material for the record with Richards soon after the trauma of the Redlands bust, later dismissed *Satanic Majesties* as music created "under the influence of bail"—an underestimation of the thing.)

But they returned to form almost immediately, jamming in a rehearsal hall in Surrey just weeks after the album's release and forcing themselves back into a rhythm-heavy rock 'n' roll groove that was far more Stones-like than Beatle-ish. Over the coming months they would record those songs at the newly located Olympic Sound Studio in Barnes, Southwest London: among the new cuts, the Dylanesque "Jigsaw Puzzle," the languid, empathetic "Salt of the Earth," the faux-folk "Factory Girl" and, most impressive, the rockers "Jumpin' Jack Flash," "Street Fighting Man" and the justifiably notorious "Sympathy for the Devil." The album *Beggars Banquet* was released at the end of 1968—just two weeks after the Beatles' White Album—after a lengthy spat with Decca about the cover design (the Stones favored an image of a graffiti-spattered bog but finally gave in and agreed, ironically, given what the Beatles were up to, to a plain white cover made to look like a formal party invitation). A year later, *Let It Bleed*, an equally fine record, was released within eight weeks of *Abbey Road*. The Stones had emerged as a group that made coherent albums as well as infectious singles and, to all purposes, were now equal to the Beatles musically as well as having surpassed them as social symbols.

Still, Mick and the boys couldn't resist striving after whatever the Beatles attempted first, even when the Fabs flopped. Take the matter of

TV movies. On Boxing Day, 1967, the Beatles aired *Magical Mystery Tour* on the BBC and got their teeth handed to them—the first bad press they'd ever had in the U.K., save for a few cranky writers complaining about their mustaches and the Maharishi.

Two weeks short of a year later, the Rolling Stones filmed their own BBC special—a projected hour-long musical variety show set in a fancifully replicated Victorian big top and entitled *The Rolling Stones' Rock and Roll Circus*. Like all those episodes of *Ready, Steady, Go!* on which the band had appeared (and, just a few months earlier, *Let It Be*), the show was directed by Michael Lindsay-Hogg, who found himself in the midst of both a literal circus and a figurative one. There were some animals on hand and genuine acrobats and clowns, as well as members of the Stones and other bands dressed in circus style: Mick Jagger as the ringmaster (a role he'd offered to Brigitte Bardot), John Lennon as a harlequin, Keith Richards as some kind of decadent one-eyed impresario.

Onstage, acts like Taj Mahal, Marianne Faithfull, Jethro Tull, The Who and Dirty Mac—a one-gig-only supergroup made up of Lennon, Richards, Eric Clapton, Mitch Mitchell and Yoko Ono—played sets over a span of nearly eighteen hours. Backstage, drugs and gossip flowed among the usual detritus of hangers-on, groupies and Stones People like Anita Pallenberg, Spanish Tony Sanchez and Sandy Lieberson, Jagger's agent for nonmusical work and one of the producers of the show.

"Everything went so far behind schedule," Lieberson remembered. "The Stones had been around since noon, and they didn't even get on to do their numbers until after one A.M. And they were so out of it: Imagine sitting around a studio for all those hours. Mick was the emcee, but everyone else was just hanging around and got wasted on booze or dope or whatever there was. We had a hard time keeping the audience: They wanted to go home. The Who stayed while the Stones played and got into the audience in costumes to help out."

Finally, trashed by whatever they'd drunk or smoked, exhausted from the length of the shoot, the Stones took the stage, performing several of their latest numbers: "Jumpin' Jack Flash," "You Can't Always Get What You Want" and, most tumultuously, "Sympathy for the Devil," during which Jagger, filled with primeval energy, ripped off his shirt to reveal a gigantic (and temporary) Luciferian tattoo on his chest: an astonishing performance in any context, otherwordly given the sort of physical strain and exhaustion to which the band had been subjected during the marathon shoot. Afterward, a mellow coda—a group sing of "Salt of the Earth"—and finis.

No, really: finis: For three decades, the film wasn't viewed by anyone outside the Stones' little circle. Jagger, it turned out, didn't have a lot of confidence in his band's performance, particularly as compared to the work of The Who, who had performed their entire operetta "A Quick One While He's Away"—which proved even more impressive live than on record. "Mick and Keith did not like their performance in the film—with some justification," Lieberson said. "But more importantly, Brian Jones was being asked to leave the band, and they did not want to put out a film that starred Brian Jones. So they said, 'Let's freeze the film; we're gonna promote the Rolling Stones with Mick Taylor,' and it never got completed and got put on the shelf. But it was made with Rolling Stones money so there was no way to get it from them. I once offered to buy it. And they gave it to Allen Klein as part of their settlement with him."

Ironically, it was the second film that Jagger made that year that wound up moldering in a film vault. In the six months preceding *Rock and Roll Circus*, Jagger had been employed in his first film as an actor, a dark, exotic, intoxicating (and intoxicated), experimental, daring and formally radical film that was known at the time of its creation as *The Performers* but eventually was entitled *Performance*.

The conception, creation and release of the film was one of the great flameouts of the London sixties. The finished product—a study of a gangster, a rock star, a couple of obliging women and a dance of lies, sex and drugs in a gothic Notting Hill mansion—would turn out to be one of the great British films of the time. But the man who dreamed it up, wrote it and codirected it found himself virtually shunned out of the film business, several of the principals in the cast had their lives spun into catastrophic spirals and the producers had to spend nearly two years to get the thing seen—and in a compromised version, at that.

Donald Cammell was the genius of the project, a man who had lived the era as darkly and decadently as any of them. He was the grandson of a Scottish ship-building magnate and was born in 1934 in the Outlook Tower adjacent to Edinburgh Castle. His father had lost most of the family fortune in the stock market crash, but held on to enough to move the household to London and dedicate his life to literary efforts with a demonic twist: He edited something called *Atlantis Quarterly: A Journal Devoted to Atlantean and Occult Studies* and wrote a fond biography of Aleister Crowley, the self-styled "magus" spoken of in his youth as "the wickedest man in the world."

Even in this world, young Donald stood out. By three, he was impressing adults with his ability to draw from life; by four, he could handle perspective drawing and foregrounding. Along with his brother, he attended Westminster public school, but he soon transferred to the Byam Shaw School of Art and then the Royal Academy of Arts. After a bit of seasoning in Tuscany, he opened his own studio in Flood Street, Chelsea, in 1953 and set out a shingle as a society portraitist; his depiction that year of the Marquess of Dufferin and Ava in the uniform he'd worn as a page at the Queen's coronation was proclaimed as the finest society painting of the year.

In 1954, Cammell married a Greek actress named Maria Andipa; the couple had a child, Amadis, but split up as Cammell's predilection for the wild life of the Chelsea Set led him into many affairs. Soon bored with painting debutantes and dukes with their dogs, Cammell left London for New York and then Paris, experimenting in abstraction and in imitations of Balthus—lots of canvases of young nude girls. By the mid-sixties, he was back in London with plans to make films. He wrote several scripts—one was made into the caper picture *Duffy*, which starred James Coburn and James Fox—and started running with the wilder (and younger) people who had enlivened his old neighborhood in his absence.

Inevitably, he bumped up against the Rolling Stones, Robert Fraser, Christopher Gibbs and the lot—as well as Sandy Lieberson, who was looking to break into feature films as a producer. Cammell pitched Lieberson his latest inspiration—the story of a gangster and a rock star initially entitled *The Liars*—as a perfect vehicle for Jagger and Marlon Brando. Brando, of course, was impossible to pin down, but Jagger was interested in working with Cammell and, more importantly, Lieberson knew it would be easy to interest financiers in working with Jagger.

He got Warner Bros. to sign on to fund and distribute the film. Of course, what the Hollywood moguls wanted was another *A Hard Day's Night*—a film made quickly and cheaply and by reliable pros and which you could take grandma to and let the kids see a dozen times. Whatever Cammell and Lieberson had in mind, they kept to themselves: "The first objective was to get Warners in," Lieberson admitted, "then reveal slowly the fact that we were all people with little or no experience."

This was no exaggeration: Lieberson had never produced; Cammell had never directed and had a sole script to his credit; Jagger had never acted. The studio wasn't willing to gamble much—£1.5 million, most of it in salaries, and most of that to Jagger, whom they were hoping to retain as a special advisor on youth-oriented projects after the completion of the film. To help stabilize the production, Cammell came up with the inspiration of codirecting with Nicolas Roeg, the gifted cinematographer of *Far from the Madding Crowd, Petulia* and *Farenheit 451,* among other films.

What remained was the crucial business of casting. Jagger, the only sure thing, was to play a reclusive former rock star named Turner whose home would be invaded by a South London gangster named Chas Devlin in need of a place to hide from a murderous boss whom he'd crossed. In the course of their time together, Turner and Chas would recognize bits of themselves in each other and, without quite realizing it, would begin to merge and swap bits of their personalities—or, more exactly, the personae they have worn as personalities. Abetting their transformations would be Turner's two paramours, Ferber and Lucy, and a lot of drugs: magic mushrooms, hashish, quote-unquote vitamin shots.

For Ferber and Lucy, Cammell had in mind Marianne Faithfull and Michele Breton, one of his Balthusian Lolitas. But Faithfull was pregnant with Jagger's child and having a rough time of it, so her part went to Anita Pallenberg—who was also, secretly, pregnant (with Keith Richards's child, probably), but was willing to have an abortion so as to be able to play the role.

For the role of Chas, Cammell had a daring inspiration: James Fox. At first blush, it seemed crazy: Fox, who had attended Harrow and served in the Coldstream Guards, was known for his quite solid work playing characters who shared his upper-class background in films like *The Loneliness of the Long-Distance Runner, King Rat* and, especially, *The Servant.* Fox's father was a famous theatrical agent who sat on the board of directors of the Royal Court Theatre, and his older brother, Edward, was also making a name as an actor. He seemed, in short, more Redgrave than radical.

But Fox had recently turned hippie, growing his hair long, experimenting with drugs, dressing in flowing clothes and running around

Rome and London with the same decadent young jet-setters who partied with the Stones. With his girlfriend, Andee Cohen, Fox had become very close to Jagger and Faithfull; the two couples often spent pleasantly smoky evenings in one another's flats—one another's beds, even—and their intimacy became known to their larger circle of friends. It was even rumored that Fox and Jagger had been lovers. *That* was the James Fox whom Cammell and Roeg reckoned they could mold into Chas—and Lieberson, who'd seen flashes of toughness in Fox's various film roles, thought it was a good bet.

That said, they knew that Fox would require some tutelage if he were to be able to pass himself off as what other gangsters would call a "chap"—a convincingly stylish hard man. "Don't come back until you're Chas," the filmmakers told him. To that end, Fox was tutored by David Litvinoff, one of the more shadowy and colorful characters of the Chelsea demimonde. Litvinoff was a ne'er-do-well East End Jew, born in 1928 to a family of eight that included two noted writers. His life was the stuff of colorful and shadowy legends amplified by his chatterbox talk and his elastic ways with the truth. He made his living as a thief, sharpie and gambler; he cruised for young boys with Ronnie Kray and Quentin Crisp; he had his face slashed over an outstanding debt and dined out on frightful accounts of the incident for years; he wove absorbing stories to astounded acquaintances for whom he never bothered to distinguish fact from fiction—perhaps because he might not have known one from the other himself.

Litvinoff took Fox 'round the Thomas à Beckett, the famous boxers' pub and gymnasium on the Old Kent Road in South London, and introduced him to various characters there, including Johnny Shannon, the magniloquent boxing trainer, and John Bindon, an authentic hard man who'd done a bit of film acting, slept with Christine Keeler and was celebrated for a party trick he'd perfected: balancing six half-pint beer mugs on his penis. In their world, Fox cut his hair, dropped the silly King's Road duds, learned to hit and to carry himself hard and even, it was rumored, went out on a dry run for a robbery and got into a tight spot with a stolen car. By the time he returned to shoot the film, he was the very stuff of Chas—he could show a nasty temper around the set— and he had incidentally acquired a pair of costars in Shannon and Bindon.

As for Jagger, no such tutelage would be necessary. "My preparation for the part was much easier, really," he said. "I just sat in the bath all day with two birds, just really lazing around." Of course, he was hiding just how much calculation he'd put into the thing. He spent many hours strategizing with Faithfull, who had made stabs at a serious acting career that included performing the first blow job in a commercial film: *I'll Never Forget What's 'Is Name.* She helped Jagger, she remembered, conceive of Turner as a cross between Brian Jones—"with his self-torment and paranoia"—and Keith Richards—"with his strength and *cool.*" Jagger dyed his hair jet black à la Olivier's Richard III and dressed in androgynous costumes: caftans and body stockings and frilly shirts all just a tad more feminine than the stuff he was already sporting in regular life.

While Mick and Fox were working on their parts, Cammell hired Christopher Gibbs to design Turner's mansion—a dark, Moroccan environment that the script actually referred to as "Gibbsian" in acknowledgment of Gibbs's efforts on the Stones' houses and his own Cheyne Walk flat. "My brief was vague," the designer recalled. "Donald just said something that's groovy and elegant, sort of Baudelaire-ish." The house was meant to be in Powis Square, Notting Hill, which is where the exteriors were filmed. But most of the production was based in Lowndes Square, Knightsbridge, in a townhouse that was unoccupied at the time the producers leased it, save for the occasional nights when it was used as an illegal casino.

In late July shooting began, even though the second half of the script was still only sketchily finished—part of Cammell's strategy of seeing how the actors would respond to the intense environment he hoped to create for them. Faithfull missed it all: She had removed herself to Ireland to rest during her pregnancy. But she completely comprehended what resulted over the following three months: In her words, the set was "a species of psycho-sexual lab" and "a seething cauldron of diabolical ingredients: drugs, incestuous sexual relationships, role reversals, art and life all whipped together into a bitch's brew."

In the coming weeks, Jagger and Fox would consume drugs before, during and after scenes; Jagger would consummate a ménage à trois with Pallenberg and Breton (the most graphic of this footage found its way to an erotic film festival in Amsterdam a few years later, where it won a prize); Pallenberg would shoplift some of Gibbs's precious props from the set; Richards would stew out in the street in his Bentley or down the road in a pub, convinced (rightly) that his girl and best mate were screwing each other and dispatching Robert Fraser and Spanish Tony Sanchez to the set as spies until they were banned; Fox would overturn desks at the production office in a fit over money; Cecil Beaton would pop in to take publicity stills; and crew members would complain that no food was available on the set, but rather a pharmacopoeia of hot-and-cold-running drugs: "You want to get a fucking joint, they're coming out of your earholes. You want a cup of tea, you've got no fuckin' chance!" ("When you went into Lowndes Square," averred art director John Clark, "you took one breath and you were stoned.")

"It was a soup made from ingredients that no one had thought of putting in the same pot before," remembered Gibbs. "And it was very experimental. There were these people from disparate backgrounds coming together, and a few sort of catalyst figures to stir it together: David Litvinoff, Robert Fraser. And it made a very fascinating and extraordinary film. The way it came to pass was a new way of making a film. Nic Roeg was a very experienced filmmaker and Donald wasn't. He was very dilettantey and aware of general culture. But he wasn't steeped in movies. I remember he was trying to get that way while he was making it. He'd watch a few movies every night. Sometimes in the afternoon. He'd come in saying, 'I got this wonderful idea. . . .' "

After a day's shooting ended, while Cammell went off to teach himself moviemaking, the cast and crew would carry the dark mood of the set into parties that grew increasingly wicked as the night wore on. Caroline Upcher, who worked in the production office on Shawfield Street, had heard that the nights could get very black indeed, though the working-class crew members who were involved—and some of the more puritanical bad guys—banned her from the really heavy scenes: "If I had been less young and innocent and well-brought up, I would've been at the *third* party of the night and seen some amazing stuff."

Warner Bros. kept their wild young film crew at arm's length for the most part, but when word got to them through an on-set representative of the bacchanalian atmosphere, executives demanded to see some footage. "In the third or fourth week of shooting," recalled Lieberson, "the distributors requested a screening. Instead of selected takes and rough sequences, we showed everything we'd shot. They hated it. Three quarters of the way through the filming, the distributors viewed the material again. They hated it." David Puttnam had just joined Lieberman's production company during the shoot and walked into a meeting with representatives of the American studio on his very first day of work: "Sandy was there," remembered Patsy Puttnam, "and someone was yelling at him, 'I'm gonna make sure you never work in this business again.' And David was thinking, I've only just come in!"

Shooting—somehow—wrapped in the fall of 1968, more or less on time and only fractionally over budget, and Cammell spent several months trying to cut the film together to match his vision of the two main characters' personalities merging. There was a moment when it seemed the whole project would disappear: A worker at a photo lab got a look at some of the more racy and violent footage and alerted a boss, who destroyed a print of the film but, fortunately, not the negative. Cammell finally got together a version of the picture suitable for a preview audience, and in July 1969, a group of people who'd come to a Santa Monica theater to see *Midnight Cowboy* sat with dozens of Warner Bros. executives as the first audience to watch *Performance*.

Very few screenings in the history of the medium could ever have gone so poorly. People shouted at the screen and fled the auditorium steadily until the Warner Bros. brass were virtually the only ones left; one studio executive's wife literally vomited onto her husband's shoes ("You couldn't have a much better reaction than *that*," crowed Cammell); Lieberson and his directors were accosted by studio bosses who demanded to know if Michele Breton was a boy or a girl and if the relationship between Turner and Chas was bi ("Bi what?" Cammell asked). The last thing the filmmakers heard that night as they were left in the lobby by their financiers: "Even the bathwater's dirty!"

Warner Bros. had the right of final cut and they insisted on some changes: trims in the violence and nudity and in some of the more exotically experimental sequences. But they also wanted Jagger to appear earlier in the film, necessitating a rethinking of the overall structure. Harried, Cammell complied. But it was for naught: Warner Bros. had no intention of letting *Performance* out into the world where it might actually be seen. (They may have had a point: "My mum saw it," revealed Jagger, "and she said she's not coming to see me anymore.")

And then *Easy Rider* changed Hollywood executives' minds about what they could show the world and Warner Bros. gave Cammell's picture an airing, however scant. The film opened in the States in the dead of August 1970 to generally blistering reviews (there were some positive notices, but not in commercially important venues) and blah business;

five months later, it opened in London, with a charity premiere benefiting Release, the drug rights organization.

In the aftermath of *Performance*, many of the people connected with the film would lose their bearings forever. "When it was being made," Christopher Gibbs recalled, "everyone was in rather a state, taking drugs and so on, and then soon after dying or being carted off to the lunatic asylum." The record would prove he wasn't kidding: Pallenberg and Breton sunk into drug addiction; Fox, who lost his father soon after shooting stopped, would convert to a form of born-again Christianity in 1970 and not work again in movies for almost a decade; and Cammell found himself unable to get another real directing job, making a few cheap thrillers and being toyed with by studios and, ironically, Marlon Brando, until he put a bullet in his head in 1996. (Keith Richards, who never forgave the director for encouraging Jagger and Pallenberg into fucking for the camera, would label *Performance* "the best work Cammell ever did, except for shooting himself.") Marianne Faithfull, who didn't even visit the set, saw the film not as a catalyst to its principals' destruction, but rather as a remarkable window that opened their true selves to the world: "Most of the people in *Performance* weren't acting at all," she remembered. "They were exhibiting themselves."

The scariest exhibition, surely, was Jagger's. According to Faithfull, who had helped him screw up his courage to act and to find a way to project daring and mystery and strength, "Mick came out of it splendidly, with a new, shining and impenetrable suit of body armor. He didn't have a drug problem and he didn't have a nervous breakdown. Nothing really touched him. In the same way that some actors get to keep their wardrobe, Mick came away from *Performance* with his *character*."

Turner became the face that Jagger would show the world: dark and decadent and sinister and fascinated with power and evil and capable of the depraved and the diabolical, even from within the shelter of his slight, fragile-seeming frame. It was a mask that people didn't dare look at and yet, because of the charisma Jagger was born with and had cultivated within himself, one from which they couldn't turn.

It was, in many ways, the epitome of all the guises he'd developed, worn and discarded over the years—a little bit bled from this or that person he'd met or read about or glimpsed across a dance floor or posh restaurant or greenroom. For years he'd been flaunting an image of sexual ambiguity—feigned, ripped-off, laced with sarcasm and flung into his audience's face with provocative glee. Now, master dissembler, he had adopted something darker—embracing, it almost seemed, the nastiness that was emerging as the decade wore on. "Street Fightin' Man," for one instance of the new Mick, had grown out of his somewhat half-assed immersion in an anti-Vietnam War protest outside the American embassy in Grosvenor Square; mobbed by fans, he signed autographs while others clashed with police. And "Sympathy for the Devil" went even further. In that epochal tune, rather than view the violent upheavals of the decade with a dilettante's eye and a rich man's shrug, he submerged into a vicious and provocative imposture that thrilled and terrified. Various members of the Stones' circle had been intrigued by aspects of the black arts for some time; Jagger, ever the dabbler and instigator, didn't dive in. But, as with so many other things, he learned enough to fake it, and his adaptation of a satanic pose in the song and onstage made him and his band take on the aspect of the five horsemen of the Apocalypse—with percussionist, piano player and backing vocals, of course.

But that was it, wasn't it? It was a *pose*. Compared to Keith, who was using heroin, or Brian, with his illegitimate children, not to mention Charlie Watts and Bill Wyman, so steady as to constitute rocks, however rolling, Mick was always the cautious one, adapting the guise of daring but staying well away from the edge of danger. He could survive unscratched events and habits that devastated everyone else.

For Marianne Faithfull, this sangfroid—the real thing—was terrifying. "Mick is so grounded as a person that he never loses his footing," she explained. "He is able to observe the car crash at the moment of impact and escape unscathed—a quality that is extremely exasperating for the victims." In November 1968, she was given ample instance: Her body massively destabilized by several years of drug-taking and her increasing use of heroin, she miscarried their child—a girl, to be named Corrina—just eight weeks shy of full term. Jagger mourned with her, she never said otherwise; but he went back to work while she sunk deeper into heroin addiction, self-neglect and ennui.

And that was nothing compared to what befell Brian Jones. Drinking and drugging himself into bloated stupefaction, harassed mercilessly by a corrupt police force that likely planted drugs in his flat and certainly had decided to make an example of him, mocked openly by the people whom he insisted to an indifferent world had usurped *his* band from him, his lover Anita Pallenberg living now with Keith, he was miserable and alone. He had always been unreliable and ill-tempered, and all the drugs had only exaggerated these tendencies. Mick and Keith, following a trend begun by Andrew Oldham, did their best to make him uncomfortable in the band and finally squeezed him out of it entirely; by the spring of '69, they were auditioning new guitarists and issuing transparently false press releases about the lack of hard feelings among the parted bandmates. Brian spent some time trying to dry out at Redlands and then bought his own country manor, Cotchford Farm, near Hartfield, Sussex, the very place where A. A. Milne wrote the majority of the Winnie the Pooh tales. In July, drunk and drugged and, it's whispered, egged on and even beset by hangers-on and employees who despised him even as they took his money, he drowned in his swimming pool.

Two days after that—the show must go on—Mick Jagger performed with the Stones in front of a quarter million people in Hyde Park. He read a few stanzas of Shelley's "Adonais"—written for the prematurely dead John Keats—as a tribute to his fallen bandmate.

Three days after *that*, in a hotel room in Sydney, Australia, where he'd gone to make a movie about a legendary nineteenth-century outlaw, Mick found Marianne in a coma. She'd swallowed dozens of sleeping pills. She was out for five days; she had visions of Brian; she came back, an emotional wreck, on the precipice of years of addiction, homelessness and self-hate.

And two days after *that*, Brian was buried in his hometown; his epitaph, which he wrote himself, was "Please don't judge me too harshly."

Mick, meanwhile, made his movie, came back to England, released *Let It Bleed* and then, with his band, toured America, ending the decade at the Altamont Raceway in Livermore, California. Bad acid; black energy; Hell's Angels; mayhem; death; the ugly, bitter end of the sixties: Ladies and Gentlemen, Mick Jagger and the Rolling Stones.

IT'S JUST NOT FUN ANYMORE

Blow-Up wasn't the last film about a Swinging London photographer. In October 1967, amid a flurry of hep films that included *Bedazzled, Poor Cow* and *Billion Dollar Brain*, appeared *Smashing Time*, a comedy about two northern girls—played by Lynn Redgrave and Rita Tushingham—who come to the capital to make their fortunes as models on Carnaby Street. The film essayed the world of boutiques, trendy restaurants, rotten pop bands, slumming aristocrats and absurd avant-garde art galleries with an amusedly jaundiced eye—screenwriter George Melly continually evoked Lewis Carroll in character and place names. But the key Londoner the girls meet is a brash young Cockney fashion snapper played by the debuting Michael York—an upper-class boy trying to make it as an East End Jack the Lad, wearing a hipster wig and false mustache to cover his normal conservative look, speaking Cockney rhyming slang when, in reality, he was educated ("He's got an awfully nice speaking voice when he's not pretending to be common," said one of the heroines).

The picture wasn't very well-received by critics or audiences. "When it opened, people actually took exception to it," remembered Tushingham. And Redgrave recalled her disappointment at how the film seemed just to miss its satiric target: "We thought as we were making it, this will be just right. But the minute it came out people said, 'It's over. Swinging London is over.' "

Well, certainly the garish, goofy, trendy, catch-a-rising-balloon minute had passed. But there were still key movers and shakers about, and if they weren't trying any longer to make the world recognize them, they were still inventing ways to express the bizarre world they'd created.

There was still David Bailey, for instance, still an object of fascination more than a half decade since he'd emerged. People loved to gossip about Bailey, and after they asked how he got all those fabulous women into bed and was *Blow-Up* really what his life was like, there was one thing they wanted to know about him: When was he going to direct a movie?

In late 1965, in fact, Bailey had seemed poised to break into films. He was prepared to make a short film called *The Assassination of Mick Jagger*, in which the singer himself was to play a pop star condemned to death by a cabal of middle-aged establishment types. Jagger changed his mind, as might have been predicted, and the picture, finally called *G. G. Passion*, was made with Eric Swayne, a photographer (and former boyfriend of the future Patti Harrison) whom Bailey had used as a model in the past, in the lead. Opposite him was Jagger's soon-to-be-ex-girlfriend, Chrissie Shrimpton; the script was by Bailey and Gerard Brach, who'd written *Repulsion* with Roman Polanski; Polanski himself produced *G. G.* for six thousand pounds after Bailey's mate Peter O'Toole pulled out of that role.

For all the famous names attached, the picture was barely released—few thirty-five-minute pictures ever saw the light of day, even in those freewheeling days—and its poor reception where it was shown may have had some effect in frustrating another movie project that Bailey had in mind: an adaptation of *A Clockwork Orange* with Jagger as the star and the rest of the Rolling Stones as his gang. Bailey blamed the failure of this project on Andrew Oldham, who owned the rights to the Anthony

Burgess novel and "wanted too much cash." But at least one friend said that Bailey just didn't like making movies: "I think he found it boring, rather lugubrious," reflected Dick Fontaine.

In order to get started in film, Bailey had aligned himself with David Puttnam, the ad world wunderkind who had begun his own company, David Puttnam Associates, to agent for photographers and, it was supposed, help steer them into film careers. Puttnam signed all the big names—Bailey, Terence Donovan, Lord Snowdon—and he managed to get at least the first two launched as directors of commercials (Bailey's first, for Cadbury chocolate, was banned for being too risqué). Puttnam said that it was just too difficult to get the photographers started in the movie business: "Photography was incredibly fashionable. They earned very good livings. They couldn't have earned anything like the same amount of money had they switched into films. I remember having a conversation with Terry Donovan at length, and when we actually analyzed it, he couldn't afford to do it." But it was also somewhat true that Bailey and Puttnam didn't mesh as well in business as they did socially— Bailey was credited for coining the immortal showbiz-ism " 'Hello,' he lied" to describe his relations with Puttnam—and they parted ways.

Actually, Bailey was getting a little loose with the lip altogether. He went on *The Eamonn Andrews Show* and said "fuck," without the calculated intent of Kenneth Tynan, who said it purposefully a few years before on the BBC, or the satiric deadliness of Lenny Bruce, who said it onstage at the Establishment club in 1963. "I was stupid then," Bailey said of the incident later. "I was just being childish and silly, and I was drunk anyway."

But as the decade wore on, what he seemed was *tired*. He described himself in 1966 as "very selfish, antisocial, quite rich, lonely and not particularly happy." "It's become an effort to keep on keeping up, to go on taking pictures," he told another interviewer. "It's just not fun anymore."

He got into other things: managing a rock band, the Golden Apples of the Sun, along with Andrew Loog Oldham; running an antique shop called Carrot on Wheels: distractions. And he declared the unimaginable in yet another interview: "I've been thinking about leaving the country for some time. I'm not all that keen on Harold Wilson. The credit squeeze affects advertising and advertising affects me. Most of my work is done in Paris anyway. I've got a studio there and my wife's apartment. She organizes me better than anyone."

Bailey's marriage to Catherine Deneuve remained a source of stability for both spouses, even as their peripatetic careers pulled them apart continually. Bailey often photographed Deneuve together with her older sister, the equally beautiful actress Françoise Dorléac; speaking of his wife and sister-in-law, he said, "Between them they made the perfect woman." Dorléac, like Deneuve, had established a significant film career while still in her early twenties, working with such directors as Roman Polanski (*Cul-de-Sac*), François Truffaut (*The Soft Skin*), Roger Vadim (*La Ronde*) and Ken Russell (*Billion Dollar Brain*). She was a handful to work with, reported Polanski, and insisted on going everywhere with her pet hairless chihuahua. In June 1967, soon after filming Jacques Demy's *The Young Girls of Rochefort* with her sister, the unthinkable befell her: Dorléac was driving near Nice in a rainstorm when her car skidded into a concrete road marker and exploded into flames, killing her on the spot.

Deneuve and Dorléac had been extraordinarily close, sharing a bedroom at their parents' home until only just a few years earlier, and the loss overwhelmed Deneuve, according to Bailey, turning her into a much more motivated career-maker than she had ever been. "Her sister's dying, that really seemed to change her a lot," he said. "She may be compensating. I just feel there's some driving force to make up for what her sister didn't do."

While respectful of his wife's grief, Bailey remained the same skirt-chaser who had moved in with Jean Shrimpton while still married. It was only a few months after Dorléac's death, in fact, that Deneuve pointed a model out to Bailey in a magazine.

"You're going to run off with this girl," she told him. "She's your type."

Bailey dismissed the idea, but looked at the picture anyway. It was an Avedon, he remembered, of a girl who looked like, in his words, "an Egyptian Jiminy Cricket."

In October 1967, Bailey got a phone call: "My English *Vogue* editor, Bea Miller, said, 'We'd like you to photograph this girl from a very important American family.' They made such a fuss about her. Straight away my curiosity was up."

He met her.

"It was love at first sight for me," he said, "and I think for her, as well."

It was: "I fell in love with him," the girl remembered. "It was pretty instant. I'd never met anyone quite so honest or sexually direct."

Her name was Penelope Tree. She was not yet eighteen years old.

Her father was Ronald Tree, a Tory member of Parliament who had overcome the handicap of American parentage (he was born in England) to become a significant figure on the English social scene, as well as a prominent editor and landowner whose family estate, Ditchley, became Winston Churchill's wartime refuge from a potential Luftwaffe bombing of his own estate, Chequers. Her mother was Marietta Tree, an heiress to the American Peabody fortune who took such diverse lovers as Adlai Stevenson and John Huston and who served as the American ambassador to the Human Rights Commission of the United Nations and was an important hostess and fund-raiser for the Democratic Party.

Penelope herself was a first-year student of anthropology at Sarah Lawrence College. But she was her mother's daughter—headstrong, rebellious, unconcerned with convention—and she had recently made a splash in the grown-up world with a scandalous outfit she wore to Truman Capote's famous Black and White Ball and with subsequent magazine photos and gossip column appearances (where she had acquired the clumsy nickname "fantas-Tree").

"Penelope was fantastic," Bailey remembered, "a real rebel. She was very aristocratic, of course—she came from the Peabodys, the Trees—but she made an effort to be outrageous. She'd shave her eyebrows off, you know, do lots of things like that."

After the *Vogue* shoot, the young model returned to the States and school, but she and Bailey realized they needed to be together, and he came to New York to fetch her from her mother's grasp. Marietta Tree tried to keep Bailey out of her house, but he stuck one of those trademark Cuban-heeled boots of his in the doorway and gained entry. "Naturally, her mother hated me," Bailey acknowledged. "I was rough, and she was a snob. I remember going to pick Penelope up once in New York to fly back to London—she was seventeen; I must've been in my thirties—and saying to her mother, 'You know, it could be worse: I could be a Rolling Stone.' God, that woman loathed me. And I loathed her. Awful woman. *Awful.*"

In January 1968, Deneuve and Bailey broke up: "It's just that things are a bit difficult, and I am not seeing him much at the moment," she told the press. (Their divorce wasn't finalized until 1972, just before Deneuve had a daughter, Chiara, by Marcello Mastroianni.) Bailey moved Tree, now eighteen, into the big house he'd bought on Gloucester Avenue—not far from the Primrose Hill flat he'd shared with Jean Shrimpton. They settled in among his dozens of parrots, and he turned her, as he had Shrimpton and Sue Murray, into a modeling superstar of the day.

But she, finally, was more of the day than he. Especially compared to the country-bred Shrimpton and the movie star Deneuve, Tree was a child of the later sixties—pot-smoking, free-speaking, politically radical. She worked with Release, the organization dedicated toward affording legal help to people charged under drug laws, and hung out with a lot of the people she met through the group. Bailey wasn't terribly fond of their company, seeing them as a gang of leeches "who would drink my brandy, smoke my dope and turn 'round and accuse me of being a capitalist."

"He was very suspicious of the people I brought home and that I had another life," Tree reflected. "But he is also very perceptive. There were some wankers around. But also he was closed to anyone who wasn't on his track. Much more than most people he is on his own track and he's not really interested in anything outside of that."

But when they worked together—which, as per Bailey's habits with previous lovers, was steadily—they were a smooth unit. Modeling for Bailey, Tree said, was "like being circled by a bird of prey. You are the only thing in his mind and vision, and that can be quite exciting."

Likewise, just turning thirty, he let her sense of vitality infuse him. "Penelope was a real exotic dresser. She had an incredibly adventuresome sense of style," Bailey remembered "In terms of fashion she did lead me up the garden path a bit. She made me grow my hair long and dye it blue. And she got me to wear things like a purple leather jacket she had Ossie Clark make."

They stayed together for six years: Bailey was a tremendous help in October 1972, when Tree was busted for drug possession and he showed up to collect her at the police station. "Suddenly they became charming," she remembered, "and took my fingerprints as if teaching me the piano." But they never married. "I was still married to Catherine," Bailey said, "and by the time I wasn't, things were sort of on the wane with Penelope."

They'd grown apart, is all, and it couldn't be blamed on a big thing so much as on little ones, such as: "I never liked drugs. I much preferred to get drunk. In a way, that's why Penelope and I split. I was a drinker; she was more into grass."

Fair enough.

So much had changed, was still changing; it was inevitable that some of the people who got the whole thing rolling should ask to be dropped off at the next stop.

The whole vibe of the scene had mutated from something dashing and smart to something frankly revolutionary, determinedly freaky and studiedly shabby: a whole new mode of cool. Young creative people who just three or four years before were vying for places at chic tables amid titled sorts and rich folks and media stars and other establishment types were beginning to reject the very notion of an establishment and any thought of buying into it.

The new magazines, for instance, bore no relation to the ones in which Bailey had made his name. *International Times*, a newspaper dedicated to hard news reporting with a leftist slant and feature stories about artists, musicians, thinkers, scenes and trends in the counterculture, had debuted in October 1966; *Oz*, a truly subversive magazine imported from Australia by its editor and chief imp, Richard Neville, turned up just three months later. Of the two, *Oz* was the more recklessly iconoclastic, featuring nudity and expressly prodrug art and writing; it eventually provoked prosecution for obscenity and was the subject of a long and sensational trial in 1970. *IT*, too, was prosecuted, even earlier: Issue number eight in March 1967 ran afoul of authorities for its use of profanities, and the paper's principals were brought to trial three years later for running personal ads for homosexual men.

New performance spaces and clubs had opened up, environments that deliberately eschewed the exclusivity and polish of places like the Ad Lib and Sibylla's. There was the Roundhouse, a former railroad turntable shed in North London where the *IT* held its launch party, an all-night fancy dress ball for two thousand attendees (including Paul McCartney, relatively incognito in Arabian headgear). As could be expected from its original use, the Roundhouse was an exceedingly uncomfortable joint: drafty, underequipped with toilets and other amenities, poor acoustically and unreliable electrically. But it was big and sufficiently removed from the surrounding homes and businesses that nobody much minded the presence of young hippies in the place all night long.

The new venues may have lacked the appointments that would have attracted the glittering melange of stars, aristocrats and beautiful people that could be found in such places as the Scotch of St. James, Blaise's and Club dell'Arethusa, all of which still catered to the old Swinging London crowd. But they were perfect settings for the new sorts of acts that were coming onto the scene. Playing lengthy, unstructured jams accompanied by slide shows and wild things done with lights, the new bands were responding to the LSD fever that had spread throughout town by seeking musical and theatrical enhancements to the experience of tripping. They thought they were approximating what they'd heard was going on in San Francisco, where acts like the Grateful Dead, the Jefferson Airplane and Quicksilver Messenger Service had begun to establish a psychedelic sound, but they'd never seen or even *heard* most of those acts. In fact, L.A. bands were more popular among the London cognoscenti: "Everybody had heard about what was going on in San Francisco," remembered Barry Miles, "but the actual influence in Britain came almost always from Los Angeles. The people that people were interested in in London were the Mothers of Invention, the Byrds, Love, the Doors. No one had actually heard any of the San Francisco stuff, and even when they did it was poorly recorded—the Grateful Dead's early records weren't representative of the Dead in full flight at all." The London acts that were trying to mimic the freak-out and acid-test music of the San Francisco bands were, in essence, inventing themselves and their own genre.

There were as many groups associated with this new wave as there had been with the Beat Boom or the R&B explosion of a few years earlier, with suitably new-sounding names that announced their affiliation with psychedelic drugs or the new ethos of communalism and harmony: The Move, Family, Creation, the Soft Machine, the Herbal Mixture, the Crazy World of Arthur Brown, the Third Ear, Geranium Pond and, of course, the group of Cambridge freaks and art students originally known as the Pink Floyd Sound.

Since coming down to London to break into the music scene in early 1966, Pink Floyd, as the band was ultimately known, played everywhere: the Free School in Notting Hill, the legendary Marquee Club, the Queen Elizabeth Hall at South Bank, the mod club Tiles, the *IT* launch party at the Roundhouse, an *IT* benefit six months later at the Alexandra Palace (the famous 14-Hour Technicolor Dream, graced by Beatle John, tripping madly) and, most famously, the UFO club, where they were informally regarded as the house band and played before such interested ears as those of Pete Townshend and Eric Clapton, both of whom were fascinated by the experimental guitar technique of Floyd founder, songwriter and lead singer, Syd Barrett.

Barrett was handsome, charismatic and a true original, but he was also one of the most notorious acidheads of the time, and his heavy drug use—coupled with what was said to be an already unsteady psychological makeup—made him one of London's first famous drug casualties. Sprightly Syd, known about town for his cockiness, sexual swagger and mischievous twinkle, became a blank-eyed golem, unable, eventually, to play a note onstage or acknowledge his surroundings. It would still be a couple of years before he was rendered utterly unable to cope with the small details of life as a London-based pop star and had to retire to his parents' care in Cambridge, but his bandmates, frustrated with his inconsistencies, dismissed him from his own group just a few months after the summer 1967 release of their first LP, *The Piper at the Gates of Dawn*.

The need to give Syd the boot had become clear on a trip to California, where Barrett mistook the corner of Hollywood and Vine for the Las Vegas Strip, freaked out Alice Cooper with his weird vibes, stood stock-still when asked questions by Pat Boone on the crooner's televised variety program and didn't bother so much as to lip-synch his lead vocal part to "See Emily Play," the band's first American single, on *American Bandstand*.

That Barrett's mortifying meltdown should come in California added irony to the pathos. Starting in 1967, the Golden State's twin cities of Los Angeles and, especially, San Francisco, had begun to draw the same sort of frenzied attention that London had been through the previous half decade. There was the burgeoning hippie scene of Haight-Ashbury, a phenomenon so renowned as to draw both Paul McCartney and George Harrison to witness it firsthand (Paul liked it okay, but George—who was tripping during his visit—was appalled by the spectacle of grubby young freaks walking barefoot through the streets and panhandling money in the name of free love, peace and good vibes). There was also, far more importantly, the Monterey International Pop Festival that spring, the first great multiday celebration of youth culture and music, where established acts like The Who and the Mamas and the Papas played alongside newcomers like Jimi Hendrix and Janis Joplin and carefully selected one-off performers like Ravi Shankar and Otis Redding. For many of those who were there, it was the most revered event of its kind—even more than Woodstock, two years later—and came to symbolize the first (and, to some minds, the last) occasion on which the global village of new-minded thinkers came together.

It meant something that it happened in California and not in London. The mood of the era had swung toward something that far more favored the sunshine, openness and wild beauty of America—and, specifically, that part of it that Theodore Roosevelt referred to as "west of the west." London had held exclusive sway on the imaginations of the young for several years, with only pockets of similarly excited activity in New York remotely on the same par. But California staked a claim to the age in 1966 with the emergence at one and the same time of countercultures on Los Angeles' Sunset Strip and in San Francisco's Haight-Ashbury district. The following year, with the Monterey Pop Festival and the Summer of Love, it seemed more the center of things than a novelty destination on the outer edge of them.

California suited the new fashions better than England: "The idea that you could have worn Flower Power in the rain!" laughed Patsy Puttnam. "Working women couldn't jump on a tube in scarves and Biba and sandals!" Agreed Nik Cohn, "Hippie was largely a summer sport. Bare feet and silks and universal brotherhoods—these things were not created for an English January." Too, the dropout mentality of hippie ran counter to the force-your-way-in attitude that had initially made London swing: Mary Quant added, "There was a change in mode. People became interested in where they lived: nesting. I started designing house stuff and bedwear. And there was the hippie thing and the growing of pot and herbs. It was kind of antifashion."

Hippie felt more like Americana, remembered Barry Miles: "In America there was a lot more freedom to pick and choose your lifestyle. It wasn't as if there was a dominant lifestyle mapped out, whereas in Britain, life was more fully described, with the Queen on top of it and everything trickling down from there. Anything even slightly different was frowned upon. Whereas in the States as long as you could portray yourself as being for freedom and the individual it seemed to be okay.

You could see an awful lot more hippie people out on the streets in America than you ever could in London. People felt quite nervous about being hippie in England unless you were on the King's Road. If you were living in Leeds, you were in trouble."

More specifically, the undeterminedness of California, its size and variety and gentle climate and long standing in the popular imagination as an El Dorado of personal freedom and Gold Rush bonanzas, seemed a bucolic counterbalance to England with its centuries of self-restraint and a class system still intact despite the titled nutters larking about with common loons, an economy in increasingly obvious tatters (the pound was devalued in late 1967 by 14.3 percent) and its awful winters and falls.

America had invented youth culture and then, frightened of its creation, found ways to stifle it. England gobbled it up, however, expanding and perfecting it and turning it loose on the world in a package that would survive for decades. But England didn't have America's energy or gumption or zealous commitment to the enterprise, not deep, deep down. While London continued to turn out new music and fashion and art, America had begun to do that and more, adding a political fervor to the sixties mix that London—for all its right-thinking—never had. In 1968, when Paris and Berlin and Rome and cities all over the United States had assassinations, protests and outright rioting, London continued in its now-familiar way acknowledging the turmoil in the air with protests of its own, but noodling as well, retreating to the country, to Spain or Greece or India, seeking meaning outside rather than in itself.

For the first time in nearly a decade, Londoners weren't creating the new sensations but seeking them outside: "Suddenly the pendulum swung back again," remembered journalist Ray Connolly. "Drugs. The antiwar thing. There was no war here, except for the big antiwar demonstrations in 1968 in Grosvenor Square outside the [American] embassy. British youth—not many—imported something to rebel against. Records coming out of the States seemed more interesting, and things going on there seemed more interesting. It's like the revolution was over in England and it was just people taking dope. The headlines came from America all the time from '67 onward."

Fashion—that fickle goddess that had capped the ascent of London in 1963 as the center and the birthplace of the pop cultural world—had turned. London wasn't *finished* finished, not yet, but it was definitely receding.

And yet there was a sense that it needed defining, even as it was still going on. But how could anybody, at the time, in the midst of it, put it all together, nitroglycerine unstable as it was?

Bailey tried—again—and, again, succeeded.

Two years after the publication of his *Box of Pin-Ups*, he set about a new book, one that would capture not a slim and cheeky pantheon of selected stars, but a full map of the cosmos that was London in the sixties: "I want to do three or four hundred people," he said. "All the people who mean something to me. I want to show what is going on now. To leave a record—a document. It's the most you can hope for in photography."

Beginning in 1967, and intending to finish the very next year, he culled a few photos from his first collection and augmented them until he had captured 150 images of models, actors, singers, writers, politicians, painters, film directors, restaurateurs, fashion designers, comedians, businessmen, journalists, charlatans and scenesters—but no gangsters, the Krays having, apparently, lost their chic when they were sent off to the pokey forever in 1968. The project finally appeared in November 1969 with the name *Goodbye Baby & Amen: A Saraband for the Sixties.*

Goodbye Baby was distinct from *Box of Pin-Ups* in a number of important ways: For five pounds, buyers got a massive, proper hardbound book of the coffee table variety with actual pages to turn and thousands of words of essays and captions by *Daily Express* showbiz writer Peter Evans. In it, there were nudes: a pregnant Marit Allen of *Vogue*, Marisa Berenson, Jane Birkin, Celia Hammond, Sharon Tate draped over Roman Polanski. There were tricked-up (and not always well) shots of the likes of Mia Farrow, Andy Warhol, Candice Bergen. There were paintings and shots by other photographers: Cecil Beaton, Bill Brandt, Bert Stern and the other famous East End boys, Terry Donovan and Brian Duffy. There were people who'd appeared on the scene since *Box of Pin-Ups*—Twiggy and Justin, Penelope Tree, Michael York and the pseudo-Bailey of *Blow-Up,* David Hemmings. And there were people who'd left the scene eerily early: Brian Epstein, Françoise Dorléac, journalist and cat-about-town Robin Douglas-Home, the artist Pauline Boty, the model Nicole de Lamarge. Bailey himself appeared in two guises: a Patrick Litchfield photo of a smoky, Mozartian madman in white tie and a Gerald Scarfe cartoon of a buck-toothed, heart-shaped head atop a tripod.

Box of Pin-Ups had displayed its idiosyncratic pantheon of heroes in stark black and white that made them look at once like emblems and lab specimens. *Goodbye Baby* was more diverse and probing, capturing its subjects not only in the controlled cool of the studio but on movie sets, in art galleries, on streets, in fields and parks and private homes. It included a brief survey of Bailey's best fashion shots, from Paulene Stone and her squirrel through some of the more amazing images of Jean Shrimpton to the spacey, diaphanous stuff that was being done that very week. It was commodious, crammed, scattershot. If the first collection was a bold "We are here," this one felt more like "Where are we?"

Peter Evans had come onboard relatively late in Bailey's planning. Over dinner one night in early 1969, the photographer asked him, as he recalled, "Why don't we kind of do a monument to Swinging London? It started out as a joke but when we mentioned it to a publisher and said, 'Would you like to do it?', they bit our arms off for it." While Bailey winnowed through his photos, Evans had to rush together the text in about six weeks' time. "It became necessary to write it quickly," he said, "because I wanted it to reflect that kind of period. It was floaty and it wasn't gonna last, and I knew it was an epitaph."

Indeed, as the two men put together their cast list, as it were, of famous and important faces, they were a little horrified to realize just how much a part death had played in their time. "A lot of people were dying," Evans recalled. "Maybe half a dozen or eight of those people were already dead when the book was published. So there was a feeling of nostalgia. Almost instant nostalgia."

The two men didn't always agree on which figures belonged in the book, Evans admitted: "Bailey, even more than a photographer's eye, had a very good journalist's eye, and he was very good with people. It was a bit prickly at the time because, obviously, two people doing a book have their own ideas." But at the same time, they were in more or less general agreement because, in truth, the population they were describing was so finite and easily identified. "A lot of people did go by the wayside," Evans said. "They had to, because of space. But the people that we decided to use were basically people we knew. London in the sixties was a very small space and a very small cast list—if we're talking about the nucleus and the essence." And the collaborators found amusement in projecting forward from their final selection and drawing up a list of which people in the book would still be alive thirty years down the line. "We had a bet on who would still be here," Evans remembered, "and since neither Bailey nor I were on that list, it couldn't have been accurate!"

When the book was submitted to the publishers, Evans was surprised to run into one very stubborn obstacle having to do with his short piece on Mary Quant. "I went to interview her," he recollected, "and we had a few drinks and she told me her husband had shaved her pubic hair into the shape of a heart. I wrote it and put it in the book, and the fight I had to keep that in the book, from lawyers, from publishers, was unbelievable: the most difficult single line I've had to argue into publication in my life. But once it was in, when people were serializing the book or lifting bits for publication, it was the part they always went for."

It was Evans who came up with the title. "I thought it was from a Cole Porter song," he revealed, "and I used it as a working title, and then we phoned up to clear the rights to it. But that phrase doesn't appear exactly in the song, and the publisher said, 'You can have it.'" He also came up with the evocative subtitle, though he later learned that his word choice was, again, just slightly off from the literal: "My impression of saraband was a slow Spanish funeral march, and no one questioned it. It was totally my idea, and I take complete blame and responsibility. But I loved it. And when it came out, some pretty smart critics couldn't find 'saraband' anywhere as describing what I thought it meant. And there was the usual bullshit arguments about that. But I don't care: A word is what it implies, and there was a wonderful poetry for me in the phrase."

The publication party for *Goodbye Baby* was held at the Club dell' Arethusa and some astonishing photos were taken, such as the ones of Bailey, with his caveman haircut and groovy necklace, in an alley off the King's Road with the trio of Christine Keeler, Marianne Faithfull and Penelope Tree—Miss 1963, '66 and '69, respectively. Standing amid them, Bailey was at once a king in his seraglio, a pop star with his backup singers, a pimp displaying his wares. Eight years after he discovered Jean Shrimpton and became a sensation, David Bailey was still a man other men envied.

And yet the little trace of merriment you could see in his eyes in those pictures seemed fleeting, if not altogether feigned. Bailey was still speaking testily about his profession in interviews—"If the others think they can do what I do they can get a leather jacket and grow their hair long; there's no trade union"—things like that. But he also began talking disparagingly of the time he had heralded and embodied and striven to capture: "It was great for two thousand people living in London, a very elitist thing, a naive kind of attitude before the accountants took over."

He would go on in this vein for years, decades: "The first half of the sixties was when it all happened. Afterward, what happened in London was no longer organic. It became manufactured, a media thing"; "It was all over by 1965. The late sixties was a hype, all the energy was dissipated by the record companies, the fashion people, *Time* and *Newsweek.*"

And it galled him to be held up as a talisman of the ills and errors of the age. In the year of *Goodbye Baby,* an odd little book by the onetime satirist Christopher Booker appeared. Moralistic, scolding and built along the lines of a bizarrely doctrinaire schema of Jungian psychology in an attempt to prove that the entire English experience from 1956 on was a mass psychotic episode, *The Neophiliacs* had several occasions to chide Bailey as a superficial sycophant who helped create the ills of the era while attempting to celebrate them. Bailey's subjects, Booker wrote, were "the leading players in some gigantic public charade," a group "as much carried away by this extraordinary make-believe as anyone."

The following year, in another jaundiced summation of the decade, *The Pendulum Years* (known in the States as *Run It Down the Flagpole,* Lord knew why), by journalist Bernard Levin, Bailey again took it hard on the chin. At first, the writing seemed at least modestly sympathetic: "For some time David Bailey, the easy insolence of his life, his public love affairs, his expensive cars bought out of his huge earnings, served as the universal hate-figure." But then Levin pointed out how few among the figures in *Box of Pin-Ups* still mattered (a dubious proposition) and, worse, how shallow to him the whole thought of *Goodbye Baby* seemed: "The cast . . . was a sad come-down from that of the earlier work, many of them, it is safe to say, being entirely unknown to more than a few score people other than their fellow subjects. . . . By the end of the decade Bailey was still earning huge sums from taking fashion photographs, but it was very clear that the world of the Sixties had moved on, and left him, and most of his world, behind."

Maybe.

But Levin was right about one thing, anyhow, as Bailey's own dyspeptic nips at his great decade bore out: The world *had* moved on.

Nineteen seventy was as rotten a year as any England had ever experienced. Obscenity charges were brought against a John Lennon lithograph show, the editorial staffs of *International Times* and *Oz* and Andy Warhol's film *Flesh*. Race rioting broke out in Notting Hill. A national dock strike, the most painful of many labor actions in that busiest year for such activity in five decades, paralyzed industry. The age of legal majority was raised from eighteen to twenty-one. And radical violence increased, from a bloody Vietnam War protest in Whitehall to the surreal attacks on the Miss World Contest, during which the underground anarchist group calling itself the Angry Brigade bombed a BBC camera van outside the Royal Albert Hall, while inside emcee Bob Hope and a parade of bathing-suited beauties were assailed from the audience by enraged feminists. (Six months later, those same Angry Brigade cutups would bomb Biba on Kensington High Street; the sensation afforded the incident meant that the shop would be subjected for several months to ongoing bomb threats from even less coherent—or well-armed—groups.)

The economy had utterly soured—the boom was a chimera—and the Conservatives were voted back in power. Taxes were driving pop stars and movie actors to look for havens on the Continent and in the Caribbean and the States. "It was a bit like Dunkirk," remembered nightclub owner John Gold. "Everyone ran for the boats."

The mood was of a place turning gray again after an unlikely decade of exploding colors.

And there was worse.

In April, two years of squabbling ended with a flurry of lawsuits: The Beatles were finished.

In September, Jimi Hendrix fell asleep on a stomach full of drugs in a Notting Hill townhouse and choked to death on his own vomit.

"There was a big cynicism toward the end," remembered tailor John Pearse. "Dropping out and all the mysticism was really mumbo jumbo. And one really just saw it for what it was. A lot of hokum. You'd actually get fed up with people giving you peace signs all day. And people were just taking too many drugs, as well. It was definitely a kind of psychosis in the latter part. All these bands whom one had held in such regard were dropping like flies: Hendrix, Brian Jones. Everybody went into a kind of self-destruct."

Good-bye baby and amen, indeed.

PART FIVE

If you're hanging on to a rising balloon, you're presented with a difficult decision: Let go before it's too late, or hang on and keep getting higher. Posing the question, How long can you keep a grip on the rope? They're sellin' hippie wigs in Woolworth's, man. The greatest decade in the history of mankind is over, and, as Presumin' Ed here has so consistently pointed out, we have failed to paint it black.

—*Withnail and I*, 1987

And when it was over, when the last traces of smoke disappeared and the final sounds faded and the laughter settled into a lull and sex and youth and life itself didn't seem all that splendid and unique anymore, what had happened?

A few had grown rich, a few had grown famous, many got stoned and many got laid and some did fabulous work and some were revealed as shams and some were hounded and some were glorified and some wandered away and some died.

Ten years earlier: boy singers and jazzbos, beatnik scruffy and a handful of mods, short back and sides and stolen knee tremblers and, if you were lucky, a shit job just like Dad's.

After the shake-up: Anything you wanted to do, pretty much, you could—or at least try—in music, fashion, hair, sex, food, living arrangements, you name it. And people would give it a minute's thought, at least, and not just write it off as a waste of time.

Forever after, you would have the license to dress, express and entertain yourself, give yourself over to sensation, investigate a wider world or things beyond it. Doors had opened—hundreds of them—and the hinges were removed from the jambs.

It wouldn't all happen in London anymore. A new dark age for England was just around the corner—race trouble, austerity, Thatcher and the gob in the eye of punk rock as the requisite retort. With everything all soft and sensual and open, other climes suited better: California, especially, where the weather fit the new hair and clothes, and the pioneering mentality still stood a chance.

But if London was no longer the undisputed mecca and center and touchstone of youth and popular culture, the model of it was still the world's great new cultural paradigm—although the craze-mad kids who were empowered by its rise were too busy chasing the next thing to know it. They did all the things that London first gathered into a life: They wore trendy clothes and grew their hair and listened to rock music and took drugs and had sex and saw groovy movies and plays and art exhibits and openly mocked their parents and the government and did it all on front pages and TV screens. They took for granted the liberties that young Swinging Londoners had first carved for themselves; they assumed that new films and LPs and works of fine art were intended for them and stood a chance of changing the world; they comported themselves as if youth itself was the feature attraction of the modern age—and they were right, even as they forgot, in seeking out warmer and more exotic climes, where the notion first made itself fully known. In time, Swinging London became a vaguely recollected phase in the American version of postwar pop history and a last groovy flare-up of British imperial might in the English.

And fair enough: If only the trappings had mattered—the clothes and the slang and some of the attitudes and the liberty with regards to drugs and sex—then it was probably to the good that it was only a fling. But Swinging London had given the world more than just the root joke of the Austin Powers films. There were cultural artifacts of lasting merit and appeal—records and films and plays and photos and paintings. There was the notion that new styles in clothing and hair should be sexy, practical, fun and affordable. There was the sense that social wrongs could not stand: racial and sexual and class oppression, bullying warfare, unchecked savaging of the environment. In England during the Swinging London years, homosexuality was decriminalized, capital punishment banned, divorce laws reformed and censorship of the arts curtailed. Governmental, corporate and social institutions that weren't utterly abolished seemed suddenly pervious to mass criticism: the class system, colonialism, the Darwinian dictates of capital. These changes—wrapped up gaily, set to a danceable beat and glowing with the optimism of youth—were genuine steps into a more just modernity. If Swinging London was a place where you got a hip haircut and outfit and danced the latest step to a groovy new 45, it was also the place where you opened your mind to a better world.

"It happened to happen," said Alvaro Maccioni, and he was right; that's how history works.

But it also *had* to happen: Nothing—*nothing*—of the modern world we share could have been the way it is without those years in London.

The music, the clothes, the hair, the sex, the drugs, the scandal, the merrymaking and the glee.

The intermingled arts and lives and classes.

The celebration of it in photo, print and song.

The ecstasy of waking up and the cold shower of people dying.

It could've taken place anywhere—New York, Paris, L.A., Rome, San Francisco, Tokyo, Amsterdam—but it didn't.

One day the world roused and decided to leap forward, and it did so on London time, with fish-and-chips breath, in a Cockney accent, with right-hand drive.

The talent was all there, and the opportunities, and—go figure—they were grabbed up and availed of. Three, four hundred people drank and smoked and danced and partied together and fucked one another and buttressed one another and were so convinced that they were right that everybody else everywhere agreed.

It was a famous moment even as it was happening. "From the very start of the sixties," Michael Caine said, "I could see myself at seventy-five on television telling people about that time. It was the time of my time; I will never have so much fun again; ever."

He wasn't alone.

From then on, the ones who continued to ascend and the ones who fell off the edge of the world—*alive*—were always still sixties people:

David Bailey the Lecher, snapping away, marrying again, grumbling about the sixties and widening the range of subjects in his lens;

Vidal Sassoon the Empire Builder, moving to America and establishing a brand name, then selling it off and devoting himself to self-discovery, eventually becoming known as much for his Jewish works as for haircutting;

Mary Quant the Molder, puttering away in a Chelsea atelier even as wilder young designers overcame her;

Terence Stamp the Seeker, off in India and then back in the business, minor but always beguiling;

Mick Jagger the Poser, pushing his band to unimaginable longevity, engaging in gossipicious marriages and affairs, becoming a daddy and a tycoon and an icon of high life;

Robert Fraser the Drifter, wandering into bootless careers and finally a death as emblematic as his life.

Nothing they did afterward—and some of them did plenty—ever obliterated the initial impressions they made.

"The volcano erupted and it threw out amazing art and energy," remembered Patsy Puttnam. "Maybe it was like Vesuvius and it froze us." And when they blew it—*if* they blew it—and the hangover set in, and them as could made off, and everyone who was left had to pick up the mess, no one complained, not really, not for long.

They'd been to the greatest party the world had ever thrown—ten years nearly, shiny and sexy and bouncy and brave and exploratory and transcendent, sleek and warm.

A group of people living in one place found one another and the thing they always wanted, and they lived it and became it and let it go or got left by it, and the ones who lived through it—and some who didn't—could rest satisfied that they had had their time.

Maybe their *only* time, yes, but maybe *our* only time, too.

The party of all parties; the time of all times; the granddaddy of all golden moments; the seed of everything we're about: Swinging London.

You hadda be there.

You are.

ACKNOWLEDGMENTS

One name goes on the title page of a book, by convention. But a book like this is, inevitably, the product of more than one mind. From the shaping of the concept to the research to the editing, I have been blessed with the assistance of dozens of foster souls.

There are the hundreds of authors of books I consulted whose names are listed in the bibliography and the thousands of authors of articles in newspapers and magazines, some anonymous, whose work was equally valuable. For that matter, given the tenor of the era about which I've written, I should mention as well the photographers, art directors, fashion designers, musicians and filmmakers who created the artifacts that I used both as evidence and telescope to get a handle on such faraway events.

Among the people who took time to look backward with me to their halcyon days and share the sensations were Marit Allen, Woody Allen, Michael Apted, John Boorman, Bill Bowen, Michael Caine, Ray Connolly, Peter Evans, Peter Fonda, Dick Fontaine, Christopher Gibbs, John Gold, Piri Halasz, Doug Hayward, Dennis Hopper, Larry Kaplan, Sandy Lieberson, Alvaro Maccioni, Charles Marowitz, Ian McKellen, Ian McLagen, Barry Miles, Ronan O'Casey, Terry O'Neill, John Pearse, Roman Polanski, David Puttnam, Patsy Puttnam, Mary Quant, Lynn Redgrave, Vidal Sassoon, Terence Stamp, Peter Stansill, Rita Tushingham, Alexander Walker and Bill Wyman.

In this context, I must make special mention of Caroline Upcher, who shared her memories and contacts and gave me and my project the gift of her imprimatur without question.

Other helpful and kindly folks who pointed me to this or that source or simply talked things over with me include Tim Appelo, Jake Arnott, Aimee Blumson, Alexander Cockburn, Trent Debord, Paul Duchene, Roger Ebert, John Foyston, Martin Harrison, Doug Holm, Marty Hughley, Jim Jarmusch, Nancy Jenkins, Frank Krutnik, Gabriel Mendoza, Kim Morgan, Roger Paulson, Wayne Pernu, Caren Rabbino, Tom Ranieri, Paul Sirett, Janet Wainwright and Mark Wigginton.

This book would have been unthinkable without the resources of the various libraries where I worked. These include the British Library at St. Pancras (*nice* joint) and its Newspaper Library at Colindale; the Multnomah County Library Central Branch; the library of the British Film Institute and the Margaret Herrick Library of the Academy of Motion Picture Arts and Sciences. And where there are libraries, there are, inevitably, bookstores, including the incomparable Powell's Foyles, Skoob, various on-line booksellers and auctioneers and all those serendipitous shops along Charing Cross Road. Particular mention must be made, too, of Movie Madness, that jewel of video stores which makes life in Portland, Oregon, that much more worth living; where do they *find* all that stuff???

For help in digging up images to illustrate and illuminate the story, I thank the London staffs of Camera Press, Rex Features and the Hulton-Getty Archive.

For freelance work that helped pay the bills during the time I worked on this project, I thank Graham Fuller at *Interview*, Nick James and Edward Lawrenson at *Sight and Sound*, Susan Pocharski at *Maximum Golf*, Craig Vasiloff at *Razor*, Andrew Pulver at *The Guardian* and my various editors at *Movieline, Pulse!* and *Travelocity*.

At *The Oregonian*, I am grateful to Fred Stickel, Sandy Rowe, Peter Bhatia and Tom Whitehouse for making it possible for me to take leave to write the thing, and to Karen Brooks, Grant Butler, Barry Johnson and my *A&E* and *ArtsWeek* teammates for indulging my various needs to vent about it and disappear.

At Doubleday, I am grateful to Kendra Harpster for expert steering and collegial prods, Amelia Zalcman for a careful legal review and Lesley Krauss for making sure that those were, in fact, p's and not q's.

My agent, Richard Pine, was a rock through the tough early phases and cool during the long gestation. Lori Andiman was a constant source of encouragement and good news.

I can't say enough about my editors. Leo Hollis was a crucial and steady point of contact and a thoughtful, inspiring intelligence when the first version of this ship sailed in. Gerry Howard was an encouraging presence and a valuable finder of oddities. Bill Thomas was enormously supportive from the outset and patient (or at least busy!) when I needed to keep my head low; he's been a touchstone for me for years, and I'm grateful. And Andy Miller was, plainly and simply, an exemplary collaborator in every important way—discussing material, touring historic sites, steering me toward this or that source, offering valuable suggestions about the text—and, more crucially, a true mate and impeccable host (and a special shout out to his lovely missus, Tina!).

On two coasts, I have enjoyed the bottomless support of family and friends. But that's especially true at home, where Mary Bartholemy patiently reassured me a million times that I was neither stupid nor crazy, and Vincent, Anthony and Paula reminded me what else there was to life besides work.

Hey kids—Dad's finished: Let's play!

The Place

Bacon, David, and Norman Maslov. *The Beatles' England: There Are Places I'll Remember.* San Francisco: 910 Press, 1982.

Bacon, Tony. *London Live: From the Yardbirds to Pink Floyd to the Sex Pistols: The Inside Story of Live Bands in the Capital's Trail-Blazing Music Clubs.* London: Balafon, 1999.

Block, David. *Carnaby Street.* London: Lord Kitchener's, undated.

Dallas, Karl, with Barry Fantoni. *Swinging London: A Guide to Where the Action Is.* London: McCarthy's, 1967.

Davies, Hunter, ed. *The New London Spy: A Discreet Guide to the City's Pleasures.* London: Anthony Blond, 1966.

Deighton, Len. *Len Deighton's London Dossier.* London: Penguin, 1967.

Halasz, Piri. *A Swinger's Guide to London.* New York: Coward-McCann, 1967.

Kiyomiya, Yumiko. *London: Swingers and Squares.* Tokyo: Kodansha International, 1973.

London (Knopf Guides). New York: Knopf, 1993.

"London: The Lives of the City." *Granta 65.* New York: Penguin, 1999.

Rebirth of Britain: A Symposium of Essays by Eighteen Writers. London: Pan, 1964.

Royds, Pamela, Nancy Tuft and Deborah Manley. *Using London.* London: Penguin, 1971.

Salter, Tom. *Carnaby Street.* Walton-on-Thames, U.K.: M&J Hobbs, 1970.

Schreuders, Piet, Mark Lewisohn and Adam Smith. *The Beatles London: The Ultimate Guide to Over 400 Beatle Sites In and Around London.* New York: St. Martin's Press, 1994.

Weinreb, Ben, and Christopher Hibbert. *The London Encyclopedia.* London: Macmillan, 1983.

Yapp, Nick, and Rupert Tenison. *London: The Secrets and the Splendour.* Cologne: Konemann, 1999.

The Times and the Faces

Aitken, Jonathan. *The Young Meteors.* New York: Atheneum, 1967.

Allen, Peter. *An Amber Glow: The Story of England's World Cup-Winning Football.* London: Mainstream, 2000.

The Angry Brigade 1967–1984, Documents and Chronology. London: Elephant Editions, 1985.

Barrow, Andrew. *Gossip 1920–1970.* New York: Coward, McCann and Geoghegan, 1979.

Bestic, Alan. *Turn Me On Man: The Drug Rave—Face to Face with Young Addicts Today.* London: Tandem, 1966.

Booker, Christopher. *The Neophiliacs; A Study of the Revolution in English Life in the Fifties and Sixties.* London: Collins, 1969.

Bracewell, Michael. *England Is Mine: Pop Life in Albion from Wilde to Goldie.* London: Flamingo, 1998.

Chaplin, Michael. *I Couldn't Smoke the Grass on My Father's Lawn: Pot, Girls, and Swingers in London's Ultra-Mod Set.* New York: Ballentine, 1967.

Cleeve, Susan. *Growing Up in the Swinging '60s.* East Sussex, U.K.: Wayland, 1980.

Connolly, Ray, ed. *In the Sixties.* London: Pavilion, 1995.

Fountain, Nigel. *Underground: The London Alternative Press 1966–1974.* London: Routledge, 1988.

Fryer, Jonathan. *Soho in the Fifties and Sixties.* London: NPG, 1998.

Gardiner, Juliet. *From the Bomb to the Beatles: The Changing Face of Post-War Britain 1945–1965.* London: Collins & Brown, 1999.

Gould, Tony. *Inside Outsider: The Life and Times of Colin MacInnes.* London: Chatto & Windus, 1983.

Green, Jonathon. *Days in the Life: Voices from the English Underground 1961–1971*. London: Pimlico, 1998.

———. *All Dressed Up: The Sixties and the Counterculture*. London: Jonathan Cape, 1998.

Gross, Nigel, Graeme Kay, Damian Wild and Sue Wood. *Collins Gem 1950s*. London: HarperCollins, 1999.

———. *Collins Gem 1960s*. London: HarperCollins, 1999.

Hamblett, Charles, and Jane Deverson. "*Generation X*." Greenwich, CT: Gold Medal, 1964.

Haynes, Jim. *Thanks for Coming: An Autobiography*. London: Faber and Faber, 1984.

Hewison, Robert. *In Anger: Culture in the Cold War 1945–1960*. London: Methuen, 1981.

———. *Too Much: Art and Society in the Sixties 1960–1975*. Oxford: Oxford University Press, 1986.

Hollingshead, Michael. *The Man Who Turned on the World*. London: Blond & Briggs, 1973.

Humphries, Steve, and John Taylor. *The Making of Modern London 1945–1985*. London: Sidgwick and Jackson, 1986.

Irving, Clive. *Pox Britannica: The Unmaking of the British*. New York: Saturday Review Press, 1974.

Levin, Bernard. *Run It Down the Flagpole: Britain in the Sixties*. New York: Atheneum, 1971.

Lownes, Victor. *The Day the Bunny Died: The Story of the Rise and Near Collapse of the Playboy Empire as Told by One of Its Principal Creators*. Secaucus, NJ: Lyle Stuart, 1983.

Maitland, Sarah. *Very Heaven: Looking Back at the 1960s*. London: Virago, 1988.

Marowitz, Charles. *Burnt Bridges: A Souvenir of the Swinging Sixties and Beyond*. London: Hodder and Stoughton, 1990.

Marwick, Arthur. *British Society Since 1945*. London: Penguin, 1984.

———. *The Sixties: Cultural Revolution in Britain, France, Italy and the United States c. 1958–c. 1974*. Oxford: Oxford University Press, 1998.

Masters, Brian. *The Swinging '60s*. London: Constable, 1985.

Melly, George. *Revolt into Style: The Pop Arts in the 50s and 60s*. Oxford: Oxford University Press, 1989.

Miller, David. *The Boys of '66: England's Last Glory*. London: Pavilion, 1986.

Neville, Richard. *Hippie Hippie Shake: The Dreams, the Trips, the Trials, the Love-Ins, the Screw-Ups, the Sixties*. London: Bloomsbury, 1996.

Obst, Lynda Rosen. *The Sixties: The Decade Remembered Now by the People Who Lived It Then*. New York: Rolling Stone, 1977.

Perry, George, ed. *London in the Sixties*. London: Pavilion, 2001.

The Permissive Society. Editors of *The Guardian*. London: Panther, 1969.

Sked, Alan, and Chris Cook. *Post-War Britain: A Political History*, 3rd edition. London: Penguin, 1990.

Slayton, Leonard. *Aly: A Biography*. New York: Random House, 1965.

Tanner, Michael. *Ali in Britain*. London: Mainstream, 1995.

Taylor, Derek. *It Was Twenty Years Ago Today*. London: Bantam, 1987.

Tennant, Emma. *Girlitude: A Portrait of the 50s and 60s*. London: Jonathan Cape, 1999.

Warhol, Andy, and Pat Hackett. *Popism: The Warhol Sixties*. New York: Harvest, 1980.

Wheen, Francis. *The Soul of Indiscretion: Tom Driberg: Poet, Philanderer, Legislator and Outlaw*. London: Fourth Estate, 2001.

Yapp, Nick. *The Hulton Getty Picture Collection 1950s*. Cologne: Konemann, 1998.

———. *The Hulton Getty Picture Collection 1960s*. Cologne: Konemann, 1998.

The Look

Armstrong-Jones, Anthony. *London*. London: Weidenfeld & Nicolson, 1958.

Bailey, David, and Francis Wyndham. *David Bailey's Box of Pin-Ups*. London: Weidenfeld & Nicolson, 1965.

Bailey, David, and Peter Evans. *Goodbye Baby & Amen*. New York: Coward-McCann, 1969.

Bailey, David, and Martin Harrison. *David Bailey's Black and White Memories*. London: J. M. Dent and Sons, 1983.

Battle-Welch, Gerald, Luca P. Marighetti and Werner Moller. *Vidal Sasson and the Bauhaus*. Ostfildern, Germany: Cantz, 1992.

Bender, Marilyn. *The Beautiful People*. New York: Coward-McCann, 1967.

Bernard, Barbara. *Fashion in the '60s*. London: Academy Editions, 1978.

Carter, Ernestine. *Magic Names of Fashion*. Englewood Cliffs, NJ: Prentice-Hall, 1980.

Cawthorne, Nigel. *Sixties Source Book: A Visual Guide to the Style of a Decade*. London: Quantum, 1998.

Cohn, Nik. *Today There Are No Gentlemen: Changes in English Men's Clothes Since the War*. London: Weidenfeld & Nicolson, 1971.

Coleridge, Nicholas, and Stephen Quinn. *The Sixties in Queen*. London: Ebury Press, 1987.

De La Haye, Amy, ed. *The Cutting Edge: 50 Years of British Fashion*. London: V&A, 1997.

Donovan, Terence. *London Photographs*. London: Museum of London, 1999.

Fishman, Diane, and Marcia Powell. *Vidal Sassoon: Fifty Years Ahead*. New York: Rizzoli, 1993.

Green, John d, with Anthony Haden-Guest. *Birds of Britain*. New York: Macmillan, 1967.

Harris, Jennifer, Sarah Hyde and Greg Smith. *1966 and All That: Design and the Consumer in Britain, 1960–1969*. London: Trefoil, 1986.

Harrison, Martin. *Appearances: Fashion Photography Since 1945*. New York: Rizzoli, 1991.

———. *Young Meteors: British Photojournalism 1957–1965*. London: Jonathan Cape, 1998.

———. *David Bailey: Archive One 1957–1969*. London: Barbican Art Gallery, 1999.

Howell, Georgina. *In Vogue: 75 Years of Style*. London: Conde Nast, 1991.

Hulanicki, Barbara. *From A to Biba*. London: Hutchinson, 1983.

Jackson, Lesley. *The Sixties: Decade of Design Revolution*. London: Phaidon, 1998.

Jobey, Liz. *The End of Innocence: Photographs from the Decades that Defined Pop: the 1950s to the 1970s*. Zurich: Scalo, 1997.

Lawson, Twiggy, and Penelope Dening. *Twiggy in Black and White*. London: Pocket, 1997.

Mellor, David. *The Sixties Art Scene in London*. London: Barbican Art Gallery, 1993.

Mellor, David Alan, and Laurent Gervereau, eds. *The Sixties: Britain and France, 1962–1973 The Utopian Years*. London: Phillip Wilson, 1997.

Moffitt, Peggy, and William Claxton. *The Rudi Gernreich Book*. Cologne: Taschen, 1999.

Quant, Mary. *Quant by Quant*. London: Cassell, 1966.

Rous, Lady Henrietta, ed. *The Ossie Clark Diaries*. London: Bloomsbury, 1998.

Sassoon, Vidal. *Sorry I Kept You Waiting, Madam*. New York: Putnam, 1968.

Seebohm, Caroline. *No Regrets: The Life of Marietta Tree*. New York: Simon & Schuster, 1997.

Shrimpton, Jean, with Unity Hall. *An Autobiography*. London: Ebury Press, 1990.

Vermorel, Fred. *Fashion and Perversity: A Life of Vivienne Westwood and the Sixties Laid Bare*. London: Bloomsbury, 1996.

Villeneuve, Justin de. *An Affectionate Punch*. London: Sidgwick & Jackson, 1986.

Vyner, Harriet. *Groovy Bob: The Life and Times of Robert Fraser*. London: Faber and Faber, 1999.

Whiteside, Thomas. *Twiggy & Justin*. New York: Farrar, Strauss and Giroux, 1968.

The Sound

Andersen, Christopher. *Jagger Unauthorized*. New York: Delacorte, 1993.

Barnes, Richard, with Johnny Moke and Jan McVeigh. *Mods!* London: Plexus, 1991.

The Beatles Anthology New York: Cassell, 2000.

Booth, Stanley. *The True Adventures of the Rolling Stones*. New York: Vintage, 1985.

Brown, Tony, with Jon Kutner and Neil Warwick. *The Complete Book of the British Charts*. London: Omnibus, 2000.

Caron, Sandra. *Alma Cogan: A Memoir*. London: Bloomsbury, 1991.

Clayson, Alan. *Beat Merchants: The Origins, History, Impact and Rock Legacy of the 1960s British Pop Groups*. London: Blandford, 1996.

Coleman, Ray. *Lennon*. New York: McGraw Hill, 1984.

———. *The Man Who Made the Beatles: An Intimate Biography of Brian Epstein*. New York: McGraw Hill, 1989.

Cooper, Michael, and Terry Southern. *The Early Stones: Legendary Photographs of a Band in the Making 1963–1973*. New York: Hyperion, 1992.

Davies, Ray. *X-Ray: The Unauthorized Autobiography*. London: Penguin, 1995.

Davis, Andy. *The Beatles Files*. London: Metro Books, 2000.

DiLello, Richard. *The Longest Cocktail Party*. New York: Playboy, 1981.

Epstein, Brian. *A Cellarful of Noise*. New York: Pocket, 1998.

Etchingham, Kathy, with Andrew Crofts. *Through Gypsy Eyes: My Life, the 60s and Jimi Hendrix*. London: Orion, 1999.

Faithfull, Marianne, with David Dalton. *Faithfull: An Autobiography*. New York: Little Brown, 1994.

Frame, Pete. *The Beatles and Some Other Guys: Rock Family Trees of the Early Sixties*. London: Omnibus, 1997.

Frith, Simon, and Howard Horne. *Art into Pop*. London: Methuen, 1987.

Geller, Debbie, with Anthony Wall. *The Brian Epstein Story*. London: Faber and Faber, 2000.

Giuliano, Geoffrey. *Behind Blue Eyes: The Life of Pete Townshend*. New York: Dutton, 1996.

Goldman, Albert. *The Lives of John Lennon*. New York: Bantam, 1988.

Goodman, Pete. *Our Own Story by the Rolling Stones*. New York: Bantam, 1965.

Guinness British Hit Albums, 4th ed. London: Guinness, 1990.

Guinness British Hit Singles 12th ed. London: Guinness, 1999.

Harrison, George, with Derek Taylor. *I, Me, Mine*. New York: Simon & Schuster, 1980.

Harry, Bill. *The Ultimate Beatles Encyclopedia*. New York: MJF, 1992.

Hinckley, David, and Debra Rodman. *The Rolling Stones: Black and White Blues, 1963*. Atlanta: Turner Publishing, 1995.

Hochner, A. E. *Blown Away*. New York: Fireside, 1991.

Jackson, Laura. *Heart of Stone: The Unauthorized Life of Mick Jagger*. London: Smyth Gryphon, 1997.

Leigh, Spencer, and John Firminger. *Halfway to Paradise: Britpop, 1955–1962*. Folkestone, Kent, U.K.: Finbarr International, 1996.

Lennon, Cynthia. *A Twist of Lennon*. New York: Avon, 1980.

Leslie, Peter. *Fab: The Anatomy of a Phenomenon*. London: MacGibbon & Kee, 1965.

Lewisohn, Mark. *The Complete Beatles Chronicle*. London: Hamlyn, 2000.

Logan, Nick, and Bob Woffindon. *The Illustrated Encyclopedia of Rock*. New York: Harmony, 1997.

Macdonald, Ian. *Revolution in the Head: The Beatles' Records & the Sixties*. London: Fourth Estate, 1997.

Marsden, Gerry, with Ray Coleman. *I'll Never Walk Alone: An Autobiography*. London: Bloomsbury, 1993.

Marsh, Dave. *Before I Get Old: The Story of The Who*. New York: St. Martin's Press, 1983.

McAleer, Dave. *Hit Parade Heroes: British Beat Before the Beatles*. London: Hamlyn, 1993.

McCabe, Peter, and Robert D. Schonfeld. *Apple to the Core: The Unmaking of the Beatles*. New York: Pocket, 1972.

McCartney, Paul, with Barry Miles. *Many Years from Now*. New York: Henry Holt, 1997.

Melly, George. *Owning Up: The Trilogy*. London: Penguin, 2000.

Miller, Jim, ed. *The Rolling Stone Illustrated History of Rock & Roll*. New York: Rolling Stone, 1976.

Miles, Barry. *Mick Jagger in His Own Words*. New York: Delilah-Putnam, 1982.

———. *The Rolling Stones: A Visual Documentary.* London: Omnibus, 1994.

———. *The Beatles: A Diary.* London: Omnibus, 1998.

Napier-Bell, Simon. *You Don't Have to Say You Love Me.* London: Ebury Press, 1998.

Oldham, Andrew Loog. *Stoned.* London: Secker & Warburg, 2000.

Palacios, Julian. *Lost in the Woods: Syd Barrett & the Pink Floyd.* London: Boxtree, 1998.

Pareles, John, and Patricia Romanowski. *The Rolling Stone Encyclopedia of Rock & Roll.* New York: Rolling Stone, 1983.

Paytrees, Mark. *The Rolling Stone Files.* London: Quadrillion, 1999.

Rawlings, Terry, and Keith Badman. *Empire Made: The Handy Parka Pocket Guide to All Things Mod.* London: Complete Music, 1997.

Rayl, A.J.S. *Beatles '64: A Hard Day's Night in America.* New York: Doubleday, 1989.

Rogan, Johnny. *Starmakers & Svengalis: The History of British Pop Management.* London: Queen Anne Press, 1988.

Sanchez, Tony. *Up and Down with the Rolling Stones.* New York: Da Capo, 1996.

Seay, David. *Jagger: The Story Behind the Rolling Stone.* New York: Birch Lane, 1993.

Schaffner, Nicholas. *Saucerful of Secrets: The Pink Floyd Odyssey.* New York: Delta, 1991.

———. *The British Invasion: From the First Wave to the New Wave.* New York: McGraw Hill, 1983.

Shapiro, Harry, and Caesar Glebeek. *Jimi Hendrix: Electric Gypsy.* New York: St. Martin's Press, 1991.

Shepherd, Billy. *The True Story of the Beatles.* New York: Bantam, 1964.

Sulphy, Doug, and Ray Schweighardt. *Get Back: The Beatles' Let It Be Disaster.* London: Helter Skelter, 1998.

Watkinson, Mike, and Peter Andrson. *Crazy Diamond: Syd Barrett and the Dawn of Pink Floyd.* London: Omnibus Press, 1991.

Whitburn, Joel. *The Billboard Book of Top 40 Hits.* New York: Billboard, 1983.

Williams, Alan, and William Marshall. *The Man Who Gave the Beatles Away.* New York: Ballantine, 1975.

Spectacles and Amusements

Aldgate, Anthony, and Jeffrey Richards. *Britain Can Take It: The British Cinema in the Second World War.* 2nd ed. Edinburgh: Edinburgh University Press, 1994.

Brown, Mick. *Performance.* London: Bloomsbury, 1999.

Caine, Michael. *What's It All About?: An Autobiography.* New York: Ballantine, 1992.

Carpenter, Humphrey. *That Was Satire That Was: The Satire Boom of the 1960s.* London: Victor Gollancz, 2000.

Connolly, Ray. *Stardust Memories: Talking About My Generation.* London: Pavillion, 1983.

Cook, Linn. *Something Like Fire: Peter Cook Remembered.* London: Methuen, 1996.

Fox, James. *Comeback: An Actor's Direction.* Grand Rapid, MI: Eerdmans, 1983.

Frost, David, and Ned Sherrin. *That Was the Week That Was.* London: W. H. Allen, 1963.

Gallagher, Elaine, with Ian Macdonald. *Candidly Caine.* London: Pan, 1991.

Gifford, Denis. *The British Film Catalogue, 1895-1985.* New York: Facts on File, 1986.

Hall, William. *Raising Caine: The Authorized Biography of Michael Caine.* New York: Prentice Hall, 1982.

Hewison, Robert. *Footlights! A Hundred Years of Cambridge Comedy.* London: Methuen, 1983.

Ingrams, Richard, ed. *The Life and Times of Private Eye, 1961-1971.* London: Penguin, 1971.

Lahr, John. *Prick Up Your Ears: The Biography of Joe Orton.* New York: Vintage, 1987.

Lanza, Joseph. *Fragile Geometry: The Films, Philosophy and Misadventures of Nicolas Roeg.* New York: PAJ, 1989.

MacCabe, Colin. *Performance.* London: BFI Publishing, 1998.

McFarlane, Brian. *An Autobiography of British Cinema by the Actors and Filmmakers Who Made It*. London: Methuen, 1997.

McKay, Peter. *Inside Private Eye*. London: Fourth Estate, 1986.

Murphy, Robert. *Sixties British Cinema*. London: BFI, 1997.

Polanski, Roman. *Roman*. New York: Ballantine, 1985.

Stamp, Terence. *Stamp Album*. London: Bloomsbury, 1987.

———. *Coming Attractions*. London: Bloomsbury, 1988.

———. *Double Feature*. London: Bloomsbury, 1989.

Thompson, Harry. *Peter Cook: A Biography*. London: Sceptre, 1997.

Tynan, Kathleen. *The Life of Kenneth Tynan*. New York: William Morrow, 1987.

Walker, Alexander. *Hollywood U.K.: The British Film Industry in the Sixties*. New York: Stein and Day, 1974.

———. *National Heroes: British Cinema in the Seventies and Eighties*. London: Harrap, 1986.

Yule, Andrew. *Enigma: David Puttnam, the Story So Far. . . .* London: Mainstream, 1988.

———. *The Man Who "Framed" the Beatles: A Biography of Richard Lester*. New York: Donald I. Fine, 1994.

Scandals

Charlton, Warwick. "Stephen Ward Speaks." London: *Today Magazine*, 1963.

Fido, Martin. *The Krays: Unfinished Business*. London: Carlton, 1990.

Fraser, Frankie, with James Morton. *Mad Frank: Memoirs of a Life of Crime*. London: Warner, 1994.

Fry, Colin. *The Kray Files*. London: Mainstream, 1998.

Green, Shirley. *Rachman*. London: Michael Joseph, 1979.

Hobbs, Dick. *Doing the Business: Entrepreneurship, the Working Class and Detectives in the East End of London*. Oxford: Oxford University Press, 1989.

Keeler, Christine. *Scandal*. New York: St. Martin's Press, 1989.

Kennedy, Ludovic. *The Trial of Stephen Ward*. New York: Simon & Schuster, 1965.

Knightley, Phillip, and Caroline Kennedy. *An Affair of State: The Profumo Case and the Framing of Stephen Ward*. New York: Atheneum, 1987.

Kray, Reg, and Ron Kray with Fred Dinenage. *Our Story*. London: Pan, 1988.

Lambrianou, Tony, with Carol Clerk. *Inside the Firm: The Untold Story of the Krays' Reign of Terror*. London: Pan, 1992.

Morton, James. *Bent Coppers: A Survey of Police Corruption*. London: Little Brown, 1993.

———. *Gangland: London's Underworld*. London: Warner, 1993.

Pearson, John. *The Profession of Violence*. New York: Saturday Review Press, 1973.

Read, Piers Paul. *The Train Robbers*. New York: Avon, 1978.

Reynolds, Bruce. *The Autobiography of a Thief*. London: Virgin, 2000.

Reynolds, Bruce, Nick Reynolds and Alan Parker. *The Great Train Robbery Files*. London: Abstract Sounds, 2000.

Rice-Davies, Mandy, with Shirley Flack. *Mandy*. London: Sphere, 1980.

Richardson, Charlie, with Bob Long. *My Manor: An Autobiography*. London: Pan, 1992.

Sparrow, Gerald. "The Profumo Affair." London: *Today Magazine*, 1963.

Williams, Emlyn. *Beyond Belief: A Chronicle of Murder and Its Detection*. London: Pan, 1968.

Instructive Diversions

Amis, Kingsley. *Lucky Jim*. London: Penguin, 1961.

Arnott, Jake. *The Long Firm*. London: Sceptre, 1999.

———. *He Kills Coppers*. London: Sceptre, 2001.

Burn, Gordon. *Alma Cogan*. London: Minerva, 1992.

Fabian, Jenny, and Johnny Byrne. *Groupie*. London: Omnibus, 1997.

Keyes, Thom. *All Night Stand*. New York: Ballantine, 1967.

MacInnes, Colin. *City of Spades*. New York: Dutton, 1985.

————. *Absolute Beginners*. New York: Dutton, 1985.

————. *Mr. Love and Justice*. New York: Dutton, 1985.

Moorcock, Michael. *Mother London*. New York: Harmony, 1989.

Norman, Phillip. *Everyone's Gone to the Moon*. London: Arrow, 1996.

Orton, Joe. *The Complete Plays*. New York: Grove Press, 1977.

© VINCENT LEVY

Shawn Levy is the author of *King of Comedy: The Life and Art of Jerry Lewis* and *Rat Pack Confidential.* His writing has appeared in the *New York Times, Los Angeles Times, Guardian* (London), *Sight and Sound, Movieline,* and *Interview.* A former editor of *American Film,* he is currently a film critic for the *Oregonian.*